Software Fault Tolerance Techniques and Implementation

Limits of Liability and Disclaimer of Warranty

For a complete listing of the *Artech House Computing Library*, turn to the back of this book.

Software Fault Tolerance Techniques and Implementation

Laura L. Pullum

A┤

Artech House
Boston • London
www.artechhouse.com

Library of Congress Cataloging-in-Publication Data
Pullum, Laura.
Software fault tolerance techniques and implementation / Laura Pullum.
p. cm. — (Artech House computing library)
Includes bibliographical references and index.
ISBN 1-58053-137-7 (alk. paper)
1. Fault-tolerant computing. 2. Computer software—Reliability.
I. Title. II. Series.
QA76.9.F38 P85 2001
005.1—dc21

2001035915

British Library Cataloguing in Publication Data
Pullum, Laura
Software fault tolerance techniques and implementation. —
(Artech House computing library)
1. Computer software—Development 2. Software failures
I. Title
005.1'2

ISBN 1-58053-137-7

Cover design by Igor Valdman

© 2001 ARTECH HOUSE, INC.
685 Canton Street
Norwood, MA 02062

International Standard Book Number: 1-58053-137-7
Library of Congress Catalog Card Number: 2001035915

10 9 8 7 6 5 4 3 2 1

Contents

Preface

The scope, complexity, and pervasiveness of computer-based and controlled systems continue to increase dramatically. The consequences of these systems failing can range from the mildly annoying to catastrophic, with serious injury occurring or lives lost, human-made and natural systems destroyed, security breached, businesses failed, or opportunities lost. As software assumes more of the responsibility of providing functionality and control in systems, it becomes more complex and more significant to the overall system performance and dependability.

It would be ideal if the processes by which software is conceptualized, created, analyzed, and tested had advanced to the state that software is developed without errors. Given the current state-of-the-practice, fewer errors are introduced, but not all errors are prevented. So even if we have the best people and use the best practices and tools, we are still imperfect beings, and it would be very risky to assume that the software we develop is error-free. This book examines the means to protect against software design faults and tolerate the operational effects of these introduced imperfections.

Chapter 1 provides definitions of several basic terms and concepts and a proposed reading guide. Chapter 2 presents various means of structuring redundancy so that it can effect software fault tolerance. Chapter 3 presents programming practices used in several software fault tolerance techniques, along with common problems and issues faced by various approaches to software fault tolerance.

The essence of this book is the presentation of the software fault tolerance techniques themselves. Design diverse techniques are presented in

Chapter 4, data diverse techniques in Chapter 5, and "other" techniques in Chapter 6. The decision mechanisms used with many of the techniques are presented in Chapter 7.

This book may be used as a reference for researchers or practitioners. It may also be used as a textbook or reference for a graduate-level software engineering course or for a course on software fault tolerance. A proposed navigational guide to reading the book is provided in Figure 1.1, Section 1.2.

Software fault tolerance is not a panacea for all our software problems. Since, at least for the near future, software fault tolerance will primarily be used in critical systems, it is even more important to emphasize that "fault tolerant" does not mean "safe," nor does it cover the other attributes comprising dependability, such as reliability, availability, confidentiality, integrity, and maintainability (as none of these covers fault tolerance). Each must be designed-in and their, at times conflicting, characteristics analyzed. Poor requirements analysis will yield poor software in most cases. Simply applying a software fault tolerance technique prior to testing or fielding a system is not sufficient. Software due diligence is required!

Acknowledgments

I am grateful to the staff at Artech House Publishers and to the reviewers for their encouragement and support during the process of writing and producing this book.

I would be happy to hear from readers who have updated research findings, implementation examples, new techniques, or other information that might enhance the usefulness of this book in any future updates. Such comments and suggestions can be sent to me via e-mail at pullum@mindspring.com.

1

Introduction

Computer-based systems have increased dramatically in scope, complexity, and pervasiveness, particularly in the past decade. Most industries are highly dependent on computers for their basic day-to-day functioning. Safe and reliable software operation is a significant requirement for many types of systems, for instance, in aircraft and air traffic control, medical devices, nuclear safety, petrochemical control, high-speed rail, electronic banking and commerce, automated manufacturing, military and nautical systems, for aeronautics and space missions, and for appliance-type applications such as automobiles, washing machines, temperature control, and telephony, to name a few. The cost and consequences of these systems failing can range from mildly annoying to catastrophic, with serious injury occurring or lives lost, systems (both human-made and natural) destroyed, security breached, businesses failed, or opportunities lost. As software assumes more of the responsibility for providing functionality in these systems, it becomes more complex and more significant to the overall system performance and dependability.

Ideally, the processes by which software is conceptualized, created, analyzed, and tested would have advanced to the point where software could be developed without errors. The current state-of-the-practice is such that fewer errors are introduced, but unfortunately not all errors are prevented. Even if the best people, practices, and tools are used, it would be very risky to assume the software developed is error-free. There may also be cases in which an error, found late in the system's life cycle and perhaps prohibitively expensive to repair, is knowingly allowed to remain in the system.

Examples of events, with a range of consequences, in which software is thought to be a contributing factor are briefly noted below. Additional examples of reported software-related accidents and incidents are related by Peter G. Neumann in *Computer Related Risks* [1] (Chapter 2) and in the archives of the Internet Risks Forum he moderates, by Nancy G. Leveson in *Safeware* [2] (appendixes), and by Debra S. Herrmann in *Software Safety and Reliability* [3] (Chapter 1).

- The aerospace industry has unique challenges and takes exceptional care in software development. Despite the care taken, several software-related incidents have caused widespread attention. A few examples include: problems in the backup tracking software delayed the launch of *Atlantis* (STS-36) for three days [4]; software on the space shuttle *Endeavor* (STS-49) effectively rounded near-zero values to zero, causing problems when attempting rendezvous with *Intelstat 6* [5–7]; and an *Apollo 11* software flaw made the moon's gravity repulsive rather than attractive [1, 8].

- In January 1990, the AT&T system suffered a nine-hour United States–wide blockade [9] when one switch experienced abnormal behavior and attempted recovery. Because of a flaw in recovery-recognition software (in all 114 switches) and a network design that permitted propagation of the effects, the problem spread to all switches.

- During the Persian Gulf War, clock drift in the Patriot system caused it to miss a scud missile that hit an American barracks in Dhahran. The missile hit killed 29 people and injured 97 others. The clock drift was reportedly caused by the software's use of two different and unequal representations (24-bit and 48-bit) of the value 0.1 [10–11]. As with most complex systems, the source of the resulting problem was multifaceted, in this case with software one of several problem sources.

- Several Airbus A320 problems (e.g., [12–16]) have been initially blamed on the pilots and their skills in handling anomalous situations. However, serious questions have been raised about the role software may have played in these incidents.

- Six known accidental massive radiation overdoses by the Therac-25 radiation therapy system had software error as their precipitating event. A thorough account of the Therac-25 accidents is provided in [17].

- A software problem caused radiation safety doors in the Sellafield, United Kingdom, nuclear reprocessing plant to be opened accidentally [18].

- A recent report outlined the impact of major system outages on various businesses, noting that the cost for a brokerage is $6.5 million per hour, the cost per hour for a credit-card authorization system is $2.6 million, and for an automated teller machine, $14,500 in automatic teller machine fees [19].

Increasing the dependability of software presents some unique challenges when compared to traditional hardware systems. Hardware faults are primarily physical faults, which can be characterized and predicted over time. Software does not physically wear out, burn out, or otherwise physically deteriorate with time (although it can be argued that the *value* of specific instances of data and software may degrade over time). Software has only logical faults, which are difficult to visualize, classify, detect, and correct. Software faults may be traced to incorrect requirements (where the software matches the requirements, but the behavior specified in the requirements is not appropriate) or to the implementation (software design and coding) not satisfying the requirements. Changes in operational usage or incorrect modifications may introduce new faults. To protect against these faults, we cannot simply add redundancy, as is typically done for hardware faults, because doing so will simply duplicate the problem. So, to provide protection against these faults, we turn to software fault tolerance.

1.1 A Few Definitions

To provide additional basis for the discussions in the remainder of this book, a few basic definitions are provided.

A *fault* is the identified or hypothesized cause of an error [20], sometimes called a "bug." It can be viewed as simply the "consequence of a failure of some other system (including the developer) that has delivered or is now delivering a service to the given system" [21]. An active fault is one that produces an error.

An *error* is part of the system state that is liable to lead to a failure [21]. It can be unrecognized as an error (i.e., latent) or detected. An error may propagate, that is, produce other errors. Faults are known to be present when errors are detected.

A *failure* occurs when the service delivered by the system deviates from the specified service, otherwise termed an incorrect result [21]. This implies that the expected service is described, typically by a specification or set of requirements.

So, with software fault tolerance, we want to prevent failures by tolerating faults whose occurrences are known when errors are detected. The cycle—...failure→fault→error→failure→fault...—indicates their general causal relationship. The causal order is maintained, however the generality is exhibited when, for example, an error leads to a fault without an observed failure (if observation capabilities are not in place or are inadequate). Another example of the generality is when one or more errors occur before a failure due to those errors occurs. The classic definition [22, 23] of *software fault tolerance* is: using a variety of software methods, faults (whose origins are related to software) are detected and recovery is accomplished.

1.2   Organization and Intended Use

This book is organized as follows. The remainder of this chapter describes how software fault tolerance is an important means to achieve dependable software, the types of recovery used in fault tolerant software, and the types of redundancy used in software fault tolerance techniques. Redundancy alone is not sufficient for detecting and tolerating software faults. It requires some form of diversity to achieve software fault tolerance. Chapter 2 presents various means of structuring redundancy, for example, via forms of diversity, so that it can effect software fault tolerance. Some programming methods are used in several different software fault tolerance techniques or are simply important enough to discuss apart from the techniques in which they are used. These programming methods are discussed in Chapter 3, along with common problems and issues faced by various approaches to software fault tolerance.

The essence of this book is the presentation of the software fault tolerance techniques themselves, including the way they operate, usage scenarios, examples, and issues. The techniques are categorized and discussed according to type of diversity—design diverse techniques in Chapter 4, data diverse techniques in Chapter 5, and the catch-all "other" techniques in Chapter 6. Just as we were able to extract some issues and programming methods common to several software fault tolerance techniques, we can also extract and discuss the decision mechanisms (DM) used with many of the techniques. This is done in Chapter 7.

A word of caution is perhaps in order now: this book is not meant to be read straight through, particularly Chapters 4, 5, and 6. End-to-end reading may turn away even the most ardent admirer of software fault tolerance. Particularly in Chapters 4, 5, and 6, it may be best to select a technique of interest to learn about and investigate, rather than reading about all the techniques in a single sitting. The book may be used as a reference for researchers or practitioners. It may also be used as a textbook or reference for a graduate-level software engineering course or for a course on software fault tolerance. Figure 1.1 provides a proposed navigational guide to reading this book.

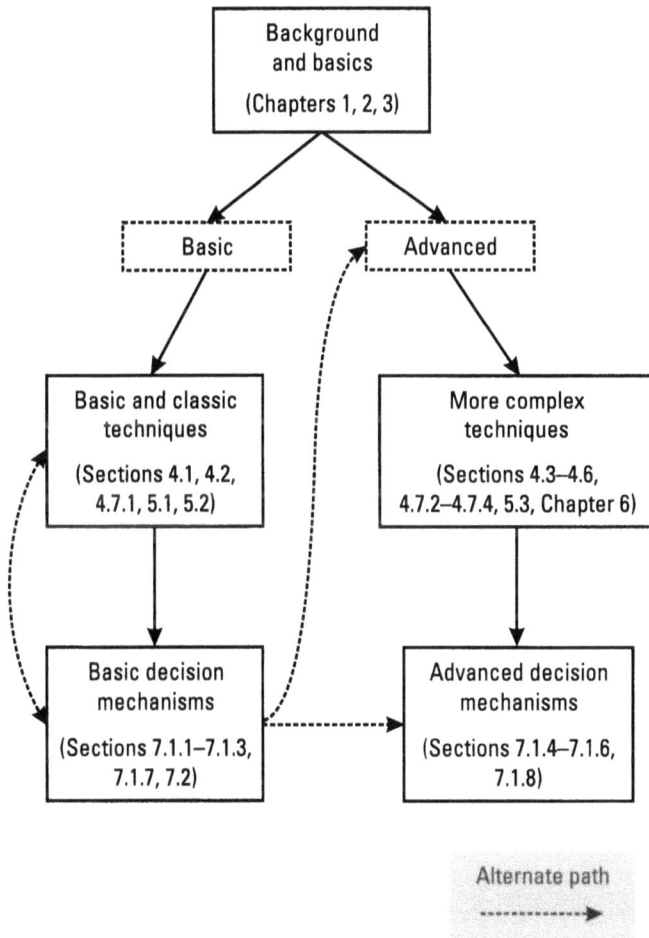

Figure 1.1 A proposed guide to reading this book.

1.3   Means to Achieve Dependable Software

We have stated that the need for dependable software in general, and soft-ware fault tolerance in particular, arises from the pervasiveness of software, its use in both critical and everyday applications, and its increasing complexity. In this section, the various technical means to achieve dependable software are briefly discussed.

The concepts related to dependable software can be classified in the form of a tree as shown in Figure 1.2 (adapted from [24]), a dependability concept classification. The tree illustrates the impairments, means, and attributes of dependability. The *impairments*, or those things that stand in the way of dependability, are faults, errors, and failures (discussed earlier). The *attributes* of dependability enable the properties of dependability and provide a way to assess achievement of those properties. Additional attributes can be derived from the properties of those listed. For example, the depend-able system attribute security is derived from the properties of integrity, availability, and confidentiality.

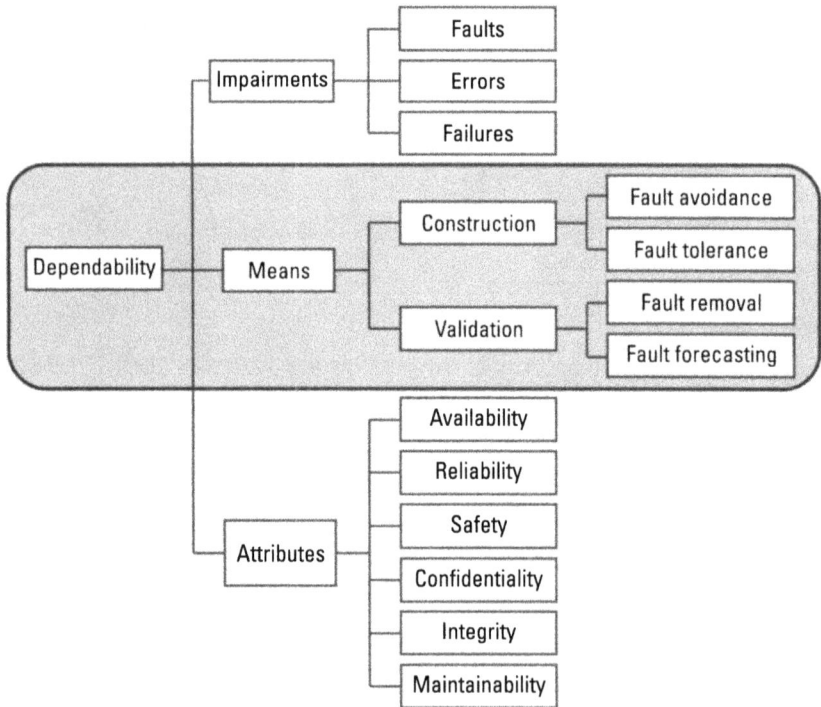

Figure 1.2 Dependability concept classification. (*After:* [24].)

The *means* to achieve dependability falls into two major groups: (1) those that are employed during the software construction process (fault avoidance and fault tolerance), and (2) those that contribute to validation of the software after it is developed (fault removal and fault forecasting). Briefly, the techniques are:

- *Fault avoidance or prevention:* to avoid or prevent fault introduction and occurrence;
- *Fault removal:* to detect the existence of faults and eliminate them;
- *Fault/failure forecasting:* to estimate the presence of faults and the occurrence and consequences of failures;
- *Fault tolerance:* to provide service complying with the specification in spite of faults.

The remainder of this section investigates each of the techniques in more detail.

1.3.1 Fault Avoidance or Prevention

Fault avoidance or prevention techniques are dependability enhancing techniques employed during software development to reduce the number of faults introduced during construction. These avoidance, or prevention, techniques may address, for example, system requirements and specifications, software design methods, reusability, or formal methods. Fault avoidance techniques contribute to system dependability through rigorous specification of system requirements, use of structured design and programming methods, use of formal methods with mathematically tractable languages and tools, and software reusability.

1.3.1.1 System Requirements Specification

The specification of system requirements is currently an imperfect process at best. A system failure may occur due to logic errors incorporated into the requirements. This results in software that is written to match the requirements, but the behavior specified in the requirements is not the expected or desired system behavior. This type of fault often occurs because software requirements specification lies at the intersection between software engineering and system engineering, and these two disciplines suffer from a lack of communication. All too often, software engineers tend to work in isolation from the rest of a system's developers. This is especially problematic from the safety standpoint, since the majority of safety problems arise from software requirements errors and not coding errors [2]. Some software engineering techniques support interactive refinement of requirements and engineering of the requirements specification process. However, a much larger part of existing software engineering techniques addresses only the errors that occur when the design and implementation of the requirements in a programming language do not match or satisfy the system requirements.

1.3.1.2 Structured Design and Programming Methods

Many structured software design and programming methods have been shown to be effective and are in common use. Most of them introduce structure to the design to reduce the complexity and interdependency of components. The principles of decoupling and modularization can be applied to software as well as system design. Further, information hiding encourages each component to encapsulate design decisions and "hide" them from other modules, while communicating only via explicit function calls and parameters. Each of these techniques reduces overall complexity of the software, making it easier to understand and implement and, hence, reduces the introduction of faults into the software.

1.3.1.3 Formal Methods

Formal methods have been used, particularly in the research community, to improve software dependability during construction. In these approaches, requirements specifications are developed and maintained using mathematically tractable languages and tools. Lyu [25] describes four goals of current formal methods studies: (1) executable specifications for systematic and precise evaluation, (2) proof mechanisms for software verification and validation, (3) development procedures that follow incremental refinement for step-by-step verification, and (4) every work item, be it a specification or a test case, is subject to mathematical verification for correctness and appropriateness.

Mathematical specifications of proofs of software properties tend to be the same size as the program, difficult to construct, and often harder to understand than the program itself. As a result, they can be just as prone to error as the software under scrutiny. Because of these concerns, formal methods have not been generally used on large projects. However, if a specific part of a system is indicated for risk mitigation, the analyst may find the size of the component small enough that the use of formal methods on that component is not prohibitive in terms of cost, time, or other resources.

1.3.1.4 Software Reuse

Software reuse is very attractive for a variety of reasons. Software reusability implies a savings in development cost, since it reduces the number of components that must be originally developed. It is also popular as a means of increasing dependability because software that has been well exercised is less likely to fail (since many faults have already been identified and corrected). In addition, object-oriented paradigms and techniques encourage and support software reuse. However, it is important to recognize that different measures of dependability may not be improved equally by reuse of software. For example, highly reliable software may not necessarily be safe.

1.3.1.5 Fault Avoidance/Prevention Summary

Interactive refinement of the user's system requirements, the engineering of the software specification process, the use of good software programming discipline, and the encouragement of writing clear code are the generally accepted and employed approaches to prevent faults in software. These are fundamental techniques in preventing software faults from being created. Formal methods are very thorough, using mathematically tractable languages and tools to verify correctness and appropriateness. The major drawback of formal methods is that the size and complexity of the verification tends to be at least as great as that of the software under scrutiny, imposing a large overhead on the development process. This overhead is usually unacceptable, except for small components that are highly critical to the entire system. Fault prevention through reusability of code components is popular and can be quite helpful when the code to be reused has been proven dependable. The pitfall here is that simply reusing code does not ensure dependability, especially if the new requirements do not match the requirements to which the code was originally written. It is difficult to quantify the impact of fault avoidance techniques on system dependability. Despite fault prevention efforts, faults are created, so fault removal is needed.

1.3.2 Fault Removal

Fault removal techniques are dependability-enhancing techniques employed during software verification and validation. These techniques improve software dependability by detecting existing faults, using verification and validation (V&V) methods, and eliminating the detected faults. Fault removal techniques contribute to system dependability using software testing, formal inspection, and formal design proofs.

1.3.2.1   Software Testing

The most common fault removal techniques involve testing. An overview of software-testing techniques is provided by the author in [26]. The difficulties encountered in testing programs are often related to the prohibitive cost and complexity of exhaustive testing [27] (testing the software under all circumstances using all possible input sets). The key to efficient testing is to maintain adequate test coverage and to derive appropriate test quality measures. It follows that minimizing component size and interrelationships maximizes accurate testing.

Additional testing may be performed on components identified as critical to the system. This additional testing may reveal unforeseen problems or may increase the confidence in the predicted probability of failure for that component.

1.3.2.2   Formal Inspection

Formal inspection [28] is another practical fault removal technique that has been widely implemented in industry and that has shown success in many companies [29]. This technique is a rigorous process, accompanied by documentation that focuses on examining source code to find faults, correcting the faults, and then verifying the corrections. Formal inspection is usually performed by small peer groups prior to the testing phase of the life cycle.

1.3.2.3   Formal Design Proofs

Formal design proofs are closely related to formal methods. This emerging technique attempts to achieve mathematical proof of correctness for programs. Using executable specifications, test cases can be automatically generated to improve the software verification process. This technique is not currently fully developed and, as with formal methods, may be a costly and complex technique to use. However, if performed on a relatively small portion of the code (identified as critical during the risk identification stage), formal design proofs may be feasible. The successful completion of a formal proof may give the designer a high degree of confidence in predicting a very low probability of failure for a software artifact.

1.3.2.4   Fault Removal Summary

Software testing and formal inspections are commonly used fault removal techniques. They introduce rigor to the process of fault removal. It is important that these techniques are used efficiently and with more emphasis on software components that are critical to the system and its dependability.

Testing has its problems, too, and these should be kept in mind: it is not currently possible to exhaustively test a large, complex system; testing can show the presence, but not the absence of faults; it may be impossible to test under realistic conditions; and specification errors may not be visible until the system is used under operational conditions.

Formal design proofs, like formal methods, are based on mathematical methods. The disadvantages of formal design proofs are that they can be costly and complex to use and the method is not currently fully developed. Fault removal techniques determine whether the software matches the specified required behavior; they do not determine whether something has been left out of the requirements. Fault removal is imperfect, so fault forecasting and fault tolerance are needed.

1.3.3 Fault/Failure Forecasting

Fault forecasting, or failure forecasting, includes dependability enhancing techniques that are used during the validation of software to estimate the presence of faults and the occurrence and consequences of failures. Fault forecasting usually focuses on the reliability measure of dependability and is also known as software reliability measurement. It involves the formulation of a fault/failure relationship, an understanding of the operational environment, the establishment of reliability models, the collection of failure data, the application of reliability models by tools, the selection of appropriate models, the analysis and interpretation of results, and guidance for management decisions [25]. Fault forecasting techniques can help predict the effectiveness of additional testing efforts. Fault forecasting includes two types of activities: reliability estimation and reliability prediction.

1.3.3.1 Reliability Estimation

Reliability estimation determines *current* software reliability by applying statistical inference techniques to failure data obtained during system testing or during system operation [25]. Reliability estimation is thus a snapshot of the reliability that has been achieved to the time of estimation.

1.3.3.2 Reliability Prediction

Reliability prediction determines *future* software reliability based upon available software metrics and measures [25]. Different techniques are used depending on the software development stage. For example, before failure data becomes available through system testing or operation, predictions can only be made using what is available. At this early stage, that typically includes information about the development process. When failure data becomes available, software reliability models can be verified so that future reliability predictions can be made.

1.3.3.3   Fault/Failure Forecasting Summary

The establishment of reliability models and their use is a complex discipline. Like fault removal techniques, fault forecasting techniques (such as operational reliability measurement) determine whether the software matches the specified required behavior. This reveals whether additional testing, fault tolerance, or other reliability-enhancing measures are needed. However, these techniques do not determine whether something has been left out of the requirements. Missing/incorrect requirements is one of the most fundamental impediments to software dependability. Fault/failure forecasting can indicate the need for fault tolerance.

1.3.4   Fault Tolerance

One way to reduce the risks of software design faults and thus enhance software dependability is to use software fault tolerance techniques. Software fault tolerance techniques are employed during the procurement, or development, of the software. They enable a system to tolerate software faults remaining in the system after its development. When a fault occurs, these techniques provide mechanisms to the software system to prevent system failure from occurring. Some of these techniques have been available for over 20 years and are well understood. There are many techniques available today for implementing software fault tolerance.

Software fault tolerance provides service complying with the relevant specification in spite of faults by typically using single version software techniques, multiple version software techniques, or multiple data representation techniques.

1.3.4.1   Single Version Software Environment

In a single version software environment, these techniques are used to partially tolerate software design faults—monitoring techniques, atomicity of actions, decision verification, and exception handling.

1.3.4.2   Multiple Version Software Environment

Design diverse techniques are used in a multiple version (or variant) software environment and utilize functionally equivalent yet independently developed software versions to provide tolerance to software design faults. Examples of such techniques include recovery blocks (RcB), *N*-version programming

(NVP), and *N* self-checking programming (NSCP). These techniques are described in Chapter 4.

1.3.4.3 Multiple Data Representation Environment

Data diverse techniques are used in a multiple data representation environment and utilize different representations of input data to provide tolerance to software design faults. Examples of such techniques include retry blocks (RtB) and *N*-copy programming (NCP). These techniques are described in Chapter 5.

1.3.4.4 Software Fault Tolerance Summary

Fault tolerance techniques are designed to allow a system to tolerate software faults that remain in the system after its development. They can provide fault tolerance capabilities for single version software environments and multiple version software environments (via design diversity and data diversity). Software fault tolerance techniques provide protection against errors in translating the requirements and algorithms into a programming language, but do not provide explicit protection against errors in specifying the requirements. Software fault tolerance techniques have been used in the aerospace, nuclear power, healthcare, telecommunications and ground transportation industries, among others.

1.4 Types of Recovery

Error recovery is part of the larger software fault tolerance process involving error (or fault) detection, diagnosis, isolation or containment, and recovery. The fault tolerance process is that set of activities whose goal is to remove errors and their effects from the computational state before a failure occurs. The process consists of:

- *Error detection:* in which an erroneous state is identified;
- *Error diagnosis:* in which the damage caused by the error is assessed and the cause of the error is determined;
- *Error containment/isolation:* in which further damages are prevented (or the error is prevented from propagating);
- *Error recovery:* in which the erroneous state is substituted with an error-free state.

Error recovery is performed using backward recovery or forward recovery.

1.4.1   Backward Recovery

When an error occurs in a program, the program generally enters a contaminated or erroneous state. Recovery techniques attempt to return the system to a correct or error-free state. Backward recovery attempts to do this by restoring or rolling back the system to a previously saved state. It is usually assumed that the previously saved state occurred before the fault manifested itself, that is, that the prior state is error-free. If it is not error-free, the same error may cause problems in the recovery attempt. System states are saved at predetermined recovery points. Recording or saving this previous state is called checkpointing. The state should be checkpointed on stable storage that will not be affected by failure. In addition to, and sometimes instead of, checkpointing, incremental checkpointing, audit trail, or logs may be used. Upon error detection, the system state is restored to the last saved state, and operations continue or restart from that state. If the failure occurred after the checkpoint was established, the checkpointed state will be error-free and after the rollback, the system state will also be error-free [30]. Figure 1.3 illustrates backward recovery.

There are several advantages to backward recovery over other recovery techniques.

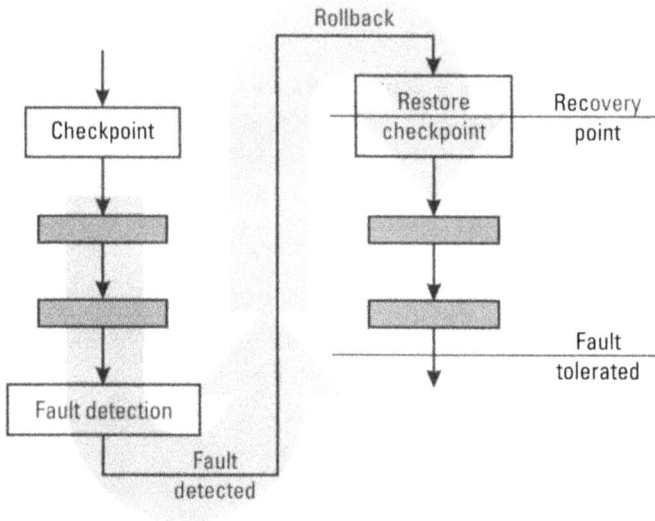

Figure 1.3 Backward recovery.

- Backward recovery can handle unpredictable errors caused by residual design faults if the errors do not affect the recovery mechanism [31].

- Backward recovery can be used regardless of the damage sustained by the state [32].

- Backward recovery provides a general recovery scheme—it has a uniform pattern of error detection and recovery, is application-independent, and does not change from program to program [32].

- Backward recovery requires no knowledge of the errors in the system state [33].

- The only knowledge required by backward recovery is that the relevant prior state is error-free [34].

- Backward recovery can handle transparent or permanent arbitrary faults.

- Backward recovery is particularly suited to recovery of transient faults. After recovery, the error may have gone away, and restarting with the checkpointed system state should not produce the same fault.

There are, however, a few disadvantages to the backward recovery approach.

- Backward recovery requires significant resources (i.e., time, computation, and stable storage) to perform checkpointing and recovery.

- The implementation of backward recovery often requires that the system be halted temporarily.

- If communication and coordination of interacting processes using backward recovery (e.g., nested recovery blocks) are not synchronized, a domino effect may occur. This happens when one process rolls back to its previous checkpoint, which in turn causes another process to roll further back (to its checkpoint), which in turn causes the first process to roll back further, and so on.

The backward recovery approach is the most generally applicable recovery technique for software fault tolerance. It is used frequently, despite its overhead. The RcB technique and most distributed systems incorporating software fault tolerance employ backward recovery.

1.4.2   Forward Recovery

As stated earlier, after an error occurs in a program, recovery techniques attempt to return the system to a correct or error-free state. Forward recovery attempts to do this by finding a new state from which the system can continue operation. This state may be a degraded mode of the previous error-free state. As an alternative to this state transitioning for recovery, forward recovery can utilize error compensation. Error compensation is based on an algorithm that uses redundancy (typically built into the system) to select or derive the correct answer or an acceptable answer. Figure 1.4 illustrates the forward-recovery concept. Note that redundant (diverse) software processes are executed in parallel. The redundancy provides a set of potential results or answers from which a fault detection and handling unit performs error compensation and selects or derives an answer deemed correct or acceptable. The NVP technique (see Chapter 4) is based on the forward-recovery concept and uses a fault detection and handling unit typically called an adjudicator (see Chapter 7 for a detailed discussion of adjudicators).

Error compensation may be performed in several ways. If used with self-checking components (see Chapter 4), then state transformation can be induced by switching from a failed component to a nonfailed one executing the same task. Error compensation may be applied all the time, whether or

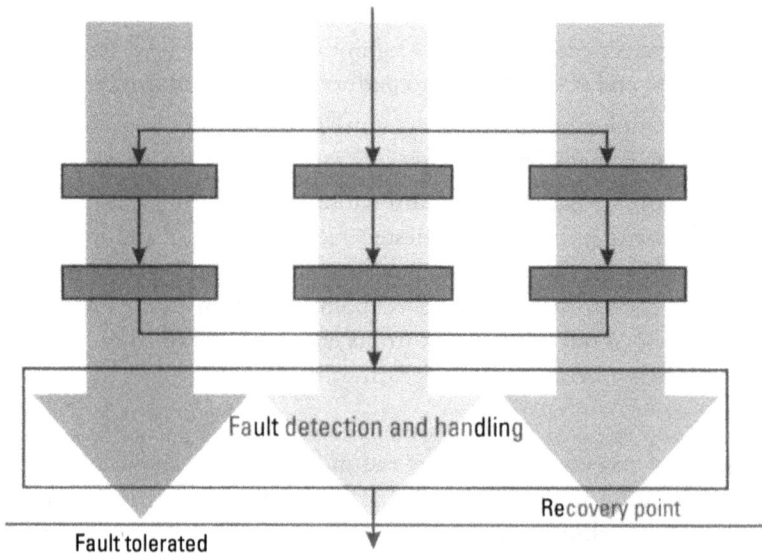

Fault detection and handling

Recovery point

Fault tolerated

Figure 1.4 Forward recovery using redundant processes.

not an error occurred. This is called *fault masking* and may be implemented using one of many available voting schemes (described in Chapter 7).

The advantages to forward recovery include:

- Forward recovery is fairly efficient in terms of the overhead (time and memory) it requires. This can be crucial in real-time applications where the time overhead of backward recovery can exceed stringent time constraints.

- If the fault is an anticipated one, such as the potential loss of data, then redundancy and forward recovery can be a useful and timely approach.

- Faults involving missed deadlines may be better recovered from using forward recovery than by introducing additional delay in rolling back and recovering.

- When the characteristics of a fault are well understood, forward recovery can provide the more efficient solution [33].

The disadvantages of forward recovery include:

- Forward recovery is application-specific, that is, it must be tailored to each situation or program.

- Forward recovery can only remove predictable errors from the system state [31].

- Forward recovery requires knowledge of the error.

- Forward recovery cannot aid in recovery if the state is damaged beyond "specificationwise recoverability" [32].

- Forward recovery depends on the ability to accurately detect the occurrence of a fault (thus initiating the recovery actions), predict potential damage from a fault, and assess the actual damage.

Forward recovery is primarily used when there is no time for backward recovery. Techniques using forward recovery include NVP, NCP, and the distributed recovery block (DRB) technique (which has the effect of forward recovery).

1.5   Types of Redundancy for Software Fault Tolerance

A key supporting concept for fault tolerance is redundancy, that is, additional resources that would not be required if fault tolerance were not being implemented. Redundancy can take several forms: hardware, software, information, and time. Redundancy provides the additional capabilities and resources needed to detect and tolerate faults.

Hardware redundancy includes replicated and supplementary hardware added to the system to support fault tolerance. It is perhaps the most common use of redundancy. Redundant or diverse software can reside on the redundant hardware to tolerate both hardware and software faults. Software redundancy includes the additional programs, modules, or objects used in the system to support fault tolerance. Information or data redundancy is sometimes grouped with software redundancy, but will be treated separately here. It includes the use of additional information with data (typically used for hardware fault tolerance) and additional data used to assist in software fault tolerance. Temporal redundancy involves the use of additional time to perform the tasks required to effect fault tolerance.

Several aspects of redundancy (e.g., hardware, software/information, and time) can be used in varying ranges (e.g., none, single, dual, and so on) in a single software fault tolerance technique. For example, the NVP technique (discussed in Chapter 4) may use three hardware units and three software variants, but no time or data redundancy. The scope of redundancy for fault tolerance is the use of any or all of the dimensions of redundancy and diversity to support software fault tolerance by a particular technique. This section describes and discusses each of these dimensions except hardware redundancy. Our focus is on those dimensions of redundancy that are used by software to protect against software failures.

1.5.1   Software Redundancy

Software redundancy (also called program, modular, or functional redundancy) includes additional programs, modules, functions, or objects used to support fault tolerance. The concept of software redundancy was borrowed from hardware fault tolerance approaches. Hardware faults are typically random, due to component aging and environmental effects. While the use of redundant hardware elements can effectively tolerate hardware faults, tolerance of software faults must employ other approaches. Software faults overwhelmingly arise from specification and design errors or implementation (coding) mistakes. To tolerate software faults, failures arising from these design and implementation problems must be detected.

Software design and implementation errors cannot be detected by simple replication of identical software units, since the same mistake will exist in each copy of the software. If the same software is copied and a failure occurs in one of the software replicas, that failure will also occur in the other replicas and there will be no way to detect the problem. (This assumes the same inputs are provided to each copy.)

A solution to the problem of replicating design and implementation faults is to introduce diversity into the software replicas. When diversity is used, the redundant software components are termed variants, versions, or alternates. Diversity can be introduced using many differing aspects of the software development process. This is discussed in detail in the following chapter.

The basic approach to adding diversity is to start with the same specification and have different programming teams develop the variants independently [35]. This results in functionally equivalent software components. The goals of increasing diversity in software components are to decrease the probability of similar, common-cause, coincident, or correlated failures and to increase the probability that the components (when they fail) fail on disjoint subsets of the input space. The achievement of these goals increases the system's reliability and increases the ability to detect failures when they occur.

The use of diverse software modules requires some means to adjudicate, arbitrate, or otherwise decide on the acceptability of the results obtained by the variants. The component that performs this task is called the adjudicator (or decision mechanism). There are many available algorithms with which to perform adjudication. Since this adjudication module is not replicated and typically does not have an alternate, it is very important that it be free from errors itself. Adjudicators are described in detail in Chapter 7.

Software redundancy can be structured in many forms. As illustrated in Figure 1.5, the structure can vary depending on the underlying hardware. That is, the system can have (a) all replicas on a single hardware component, (b) replicas on multiple hardware components, or (c) the adjudicator on a separate hardware component. In addition, the software that is replicated can range from an entire program to a few lines of code (program segment) as shown in Figure 1.5(d). The choices to be made in structuring software redundancy are based on available resources and the specific application.

1.5.2   Information or Data Redundancy

As stated earlier, information (or data) redundancy is sometimes grouped with software redundancy. However, it will be treated separately to introduce

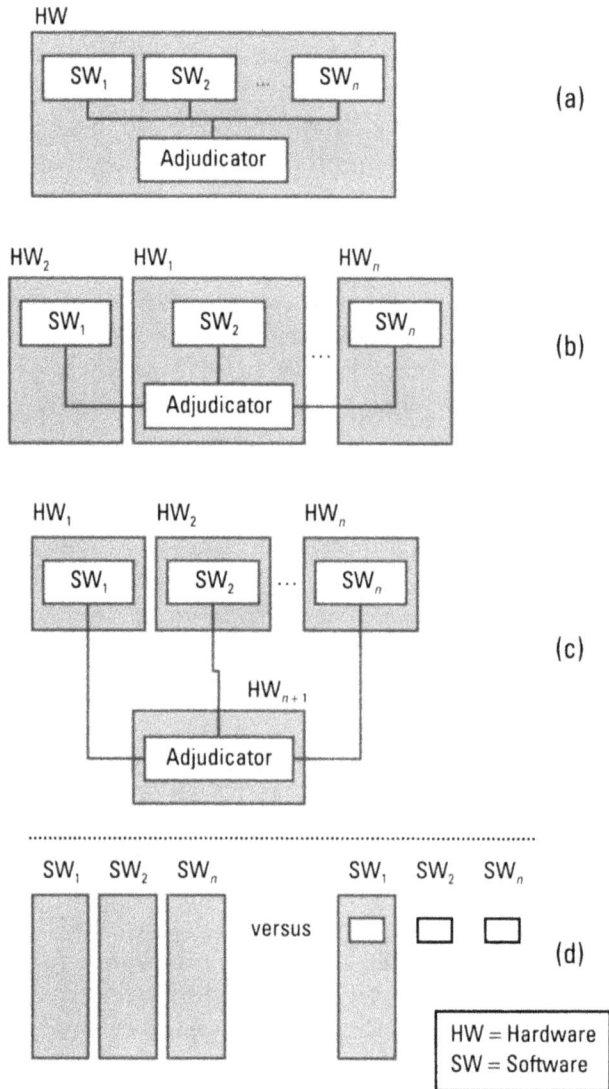

Figure 1.5 Various views of redundant software: (a) all replicas on a single hardware componenet, (b) replicas on multiple hardware components, (c) adjudicator on separate hardward component, and (d) complete program replicas versus program segment replicas.

the concept of data diversity. Information or data redundancy includes the use of information with data and the use of additional forms of data to assist in fault tolerance. The addition of data to information is typically used for hardware fault tolerance. Examples of this type of information redundancy include error-detecting and error-correcting codes.

Diverse data (not simple redundant copies) can be used for tolerating software faults. A data re-expression algorithm (DRA) produces different representations of a module's input data. This transformed data is input to copies of the module in data diverse software fault tolerance techniques. Data diversity is presented in more detail in the following chapter. Techniques that utilize diverse data are described in Chapter 5.

1.5.3 Temporal Redundancy

Temporal redundancy involves the use of additional time to perform tasks related to fault tolerance. It is used for both hardware and software fault tolerance. Temporal redundancy commonly comprises repeating an execution using the same software and hardware resources involved in the initial, failed execution. This is typical of hardware backward recovery (roll-back) schemes. Backward recovery schemes used to recover from software faults typically use a combination of temporal and software redundancy.

Timing or transient faults arise from the often complex interaction of hardware, software, and the operating system. These failures, which are difficult to duplicate and diagnose, are called Heisenbugs [36]. Simple replication of redundant software or of the same software can overcome transient faults because prior to the reexecution time, the temporary circumstances causing the fault are then usually absent. If the conditions causing the fault persist at the time of reexecution, the reexecution will again result in failure.

Temporal redundancy has a great advantage for some applications—it does not require redundant hardware or software. It simply requires the availability of additional time to reexecute the failed process. Temporal redundancy can then be used in applications in which time is readily available, such as many human-interactive programs. Applications with hard real-time constraints, however, are not likely candidates for using temporal redundancy. The additional time used for reexecution may cause missed deadlines. Forward recovery techniques using software redundancy are more appropriate for these applications.

1.6 Summary

The need for dependable systems of all types and especially those controlled by software was posed and illustrated by example. We humans, being imperfect creatures, create imperfect software. These imperfections cannot presently be tested or proven away, and it would be far too risky to simply ignore them. So, we will examine means to tolerate the effects of the imperfections during system operation until the problem "disappears" or is handled in another manner and brought to conclusion (for example, by system shutdown and repair). To give a basis for the software fault tolerance technique discussion, we provide definitions of several basic terms—fault, error, failure, and software fault tolerance. The basic organization of the book and a proposed reading guide were presented, illustrating both basic and advanced tours of the techniques.

To achieve dependable systems, it is necessary to use a combination of techniques from four risk mitigation areas: fault avoidance, fault removal, fault forecasting, and fault tolerance. Unfortunately, there is no single combination of these techniques that is significantly better in all situations. The conventional wisdom that system and software requirements should be addressed early and thoroughly becomes more apparent as it is seen that later efforts at risk mitigation cannot determine or compensate for requirements specification errors. However, the effective use of risk mitigation techniques does increase system dependability. In each case, one must creatively combine techniques from each of the four areas to best address system constraints in terms of cost, complexity, and effectiveness.

We have seen that neither forward nor backward recovery is ideal. Their advantages and disadvantages were identified in this chapter. These recovery techniques do not have to be used in exclusion of each other. For instance, one can try forward recovery after using backward recovery if the error persists [20].

Most, if not all, software fault tolerance techniques are based on some type of redundancy—software, information, and/or time. The selection of which type of redundancy to use is dependent on the application's requirements, its available resources, and the available techniques. The detection and tolerance of software faults usually require diversity (except in the case of temporal redundancy used against transient faults).

Software fault tolerance is not a panacea for all our software problems. Since, at least for the near future, software fault tolerance will primarily be used in critical (for one reason or another) systems, it is even more important to emphasize that "fault tolerant" does not mean "safe," nor does it cover the other attributes comprising dependability (as none of these covers fault tolerance). Each must be designed-in and their, at times conflicting, characteristics analyzed. Poor requirements analysis will yield poor software in most cases. Simply applying a software fault tolerance technique prior to testing or fielding a system is not sufficient. Software due diligence is required!

References

[1]   Neumann, P. G., *Computer Related Risks*, Reading, MA: Addison-Wesley, 1995.

[2]   Leveson, N. G., *SAFEWARE: System Safety and Computers*, Reading, MA: Addison-Wesley, 1995.

[3]   Herrmann, D. S., *Software Safety and Reliability: Techniques, Approaches, and Standards of Key Industrial Sectors*, Los Alamitos, CA: IEEE Computer Society, 1999.

[4]   ACM SIGSOFT, *RISKS* Section, *Software Engineering Notes*, Vol. 15, No. 2, 1990.

[5]   "Mission Control Saves Inselat Rescue from Software Checklist Problems," *Aviation Week and Space Technology*, May 25, 1992, p. 79.

[6]   Asker, J. R., "Space Station Designers Intensify Effort to Counter Orbital Debris," *Aviation Week and Space Technology*, June 8, 1992, pp. 68–69.

[7]   ACM SIGSOFT, *RISKS* Section, *Software Engineering Notes*, Vol. 17, No. 3, 1992.

[8]   ACM SIGSOFT, *RISKS* Section, *Software Engineering Notes*, Vol. 9, No. 5, 1984.

[9]   "Software Glitch Cripples AT&T," *Telephony*, January 22, 1990, pp. 10–11.

[10] ACM SIGSOFT, *RISKS* Section, *Software Engineering Notes*, Vol. 18, No. 1, 1993.

[11] ACM SIGSOFT, *RISKS* Section, *Software Engineering Notes*, Vol. 18, No. 25, 1993.

[12] Denning, P. J. (ed.), *Computers Under Attack: Intruders, Worms, and Viruses*, New York: ACM Press, and Reading, MA: Addison-Wesley, 1990.

[13] DeTreville, J., "A Cautionary Tale," *Software Engineering Notes*, Vol. 16, No. 2, 1991, pp. 19–22.

[14] ACM SIGSOFT, *RISKS* Section, *Software Engineering Notes*, Vol. 15, No. 2, 1990.

[15] ACM SIGSOFT, *RISKS* Section, *Software Engineering Notes*, Vol. 15, No. 3, 1990.

[16] ACM SIGSOFT, *RISKS* Section, *Software Engineering Notes*, Vol. 15, No. 5, 1990.

[17] Leveson, N. G., and C. Turner, "An Investigation of the Therac-25 Accidents," *IEEE Computer*, 1993, pp. 18–41.

[18] Neumann, P. G., et al., *A Provably Secure Operating System: The System, Its Applications, and Proofs*, (2nd ed.) SRI International Computer Science Lab, Technical Report CSL-116, Menlo Park, CA, 1980.

[19] Eklund, B., "Down and Out: Distributed Computing Has Made Failure Even More Dangerous," *Red Herring*, Dec. 18, 2000, pp. 186–188.

[20] Laprie, J. -C., "Computing Systems Dependability and Fault Tolerance: Basic Concepts and Terminology," *Fault Tolerant Considerations and Methods for Guidance and Control Systems*, NATO Advisory Group for Aerospace Research and Development, AGARDograph No. 289, M. J. Pelegrin (ed.), Toulouse Cedex, France, 1987.

[21]   Laprie, J. -C., "Dependability—Its Attributes, Impairments and Means," in B. Randell, et al. (eds.), *Predictably Dependable Computing Systems*, New York: Springer, 1995, pp. 3–24.

[22]   Randell, B., "System Structure for Software Fault Tolerance," *IEEE Transactions on Software Engineering*, Vol. SE-1, No. 2, 1975, pp. 220–232.

[23]   Avizienis, A., "On the Implementation of N-Version Programming for Software Fault-Tolerance During Execution," *COMPSAC '77*, 1977, pp. 149–155.

[24]   Laprie, J. -C., "Dependable Computing: Concepts, Limits, Challenges," *Proceedings of FTCS-25*, Pasadena, 1995, pp. 42–54.

[25]   Lyu, M. R. (ed.), *Handbook of Software Reliability Engineering*, New York: IEEE Computer Society Press, McGraw-Hill, 1996.

[26]   Pullum, L. L., and S. A. Doyle, "Tutorial: Software Testing," *Annual Reliability and Maintainability Symposium*, Los Angeles, CA, 1998.

[27]   Myers, G. J., *Software Reliability, Principles and Practices*, New York: John Wiley and Sons, 1976.

[28]   Fagan, M. E., "Design and Code Inspections to Reduce Errors in Program Development," *IBM Systems Journal*, Vol. 15, No. 3, 1976, pp. 219–248.

[29]   Grady, R. B., *Practical Software Metrics for Project Management and Process Improvement*, Englewood Cliffs, NJ: Prentice-Hall, 1992.

[30]   Jalote, P., *Fault Tolerance in Distributed Systems*, Englewood Cliffs, NJ: Prentice Hall, 1994.

[31]   Randell, B., and J. Xu, "The Evolution of the Recovery Block Concept," in M. R. Lyu (ed.), *Software Fault Tolerance*, New York: John Wiley and Sons, 1995, pp. 1–21.

[32]   Mili, A., *An Introduction to Program Fault Tolerance: A Structured Programming Approach*, New York: Prentice Hall, 1990.

[33]   Xu, J., and B. Randell, *Object-Oriented Construction of Fault-Tolerant Software*, University of Newcastle upon Tyne, Technical Report Series, No. 444, 1993.

[34]   Levi, S. -T., and A. K. Agrawala, *Fault Tolerant System Design*, New York: McGraw-Hill, 1994.

[35]   Avizienis, A., "The N-Version Approach to Fault-Tolerant Software," *IEEE Transactions on Software Engineering*, Vol. SE-11, No. 12, 1985, pp. 1491–1501.

[36]   Gray, J., "A Census of Tandem System Availability Between 1985 and 1990," *IEEE Transactions on Reliability*, Vol. 39, No. 4, 1990, pp. 409–418.

2

Structuring Redundancy for Software Fault Tolerance

In the previous chapter, we reviewed several types of redundancy often used in fault tolerant systems. It was noted then that redundancy alone is not sufficient for tolerance of software design faults—some form of diversity must accompany the redundancy. Diversity can be applied at several different levels in dependable systems. In fact, some regulatory agencies require the implementation of diversity in the systems over which they preside, in particular the nuclear regulatory agencies.

For instance, the U.S. Nuclear Regulatory Agency, in its "Digital Instrumentation and Control Systems in Advanced Plants" [1] states that

1. The applicant shall assess the defense-in-depth and diversity of the proposed instrumentation and control system to demonstrate that vulnerabilities to common-mode failures have been adequately addressed. The staff considers software design errors to be credible common-mode failures that must be specifically included in the evaluation.

2. In performing the assessment, the vendor or applicant shall analyze each postulated common-mode failure for each event that is evaluated in the analysis section of the safety analysis report (SAR) using best-estimate methods. The vendor or applicant shall demonstrate adequate diversity within the design for each of these events.

The digital instrumentation and control systems of which they speak are used to detect failures so that failed subsystems can be isolated and shut down. These protection systems typically use a two-out-of-four voting scheme that reverts to a two-out-of-three voter if one of the channels fails. The failed channel is taken out of service, but the overall service continues with the remaining channels.

The Canadian Atomic Energy Control (AECB) takes a similar stance in "Software in Protection and Control Systems" [2], as stated below:

> To achieve the required levels of safety and reliability, the system may need to be designed to use multiple, diverse components performing the same or similar functions. For example, AECB Reg. Docs. R-8 and R-10 require 2 independent and diverse protective shutdown systems in Canadian nuclear power reactors. ... The design should address this danger by enforcing other types of diversity [other than design diversity] such as functional diversity, independent and diverse sensors, and timing diversity.

In aviation, the regulatory situation differs, but the use of diversity is fairly common. In terms of regulation, the U.S. Federal Aviation Administration states in [3] that "since the degree of protection afforded by design diversity is not quantifiable, employing diversity will only be counted as an additional protection beyond the already required levels of assurance."

To illustrate the use of diversity in an aviation system, look at Airbus, in which diversity is employed at several levels. Diverse software is used in the Airbus A-310, A-320, A-330, and A-340 flight control systems [4, 5]. The A-320 flight control system uses two types of computers that are manufactured by different companies, resulting in different architectures and microprocessors. The computers are based on different functional specifications. One of four diverse software packages resides on each control and monitoring channel on the two computers. The controller uses N-version programming (NVP) to manage the diverse software, enabling software fault tolerance.

This chapter will illustrate how redundancy is structured for software fault tolerance. We will start by taking a step back to examine robust software—software that does not use redundancy to implement fault tolerance. The majority of the chapter will examine design diversity, including issues surrounding its use and cost, case studies examining its effectiveness, levels of diversity application, and factors that influence diversity. Next, we will examine two additional means of introducing diversity for fault tolerance purposes—data and temporal diversity. To assist in developing and evaluating software fault tolerance techniques, several researchers and practitioners have described hardware/software architectures underlying the techniques and design/implementation components with which to build the techniques. We will provide these results to assist the reader in developing and evaluating his or her own implementations of the techniques.

2.1 Robust Software

Although most of the techniques and approaches to software fault tolerance use some form of redundancy, the robust software approach does not. The software property *robustness* is defined as "the extent to which software can continue to operate correctly despite the introduction of invalid inputs" [6]. The invalid inputs are defined in the program specification. The definition of robustness could be taken literally and include all software fault tolerance techniques. However, as it is used here, robust software will include only nonredundant software that, at a minimum, properly handles the following:

- Out of range inputs;
- Inputs of the wrong type;
- Inputs in the wrong format.

It must handle these without degradation of those functions not dependent on the invalid input(s).

As shown in Figure 2.1, when invalid inputs are detected, several optional courses of action may be taken by the robust software. These include:

- Requesting a new input (to the input source, in this case, most likely a human operator);
- Using the last acceptable value for the input variable(s) in question;
- Using a predefined default value for the input.

After detection and initial tolerance of the invalid input, the robust software raises an exception flag indicating the need for another program element to handle the exception condition.

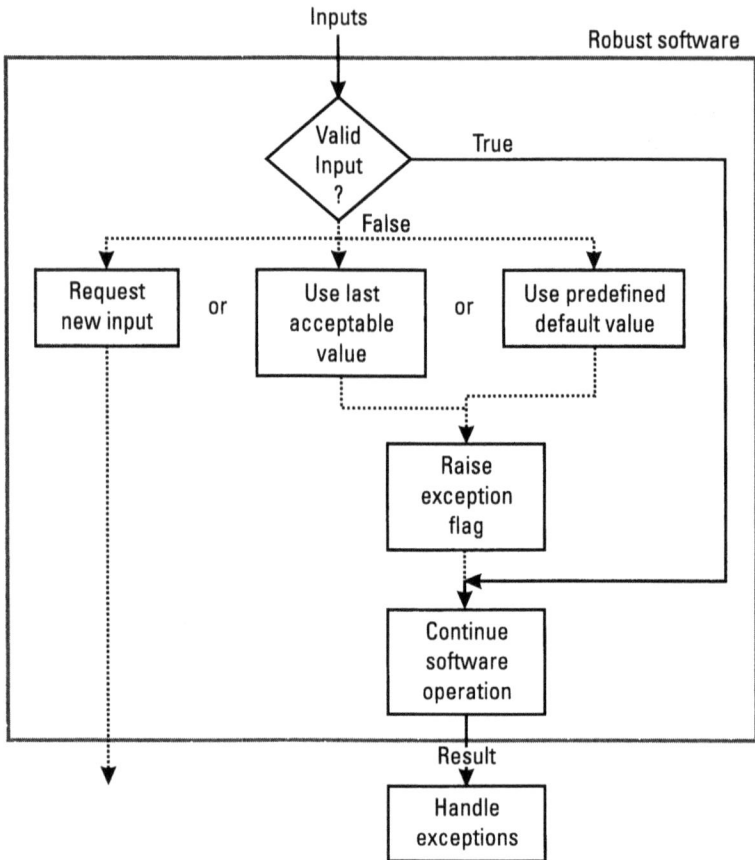

Figure 2.1 Robust software operation.

Examination of self-checking software [7] features reveal that it can reside under the definition of robust software. Those features are:

- Testing the input data by, for example, error detecting code and data type checks;

- Testing the control sequences by, for example, setting bounds on loop iterations;

- Testing the function of the process by, for example, performing a reasonableness check on the output.

An advantage of robust software is that, since it provides protection against predefined, input-related problems, these errors are typically detected early in the development and test process. A disadvantage of using robust software is that, since its checks are specific to input-related faults as defined in the specification, it usually cannot detect and tolerate any other less specific faults. Hence, the need exists for other means to tolerate such faults, mainly through the use of design, data, or temporal diversity.

2.2 Design Diversity

Design diversity [8] is the provision of identical services through separate design and implementations [9–11]. As noted earlier, redundant, exact copies of software components alone cannot increase reliability in the face of software design faults. One solution is to provide diversity in the design and implementation of the software. These different components are alternatively called modules, versions, variants, or alternatives. The goal of design diversity is to make the modules as diverse and independent as possible, with the ultimate objective being the minimization of identical error causes. We want to increase the probability that when the software variants fail, they fail on disjoint subsets of the input space. In addition, we want the reliability of the variants as high as possible, so that at least one variant will be operational at all times.

Design diversity begins with an initial requirements specification. The specification states the functional requirements of the software, when the decisions (adjudications) are to be made, and upon what data the decision-making will be performed. Note that the specifications may also employ diversity as long as the system's functional equivalency is maintained. (When coupled with different inputs for each variant, the use of diverse specifications is termed *functional diversity*.) Each developer or development organization responsible for a variant implements the variant to the specification and provides the outputs required by the specification.

Figure 2.2 illustrates the basic design diversity concept. Inputs (from the same or diverse sources) are provided to the variants. The variants perform their operations using these inputs. Since there are multiple results, this redundancy requires a means to decide which result to use. The variant outputs are examined by a decider or adjudicator. The adjudicator determines which, if any, variant result is correct or acceptable to forward to the next part of the software system. There are a number of adjudication algorithms available. These are discussed in Chapter 7.

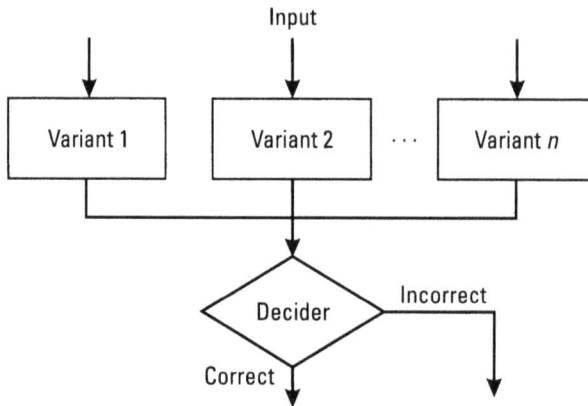

Figure 2.2 Basic design diversity.

When significant independence in the variants' failure profile can be achieved, a simple and efficient adjudicator can be used, and design diversity provides effective error recovery from design faults. It is likely, however, that completely independent development cannot be achieved in practice [12]. Given the higher cost of design diversity, it has thus typically been used only in ultrareliable systems (i.e., those with failure intensity objectives less than 10^{-6} failure/CPU hour) [12].

A word about the cost of design diversity before we continue. It has been often stated that design diversity is prohibitively costly. Studies have shown, however, that the cost of an additional diverse variant does not double the cost of the system [13–16]. More recently, a study on industrial software [17] showed that the cost of a design diverse variant is between 0.7 and 0.85 times the cost of a nondiverse software module. The reason for the less-than-double cost is that even though some parts of the development process are performed separately for each variant (namely detailed design, coding, and unit and integration testing), others are performed for the software system as a whole (specifications, high-level design, and system tests). Note that the systemwide processes can limit the amount of diversity possible. In addition, the process of developing diverse software can take advantage of the existence of more than one variant, specifically, through back-to-back testing.

The remainder of this discussion on design diversity presents the results of case studies and experiments in design diversity, the layers or levels at which design diversity can be applied, and the factors that influence diversity.

2.2.1 Case Studies and Experiments in Design Diversity

There have been numerous experiments and case studies on design diversity, mainly on the NVP technique that employs design diversity. Bishop [18] presents a useful review of the research in this area. The focus of most of the research centers around the factors affecting the diversity of the faults encountered, the reliability improvement using NVP, and investigation of the independence assumption. (The independence assumption states that the failures of diverse versions will be independent and thus detectable.) Table 2.1 summarizes some typical experiments.

The summarized findings of the experiments are provided below [18].

- A significant proportion of the faults found in the experiments were similar.

- The major cause of the common faults was the specification. [Attempts to avoid this include use of diverse specifications and the *N*-version software process (see Section 3.3.3).]

- The major deficiencies in the specifications were incompleteness and ambiguity. This caused the programmer to make sometimes incorrect and potentially common, design choices.

- Diverse design specifications can potentially reduce specification-related common faults.

Table 2.1
Summary of Some *N*-Version Programming Experiments.
(*From:* [18], © 1995, John Wiley & Sons, Ltd. Reproduced with permission.)

Experiment	Specifications	Languages	Versions	Reference
Halden, Reactor Trip	1	2	2	[19]
NASA, First Generation	3	1	18	[20]
KFK, Reactor Trip	1	3	3	[21]
NASA/RTI, Launch Interceptor	1	3	3	[22]
UCI/UVA, Launch Interceptor	1	1	27	[23]
Halden (PODS), Reactor Trip	2	2	3	[24]
UCLA, Flight Control	1	6	6	[25]
NASA (2nd Generation), Inertial Guidance	1	1	20	[26]
UI/Rockwell, Flight Control	1	1	15	[27]

- It was found that the use of relatively formal notations (see [20, 28]) was effective in reducing specification-related faults caused by incompleteness and ambiguity. The use of diverse specifications raises additional concerns, however, because the specifications may not be equivalent. In practice, a single good requirements specification is used unless it is shown that the diverse specifications are mathematically equivalent.

- In general, fewer faults seem to occur in strongly typed, tightly structured languages such as Modula 2 and Ada, while low-level assembler has the worst performance in terms of fault occurrence.

- The protocol for communication between the development teams and the project coordinator in the N-version design paradigm [25, 27] is key to the success of the resulting software. Also key is the presence of a good initial specification.

- A significant improvement in the reduction of identical and very similar faults was found by using the N-version design paradigm.

- An experimental test of the independence assumption [23, 29] rejected the assumption to a high level of confidence. The dependent failures were claimed to be due to design faults only, and not due to faults in the specification. Analysis of the faults showed that the programmers tended to make similar mistakes.

- A theoretical analysis of coincident failures [26] showed that if mistakes were more likely for some specific input values, then dependent failures would be observed.

- Littlewood and Miller [30] refined the previous finding to show that it was possible to have cases in which dependent failures occurred less frequently than predicted by the independence assumption. It is noted that the "degree of difficulty" distribution is not the same for all programmers and if this distribution can be altered using different development processes, then failures are likely to occur in different regions of the input space, and hence the failures would not be correlated.

- Masking of internal errors causes dependent failures to be observed even if the internal error rates are independent. Any output variable whose computation relies on masking functions (e.g., AND gates, OR gates, MIN and MAX functions, and selection functions such as IF/THEN/ELSE, case statements, and such) is likely to exhibit some dependent failures in diverse implementations.

- The reliability improvement in one study [27] showed an improvement factor of 13 for an average triple (set of three variants), not
  including the error correction capabilities of the voting system. With
  the voting system included, the average reliability improvement is
  increased to approximately 58.

Given these results, the main lesson to be gained from these experiments is that the performance of N-version software (diverse software) is
severely limited if common faults are likely. The sources for these common
failures are most probably common implementation mistakes and omissions
and ambiguities in the requirements specification. Use of the N-version programming paradigm has been helpful in minimizing these risks. In addition,
the use of metrics for identification of trouble spots in the program [31] may
be useful in focusing diversification efforts.

2.2.2 Levels of Diversity and Fault Tolerance Application

There are two aspects of the level of fault tolerance application to consider.
One is determining at what level of detail to decompose the system into
modules that will be diversified. The other involves the determination of
which layers of the system to diversify. To determine the level of decomposition for diversification, we must examine the trade-offs between small-
and large-size components. Small components are generally less complex,
and their use leads to DMs, or adjudicators, that are easier to handle. Larger
components, however, are more favorable for effective diversity. Note also
that those places where a decision takes place (decision points) are "nondiver-
sity" points (and synchronization points for techniques such as NVP and
N-self-checking programming (NSCP)) and must be limited [32]. These
decision points are only required *a priori* for interaction with the environment in, for example, sensor data acquisition, delivery of orders to actuators,
and interactions with operators [32].

Diversity can be applied to several layers of the system—hardware,
application software, system software, operators, and the interfaces between
these components. When diversity is applied to more than one of these layers, it is generally termed *multilayer diversity*.

The use of diverse hardware architectures provides the benefits of hardware diversity—protection of faults in the hardware manufacturing process
and subsequent physical faults. This diversity has been primarily used to tolerate hardware component failures and external physical faults.

We have discussed the use of diversity at the application software level (and will examine the specific fault tolerance techniques in a later chapter). This is the most common form of diversity, typically used in safety-critical systems to provide either a fail-halt property or to ensure continuity of service. It has also been examined by several researchers (e.g., [33, 34], and others) as a guard against malicious faults. Several multiversion systems using both diverse hardware and software have been built—flight control computers for the Boeing 737-300 [35] and 7J7 [36]; the ATR.42, Airbus A-310, A-320 [37], A-330, and A-340 aircraft; and the four-version MAFT system [38].

Diversity at the operator-machine interface has been used to tolerate both hardware and software design faults. Dual or triple displays of diverse design and component technologies can be used by human operators in many types of systems, including air traffic control, airliner cockpits, nuclear power plant control rooms, and hospital intensive care facilities [39].

The major disadvantages of multilayer diversity are cost and speed. The cost of designing and implementing diversity in multiple layers can be prohibitive. In addition, the requirement to wait for the slowest component at each diversified layer is a critical drawback for real-time systems.

One way to add diversity at a potentially lower cost is systematic diversity, although it is typically used as a software technique for tolerating hardware faults. Some examples of systematic diversity are [40]:

- Utilization of different processor registers in the variants;
- Transformation of mathematical expressions;
- Different implementation of programming structures;
- Different memory usage;
- Using complementary branching conditions in the variants by transforming the branch statements;
- Different compilers and libraries;
- Different optimization and code-generation options.

2.2.3 Factors Influencing Diversity

It is important to understand the factors that influence the diversity of software so that resources may be put to use most effectively. The ultimate goal is to determine those factors whose influence on software diversity most affect a reduction in the likelihood of common mode failures. The collection of a set of attributes that influence software diversity (in this case, the differences between two pieces of software) was gathered by Burke and Wall [41].

A model was developed to represent the resulting software in terms of both product and process attributes and the relationships between the attributes. The attributes include both those that have the potential to enhance and to inhibit diversity. For example, the *software product* attribute is decomposed into *use* and *product profile* attributes. These attributes are further broken down until leaf nodes such as *number of loops* and *hazards containment techniques* are found. The *software process* attribute is decomposed into the following subattributes: *process profile*, *tools*, *personnel*, and *machines*. Leaf nodes on this major branch include the attributes *skill level* and *assurance of software tool.* Some of these attributes may only be applicable to certain applications.

Inputs to the model are provided for the leaf nodes only, such as *skill level*, *number of decision points*, *hardware dependencies*, *throughput*, *use of recursion*, *standards compliance*, *consistency*, and *actual proof coverage*, to name a few. The resulting model output is a numerical measure indicating the degree of belief that the two software versions under consideration are diverse. Burke and Wall provide definitions for each of the attributes used in the model [41]. Wall elsewhere [42] gives the rules used in the model. Once a measure of diversity is known, it remains to be seen how that diversity in fact influences the reduction of the likelihood of occurrence of common-mode failures.

2.3 Data Diversity

Limitations of some design diverse techniques led to the development of data diverse software fault tolerance techniques. The data diverse techniques are meant to complement, rather than replace, design diverse techniques.

Ammann and Knight [43–45] proposed data diversity as a software fault tolerance strategy to complement design diversity. The employment of data diversity involves obtaining a related set of points in the program data space, executing the same software on those points, then using a decision algorithm to determine the resulting output. Data diversity is based on a generalization of the works of Gray, Martin, and Morris [46–48], which utilize data diverse approaches relying on circumstantial changes in execution conditions. These execution conditions can be changed deliberately to effect data diversity [45]. This is done using data re-expression to obtain logically equivalent variants of the input data. Data diverse techniques use data re-expression algorithms (DRAs) to obtain their input data. Through a pilot study on data diversity [43–45], the *N*-copy programming (NCP) and retry block (RtB) data diverse software fault tolerance structures were developed. These techniques are discussed in Chapter 5.

The performance of data diverse software fault tolerance techniques depends on the performance of the re-expression algorithm used. Ammann and Knight [43–45] suggest that there are several ways to perform data re-expression and provide some insight on actual re-expression algorithms and their use. DRAs are very application dependent. Development of a DRA also requires a careful analysis of the type and magnitude of re-expression appropriate for each data that is a candidate for re-expression [45]. There is no general rule for the derivation of DRAs for all applications; however, this can be done for some special cases [49]. It has also been shown that DRAs exist for a fairly wide range of applications [50]. Of course, a simple DRA is more desirable than a complex one because the simpler algorithm is less likely to contain design faults.

A *failure domain* is the set of input points that cause program failure [51]. The *failure region* is the geometry of the failure domain. It describes the distributions of points in the failure domain and determines the effectiveness of data diversity. The input space of most programs is a hyperspace of many dimensions. For example, if a program reads and processes a set of 25 floating-point numbers, its input space has 25 dimensions. The valid program space is defined by the specifications and by tested values and ranges. Failure regions tend to be associated with transitions in the output space [45].

The fault tolerance of a system employing data diversity depends upon the ability of the DRA to produce data points that lie outside of a failure region, given an initial data point within a failure region. The program executes correctly on re-expressed data points only if they lie outside a failure region. If the failure region has a small cross section in some dimensions, then re-expression should have a high probability of translating the data point out of the failure region. Many real-time control systems and other applications can use DRAs. For example, sensors typically provide noisy and imprecise data; hence small modifications to those data would not adversely affect the application [43] and can yield a means of implementing fault tolerance. The performance of the DRA is much more important than the program structure (e.g., NCP, RtB, and so on) in which it is embedded [52].

Not all applications can employ data diversity. Those that cannot do so include applications in which an effective DRA cannot be found. This may include: applications that do not primarily use numerical data (although character data re-expressions are possible), some that use primarily integer data, some for which an exact re-expression algorithm is required (or where approximation is not useful or that cannot afford or perform postexecution adjustment), those for which a DRA that escapes the failure region cannot be developed, and those for which the known re-expression algorithm(s) that escape the failure region are resource-ineffective.

The remainder of this section provides an overview of data re-expression, describes output sets and related types of data re-expression, and illustrates examples of DRAs.

2.3.1 Overview of Data Re-Expression

Data re-expression is used to obtain alternate (or diverse) input data by generating logically equivalent input data sets. Given initial data within the program failure region, the re-expressed input data should exist outside that failure region. A re-expression algorithm, R, transforms the original input x to produce the new input, $y = R(x)$. The input y may either approximate x or contain x's information in a different form. The program, P, and R determine the relationship between $P(x)$ and $P(y)$. Figure 2.3 illustrates basic data re-expression. The requirements for the DRA can be derived from characteristics of the outputs.

Other re-expression structures exist. Re-expression with postexecution adjustment (Figure 2.4) allows the DRA to produce more diverse inputs than those produced using the basic structure. A correction, A, is performed on $P(y)$ to undo the distortion produced by the re-expression algorithm, R. If the distortion induced by R can be removed after execution, then this approach allows major changes to the inputs and allows copies of the program to operate in widely separated regions of the input space [45].

In another approach, data re-expression via decomposition and recombination (Figure 2.5), an input x is decomposed into a related set of inputs

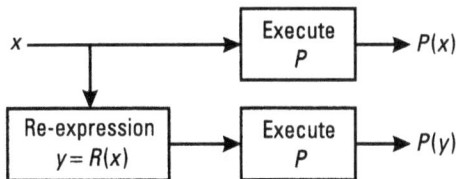

Figure 2.3 Basic data re-expression method. (*Source:* [45], © 1988, IEEE. Reprinted with permission.) New data re-expression methods may be developed by variation on the basic method or by entirely new methods and algorithms.

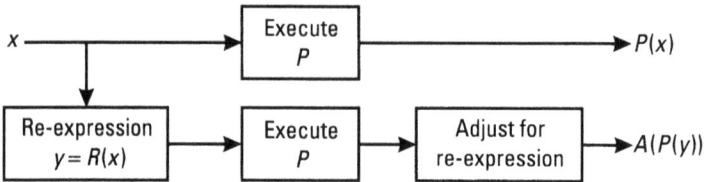

Figure 2.4 Data re-expression with postexecution adjustment. (*Source:* [45], © 1988, IEEE. Reprinted with permission.) Data re-expression with postexecution adjustment can provide even more diversity than basic data re-expression.

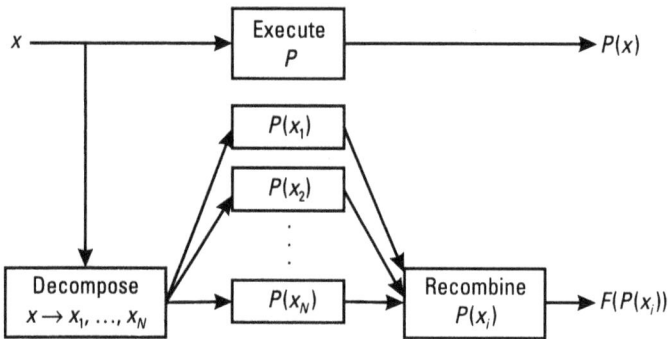

Figure 2.5 Data re-expression via decomposition and recombination. (*Source:* [45], © 1988, IEEE. Reprinted with permission.) Data re-expression via decomposition and recombination can also provide more diversity than basic data re-expression.

and the program is then run on each of these related inputs. The results are then recombined. Basic data re-expression and re-expression with postexecution adjustment allow for both exact and approximate DRAs (defined in the following section).

2.3.2 Output Types and Related Data Re-Expression

Requirements for a DRA can be derived from characteristics of the outputs. There exist three sets in the output space for a given input x (see Figures 2.6 and 2.7). The identical output set I contains all inputs y for which the correct output is the same (up to numerical error) as the correct output, given x as an input. *Correct*(in, out) is true if and only if (IFF), out is the output required by the specifi- cation for input in. $P_{correct}$ represents a correctly implemented specification. $P_{correct}(x)$ is the correct output for input x.

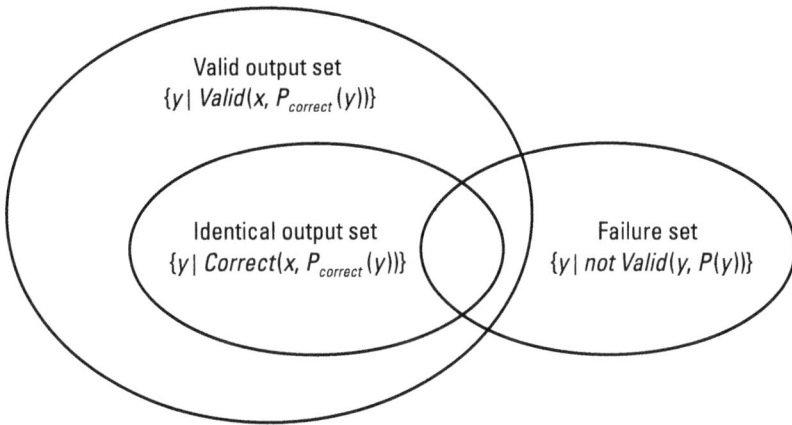

Figure 2.6 Sets in the output space for a given *x*. These sets are important in the development of data re-expression algorithms.

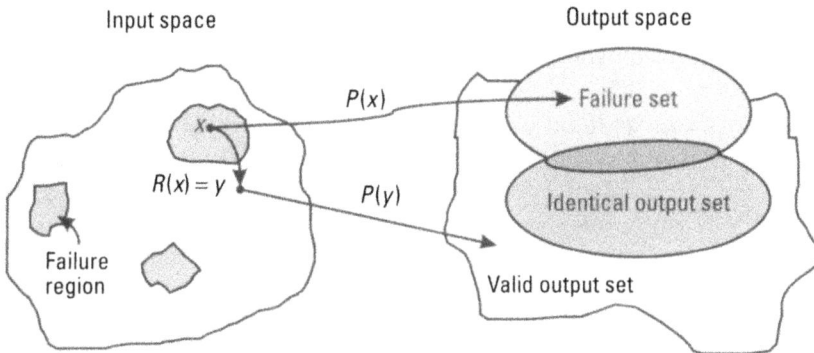

Figure 2.7 Data re-expression. Data re-expression alters the original input to yield a valid result.

The valid output set *V* is the set of all inputs *y* for which a correct program produces an acceptable output, given *x* as the actual input. *Valid*(*in*, *out*) is true IFF *out* is a valid or acceptable output for input *in*. Hence, *V* is the set of all inputs *y* for which a correct program produces an acceptable output given *x* as the actual input.

The failure set *F* represents all inputs *y* for which the program fails to produce a correct or acceptable output. Elements of *F* are, by definition, not enumerated. However, the effectiveness of data diversity is determined by the proportion of re-expressed points that lie in *F*.

Data re-expression in the set I, that is, selection of re-expressed inputs y from I, is desirable because it is transparent outside the program and implementation of the error detection mechanism is simplified. DRAs resulting in values belonging to I are called *exact*. These algorithms may preserve those aspects of the data that cause failure. It is easier to produce values in the set V than in I, but error detection for members of V is more difficult because of the problem of voting with multiple correct outputs. DRAs resulting in values belonging to the set V are called *approximate*. Approximate DRAs may have a better chance than exact DRAs of escaping a failure region [45].

2.3.3   Example Data Re-Expression Algorithms

This section provides several examples of exact and approximate DRAs. An example of re-expression with postexecution adjustment provided in [45] follows. Suppose a program computes intersections of line segments. A DRA could alter the representation of the input by multiplying the input by a nonsingular matrix. After execution of P, the distortion could be recovered by multiplying the program output by the inverse of the matrix.

For an example of an exact DRA, suppose we have a program that processes Cartesian input points. Also suppose that only the relative position of the points is relevant to the application at hand. An example of an exact DRA for this program would be one that translates the coordinate system to a new origin or one that rotates the coordinate system about an arbitrary point [45].

Another example of an exact DRA, this time for a sort function, is random permutation of the input. The re-expressed data is different from the original data, and it should yield identical output. Another exact DRA, this one for a sort function, is to subtract each input data value from a value larger than all the input data values. The output is simply related to the original and can be easily recovered through postexecution adjustment.

An example of an approximate DRA for sensor values is to introduce a low-intensity noise term into the sensor values used by a control system. Since sensor data generally has limited accuracy, this DRA should have little or no impact on the application, other than the desired fault tolerance contribution. Perturbing real-valued quantities within specified bounds provides this type of data diversity. This example is from [43]. One of the inputs to the programs the authors of [43] studied is a list of (x, y) pairs representing radar tracks. To use data diversity, it was assumed that data obtained from the radar was of limited precision. A DRA moved each (x, y) point to a random location on the circumference of a circle centered at (x, y) and of some small, fixed radius. Figure 2.8 shows how this algorithm re-expresses a set of three radar points.

An example of an exact DRA of the "re-expression via decomposition and recombination" type [45] considers a data diverse computation of the sine function. Assume the failure probability for the sine function in this example, on a randomly chosen input x, is p, where $p \ll 1$. Use the following trigonometric identifiers for computing $\sin(x)$

$$\sin(a + b) = \sin(a)\cos(b) + \cos(a)\sin(b)$$
$$\cos(a) = \sin(\pi/2 - a)$$

to rewrite

$$\sin(x) = \sin(a)\sin(\pi/2 - b) + \sin(\pi/2 - a)\sin(b)$$

a and b are real numbers such that $a + b = x$. Suppose that $\sin(x)$ is computed using three independent decompositions for x obtained by using three different values for each a and b, and that a simple majority voter selects the output. Using the worst case assumption that all incorrect answers appear identical to the voter, a conservative estimate of the probability of computing an incorrect value for $\sin(x)$ can be shown to be on the order of $48p^2$ [44].

Data re-expression can be used on numeric data, character strings, differential equations, and other data representations. For example, combining tree transformations, data storage reordering, and code storage reordering (generation of code for subprograms in an arbitrary order) provide considerable diversity in the data processed by large fractions of a conventional compiler [45]. For example, Figure 2.9 [52] illustrates a simple tree

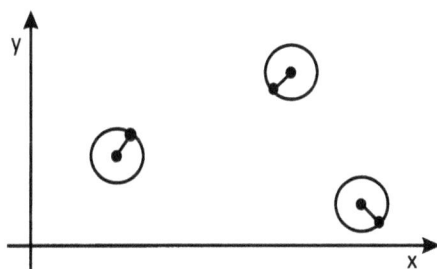

Figure 2.8 Re-expression of three radar points [43]. © 1987 IEEE. Reprinted with permission. This type of re-expression yields values in set *V* and is thus termed an approximate data re-expression algorithm.

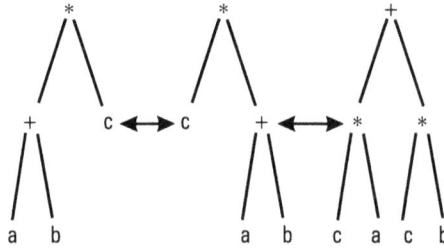

Figure 2.9 Invariant tree transformations. (*Source:* [52], © 1990, Springer-Verlag, Figure 6, p. 49. Reprinted with permission.) This example illustrates that data re-expression algorithms do not have to be performed solely on numeric data.

transformation for evaluating the expression $(a + b) * c$. The figure shows three semantically identical trees that represent the given expression. Normally, compilers are designed to optimize such trees. For example, the third tree is undesirable from a performance standpoint because the variable c must be evaluated twice. From a data diverse standpoint, however, performance is not the major issue. In this example, the goal is to convert different trees representing the same expression into code. The different representations will encourage, for instance, a different allocation of registers to the values a, b, and c.

Ammann and Knight [52] also caution that exact re-expression algorithms may have the defect of preserving precisely those aspects of the data that cause program failure. An exact re-expression algorithm may cause all inputs in the failure region to be re-expressed as other inputs in the failure region. An approximate DRA may have a higher probability of escaping the failure region. The DRA designer must fully understand the program and the characteristics of its input failure region (e.g., cross section) to provide a DRA that enables effective data diversity.

2.4 Temporal Diversity

Temporal diversity involves the performance or occurrence of an event at different times. For example, temporal diversity can be implemented by beginning software execution at different times or using inputs that are produced or read at different times. Temporal diversity can be an effective means of overcoming transient faults (as discussed in Section 1.5.3) because the temporary conditions that cause problems in one execution may be absent when the software is reexecuted.

Temporal diversity by using data produced at different times can also provide diverse inputs to a data diverse technique. Temporal skewing of input data was proposed by Martin [47] and by Morris [48]. Their two-version systems use data from adjacent real-time frames rather than from the same frame. The data differs because it is read from the sensors at different times. Each version is provided inputs from different time frames. A correction may be necessary prior to voting on the results to account for the different read times.

Figure 2.10 illustrates event timing for a sample temporally diverse system. Inputs are received at times t_i, t_{i+1}, and t_{i+2}. The input received at time t_i is used by the software to produce its results. The results are checked by an adjudicator, say in this case, an acceptance test (AT). (Chapter 7 describes ATs, but for this example let's assume the test checks the result against a maximum. That is, if the result is less than or equal to the maximum allowed value, it passes the AT. Otherwise, it fails the AT.) Suppose the result produced using the input received at time t_i fails the AT. Given this failure, our program accepts an input retrieved at time t_{i+1}. The resulting program output passes the AT. If our scheme is set up to receive three inputs and accept the first that passes the AT, then the input retrieved at time t_{i+2} is discarded.

Temporal diversity can be used to tolerate transient faults by re-execution. It can also be used to provide diverse inputs for data or design diverse systems or, as illustrated in our example, for a simple temporally diverse, sequentially executed fault tolerance technique.

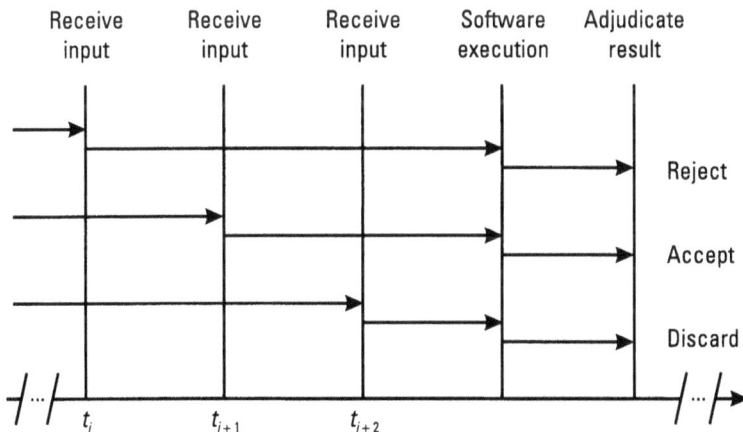

Figure 2.10 Sample illustration of temporal diversity.

2.5   Architectural Structure for Diverse Software

The typical systems for which software fault tolerance is applicable are highly complex. To aid in the avoidance of faults in the first place and the tolerance of those remaining faults, the system complexity must be controlled. Structuring the hardware and software components that comprise these systems is a key factor to controlling the complexity.

Laprie, et al. [32] describe two such structuring mechanisms—layering and error confinement areas. In structuring the system into layers, we want each layer to have the fault tolerance mechanisms to handle the errors produced in that layer. The fault tolerance mechanisms in each layer should handle the error recovery time performance and containment of error data propagation.

Error confinement areas [53] are described in terms of the system hardware and software architecture elements. These architectural elements are [32]:

- The elements providing the services necessary for application software to be executed, that is, hardware and executive software (termed a hardware component in this usage [32]);

- The application software variants.

Laprie, et al. [32] define a hardware error confinement area (HECA) as covering at least one hardware component. A software error confinement area (SECA) covers at least one software variant.

2.6   Structure for Development of Diverse Software

Another way to control the complexity of software fault tolerant systems is to provide a framework or structure for design and implementation. Several such frameworks exist (e.g., [54–57]) and share, in general, the following characteristics.

- They are based on the concept of an idealized fault-tolerant component [58, 59].

- They are recursive in nature—each component can be viewed as a system in itself [60].

- Many details of their implementation are made transparent to the users.

- They provide well-defined interfaces for the definition and implementation of fault tolerance schemes.

- They consist, in general, of three parts of a fault-tolerant component: the controller, redundant variants, and an adjudicator.

The *controller* orchestrates the operation of the fault tolerance technique by invoking the variants and using an adjudicator to determine the system result. The *variants* provide the same service, but through diverse software or data. The *adjudicator* selects a presumably correct system result from the results provided by the variants.

We will present the frameworks of Xu and Randell [54, 55] and Daniels, Kim, and Vouk [56] in this section. The Pullum and Duncan approach is presented in [57, 61].

2.6.1   Xu and Randell Framework

The basic building block used in the Xu and Randell framework is an idealized fault-tolerant component [55]. It receives requests for service and produces responses. If the component cannot satisfy a service request, it returns an exception. The idealized fault-tolerant component provides both normal and abnormal (i.e., exception) responses in the interface between interacting components. There are three classes of exceptional situations, in which some fault tolerance response is needed, identified for this framework as follows [55]:

- *Interface exceptions:* signaled when interface checks find that an invalid service request has been made to a component;

- *Local exceptions:* raised when a component detects an error that its own fault tolerance capabilities could or should deal with in the hope that the component would return to normal operations after exception handling;

- *Failure exception:* signaled to notify the component that made the service request that, despite the use of its own fault tolerance capabilities, it has been unable to provide the service requested of it.

The framework [54] for describing, comparing, and implementing various software fault tolerance schemes is illustrated in Figure 2.11. The framework consists of an idealized component that in turn consists of an

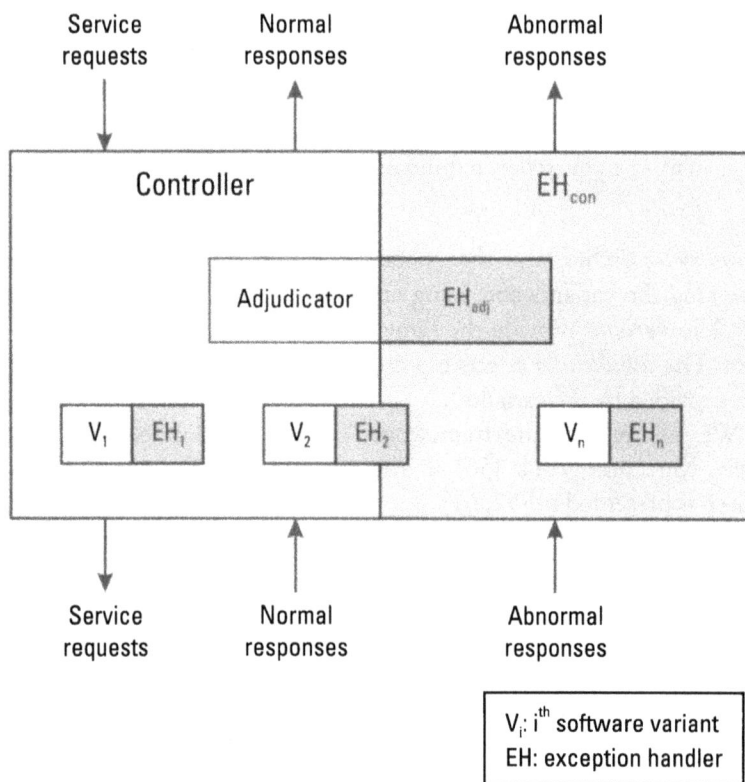

Figure 2.11 Idealized component with design redundancy. (*Source:* [55], © 1995 John Wiley and Sons. Reproduced with permission.)

adjudicator subcomponent and a set of software variants. The controller invokes one or more of the variants, waits as necessary for such variants to complete their execution, and invokes the adjudicator to check on the results produced by the variants. As shown, each of the components can contain its own exception handler, and the framework structure is fully recursive.

The class hierarchy of Figure 2.12 illustrates how the application-specific software fault tolerance is constructed and how application programmers can define their own class hierarchies by inheritance. The control architecture is implemented by class sftFramework, which controls two abstract base classes—adjudicator and variant. The remainder of this subsection provides some details on the classes and use of the framework to develop a fault tolerant application. This information is derived from Xu and Randell [54], which may be referred to for additional details.

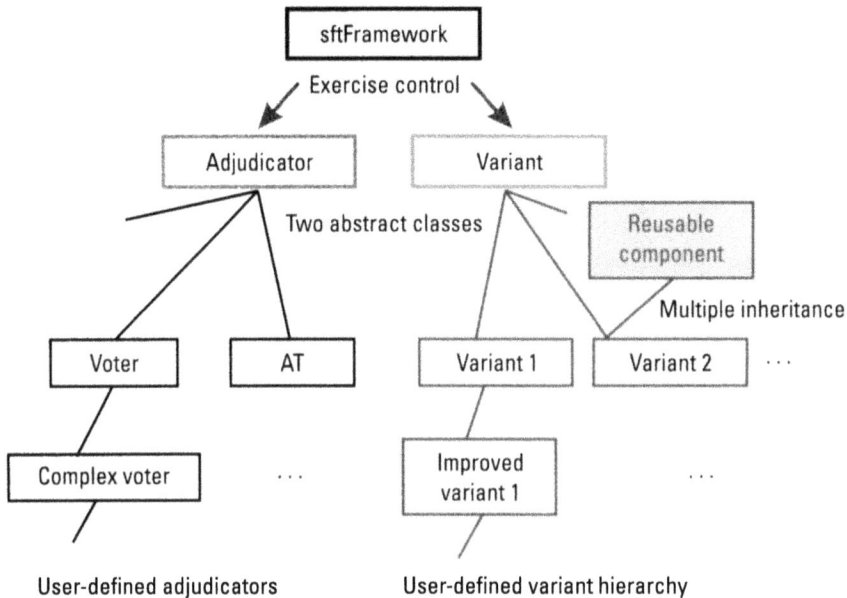

Figure 2.12 Construction of the framework and user-defined class hierarchy. (*Source:* [54].)

Software variants are implemented with the abstract base class variant [54]. (Code examples from Xu and Randell [54] are reproduced here with permission.)

```
class variant
{ ... ...      //private variables and operations
public:
    virtual void variantDefinition();  //interface
    virtual void exceptionHandler1(...);
    virtual void exceptionHandler2(...);
    ... ...
};
```

The purpose of the variant class is to provide an interface through which the application programmer can develop specific program variants and, furthermore, the control architecture can organize the execution of these user-defined variants in order to provide either static or dynamic redundancy, as chosen by the application designer. Class variant is an abstract class. It is used only for deriving other classes, and not for creating class objects. The variantDefinition() function is intended to be overridden in the derived classes, providing the application-specific variant definitions.

An example application-specific variant, quickSort, is written in the form of a derived class [54]. This part is developed by the application programmer.

```
class quickSort : public variant
{ ... ...  //private attributes and class invariant
public:
    //user-defined sorting and other operations
    int variantDefinition(int);
    ... ...
    //user-defined handlers
    void exceptionHandler1(...);
    void exceptionHandler2(...);
    ... ...
};
```

Adjudicators are implemented with the base class adjudicator [54].

```
class adjudicator
{ ... ...  //private variables and operations
public:
    //standard adjudication operations
    virtual boolean acceptanceTest();
    virtual void voting(...);
    ... ...
    //handlers for errors in adjudicators
    void exceptionHandler1(...);
    void exceptionHandler2(...);
    ... ...
};
```

In practice, adjudication algorithms are usually application-specific. Similar to the way application-specific variants are developed, the application programmer can develop application-specific adjudication algorithms.

The function of the control architecture is to control the execution of variants, to invoke the adjudicator, and to output the results or to report an exception to the next higher level of the system. The control architecture is implemented by the class sftFramework [54].

```
enum sftStatus {NORMAL, EXCEPTION, FAILURE...}
class sftFramework
{ ...      ...          //private variables and operations
    adjudicator* pa;  //pointer to adjudicator
    variant* pv1;      //pointers to variants
    variant* pv2;
    ...      ...
public:
    //execution modes
    sftStatus recoveryBlock(...);
    sftStatus nVersionProgramming(...);
    sftStatus sequentialExecution(...);
    sftStatus dynamicExecution(...);
    ...      ...
    void exceptionHandler1(...);
    void exceptionHandler2(...);
    ...      ...
};
```

Class `sftFramework` involves a set of control modes corresponding to different software fault tolerance techniques, from which the programmer chooses the appropriate control modes to implement the desired fault-tolerant technique. The enum structure, `sftStatus`, enumerates the possible execution states of an execution mode. The return states are:

- NORMAL: A normal service;
- EXCEPTION: A possibly degraded service;
- FAILURE: No service.

The control modes available are defined as follows.

- Mode 1: *Conditionally sequential execution.* In this mode, the control program first saves the state of the system (providing for backward error recovery), then invokes variant 1 and calls the adjudicator. If variant 1 fails the adjudication check, the control program restores the state of the system and invokes another variant. An example technique using this mode is the recovery block (RcB) technique.
- Mode 2: *Full parallel execution.* In this mode, the control algorithm invokes all the variants and coordinates their execution through a synchronization regime. It then calls the adjudicator. If no single, presumably correct result is determined, an exception is signaled to

the higher level of the system. The NVP, NSCP, and $t/(n-1)$-variant programming techniques are typical examples of this mode.

- Mode 3: *Fully sequential execution.* In this mode, the control architecture executes all the variants sequentially and then invokes the adjudicator for the selection of a correct result. Sequential NVP [62] and the certification trail scheme [63] are examples of this mode.

- Mode 4: *Dynamically adaptive execution.* In this mode, the control program organizes the execution of variants in a dynamic fashion. It always invokes a currently active set of variants and then calls the adjudicator. Once a correct result is obtained, it stops any further action immediately. If the current execution fails the adjudicator, the control program configures another set of variants to execute. The self-configuring optimal programming (SCOP) method [64, 65] employs this structure.

Given this framework, all the application programmer has to do to implement their fault-tolerant application is:

- Develop redundant variants of the parts of the overall program that they want to make fault-tolerant;

- Select a basic adjudication function or define a new adjudication function;

- Choose an appropriate control mode effective for the particular application requirements (reliability, performance, timeliness, efficiency, etc.) [54].

Suppose the programmer wants to implement a fault-tolerant application using the RcB technique. The programmer simply develops a module that defines the elements listed above, as shown in the sample below [54].

```
sft_module
{ ...      ...
    sftFramework* pf;
    acceptanceTest* pa;            //user-defined AT test
    variant1* pv[1] = &primary;    //user-defined primary
    variant2* pv[2] = &alternate1; //user-defined alternates
    ...      ...
    status = pf->recoveryBlock(pa, pv[], ... );
    ...      ...
};
```

To use the NVP technique, the elements are defined as illustrated below [54].

```
sft_module
{    ...       ...
     sftFramework* pf;
     exactVoting* pe;                //user-defined voter
     variant1* pv[1] = &version1; //user-defined versions
     variant2* pv[2] = &version2;
     variant3* pv[3] = &version3;
     ...      ...
     status = pf-nVersionProgramming(pe, pv[], ...);
     ...      ...
};
```

2.6.2　Daniels, Kim, and Vouk Framework

Daniels, Kim, and Vouk [56] developed a general pattern for designing fault tolerant software applications—the *reliable hybrid pattern*. The pattern can be used to support development of fault-tolerant applications based on the classic NVP and RcB techniques, and those based on hybrid techniques such as consensus recovery block (CRB), acceptance voting (AV), and NSCP. This section describes the pattern as presented in [56] (with permission). For additional details, the reader is referred to [56].

The structure of the reliable hybrid pattern is illustrated in Figure 2.13. The elements in the pattern are defined below [56].

- *Client:* invokes the services of the reliable hybrid pattern master component when a fault tolerant service is requested.

- *Master:* requests service from two or more functionally equivalent but diverse software versions; sends the results of the version executions to the adjudicator subsystem; and receives results back from the adjudication subsystem and reports results back to the client.

- *Version:* abstract class that declares the common interface for software versions.

- *Version1..N:* executes the requested service and reports the results of execution back to the master.

- *Adjudicator:* abstract class that declares the common interface for adjudication algorithms.

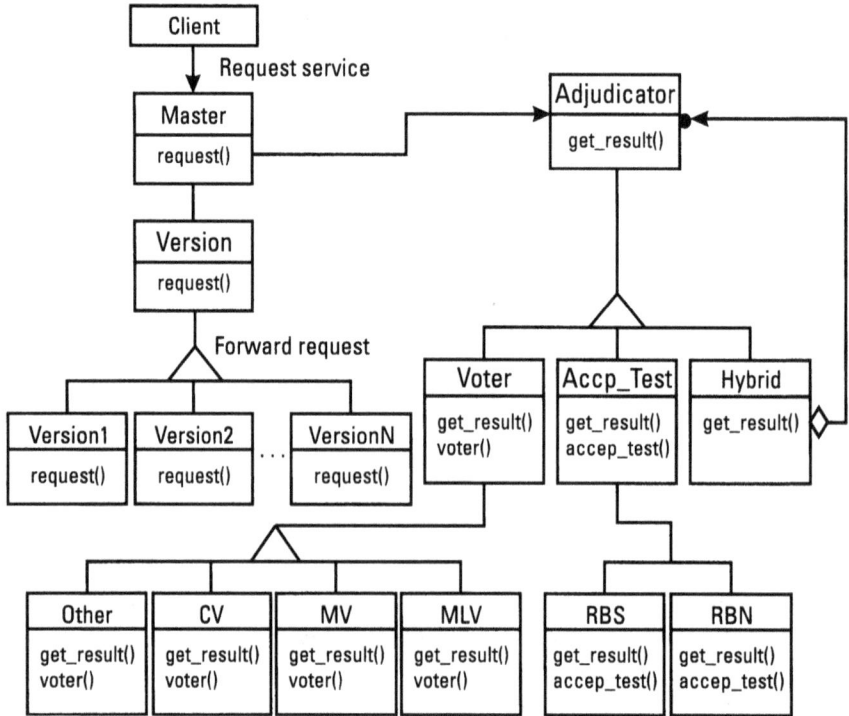

Figure 2.13 Reliable hybrid pattern structure. (*Source:* [56].)

- *Voter:* abstract class that declares the common interface for objects that implement voter-based techniques.

- *CV, MV, MLV, and other:* implements consensus voting (CV), majority voting (MV), maximum likelihood voting (MLV) and any other voting technique suitable for use with the voting interface.

- *Accp_Test:* abstract class that declares the common interface for objects that implement an RcB technique.

- *Recovery block simple (RBS):* implements an RcB scheme and runs a simple acceptance test on the given version outputs.

- *Recovery block version (RBN):* implements an RcB and uses version $N+1$ as the acceptance test on the given version outputs.

- *Hybrid:* declares and implements the common interface for objects that implement fault-tolerant techniques by recursively combining NVP, RcB, and already generated hybrid solutions.

The reliable hybrid pattern can be used to design many software fault tolerance techniques. Kim and Vouk provide the CRB design in [56]. We will postpone further discussion of specific techniques until Chapter 4.

2.7 Summary

Since redundancy alone is not sufficient to help detect and tolerate software design faults, some type of diversity must be present. This diversity can be applied at several levels and in several forms. This chapter explored the diversity of diversity as it can be used in software fault tolerance.

Robust software was examined first, just to mix things up, since it is an approach that does not use redundancy. Rather, it uses various means to check for and then handle invalid inputs.

Design diversity is the form of diversity most common and most studied in software fault tolerance techniques. Separate designs and implementations are used to provide identical services. Many studies and experiences have illustrated all sides of the issue of design diversity efficacy in avoiding dependent failures. Findings of these experiments were summarized and the reader was provided pointers to additional information and the original references.

Data diversity is based on the provision of different input data to the program to avoid anomalous areas in the input data space that cause faults. Several ways of providing data re-expression were described. We briefly touched on temporal diversity. It enables the production of data at different times to provide diverse inputs.

Frameworks for controlling complexity were presented—the Xu and Randell framework (based on an idealized fault-tolerant component) and the Daniels, Kim, and Vouk framework (based on the reliable hybrid pattern). Other frameworks exist, including the author's [57, 61].

Inherent in any successful development of dependable software is the existence of a good requirements specification. It must exist for current software fault tolerance techniques to be successful, regardless of the amount and type of diversity.

References

[1]   U.S. Nuclear Regulatory Commission, *Draft Branch Technical Position*, 1994.

[2]   Atomic Energy Control Board, *Draft Regulatory Guide C-138*, 1996.

[3]   Federal Aviation Administration, *Software Considerations in Airborne Systems and Equipment Certification*, Document No. RTCA/DO-178B, RTCA, Inc., 1992.

[4]   Traverse, P., "Dependability of Digital Computers on Board Airplanes," *Proceedings of DCCA-1*, Santa Barbara, CA, Aug. 1989.

[5]   Briere, D., and P. Traverse, "AIRBUS A320/A330/A340 Electrical Flight Controls— A Family of Fault-Tolerant Systems," *Proceedings of FTCS-23*, Toulouse, France, 1993, pp. 616–623.

[6]   IEEE Standard 729-1982, "IEEE Glossary of Software Engineering Terminology," The Institute of Electrical and Electronics Engineers, Inc., 1982.

[7]   Yau, S. S., and R. C. Cheung, "Design of Self-Checking Software," *Proceedings of the 1975 International Conference on Reliability*, Los Angeles, CA, April 1975, pp. 450–457.

[8]   Avizienis, A., and J. P. J. Kelly, "Fault Tolerance by Design Diversity: Concepts and Experiments," *IEEE Computer*, Vol. 17, No. 8, 1984, pp. 67–80.

[9]   Avizienis, A., "Fault Tolerance, the Survival Attribute of Digital Systems," *Proceedings of the IEEE*, Vol. 66, No. 10, 1978, pp. 1109–1125.

[10] Elmendorf, W. R., "Fault-Tolerant Programming" *Proceedings of FTCS-2*, Newton, MA, 1972, pp. 79–83.

[11] Randell, B., "System Structure for Software Fault Tolerance," *IEEE Transactions on Software Engineering*, Vol. SE-1, No. 2, 1975, pp. 220–232.

[12] Donnelly, M., et al., "Best Current Practice of SRE," in M. R. Lyu (ed.), *Handbook of Software Reliability Engineering*, New York: McGraw-Hill, 1996, pp. 219–254.

[13] Anderson, T., et al., "Software Fault Tolerance: An Evaluation," *IEEE Transactions on Software Engineering*, Vol. SE-11, 1985, pp. 1502–1510.

[14] Avizienis, A., et al., "DEDIX 87—A Supervisory System for Design Diversity Experiments at UCLA," in U. Voges (ed.), *Software Diversity in Computerized Control Systems, Dependable Computing and Fault-Tolerant Systems*, Vol. 2, New York: Springer-Verlag, 1988, pp. 127–168.

[15] Hagelin, G., "'ERICSSON Safety System for Railway Control," in U. Voges (ed.), *Software Diversity in Computerized Control Systems, Dependable Computing and Fault-Tolerant Systems*, Vol. 2, New York: Springer-Verlag, 1988, pp. 9–21.

[16] Laprie, J.-C., et al., "Architectural Issues in Software Fault Tolerance," in M. R. Lyu (ed.), *Software Fault Tolerance*, New York: John Wiley and Sons, 1995, pp. 45–80.

[17] Kanoun, K., "Cost of Software Design Diversity—An Empirical Evaluation," *Proceedings 10th International Symposium on Software Reliability Engineering (ISSRE'99)*, Boca Raton, FL, 1999.

[18] Bishop, P., "Software Fault Tolerance by Design Diversity," in M. R. Lyu (ed.), *Software Fault Tolerance*, New York: John Wiley and Sons, 1995, pp. 211–229.

[19] Dahll, G., and J. Lahti, "An Investigation into the Methods of Production and Verification of Highly Reliable Software," *Proceedings SAFECOMP 79*, 1979.

[20] Kelly, J. P. J., and A. Avizienis, "A Specification-Oriented Multi-Version Software Experiment," *Proceedings of FTCS-13*, Milan, Italy, June 1983, pp. 120–126.

[21] Gmeiner, L., and U. Voges, "Software Diversity in Reactor Protection Systems: An Experiment," *Proceedings SAFECOMP 79*, 1979, pp. 89–93.

[22] Dunham, J. R., "Experiments in Software Reliability: Life Critical Applications," *IEEE Transactions on Software Engineering*, Vol. SE-12, No. 1, 1986.

[23] Knight, J. C., and N. G. Leveson, "An Experimental Evaluation of the Assumption of Independence in Multiversion Programming," *IEEE Transactions on Software Engineering*, Vol. SE-12, No. 1, 1986, pp. 96–109.

[24] Bishop, P. G., et al., "PODS—A Project on Diverse Software," *IEEE Transactions on Software Engineering*, Vol. SE-12, No. 9, 1986, pp. 929–940.

[25] Avizienis, A., M. R. Lyu, and W. Schuetz, "In Search of Effective Diversity: a Six Language Study of Fault Tolerant Flight Control Software," *Proceedings of FTCS-18*, Tokyo, June 1988, pp. 15–22.

[26] Eckhardt, D. E., et al., "An Experimental Evaluation of Software Redundancy as a Strategy for Improving Reliability," *IEEE Transactions on Software Engineering*, Vol. SE-17, No. 7, 1991, pp. 692–702.

[27] Lyu, M. R., and Y. He, "Improving the N-Version Programming Process Through the Evolution of a Design Paradigm," *IEEE Transactions on Reliability*, Vol. 42, No. 2, 1993, pp. 179–189.

[28] Caine, S. H., and E. K. Gordon, "PDL—A Tool for Software Design," *Proc. NCC*, 1975.

[29] Knight, J. C., and N. G. Leveson, "An Empirical Study of the Failure Probabilities in Multi-Version Software," *Proceedings of FTCS-16*, Vienna, Austria, July 1986, pp. 165–170.

[30] Littlewood, B., and D. Miller, "Conceptual Modeling of Coincident Failures in Multi-Version Software," *IEEE Transactions on Software Engineering*, Vol. SE-15, No. 12, 1989, pp. 1596–1614.

[31] Lyu, M. R., J.-H. Chen, and A. Avizienis, "Experience in Metrics and Measurements for N-Version Programming," *International Journal of Reliability, Quality, and Safety Engineering*, Vol. 1, No. 1, 1994.

[32] Laprie, J.-C., et al., "Definition and Analysis of Hardware-and-Software Fault-Tolerant Architectures." in B. Randell, et al. (eds.), *Predictably Dependable Computing Systems*, New York: Springer, 1995, pp. 103–122.

[33] Joseph, M. K., and A. Avizienis, "A Fault Tolerance Approach to Computer Viruses," *Proc. of the Intl. Symposium on Security and Privacy*, Oakland, CA, 1988, pp. 52–58.

[34] Duncan, R. V., and L. L. Pullum, *Executable Object-Oriented Cyberspace Models for System Design and Risk Assessment*, Quality Research Associates, Technical Report, Sept. 1999.

[35] Williams, J. F., L. J. Yount, and J. B. Flannigan, "Advanced Autopilot Flight Director System Computer Architecture for Boeing 737-300 Aircraft," *AIAA/IEEE 5th Digital Avionics Systems Conference*, Seattle, WA, Nov. 1983.

[36] Hills, A. D., and N. A. Mirza, ""Fault Tolerant Avionics," *AIAA/IEEE 8th Digital Avionics Systems Conference*, San Jose, CA, Oct. 1988, pp. 407–414.

[37] Traverse, P., "AIRBUS and ATR System Architecture and Specification," in U. Voges (ed.), *Software Diversity in Computerized Control Systems*, New York: Springer, 1988, pp. 95–104.

[38] Walter, C. J., "MAFT: An Architecture for Reliable Fly-by-Wire Flight Control," *8th Digital Avionics Systems Conference*, San Jose, CA, Oct. 1988, pp. 415–421.

[39] Avizienis, A., "The Methodology of N-Version Programming," in M. R. Lyu (ed.), *Software Fault Tolerance*, New York: John Wiley and Sons, 1995, pp. 23–46.

[40] Lovric, T., "Systematic and Design Diversity—Software Techniques for Hardware Fault Detection," *Proc. 1st Euro. Dependable Computing Conf. EDCC-1*, 1994, pp. 309–326.

[41] Burke, M. M., and D. N. Wall, "The FRIL Model Approach for Software Diversity Assessment," in M. Kersken and F. Saglietti (eds.), *Software Fault Tolerance: Achievement and Assessment Strategies*, New York: Springer-Verlag, 1992, pp. 147–175.

[42] Wall, D. N., "Software Diversity—Its Role and Measurement," Phase 2, REQUEST Report R2.3.6, 1989.

[43] Ammann, P. E., and J. C. Knight, "Data Diversity: An Approach to Software Fault Tolerance," *Proceedings of FTCS-17*, Pittsburgh, PA, 1987, pp. 122–126.

[44] Ammann, P. E., "Data Diversity: An Approach to Software Fault Tolerance," Ph.D. dissertation, University of Virginia, 1988.

[45] Ammann, P. E., and J. C. Knight, "Data Diversity: An Approach to Software Fault Tolerance," *IEEE Transactions on Computers*, Vol. 37, 1988, pp. 418–425.

[46] Gray, J., "Why Do Computers Stop and What Can Be Done About It?" Tandem, Technical Report 85.7, June 1985.

[47] Martin, D. J., "Dissimilar Software in High Integrity Applications in Flight Control," *Software for Avionics, AGARD Conference Proceedings*, 1982, pp. 36-1–36-13.

[48] Morris, M. A., "An Approach to the Design of Fault Tolerant Software," M. Sc. thesis, Cranfield Institute of Technology, 1981.

[49] Ammann, P. E., D. L. Lukes, and J. C. Knight, "Applying Data Diversity to Differential Equation Solvers," in *Software Fault Tolerance Using Data Diversity*, Univ. of Virginia, Tech. Report No. UVA/528344/CS92/101, for NASA LaRC, July 1991.

[50] Ammann, P. E., and J. C. Knight, *Data Re-expression Techniques for Fault Tolerant Systems*, Tech. Report, Report No. TR90-32, CS Dept., Univ. of Virginia, Nov. 1990.

[51] Cristian, F., "Exception Handling," in T. Anderson (ed.), *Resilient Computing Systems*, Vol. 2, New York: John Wiley and Sons, 1989.

[52] Ammann, P. E., "Data Redundancy for the Detection and Tolerance of Software Faults," *Proceedings: Interface '90*, East Lansing, MI, May 1990.

[53] Siewiorek, D. P., and D. Johnson, "A Design Methodology," in D. P. Siewiorek and R. S. Swarz (eds.), *Reliable Computer Systems—Design and Evaluation*, Bedford, MA: Digital Press, 1992, pp. 739–767.

[54] Xu, J., and B. Randell, *Object-Oriented Construction of Fault-Tolerant Software*, University of Newcastle upon Tyne, Technical Report Series, No. 444, July 1993.

[55] Randell, B., and J. Xu, "The Evolution of the Recovery Block Concept," in M. R. Lyu (ed.), *Software Fault Tolerance*, New York: John Wiley and Sons, 1995, pp. 1–21.

[56] Daniels, F., K. Kim, and M. Vouk. "The Reliable Hybrid Pattern—A Generalized Software Fault Tolerant Design Pattern," *Proceedings: PloP 1997 Conference*, 1997.

[57] Pullum, L. L., and R. V. Duncan, Jr., *Fault-Tolerant Object-Oriented Code Generator: Phase I Final Report*, Quality Research Associates, Tech. Rep., NASA Contract, 1999.

[58] Anderson, T., and P. A. Lee, *Fault Tolerance: Principles and Practice*, Upper Saddle River, NJ: Prentice-Hall, 1981.

[59] Randell, B., "Fault Tolerance and System Structuring," *Proceedings 4th Jerusalem Conference on Information Technology*, Jerusalem, 1984, pp. 182–191.

[60] Lee, P. A., and T. Anderson, *Fault Tolerance: Principles and Practice*, New York: Springer-Verlag, 2nd ed., 1990.

[61] Duncan, R. V., Jr., and L. L. Pullum, "Object-Oriented Executives and Components for Fault Tolerance," *IEEE Aerospace Conference*, Big Sky, MT, 2001.

[62] Grnarov, A., J. Arlat, and A. Avizienis, "On the Performance of Software Fault-Tolerance Strategies," *Proceedings of FTCS-10*, Kyoto, Japan, 1980, pp. 251–256.

[63] Sullivan, G., and G. Masson, "Using Certification Trails to Achieve Software Fault Tolerance," *Proceedings of FTCS-20*, Newcastle, 1990, pp. 423–431.

[64] Bondavalli, A., F. DiGiandomenico, and J. Xu, *A Cost-Effective and Flexible Scheme for Software Fault Tolerance*, Univ. of Newcastle upon Tyne, Tech. Rep. No. 372, 1992.

[65] Xu, J., A. Bondavalli, and F. DiGiandomenico, *Software Fault Tolerance: Dynamic Combination of Dependability and Efficiency*, Univ. of Newcastle upon Tyne, Tech. Rep. No. 442, 1993.

3

Design Methods, Programming Techniques, and Issues

Developing dependable, critical applications is not an easy task. The trend toward increasing complexity and size, distribution on heterogeneous platforms, diverse accidental and malicious origins of system failures, the consequences of failures, and the severity of those consequences combine to thwart the best human efforts at developing these applications. In this chapter, we will examine some of the problems and issues that most, if not all, software fault tolerance techniques face. (Issues related to specific techniques are discussed in Chapters 4 through 6 along with the associated technique.) After examining some of the problems and issues, we describe programming or implementation methods used by several techniques: assertions, checkpointing, and atomic actions. To assist in the design and development of critical, fault-tolerant software systems, we then provide design hints and tips, and describe a development model for dependable systems and a design paradigm specific to N-version programming (NVP).

3.1 Problems and Issues

The advantages of software fault tolerance are not without their attendant disadvantages, issues, and costs. In this section, we examine these issues and potential problems: similar errors, the consistent comparison problem (CCP), the domino effect, and overhead. These are the issues common to many types of software fault tolerance techniques. Issues that are specific to individual techniques are discussed in Chapters 4 through 6, along with the associated technique. Knowing the existence of these problems and understanding the problems may help the developer avoid their effects or at least understand the limitations of the techniques so that knowledgeable choices can be made.

3.1.1   Similar Errors and a Lack of Diversity

As stated in the introductory chapter, the type of software fault tolerance examined in this book is *application* fault tolerance. The faults to be tolerated arise from software design and implementation errors. These cannot be detected by simple replication of the software because such faults will be the same in all replicated copies—hence the need for diversity. (We discussed the need for and experiments on diversity in Chapter 2.) Diversity allows us to be able to detect faults using multiple versions of software and an adjudicator (see Chapter 7). In this section, we examine the faults arising from a lack of adequate diversity in the variants used in design diverse software fault tolerance techniques and the problems resulting from a lack of diversity.

One of the fundamental premises of the NVP software fault tolerance technique (described in Section 4.2) and other design diverse techniques, especially forward recovery ones, is that the lack of "independence of programming efforts will assure that residual software design faults will lead to an erroneous decision by causing similar errors to occur at the same [decision point]" [1] in two or more versions. Another major observation is that "[NVP's] success as a method for run-time tolerance of software faults depends on whether the residual software faults in each version are distinguishable" [2, 3]. The reason errors need to be distinguishable is because of the adjudicator—forward recovery design diverse techniques typically use some type of voter to decide upon or adjudicate the correct result from the results obtained from the variants. (Adjudicators are discussed in Chapter 7.)

The use of floating-point arithmetic (FPA) in general computing produces a result that is accurate only within a certain range. The use of design diversity can also produce individual variant results that differ within a certain range, especially if FPA is used. A tolerance is a variance allowed by a decision algorithm. Two or more results that are approximately equal within a specified tolerance are called *similar results*. Whether the results are correct or incorrect, a decision algorithm that allows that tolerance will view the similar results as correct. Two or more similar results that are erroneous are referred to as *similar errors* [1, 4], also called identical and wrong answers

(IAW). If the variants (functionally equivalent components) fail on the same input case, then a *coincident failure* [5] is said to have occurred. If the actual, measured probability of coincident variant failures is significantly different from what would be expected by chance occurrence of these failures (assuming failure independence), then the observed coincident failures are *correlated* or dependent [6–9].

When two or more correct answers exist for the same problem, for the same input, then we have multiple correct results (MCR) [10, 11]. An example of MCR is finding the roots of an nth order equation, which has n different correct answers. The current algorithms for finding these roots often converge to different roots, and even the same algorithm may find different roots if the search is started from different points. Figure 3.1 presents a taxonomy of variant results, the type of error they may indicate, the type of

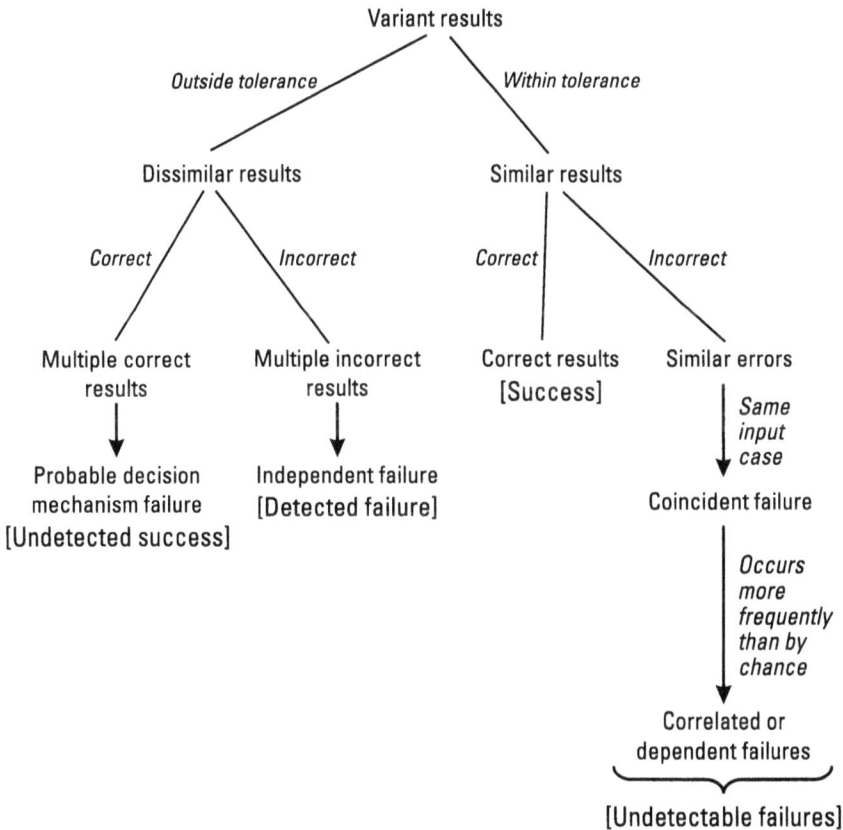

Figure 3.1 A taxonomy of variant results.

failure the error may invoke, and the resulting success or failure detected. The arrows show the errors causing the failures to which they point.

Figure 3.2 illustrates some of these errors and why they pose problems for fault-tolerant software. In this example, the same input, A, is provided to each variant. Variants 1 and 2 produce results, r_1 and r_2, respectively, that are within a predefined tolerance of each other. Suppose a majority voter-type decision mechanism (DM) is being used. Then, the result returned by the decision mechanism, $r*$, is equal to r_1 or r_2 (or some combination of r_1 and r_2 such as an average, depending on the specific decision algorithm). If r_1 and r_2 are correct, then the system continues this pass without failure. However, if r_1 and r_2 are erroneous, then we have similar errors (or IAW answers) and an incorrect result will be returned as the "valid" result of the fault-tolerant subsystem. Since variants 1 and 2 received the same input, A, we also have a coincident failure (assuming a failure in our example results from the inability to produce a correct result). With the information given in this example, we cannot determine if correlated or dependent failures have occurred. This example has illustrated the havoc that similar errors can play with multiversion software fault tolerance techniques.

3.1.2   Consistent Comparison Problem

Another fundamental problem is the CCP, which limits the generality of the voting approach for error detection. The CCP [12, 13] occurs as a result of

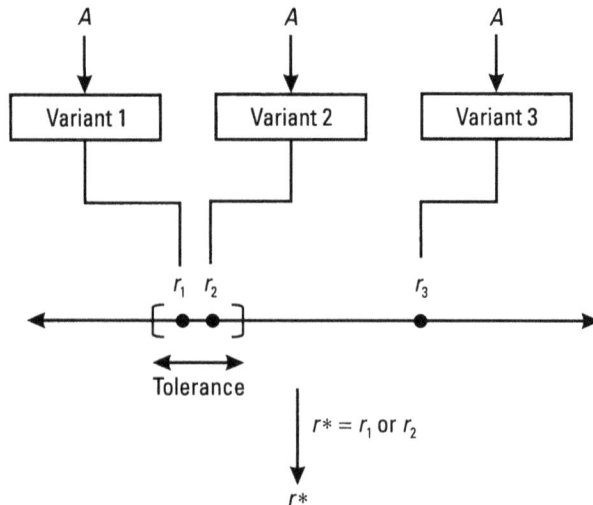

Figure 3.2 Example of similar results.

finite-precision arithmetic and different paths taken by the variants based on specification-required computations. Informally stated, "the difficulty is that if N versions operate independently, then whenever the specification requires that they perform a comparison, it is not possible to guarantee that the versions arrive at the same decision, i.e., make comparisons that are consistent" [14]. These isolated comparisons can lead to output values that are completely different rather than values that differ by a small tolerance. This is illustrated in Figure 3.3. The following example is from [12].

Suppose the application is a system in which the specification requires that the actions of the system depend upon quantities, x, that are measured by sensors. The values used within a variant may be the result of extensive computation on the sensor measurements. Suppose such an application is

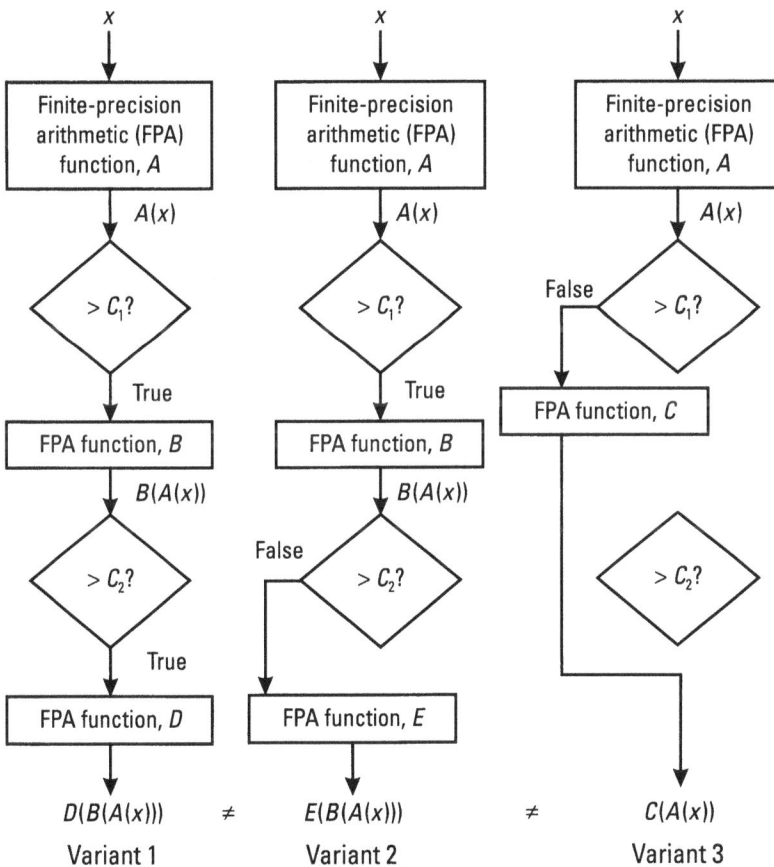

Figure 3.3 Consistent comparison problem yields variant result disagreement.

implemented using a three-variant software system and that at some point within the computation, an intermediate quantity, $A(x)$, has to be compared with an application-specific constant C_1 to determine the required processing. Because of finite-precision arithmetic, the three variants will likely have slightly different values for the computed intermediate result. If these intermediate result values are very close to C_1, then it is possible that their relationships to C_1 are different. Suppose that two of the values are less than C_1 and the third is greater than C_1. If the variants base their execution flow on the relationships between the intermediate values and C_1, then two will follow one path and the third a different path. These differences in execution paths may cause the third variant to send the decision algorithm a final result that differs substantially from the other two, $B(A(x))$ and $C(A(x))$.

It may be argued that the difference is irrelevant because at least two variants will agree, and, since the intermediate results were very close to C_1, either of the two possible results would be satisfactory for the application. If only a single comparison is involved, this is correct. However, suppose that a comparison with another intermediate value is required by the application. Let the constant involved in this decision be C_2. Only two of the variants will arrive at the comparison with C_2 (since they took the same path after comparison with C_1). Suppose that the intermediate values computed by these two variants base their control flow on this comparison with C_2, then again their behavior will differ. The effect of the two comparisons, one with each constant, is that all variants might take different paths and obtain three completely different final results, for example, $D(B(A(x)))$, $E(B(A(x)))$, and $C(A(x))$. All of the results are likely to be acceptable to the application, but it might not be possible for the decision algorithm to select a single correct output. The order of the comparisons is irrelevant, in fact, since different orders of operation are likely if the variants were developed independently. The problem is also not limited to comparison with constants because if two floating-point numbers are compared, it is the same as comparing their differences with zero.

The problem does not lie in the application itself, but in the specification. Specifications do not (and probably cannot) describe required results down to the bit level for every computation and every input to every computation. This level of detail is necessary, however, if the specification is to describe a function in which one, and only one, output is valid for every input [15]. It has been shown that, without communication between the variants, there is no solution to the CCP [12].

Since the CCP does not result from software faults, an n-version system built from fault-free variants may have a nonzero probability of being unable to reach a consensus. Hence, if not avoided, the CCP may cause failures to occur that would not have occurred in non-fault-tolerant systems. The CCP has been observed in several NVP experiments. There is no way of estimating the probability of such failures in general, but the failure probability will depend heavily on the application and its implementation [14]. Although this failure probability may be small, such causes of failure need to be taken into account in estimating the reliability of NVP, especially for critical applications.

Brilliant, Knight, and Leveson [12] provide the following formal definition of CCP:

> Suppose that each of N programs has computed a value. Assuming that the computed values differ by less than ε ($\varepsilon > 0$) and that the programs do not communicate, the programs must obtain the same order relationship when comparing their computed value with any given constant.

Approximate comparison and rounding are not solutions to this problem. Approximate comparison regards two numbers as equal if they differ by less than a tolerance δ [16]. It is not a solution because the problem arises again with $C + \delta$ (where C is a constant against which values are compared). Impractical avoidance techniques include random selection of a result, exact arithmetic, and the use of cross-check points (to force agreement among variants on their floating-point values before any comparisons are made that involve the values).

When two variants compare their computed values with a constant, the two computed values must be identical in order for the variants to obtain the same order relationship. To solve the CCP, an algorithm is needed that can be applied independently by each correct variant to transform its computed value to the same representation as all other correct variants [12]. No matter how close the values are to each other, their relationships to the constant may still be different. The algorithm must operate with a single value and no communication between variants to exchange values can occur since these are values produced by intermediate computation and are not final outputs. As shown by the following theorem, there is no such algorithm, and hence, no solution to the CCP [12].

> Other than the trivial mapping to a predefined constant, no algorithm exists which, when applied to each of two n-bit integers that differ by less than $2k$, will map them to the same m-bit representation ($m + k \leq n$).

In the investigation of practical avoidance techniques for the CCP, the major characteristic that needs to be considered is whether or not the application has state information that is maintained from frame to frame, that is, whether or not the application maintains its history [12]. Systems and associated CCP avoidance techniques can be characterized as shown in Figure 3.4. Each of these types of systems and the avoidance technique proposed by Brilliant, Knight, and Leveson [12] are discussed in the following paragraphs. The immediate effect of inconsistent comparison on a system is that a consensus might not be reached. The extent of the resulting damage varies with the application and has a substantial impact on the effectiveness of measures designed to handle the damage [12]. The avoidance approach requires that enhancements be made to the implementation of an NVP system.

3.1.2.1   Systems with No History

Some simple control systems have no history and thus compute their outputs for a given frame using only constants and the inputs for that frame. If no consensus is reached in one frame and if the inputs are changing, then it is extremely unlikely that the lack of consensus will last for more than a short time. After a brief interval, the inputs should leave the region of difficulty. Doing so, subsequent comparisons will be consistent among the variants. Hence, the effects of the CCP in systems with no history are transient.

An avoidance approach, using confidence signals, for the CCP in systems with no history is described in [12]. Each variant determines, for itself, whether the values used in comparisons were close enough to warrant

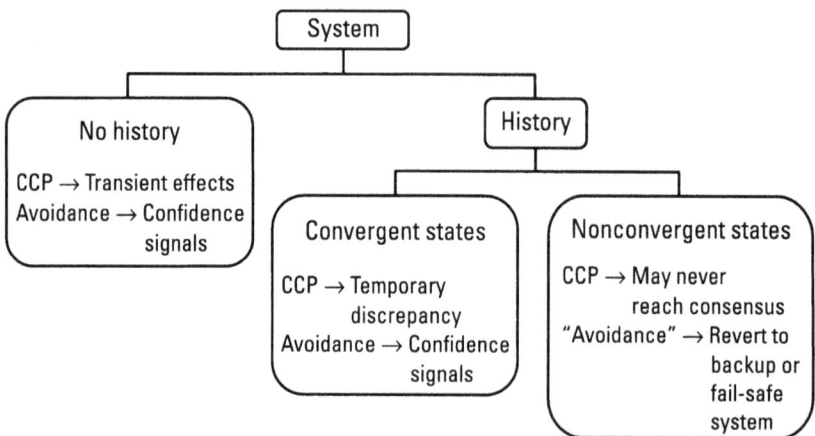

Figure 3.4 Consistent comparison problem avoidance techniques depend on system history maintenance.

suspicion of inconsistency. If a possibly inconsistent solution is detected by the variant, it signals the voter of the event. The voter is unable to tell the difference between the occurrence of an inconsistent comparison and a failed variant, so it ignores the flagged variants' results. The voter can then vote using the results from the variants that indicated confidence in their results. Hence, the fault tolerance may be reduced or even eliminated in this situation. System recovery under these circumstances is application dependent, but it may be possible to treat the situation as a single-cycle failure [12]. This approach requires fairly extensive modifications to the system structure. For example, each variant result would have to be supplemented by a confidence signal, and the voter would have to be modified to incorporate these signals into its decision-making logic.

3.1.2.2 Systems with Convergent States

The situation is much more complex for systems with history, that is, those that maintain internal state information over time. In these systems, the failure to reach a consensus may coincide with differences in the internal state information among the variants [12]. The duration of these internal state differences varies among applications.

In some applications, the state information is revised with the passage of time and, once the inputs have changed so that comparisons are again consistent, the variants may revise their states to also be consistent. In these systems with convergent states, the entire system is once again consistent and operation can safely proceed. An example [12] of this type of application is an avionics system in which the flight mode is maintained as internal state information. If the flight mode is determined by height above ground, then if a measurement is taken that is close to the value at which the mode is changed, different variants might reach different conclusions about which mode to enter. If the variants continue to monitor the height sensor, any inconsistency that occurs should be rapidly corrected.

Inconsistent comparisons may cause a temporary discrepancy among variant states in systems with convergent states. A confidence signal approach may also be used with these systems [12]. Each variant must maintain confidence information as part of its state. If a part of the system's state information is based on a comparison that may be inconsistent, then the variant must indicate a "No confidence" signal to the voter for its results. The no confidence state for this variant remains until the system state is reevaluated. The time required to reevaluate the state is application dependent. During the reevaluation period the system is not fault tolerant. In addition, the time to reevaluate the state may be unacceptably long.

3.1.2.3   Systems with Nonconvergent States

Other applications (i.e., systems with nonconvergent states) determine and then never reevaluate some state information. An example [12] of this type system is sensor processing in which one variant may determine that a sensor has failed and subsequently ignore it. Other variants may not make the same decision at the same point in time, and, depending on subsequent sensor behavior, may never conclude that the sensor has failed. Hence, although the inputs change, the variants may continue to arrive at different correct outputs long after comparisons become consistent because the sets of state information maintained by the individual variants are different.

Once the variants in a system with nonconvergent states acquire different states, the inconsistency may persist indefinitely. Though no variant has failed, the variants may continue to produce different outputs. In the worst case, the NVP system may never again reach a consensus on a vote. There is no simple avoidance technique that can be used for systems with nonconvergent states. The only practical approach in systems of this type seems to be to revert to a backup or a fail-safe system [12].

3.1.3   Domino Effect

While the CCP of the previous section can generally affect design diverse forward recovery software fault tolerance techniques, the domino effect discussed here can generally affect backward recovery techniques. The *domino effect* [17] refers to the successive rolling back of communicating processes when a failure is detected in any one of the processes.

To implement software fault tolerance in concurrent systems (of multiple cooperating processes that communicate with each other via messages), one cannot simply apply some fault tolerance technique in each separate process. If this is done, then each process will have its own error detection mechanism and would establish its own recovery point(s). When one process detects an error and attempts recovery to its recovery point or checkpoint, this can result in an inconsistent global system state unless the other relevant processes are also rolled back. When rolling back the faulty process to its recovery point, the messages issued by that process may also be faulty, so they must be recalled [17, 18]. This recall will force the other processes to roll back to their recovery points that precede receipt of the recalled messages. This recovery and recall continues until the system reaches a stable state, which may be the initial state. This continual rollback and recall is the domino effect, resulting when recovery and communication operations are not coordinated. This causes the loss of the entire computation that was performed prior to the detection of the initial error.

An example will help illustrate the domino effect (see Figure 3.5). (Similar examples are provided in [18–21] and others. The example provided here is derived from [22].) In the figure below, the communicating processes are labeled P1 and P2. At time T1, P1 detects an error and must roll back to recovery point R6. Because of the communications, C5, between P1 and P2, process P2 has to roll back to its recovery point R5. Because of this rollback, the effect of C4 has to be removed, so P1 has to roll back to R4. Because of C3, P2 has to roll back to R3. Because of C2, P1 has to roll back to R1 and because of C1, P2 has to roll back to R2. Now both processes have rolled back to their initial state at T0 and lost the computations performed between T0 and T1.

The avoidance of the uncontrolled rolling back evidenced by the domino effect is achieved if system consistent states, which serve as recovery points, can be established. A consistent state of a system conforms to the system's correctly reachable states and the events history as reflected in the system behavior (its interface) [23]. A consistent state allows the system to achieve an error-free state that leads to no contradictions and conflicts within the system and its interfaces. All communications between processes and their order of occurrence are taken into account. To support consistency, some restrictions on the communication system must be enforced [23]:

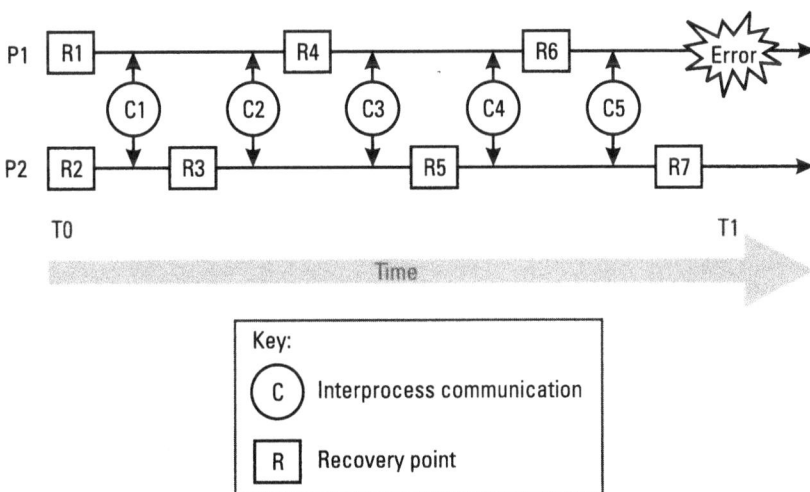

Figure 3.5 The domino effect. (*Source:* [22], © 1991, IEEE. Reprinted with permission.)

- Communication delay is negligible and can be considered zero.

- Communication maintains a partial order of data transfer. All messages sent between a particular pair of processes are received at the destination in the order they were sent.

Consistent states can be determined statically or dynamically. The static approach is a language-based approach in which the consistent state is determined at compile time. At compile time a recovery line is set comprising a set of recovery points, one for each process, to which the processes will roll back. The conversation scheme [17, 24] is a well-known static approach and the oldest approach for overcoming the domino effect. In the conversation scheme, processes that are members of a conversation may communicate with each other, but not with processes outside the conversation. The processes must establish a recovery point when they enter a conversation, and all processes must leave the conversation together. This technique is discussed more in Chapter 4.

The dynamic approach uses stored information about communication and recovery points to set up a recovery line only after an error occurs. The programmer-transparent coordination scheme [18, 25, 26] is a dynamic approach that overcomes the domino effect by relying on an intelligent underlying machine. Detailed implementations of models and recovery protocols based on state descriptions can be found in the literature, such as in [27].

3.1.4   Overhead

The benefits of software fault tolerance do not come without a price. In this section, we examine the overhead incurred in the use of software fault tolerance in terms of space (memory), time, and cost. Given this information (and information specific to individual techniques presented in Chapter 4), one can make a more informed decision on the use of software fault tolerance.

Table 3.1 [28] provides a summary of the overhead involved in software fault tolerance for tolerating one fault. Overhead is described in terms of both structural overhead and operational time overhead. The table does not include overhead that is common to all approaches (including that overhead that should be present in non-fault-tolerant software) such as checking input variables to ensure their values are within a valid range or checking for results that are obviously grossly wrong. For example, the recovery block

Table 3.1
Software Fault Tolerance Overhead for Tolerating One Fault (*From:* [28], © 1995 John Wiley & Sons, Ltd. Reproduced with permission.)

Method Name		Structural Overhead		Operational Time Overhead		
		Diversified Software Layer	Mechanisms (Layers Supporting the Diversified Software Layer)	Systematic		On Error Occurrence
				Decider	Variants Execution	
RcB		One variant and one AT	Recovery cache	Acceptance test execution	Accesses to recovery cache	One variant and AT execution
NSCP	Error detection by ATs	One variant and two ATs	Result switching			Possible result switching
	Error detection by comparison	Three variants	Comparators and result switching	Comparison execution	Input data consistency and variants execution synchronization	
NVP		Two variants	Voters	Vote execution		Usually neglectable

(RcB) technique includes structural overhead for one variant, an acceptance test (AT), and its recovery cache and operational time overhead for executing the AT, accessing the recovery cache, and when an error is detected, executing an additional variant and the AT on the second variant's results. We hold further discussion of the details of this table for the technique discussions of Chapters 4 through 6. It is provided here to briefly illustrate some of the non-cost-related overhead.

As discussed in Chapter 2, all the software fault tolerance techniques require diversity in some form and this diversity in turn requires additional space or time, or both. Xu, Bondavalli, and Di Giandomenico [29] provide an illustration (see Figure 3.6) that summarizes the space and time overheads of software fault tolerance techniques. Space is defined here as the amount of hardware, such as the number of processors, needed to support parallel execution of multiple variants. Time is defined for the figure as the physical time required to execute the variants sequentially. For example, the NVP technique requires additional space for its n variants, so it is to the upper (right) side of the space continuum on the figure. It is also on the lower (top) side of the time continuum because all the variants are executed in parallel. (Xu, Bondavalli, and Di Giandomenico [29] developed a technique, self-configuring optimal programming (SCOP), presented in Chapter 6, that attempts to optimize

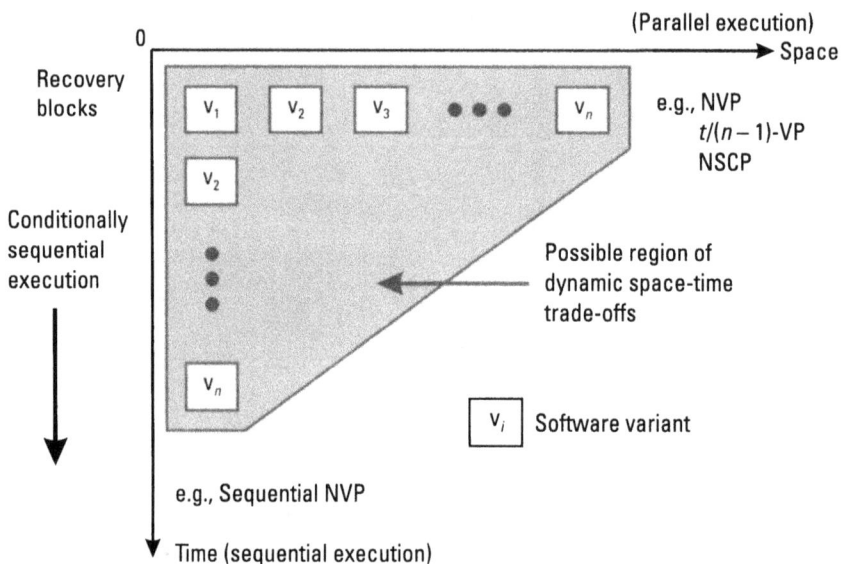

Figure 3.6 Space and time redundancy in software fault tolerance. (*Source:* [29], © 1995, Springer-Verlag, Figure 1, p. 158.)

these overheads.) For use here, the figure provides a basis for understanding the space and time requirements of, and possible trade-offs between, the software fault tolerance techniques being considered for use.

Software fault tolerance also introduces additional overhead in terms of costs. The cost-effectiveness of software has been the subject of debate for many years. The question usually posed is this: Is it better to devote the extra effort to develop the additional variants for diverse software or to devote that effort to the verification and validation (V&V) of one "really good" piece of software? (Halton [30] provides an interesting discussion of this question, favoring diversity.) Below we provide brief descriptions of experimental results on the cost of diversity, then continue with more specific cost information.

The following summaries provide brief overviews of experimental results on the costs of diversity. Note that, in general, the results indicate that the cost of threefold diversity (e.g., NVP with $n = 3$) is not three times that of a single development (it is less) and the cost of twofold diversity is less than twice that of a single development. In addition, not all parts of the software's functionality are critical; that is, only a small part of the software may need to be made fault tolerant. Software fault tolerance may also be less expensive than alternative means of assurance. When examining the cost of software fault tolerance, it is useful to keep the focus on the cost implications on the overall project.

- Several experiments, for example [31–33], have shown that the development and maintenance costs for three-variant diversity can be twice that of a single development and less than double for two-variant diversity.

- The Ericsson company [32] found that, for their railway interlocking system, the costs of developing two functionally equivalent software variants is not double the cost of a single variant because: (a) not all parts of the system are critical, hence only the critical parts may require fault tolerance; (b) while the cost of program specification (design), coding, and testing is doubled, the cost of requirement specification, system specification, test specification, and system test execution is not doubled. In the Ericsson system [32], the majority of the system is concerned with complex computations to make train control decisions. The control commands are submitted to the interlocking software and only the interlocking software is diversely implemented.

- Panzl [34] found that two-variant development with back-to-back (comparison) testing increases the initial development cost by 77% (not a factor of 2), but reduced the number of residual errors from 69 to 2.

- Laprie, et al. [35] analyzed the cost of several software fault tolerance techniques and found that in a multiple variant software development project typical component cost is about 75% to 80% of single-variant costs.

- An experiment at the University of Newcastle upon Tyne estimated the RcB technique's overhead for two variants to be 60% [36] (i.e., 0.8 times the cost of a non-fault-tolerant variant, a cost increase factor of 1.6).

- Another experiment estimated the cost of NVP for $n = 3$ variants at 2.26 times the cost of a one-variant program [37] (and a cost increase factor of 1.5 for $n = 2$). Hence, the cost of a variant in NVP was evaluated as 0.75 times the cost of a non-fault-tolerant variant.

- There are a number of models of the cost of fault-tolerant software [35, 38–43]. We will examine one of these in detail later in this section.

- Some industries, such as aircraft and nuclear power, are subject to official regulation. The costs of demonstrating safety in these industries can far outweigh the development costs. For example, over 500 person-years of effort in safety assessment [44, 45] (not including lost income associated with licensing delays) have been used in the Sizewell B nuclear power station computer-based protection system. In some cases, diversity (not necessarily *software* diversity) has been used to make a more convincing safety case.

- Acceptable alternatives to software fault tolerance may also increase the system's cost. For example, formal methods can be used to prove that a program meets its specification (see Section 1.3.1.3). However, there are high costs associated with these alternatives and there remains the risk of faults within the process and results of these approaches.

Kanoun [46] provides the results of examining working hours recorded during the development of a real-life software system (composed of two self-checking diverse variants). Kanoun evaluated the cost overhead induced by the development of the second variant with respect to the cost of the principal variant, which was considered as a reference. The results indicate this overhead varies from 15% to 134% according to the development phase (134% for coding and unit tests together; about 100% for integration tests, general tests, maintenance, and analysis; about 60% for specification analysis, design, and documentation; and 25% for functional specifications). The average was around 64% for all phases excluding the effort spent for requirement specifications and system tests. The average is between 42% and 71% if the requirement specification phase only is excluded (assuming the system test overhead is 0% and 100%, respectively). Kanoun's results confirm those published in previous work (see above). The results are especially valuable since they were observed for a real system in an industrial environment (versus an experimental environment).

We will examine one of the cost models mentioned above in more detail. Laprie, et al. [35] examined the costs of several software fault tolerance techniques and provided a model for determining the cost of fault-tolerant software with respect to the cost of non-fault-tolerant software. Laprie starts with a cost distribution across life cycle phases for classical, non-fault-tolerant software (see Table 3.2, with these entries based on [47]). Since fault-tolerant software is used mainly with critical applications and the cost distribution is based on no specific class of software, [35] provides some multiplicative factors that depend on the particular lifecycle activity (from [48]).

To determine the cost of fault-tolerant software, factors are used to account for the overheads associated with the decision points and the DMs, and to account for the cost reduction in V&V caused by commonalities among variants. The commonalities include actual V&V activities (e.g., back-to-back testing) and V&V tools (e.g., test harnesses). Given the current state of the art, the values of these factors cannot be accurately estimated, but [35] provides reasonable ranges of values for the factors. The factors and their ranges from [35] are provided below.

- r is the multiplier associated with the decision points, with $1 < r < 1.2$.

- s is the multiplier associated with the decider, with $1 < s < 1.1$ for NVP (Section 4.2) and N self-checking programming (NSCP) (Section 4.4) when error detection is performed through comparison, and $1 < s < 1.3$ for RcB (Section 4.1) and NSCP when error detection is performed through AT (Section 7.2). This difference reflects the differences in the deciders, that is, the fact that the deciders are specific when they decide by AT and generic when they decide by comparison or vote.

- u is the proportion of testing performed once for all variants (such as provision for test environments and harnesses), with $0.2 < u < 0.5$.

- v is the proportion of testing, performed for each variant, that takes advantage of the existence of several variants (such as back-to-back testing), with $0.3 < v < 0.6$.

- w is the cost-reduction factor for testing performed in common for several variants, with $0.2 < w < 0.8$.

The following expression gives the cost of fault-tolerant software (C_{FT}) with respect to the cost of non-fault-tolerant software (C_{NFT}):

$$C_{FT}/C_{NFT} = \rho_{Req} + rs\,\rho_{Spe} + \left[Nr + (s-1)\right]\left(\rho_{Des} + \rho_{Imp}\right)$$
$$+ r\left\{us + (1-u)N\left[vw + (1-v)\right]\right\}\rho_{V\&V}$$

where N is the number of variants, and ρ_{Req}, ρ_{Spe}, ρ_{Des}, ρ_{Imp}, and $\rho_{V\&V}$ are the cost distribution percentages for requirements, specification, design, implementation, and V&V, respectively.

Table 3.3 gives the ranges for the ratio C_{FT}/C_{NFT} as well as the average values and the average values per variant. Examining this table's results provides quantitative evidence for the qualitative statement that N-variant software is less costly than N times a non-fault-tolerant software. The experimental cost results noted earlier in this section fall within the ranges noted in Table 3.3.

3.2 Programming Techniques

In this section, we describe several programming or implementation techniques used by several software fault tolerance techniques. The programming techniques covered are assertions, checkpointing, and atomic actions. Assertions can be used by any software fault tolerance technique, and by non-fault-tolerant software. Checkpointing is typically used by techniques that employ backward recovery. Atomic actions can also be used in non-fault-tolerant software, but are presented here primarily in the context of software fault tolerance in concurrent systems.

Table 3.2
Software Cost Elements for Non-Fault-Tolerant Software
(*From:* [35], © 1990, IEEE. Reprinted with permission.)

Activity	Life-Cycle Cost Breakdown [47]	Multipliers for Critical Applications [48]	Cost Distribution	
			Development	Development and Maintenance
Development				
Requirements	3%	1.3	8%	6%
Specification	3%	1.3	8%	7%
Design	5%	1.3	13%	14%
Implementation	7%	1.3	19%	19%
V&V	15%	1.8	52%	54%
Maintenance*	67%			

*Of this, 20% is for corrective maintenance, 25% is for adaptive maintenance, and 55% is for perfective maintenance [47].

Table 3.3
Cost of Fault-Tolerant Software Versus Non-Fault-Tolerant Software
(*From:* [35], © 1990, IEEE. Reprinted with permission.)

Faults Tolerated	Fault Tolerance Method	N	(C_{FT}/C_{NFT}) Minimum	(C_{FT}/C_{NFT}) Maximum	(C_{FT}/C_{NFT}) Average	(C_{FT}/NC_{NFT}) Average
1	RcB	2	1.33	2.17	1.75	0.88
1	NSCP					
	AT	2	1.33	2.17	1.75	0.88
	Comparison	4	2.24	3.77	3.01	0.75
1	NVP	3	1.78	2.71	2.25	0.75
2	RcB	3	1.78	2.96	2.37	0.79
2	NSCP					
	AT	3	1.78	2.96	2.37	0.79
	Comparison	6	3.71	5.54	4.63	0.77
2	NVP	4	2.24	3.77	3.01	0.75

3.2.1 Assertions

Assertions are a fairly common means of program validation and error detection. As early as 1975, Randell [17] presented executable assertions as central to the design of fault-tolerant programs. An executable assertion is a statement that checks whether a certain condition holds among various program variables, and, if that condition does not hold, takes some action. In essence, they check the current program state to determine if it is corrupt by testing for out-of-range variable values, the relationships between variables and inputs, and known corrupted states. These assertion conditions are derived from the specification, and the assertion can be made arbitrarily stringent in its checking. Assertions may be set up to only produce a warning upon detection of a corrupt state or they may take or initiate corrective action. For example, upon the detection of a corrupt state, the assertion may halt program execution or attempt to recover from the corrupt state. What the assertion does upon firing (detecting a corrupt state) is application-dependent. Assertions can be used as part of a "reasonableness-checking AT" such as a range bounds AT (see Section 7.2.3).

Traditional assertions produce warnings when the condition being checked is not met. They do not typically attempt recovery. Recovery assertions, on the other hand, are forward recovery mechanisms that attempt to replace the current corrupt state with a correct state. As with checkpointing (discussed in the next subsection), the entire state can be replaced or only specific variables, depending on the system constraints and overhead (e.g., time and memory) involved in the saving and restoration of the variables' or state's values. Assertions can also be used to reset variables periodically (i.e., without necessarily testing for a corrupt state) in, for example, safety-critical real-time systems to limit the propagation of corrupt data values [49].

Some programming languages provide special constructs for executable assertions. However, executable assertions are essentially Boolean functions that evaluate to TRUE when the condition holds, and FALSE otherwise. Using a generic pseudocode language, we can present the simplest form of an executable assertion as

```
if not assertion then action
```

where assertion is a Boolean expression and action is a method or procedure.

The most general form of an assertion must refer to the current state and to a previous state. Primary choices for the previous state are:

- The initial state, s_0;

- An intermediate state between s_0 and the current state that was reached along the path the program execution has taken.

Mili [50] provides three reasons for which an intermediate state should be chosen over the initial state in an executable assertion:

1. *Modularity:* We can think of the assertion *a* as checking a local program segment *b* by referring to the state of the program before execution of *b* and after execution of *b*. The program segment *b* and its assertion-checking facilities then form a modular unit that is context independent—it does not depend on where it is in the program [50].

2. *Time parsimony:* Block *b* can be arbitrarily short, and the function it computes arbitrarily simple. Hence the assertion that checks it can be arbitrarily easy to compute and arbitrarily time efficient. By contrast, referring to s_0 means that, at milestone *m*, we check expected past functional properties of program *P* at *m*, whose complexity we do not choose [50].

3. *Space parsimony:* Block *b* can be arbitrarily short, and the variables it affects arbitrarily few. Hence the memory space required to save the variables modified by block *b* is arbitrarily small. By contrast, referring to s_0 means that sufficient memory space must be set aside to save all of s_0, whose size we do not choose [50].

The initial state or intermediate state, the block *b* to be checked, and the statement that saves all or part of the previous state comprise an elementary asserted block (EAB). The general form of an EAB is [50]:

```
ŝ = s;
b;  // modifies s, but not ŝ
if not a(ŝ, s) then action;
```

In the above EAB, the assignment statement $\hat{s} = s$ means saving state s in $\hat{s}$. The expression $a(\hat{s}, s)$ is the assertion. As stated earlier, we may only want to save some variables, such as those that are going to be modified by *b* and/or those that are involved in the expression of assertion *a*.

Let's look at an example. Suppose $s \in S$ is an integer. Also, suppose that program block *b* determines the square of *s*, that is, $b = (s = s * s)$. The following three simple assertions [50] illustrate different assertions we can use with the defined program block, *b*.

```
ŝ = s;
b;
if not (s = ŝ²) then action;

ŝ = s;
b;
if not (ŝ > 1 ⟹ s > ŝ) then action;

ŝ = s;
b;
if not (s > 0) then action;
```

In typical practice, *b* would be an intricate block of code that is difficult to analyze and $a(\hat{s}, s)$ would be a simple assertion [50].

When an error is detected in the current state, action should be taken to notify the designer (so that corrective action—fault removal—can be taken) and a procedure is invoked to perform damage assessment and take appropriate recovery action.

An assertion, *sc*, can be used to detect strict correctness (or freedom from errors) in the program. The following pseudocode sample (after [50]) illustrates the pattern for such an assertion.

```
perform_error_management
{
if not sc(ŝ = s) then {
        //  erroneous state
    produce_warning(UI_or_errorfile, detected_error);
        //  UI - User Interface
    perform_damage_assessment_and_recovery; }
}
```

3.2.2 Checkpointing

Checkpointing is used in (typically backward) error recovery, which we recall restores a previously saved state of the system when a failure is detected. Recovery points, points in time during the process execution at which the system state is saved, are established. The recovery point is discarded when the process result is accepted, and it is restored when a failure is detected. Checkpoints are one of several mechanisms used to establish these recovery points. Other mechanisms include the audit trail [51] and the recovery cache [52, 53]:

- *Checkpoint:* saves a complete copy of the state when a recovery point is established.

- *Recovery cache:* saves only the original state of the objects whose values have changed after the latest recovery point.

- *Audit trail:* records all the changes made to the process state.

In the discussion that follows, the generic term "checkpoint" will be used and will include all three mechanisms, unless otherwise stated.

The information saved by checkpoints includes the values of variables in the process, its environment, control information, register values, and so on. The information should be saved on stable storage so that even if the node fails, the saved checkpoint information will be safe. For single node, single process systems, checkpointing and recovery are simpler than in systems with multiple communicating processes on multiple nodes.

For single process checkpointing, there are different strategies for setting the checkpoints. Some strategies use randomly selected points, some maintain a specified time interval between checkpoints, and others set a checkpoint after a certain number of successful transactions have been completed. For example, [54, 55] examine the location of checkpoints based on the principle of information reduction. There is a trade-off between the frequency and amount of information checkpointed, and various performance measures (e.g., information integrity, system availability, program correctness, and expected execution time). For example, the code size between checkpoints can be a determining factor in the effectiveness and cost of a fault tolerance strategy. If the intermediate results are checked after small pieces of code have been executed, then there is lower error latency, but also a higher execution time overhead. In addition, decision points limit design diversity, since an increase in the frequency or number of decisions requires the agreement of variants at a higher level of detail. However, a large modular decomposition (and thus larger code segments between decisions or checkpoints) ensures higher variant independence and lower execution overheads. Larger code segments between checkpoints and decisions may result in a cursory acceptance test that is incapable of localizing the errors that occur. Models of the various approaches to checkpointing have been compared and their effects on system performance examined [54, 56–58].

There are generally two approaches to multiprocess backward recovery—asynchronous and synchronous checkpointing. In asynchronous checkpointing, the checkpointing by the various nodes in the system is not coordinated. However, sufficient information is maintained in the system so that when rollback and recovery is required, the system can be rolled back to a consistent state. The cost of asynchronous checkpointing is lower than synchronous checkpointing, but the risk of unbounded rollback (the domino effect, discussed earlier in this chapter) remains. Many checkpoints for a given process may need to be saved because during rollback, a remote (in time) state can be restored. Asynchronous checkpointing is simpler than synchronous checkpointing, but can be useful *only* where expected failures are rare and there is limited communication between the system processes. State saving and restoration protocols for asynchronous checkpointing include [59–62] and others.

In synchronous checkpointing (or distributed checkpointing), establishing checkpoints is coordinated so that the set of checkpoints as a whole comprise a consistent system state. This limits the amount of rollback required, but the cost of establishing the checkpoints is higher than in asynchronous checkpointing because of the coordination required. Also, only a few checkpoints of a process need to be saved at a time. State saving and restoration protocols for synchronous checkpointing include [63–69] and others. Consistency criteria for distributed checkpoints (independent of the communication model) are investigated in [70].

Calsavara and Stroud [71] provide example C++ code for checkpointing and discuss some implementation issues. A very simple technique for implementing backward error recovery as part of a generic recovery block is to make a copy of the original object before invoking each alternate, as shown below [71] (reproduced here with permission):

```
try
{
    T oldobject = object;
    alternate(object);
    if( accept(object) )
    {
        return;
    }
}
catch (...)
{
    object = oldobject;
    continue;
}
```

An alternative implementation of backward recovery has each alternate returning a new object (shown below, [71], with permission) rather than modifying the old object in place.

```
try
{
    T newobject = alternate(object);
    if ( accept(newobject) )
    {
        object = newobject;
        return;
    }
}
catch(...)
{
    continue;
}
```

The first approach may be preferable because it only involves an initialization in the normal case, where the second approach requires both an initialization and an assignment. Both approaches make crude copies of the entire state of what could be a very large object. It is preferable to only save and restore the state that has changed.

Using C++, the designer can specify what it means to make a copy of an object. The compiler supplies default implementations of these copy operations if they are not supplied by the implementer, however, the default implementations are recursively defined in terms of their implementation for each subcomponent of the object. By overriding the assignment operator and defining the copy for classes, one has the freedom to copy objects fully or partially on demand, or to copy them using reference counting ("lazy" copy). This control may be exercised at any level of the object hierarchy. So, if each subcomponent of a large object is made up of a smaller object that makes a lazy copy of itself and only makes a full copy when it is modified, then without much effort, the copying operations used in the implementation of the recovery block algorithm above will in fact copy only the state which is modified and no more [71]. Hence, one can use these C++ mechanisms to implement a hardware recovery cache in software.

There has been much research in checkpointing over the years, for example, in protocols and performance modeling (references mentioned earlier), for different application environments (e.g., [63], mobile environments

[72]), and in object-oriented development (e.g., [71, 73, 74]). The reader is referred to the literature referenced in this section and the references therein for further details on checkpointing.

3.2.3 Atomic Actions

Atomic actions are used for error recovery, primarily in concurrent systems (and are widely used in transaction systems, which are not covered specifically in this text). Critical concurrent systems must be structured so that their complex asynchronous activities, such as those related to fault tolerance, can be achieved. One way to approach this requirement is to use atomic actions, which have been shown [75] to increase the quality and reusability of code and to reduce code complexity significantly. The activity of a group of components constitutes an atomic action if no information flows between that group and the rest of the system for the duration of the activity [76]. An *atomic action* [77–79] is an action that is:

- *Indivisible:* Either all the steps in the atomic action complete or none of them does, that is, the "all-or-nothing" property.

- *Serializable:* All computation steps that are not in the atomic action either precede or succeed all the steps in the atomic action.

- *Recoverable:* The external effects of all the steps in the atomic action either occur or not; that is, either the entire action completes or no steps are completed.

The property of atomicity guarantees that if an action successfully executes, its results and the changes it made on shared data become visible for subsequent actions. On the other hand, if a failure occurs inside of an action, the failure is detected and the action returns without changes on shared data. This enables easy damage containment and error handling, since the fault, error propagation, and error recovery all occur within a single atomic action. Therefore, the fault and associated recovery activities will not affect other system activities. If the activity of a system can be decomposed into atomic actions, fault tolerance measures can be constructed for each of the atomic actions independently [80].

The "indivisibility" property of atomic actions may seem to imply that an atomic action itself cannot have structure. However, an action can be composed of other actions that are not necessarily primitive operations. These are called *nested atomic actions* [81]. Since a procedure (or operation or method) may invoke other procedures, which may invoke other procedures, and so on, we can naturally get a nested atomic action.

The structure of a nested action atomic cannot be visible from outside the nested atomic action. A nested atomic action consists of subactions (not visible from outside), which are seen as atomic actions to the other subactions of the same action. That is, within the nested atomic action, each subaction is an atomic action, and hence the structure of a subaction is not visible to another subaction. This enables a safe method of supporting concurrency within an action.

Although atomic actions were developed some time ago, few of the mainstream programming languages or operating systems provide direct support for atomic actions [82]. Supporting atomicity in a single process environment is straightforward. Suppose we have an action, *a*, that we wish to execute atomically. Prior to beginning the execution of *a*, checkpoint the state of the system. If no failure occurs before the completion of *a*'s execution, then the "all" part of the atomic action's "all-or-nothing" property is satisfied. If, however, a failure occurs prior to the completion of *a*'s execution, then restore the checkpointed state. This removes the effects of *a*'s partial execution and effectively satisfies the "nothing" part of the "all-or-nothing" property.

In a distributed system, supporting atomic actions is more complicated. Without proper coordination of concurrent data access, this access to shared data by different processes can cause the system state to become inconsistent. Some efforts to provide support for atomic actions in distributed systems are noted below.

- In Pact (the *parallel act*ions parallel programming environment), atomic actions are used to achieve fully user-transparent fault tolerance with low run-time overhead [62].

- Wellings and Burns [83] show how atomic actions can be implemented in Ada 95, and how they can be used to implement software fault tolerance techniques.

- Avalon/C++ [84] takes advantage of inheritance to implement atomic actions in object-oriented applications.

- The Arjuna system [85] uses inheritance, in a manner similar to Avalon/C++, and object extensions to implement atomic actions in object-oriented applications.

We will examine Arjuna a bit more closely.

To implement atomic actions, the Arjuna toolkit requires the following:

- Every object used within an atomic action must be recoverable; that is, it must provide its own state preservation and recovery operations.

- Each object is also required to state explicitly within the atomic action when it is modified.

- All persistent objects are derived from a special class, LockManager, which is known to the implementation of class AtomicAction. LockManager has two pure virtual functions, save_state and restore_state, which each subclass of LockManager is required to define.

- To ensure that the state's save and restore operations are invoked at appropriate points during the atomic action, an object that is about to modify itself must first acquire a write lock.

There are similarities between the Arjuna mechanism and the recursive definition of default copy operations provided by the C++ compiler itself [71], described earlier.

The class declaration below [85] (boldface indicates keywords) shows the important operations provided by the Arjuna AtomicAction class. To create an atomic action using Arjuna, one declares an AtomicAction instance in the program and invokes the Begin operation. To create nested atomic actions, declare multiple instances of the class so nesting occurs when a Begin operation is invoked within the scope of another atomic action. (Code and discussion from [85] are reproduced here with permission.)

```
class AtomicAction : public StateManager
{
    // private instance variables
    RecordList List;
    ...
protected:    // protected operations
    PrepareOutcome Prepare();
    void Commit();
public:
    // global class variable
    static AtomicAction *Current;
    AtomicAction();
    ~AtomicAction();

    virtual Action_Status Begin();
    virtual Action_Status End();
    virtual Action_Status Abort();
    ...
    bool add(AbstractRecord*);
    AtomicAction*Parent();
    ...
}
```

The following code [85] shows two atomic actions, one of which is committed (A) and the other aborted (B). Arjuna also supports nested concurrent atomic actions, implemented by the class ConcurrentAtomicAction [85].

```
AtomicAction A, B;
A.Begin();        // start of atomic action A
    B.Begin();    // start of atomic action B
    B.Abort();    // abortion of atomic action B
A.End();          // commitment of atomic action A
```

The basic structure for state-based recovery using atomic actions in Arjuna is illustrated in the pseudocode below (from [71]).

```
for (each alternate)
{
    AtomicAction A;
    A.Begin();
    try
    {
        alternate(object);
        if ( accept(object) )
        {
            A.Commit();
            return;
        }
    }
    catch(...)
    {
        A.Abort();
        continue;
    }
}
```

3.3 Dependable System Development Model and *N*-Version Software Paradigm

As stated in the introduction to this chapter, developing dependable, critical applications is not an easy task. The trend toward increasing complexity and size, distribution on heterogeneous platforms, diverse accidental and malicious origins of system failures, the consequences of failures, and the severity of those consequences combine to thwart the best human efforts at developing these applications. In this section, we describe methods to assist in the design and development of these critical, fault-tolerant software systems. In doing so, the following topics are covered: design considerations, a development model for dependable systems, and a design paradigm specific to NVP.

3.3.1 Design Considerations

This section provides a brief introduction to some of the design considerations to be examined when developing fault-tolerant software. These issues are primarily related to design diverse software fault tolerance techniques, but are also useful to consider for other types of software fault tolerance techniques.

3.3.1.1 Component Selection

One of the first major decisions to make is to determine which software functions or components to make fault tolerant. Specifications, simulation and modeling, cost-effectiveness analysis, and expert opinion from those familiar with the application and with software fault tolerance can be helpful in this determination.

3.3.1.2 Level of Application of Fault Tolerance

One of the most important early decisions impacting the system architecture is the level of fault tolerance application. There are two major questions determining the level of application of fault tolerance: (1) At what level of detail should one perform the decomposition of the system into components that will be diversified? and (2) Which layers (application software, executive, hardware) must be diversified [86]?

Level of Decomposition/Granularity

While discussing checkpointing, we touched on this question. There is a trade-off between large and small components, that is, the granularity of fault tolerance application. Component size can be a determining factor in the effectiveness and cost of a fault tolerance strategy. Small pieces of code enable lower error latency and make decision algorithms simpler and more precise. However, small components will increase the number of decision points, which limits design diversity, since an increase in the frequency or number of decisions requires the agreement of variants at a higher level of detail. A smaller modular decomposition (i.e., smaller code segments between decision or checkpoints) increases execution overhead in decision making and fault tolerance control.

Larger components favor diversity and higher variant independence. In addition, larger components result in lower execution overheads because of the lower frequency of executing the decision algorithm. However, larger component size increases the error latency because of increased synchronization delays (e.g., for NVP or NSCP) or rollback distance (e.g., for RcB). Having larger code segments between checkpoints and decisions may result in a cursory decision mechanism that is incapable of localizing the errors that occur.

Related to this decomposition/granularity decision is a lower-level design issue regarding the placement of decision and recovery points within a fault-tolerant section of code and the choice of the data upon which to perform decision making.

What Layer(s) to Diversify/Extent of Diversity

As discussed in Chapter 2, diversity can be applied at several layers of the system (e.g., the application software, executive software or operating system, and hardware) and throughout the development effort (e.g., languages, development teams and tools, and so on). Additional diversity is likely to increase reliability, but must be balanced against cost and management of the resulting diversity.

3.3.1.3 Technique Selection

Selection of which technique(s) to use is an important design consideration. This decision can be helped by input from performance analysis, simulation and modeling, cost-effectiveness analysis, design tools (e.g., [87]), and expert opinion (again, from those familiar with the application (domain) and with software fault tolerance). The information provided in Chapters 4–6 should also be useful in making this decision.

3.3.1.4 Number of Variants

Not considering any economic impact, the number of variants to be produced for a given software fault tolerance method is directly related to the number of faults to be tolerated [86]. There are, of course, both cost and performance effects to consider. A larger number of variants should increase reliability (if the number of related faults does not also increase). However, a larger number of variants in a recovery block scheme will also increase the execution time and cost. Similarly, in multiversion software (such as NVP), an increase in the number of variants will result in higher development and support costs.

3.3.1.5 Design Methodology

Using a design methodology that effectively considers dependable, fault-tolerant software needs will assist in managing the complexities, realizing and handling the design and development issues particular to fault-tolerant software, and developing a dependable system. The guidance in the methodologies presented in the following sections can provide valuable assistance.

3.3.1.6 Decision Mechanism Algorithm

Selection of which DM to use is another important design consideration. This selection can be helped by input from fault-handling simulation, design tools (e.g., [87]), and expert opinion. The information provided in Chapter 7 should also be useful in selecting an appropriate DM.

3.3.1.7 Summary of Design Considerations

Little specific assistance is available to make the required decisions about design, particularly since many of them are at least partially application-dependent. However, cost and overhead information (such as that described earlier in this chapter), performance analysis (such as that described in [63]), design methodologies (e.g., those described in the next sections), and prototype design assistance tools (e.g., the Software Fault Tolerance Design Assistant (SFTDA) [87]) provide valuable guidance and input to the necessary decisions.

3.3.2 Dependable System Development Model

Given the complexity of computer-based critical software, the diversity of faults to be handled by these systems, and the consequences and severity of their failure, a systematic and structured design framework that integrates dependability concerns and requirements at the early stages of (and throughout) the development process is needed [88–90]. Software design faults are recognized as the current obstacle to successful dependable systems development [91]. Conventional development methods do not incorporate the processes and key activities required for effective development of dependable systems. To fill this need, Kaaniche, Blanquart, Laprie, and colleagues [91, 92] developed the dependability-explicit development model. The model provides guidelines emphasizing the key issues to be addressed during the main stages of dependable systems development [91, 92]. In this section, we provide an overview of the development model's key activities for the fault tolerance process and refer the reader to the sources [91, 92] for additional details and activities in other processes.

The dependability-explicit development model provides lists of key activities related to system development phases. The requirements phase begins with a detailed description of the system's intended functions and definition of the system's dependability objectives. The following list [91, 92] summarizes the key activities in the fault tolerance process for this phase.

- Description of system behavior in the presence of failures:
  - Identification of relevant dependability attributes and necessary trade-offs;
  - Failure modes and acceptable degraded operation modes;

- Maximum tolerable duration of service interruption for each degraded operation mode;
- Number of consecutive and simultaneous failures to be tolerated for each degraded operation mode.

The main objective of the design phase is to define an architecture that will allow the system requirements to be met. The following list [91, 92] summarizes the key fault tolerance activities and issues for this phase.

- Description of system behavior in presence of faults:
  - Fault assumptions (faults considered, faults discarded);
- System partitioning:
  - Fault tolerance structuring: fault-containment regions, error-containment regions;
  - Fault tolerance application layers;
- Fault tolerance strategies:
  - Redundancy, functional diversity, defensive programming, protection techniques and others;
- Error-handling mechanisms:
  - Error detection, error diagnosis, error recovery;
- Fault-handling mechanisms:
  - Fault diagnosis, fault passivation, reconfiguration;
- Identification of single points of failure.

The realization phase consists of implementing the system components based on the design specification. Below is a summary of the key fault tolerance process activities for the implementation or realization phase [91, 92].

- Collect the number of faults discovered during this stage:
  - Use as indicator of component dependability;
  - Use to identify system components requiring reengineering.

The integration phase consists of assembling the system components and integrating the system into its environment to make sure that the final product meets its requirements. Following is a summary of the key fault tolerance activities for the integration phase [91, 92].

- Verification of integration of fault and error processing mechanisms:
  - Use analysis and experimentation to ensure validated fault-tolerant subsystems satisfy dependability requirements when integrated;
  - Use fault injection (multiple and near-coincident faults);
- Evaluate fault tolerance mechanisms' efficiency;
- Estimate fault tolerance mechanism coverage—fault injection experiments.

The dependability-explicit development model is provided to ensure that dependability related issues are considered at each stage of the development process. The model is generic enough to be applied to a wide range of systems and application domains and can be customized as needed. Since the key activities and guidelines of the model focus on the nature of activities to be performed and the objectives to be met, they can be applied regardless of which development methods are used.

3.3.3 Design Paradigm for *N*-Version Programming

Although the NVP technique is presented in Section 4.2, we describe in this section a design paradigm for NVP because it contains guidelines and rules that can be useful in the design of many software fault tolerance techniques. It is generally agreed that a high degree of variant independence and a low probability of failure correlation are vital to successful operation of *N*-version software (NVS). This requires attaining the lowest possible probability that the effects of similar errors in the variants will coincide at the DM. The design paradigm for NVP was developed and refined by Lyu and Avizienis [93–96] to achieve these goals. Hence, the objectives of the design paradigm, as stated in [96] are:

- To reduce the possibility of oversights, mistakes, and inconsistencies in the process of software development and testing;
- To eliminate most perceivable causes of related design faults in the independently generated versions of a program, and to identify causes of those that slip through the design process;

- To minimize the probability that two or more versions will produce similar erroneous results that coincide in time for a decision (consensus) action of the *N*-version executive (NVX).

The design paradigm for NVP is illustrated in Figure 3.7 [96]. As shown, it consists of two groups of activities. On the left side of the figure are the standard software development activities. To the right are the activities specifying the concurrent implementation of NVS. Table 3.4 summarizes the NVS design paradigm's activities and guidelines incorporated into the software development life cycle. (The table was developed by combining information found in [95] (the table structure and initial entries) and [96] (updated information on the refined paradigm). For more detail on the paradigm and a discussion of the associated issues, the reader is referred to [95, 96].

3.4 Summary

This chapter presented software fault tolerance problems and issues, programming techniques, and design and development considerations and models. The advantages of software fault tolerance are accompanied by disadvantages, issues to consider, and costs. Those common to most techniques were covered here. We covered perhaps the greatest bane of design diversity—similar errors. If these are not avoided then software fault tolerance techniques based on design diversity will not be effective. Other issues and potential problems to be considered were covered, including the CCP with FPA applications, the domino effect in backward recovery, and overhead (not just cost, but time, operation overhead, redundancy, and memory).

Then, to help in development, we described several programming methods that are used by several software fault tolerance techniques. These include assertions (that can be used by fault tolerant or non-fault-tolerant software), checkpointing (typically used in techniques employing backward recovery), and atomic actions (also used in non-fault-tolerant software, but presented here in reference to concurrent systems).

Backing out the scope, we then present methods to assist in the design and development of critical, fault-tolerant software systems. Design considerations, a development model for dependable systems, and a design paradigm specific to NVP are presented.

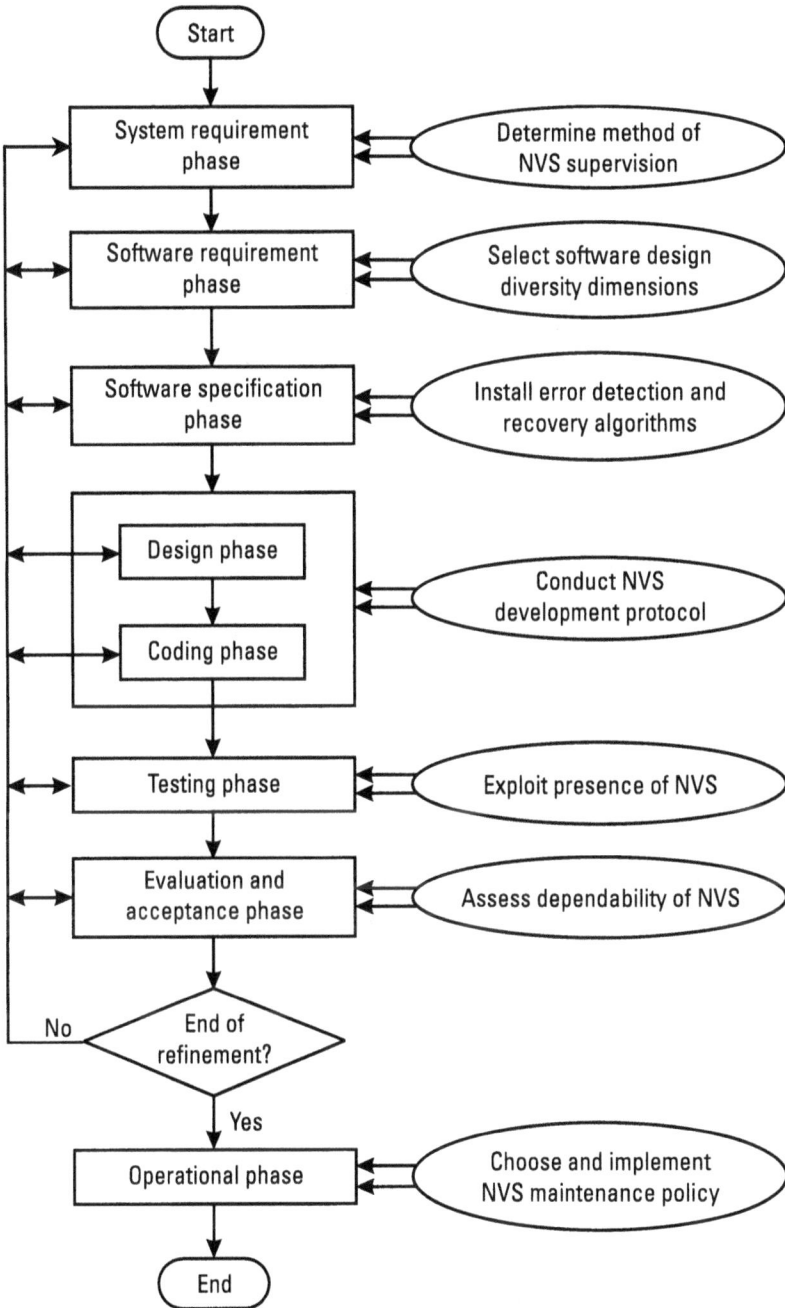

Figure 3.7 Design paradigm for *N*-version programming. (*Source:* [96], © 1995 John Wiley and Sons. Reproduced with permission.)

Table 3.4
N-Version Programming Design Paradigm Activities and Guidelines

Software Life Cycle Phase	Enforcement of Fault Tolerance	Design Guidelines and Rules
System requirement	Determine method of NVS supervision	1. Choose NVS execution method and allocate required resources 2. Develop support mechanisms and tools 3. Select hardware architecture
Software requirement	Select software design diversity dimensions	1. Assess random diversity versus required diversity 2. Evaluate required design diversity 3. Specify diversity under application constraints
Software specification	Install error detection and recovery algorithms	1. Specify the matching features needed by NVX 2. Avoid diversity-limiting factors 3. Diversify the specification
Design and coding	Conduct NVS development protocol	1. Impose a set of mandatory rules of isolation 2. Define a rigorous communication and documentation protocol 3. Form a coordinating team
Testing	Exploit presence of NVS	1. Support for verification procedures 2. Opportunities for back-to-back testing
Evaluation and acceptance	Assess the dependability of NVS	1. Define NVS acceptance criteria 2. Assess evidence of diversity 3. Make NVS dependability predictions
Operational	Choose and implement an NVS maintenance policy	1. Assure and monitor NVX functionality 2. Follow the NVP paradigm for NVS modification

This chapter has focused on issues that are fairly common across software fault tolerance techniques. In the following Chapters 4, 5, and 6, we examine individual techniques, including technique-specific issues.

References

[1] Avizienis, A., "The *N*-Version Approach to Fault-Tolerant Software," *IEEE Transactions on Software Engineering*, Vol. SE-11, No. 12, 1985, pp. 1491–1501.

[2] Chen, L., and A. Avizienis, "N-Version Programming: A Fault-Tolerance Approach to Reliability of Software Operation," *Proceedings of FTCS-8*, Toulouse, France, 1978, pp. 3–9.

[3] Avizienis, A., and L. Chen, "On the Implementation of N-Version Programming for Software Fault-Tolerance During Program Execution," *COMPSAC '77*, 1977, pp. 149–155.

[4] Avizienis, A., and J. P. J. Kelly, "Fault-Tolerance by Design Diversity: Concepts and Experiments," *IEEE Computer*, Vol. 17, No. 8, 1984, pp. 67–80.

[5] Eckhardt, D. E., and L. D. Lee, "A Theoretical Basis for the Analysis of Multiversion Software Subject to Coincident Errors," *IEEE Transactions on Software Engineering*, Vol. SE-11, No. 12, 1985, pp. 1511–1517.

[6] Littlewood, B., and D. R. Miller, "Conceptual Modeling of Coincident Failures in Multiversion Software," *IEEE Transactions on Software Engineering*, Vol. 15, No. 12, 1989, pp. 1596–1614.

[7] Kelly, J. P. J., et al., "A Large Scale Second Generation Experiment in Multi-Version Software: Description and Early Results," *Proceedings of FTCS-18*, Tokyo, 1988, pp. 9–14.

[8] Eckhardt, D. E., et al., "An Experimental Evaluation of Software Redundancy as a Strategy for Improving Reliability," *IEEE Transactions on Software Engineering*, Vol. 17, No. 7, 1991, pp. 692–702.

[9] Vouk, M. A., et al., "An Empirical Evaluation of Consensus Voting and Consensus Recovery Block Reliability in the Presence of Failure Correlation," *Journal of Computer and Software Engineering*, Vol. 1, No. 4, 1993, pp. 367–388.

[10] Anderson, T., and P. A. Lee, *Fault Tolerance: Principles and Practice*, Englewood Cliffs, NJ: Prentice-Hall, 1981.

[11] Pullum, L. L., "Fault Tolerant Software Decision-Making Under the Occurrence of Multiple Correct Results," Doctoral dissertation, Southeastern Institute of Technology, 1992.

[12] Brilliant, S., J. C. Knight, and N. G. Leveson, "The Consistent Comparison Problem in *N*-Version Software," *ACM SIGSOFT Software Engineering Notes*, Vol. 12, No. 1, 1987, pp. 29–34.

[13] Brilliant, S., J. C. Knight, and N. G. Leveson, "The Consistent Comparison Problem in *N*-Version Software," *IEEE Transactions on Software Engineering*, Vol. 15, No. 11, 1989, pp. 1481–1485.

[14]   Knight, J. C., and P. E. Ammann, "Issues Influencing the Use of N-Version Programming," *Information Processing '89*, 1989, pp. 217–222.

[15]   Ammann, P. E., and J. C. Knight, "Data Diversity: An Approach to Software Fault Tolerance," *IEEE Transactions on Computers*, Vol. 37, No. 4, 1989, pp. 418–425.

[16]   Knuth, D. E., *The Art of Computer Programming*, Reading, MA: Addison-Wesley, 1969.

[17]   Randell, B., "System Structure for Software Fault Tolerance," *IEEE Transactions on Software Engineering*, Vol. SE-1, No. 2, 1975, pp. 220–232.

[18]   Kim, K. H., "An Approach to Programmer-Transparent Coordination of Recovering Parallel Processes and Its Efficient Implementation Rules," *Proceedings IEEE Computer Society's International Conference on Parallel Processing*, 1978, pp. 58–68.

[19]   Nelson, V. P., and B. D. Carroll, "Software Fault Tolerance," in V. P. Nelson and B. D. Carroll (eds.), *IEEE Tutorial on Fault Tolerant Computing*, Washington, D.C.: IEEE Computer Society Press, 1987, pp. 247–256.

[20]   Randell, B., and J. Xu, "The Evolution of the Recovery Block Concept," in M. R. Lyu (ed.), *Software Fault Tolerance*, New York: John Wiley and Sons, 1995, pp. 1–21.

[21]   Anderson, T., and J. Knight, "A Framework for Software Fault Tolerance in Real-Time Systems," *IEEE Trans. on Software Engineering*, Vol. SE-9, No. 5, 1983, pp. 355–364.

[22]   Kelly, J. P. J., T. I. McVittie, and W. I. Yamamoto, "Implementing Design Diversity to Achieve Fault Tolerance," *IEEE Software*, July 1991, pp. 61–71.

[23]   Levi, S.-T., and A. K. Agrawala, *Fault-Tolerant System Design*, New York: McGraw-Hill, 1994.

[24]   Kim, K. H., "Approaches to Mechanization of the Conversation Scheme Based on Monitors," *IEEE Trans. on Software Engineering*, Vol. SE-8, No. 5, 1993, pp. 189–197.

[25]   Kim, K. H., "Distributed Execution of Recovery Blocks: Approach to Uniform Treatment of Hardware and Software Faults," *Proceedings IEEE 4th International Conference on Distributed Computing Systems*, 1984, pp. 526–532.

[26]   Kim, K. H., "Programmer-Transparent Coordination of Recovering Concurrent Processes: Philosophy & Rules," *IEEE Transactions on Software Engineering*, Vol. 14, No. 6, 1988, pp. 810–817.

[27]   Merlin, P. M., and B. Randell, "State Restoration in Distributed Systems," *Proceedings of FTCS-8*, Toulouse, France, 1978, pp. 129–134.

[28]   Laprie, J. -C., et al., "Architectural Issues in Software Fault Tolerance," in M. R. Lyu (ed.), *Software Fault Tolerance*, New York: John Wiley & Sons, 1995, pp. 47–80.

[29]   Xu, J., A. Bondavalli, and F. Di Giandomenico, "Dynamic Adjustment of Dependability and Efficiency in Fault-Tolerant Software," in B. Randell, et al. (eds.), *Predictably Dependable Computing Systems*, New York: Springer-Verlag, 1995, pp. 155–172.

[30]   Halton, L., "N-Version Design Versus One Good Design," *IEEE Software*, Nov./Dec. 1997, pp. 71–76.

[31]   Bishop, P. G., et al., "PODS—A Project on Diverse Software," *IEEE Transactions on Software Engineering*, Vol. SE-12, No. 9, 1986, pp. 929–940.

[32]   Hagelin, G., "Ericsson Safety System for Railway Control," in U. Voges (ed.), *Software Diversity in Computerized Control Systems*, Vienna, Austria: Springer-Verlag, 1988, pp. 11–21.

[33]   Voges, U., "Software Diversity," *Reliability Engineering and System Safety*, Vol. 43, 1994.

[34]   Panzl, D. J., "A Method for Evaluating Software Development Techniques," *The Journal of Systems Software*, Vol. 2, 1981, pp. 133–137.

[35]   Laprie, J. -C., et al., "Definition and Analysis of Hardware- and Software-Fault-Tolerant Architectures," *IEEE Computer*, Vol. 23, No. 7, 1990, pp. 39–51.

[36]   Anderson, T., et al., "Software Fault Tolerance: An Evaluation," *IEEE Transactions on Software Engineering*, Vol. SE-11, No. 12, 1985, pp. 1502–1510.

[37]   Avizienis, A., et al., "DEDIX 87—A Supervisory System for Design Diversity Experiments at UCLA," in U. Voges (ed.), *Software Diversity in Computerized Control Systems*, Vienna, Austria: Springer-Verlag, 1988, pp. 127–168.

[38]   Bhargava, B., and C. Hua, "Cost Analysis of Recovery Block Scheme and Its Implementation Issues," *International Journal of Computer and Information Sciences*, Vol. 10, No. 6, 1981, pp. 359–382.

[39]   McAllister, D. F., "Some Observations on Costs and Reliability in Software Fault-Tolerant Techniques," *Proceedings TIMS-ORSA Conference*, Boston, MA, 1985.

[40]   Saglietti, F., and W. Ehrenberger, "Software Diversity—Some Considerations about Benefits and Its Limitations," *Proceedings IFAC SAFECOMP '86*, Sarlet, France, 1986, pp. 27–34.

[41]   Vouk, M. A., "Back-to-Back Testing," *Journal of Information and Software Technology*, Vol. 32, No. 1, 1990, pp. 34–45.

[42]   McAllister, D. F., and R. K. Scott, "Cost Models for Fault-Tolerant Software," *Journal of Information and Software Technology*, Vol. 33, No. 8, 1991, pp. 594–603.

[43]   Lyu, M. R. (ed.), *Software Fault Tolerance*, New York: John Wiley & Sons, 1995.

[44]   Betts, A. E., and D. Wellbourne, "Software Safety Assessment and the Sizewell B Applications," *International Conference on Electrical and Control Aspects of the Sizewell B PWR*, Churchill College, Cambridge, 1992.

[45]   Ward, N. J., "Rigorous Retrospective Static Analysis of the Sizewell B Primary Protection System Software," *Proceedings IFAC SAFECOMP '93*, Poznan-Kiekrz, Poland, 1993.

[46]   Kanoun, K., "Cost of Software Design Diversity: An Empirical Evaluation," LAAS Report No. 9163, Toulouse, France: LAAS, 1999.

[47]   Ramamoorthy, C. V., et al., "Software Engineering: Problems and Perspectives," *Computer*, Vol. 17, No. 10, 1984, pp. 191–209.

[48]   Boehm, B. W., *Software Engineering Economics*, Englewood Cliffs, NJ: Prentice-Hall, 1981.

[49]   Parnas, D. L., A. J. Van Schouwen, and A. Po Kwan, "Evaluation of Safety-Critical Software," *Communications of the ACM*, June 1990, pp. 636–648.

[50]   Mili, A., *An Introduction to Program Fault Tolerance: A Structured Programming Approach*, New York: Prentice-Hall, 1990.

[51]   Bjork, L. A., "Generalized Audit Trail Requirements and Concepts for Data Base Applications," *IBM Systems Journal*, Vol. 14, No. 3, 1975, pp. 229–245.

[52]   Horning, J., et al., "A Program Structure for Error Detection and Recovery," in *Lecture Notes in Computer Science*, Vol. 16, New York: Springer-Verlag, 1974, pp. 171–187.

[53]   Lee, P. A., N. Ghani, and K. Heron, "A Recovery Cache for the PDP-11," *IEEE Transactions on Computers*, June 1980, pp. 546–549.

[54]   Saglietti, F., "Location of Checkpoints by Considering Information Reduction," in M. Kersken and F. Saglietti (eds.), *Software Fault Tolerance: Achievement and Assessment Strategies*, New York: Springer-Verlag, 1992, pp. 225–236.

[55]   Saglietti, F., "Location of Checkpoints in Fault-Tolerant Software," *IEEE*, 1990, pp. 270–277.

[56]   Nicola, V. F., and J. M. Spanje, "Comparative Analysis of Different Models of Checkpointing and Recovery," *IEEE Transactions on Software Engineering*, Vol. 16, No. 8, 1990, pp. 807–821.

[57]   Nicola, V. F., "Checkpointing and the Modeling of Program Execution Time," in M. R. Lyu (ed.), *Software Fault Tolerance*, New York: John Wiley & Sons, 1995, pp. 167–188.

[58]   Kulkarni, V. G., V. F. Nicola, and K. S. Trivedi, "Effects of Checkpointing and Queuing on Program Performance," *Communications on Statistics—Stochastic Models*, Vol. 6, No. 4, 1990, pp. 615–648.

[59]   Wood, W. G., "A Decentralized Recovery Protocol," *Proceedings of FTCS-11*, Portland, OR, 1981, pp. 159–164.

[60] Juang, T. T. Y., and S. Venkatesan, "Efficient Algorithm for Crash Recovery in Distributed Systems," *10th Conference on Foundations of Software Technology and Theoretical Computer Science (LNCS)*, 1990, pp. 349–361.

[61] Juang, T. T. Y., and S. Venkatesan, "Crash Recovery with Little Overhead," *11th International Conference on Distributed Computing Systems*, 1991, pp. 454–461.

[62] Maier, J., "Fault-Tolerant Parallel Programming with Atomic Actions," in D. Pradhan and D. Avresky (eds.), *Fault-Tolerant Parallel and Distributed Systems*, Los Alamitos, CA: IEEE Computer Society Press, 1995, pp. 210–219.

[63] Tai, A. T., J. F. Meyer, and A. Avizienis, *Software Performability: From Concepts to Applications*, Norwell, MA: Kluwer Academic Publishers, 1996.

[64] Chandy, K. M., and L. Lamport, "Distributed Snapshots: Determining Global States of Distributed Systems," *ACM Transactions on Computer Systems*, Vol. 3, No. 1, 1985, pp. 63–75.

[65] Koo, R., and S. Toueg, "Checkpointing and Rollback-Recovery for Distributed Systems," *IEEE Transactions on Software Engineering*, Vol. SE-13, No. 1, 1987, pp. 23–31.

[66] Cristian, F., and F. Jahanian, "A Timestamp-Based Checkpointing Protocol for Long-Lived Distributed Computations," *Proceedings of Reliable Distributed Software and Database Systems*, Pisa, Italy, 1991, pp. 12–20.

[67] Tong, Z., R. Y. Kain, and W. T. Tsai, "Rollback Recovery in Distributed Systems Using Loosely Synchronized Clocks," *IEEE Transactions on Parallel and Distributed Systems*, Vol. 3, No. 2, 1992, pp. 246–251.

[68] Venkatesh, K., T. Radhakrishnan, and H. F. Li, "Optimal Checkpointing and Local Recording for Domino-Free Rollback Recovery," *Proceedings of FTCS-11*, Portland, OR, 1981, pp. 159–164.

[69] Shin, K. G., and Y. -H. Lee, "Evaluation of Error Recovery Blocks used for Cooperating Processes," *IEEE Transactions on Software Engineering*, Vol. SE-10, No. 11, 1984, pp. 692–700.

[70] Helary, J.-M., R. H. B. Netzer, and M. Raynal, "Consistency Issues in Distributed Checkpoints," *IEEE Transactions on Software Engineering*, Vol. 25, No. 2, 1999, pp. 274–281.

[71] Calsavara, C. M. F. R., and R. J. Stroud, "Forward and Backward Error Recovery in C++," University of Newcastle upon Tyne, Technical Report No. 417, 1993.

[72] Ssu, K. -F., et al., "Adaptive Checkpointing with Storage Management for Mobile Environments," *IEEE Transactions on Reliability*, Vol. 48, No. 4, 1999, pp. 315–323.

[73] Kasbekar, M., C. Narayanan, and C. R. Das, "Selective Checkpointing and Rollbacks in Multi-Threaded Object-Oriented Environment," *IEEE Transactions on Reliability*, Vol. 48, No. 4, 1999, pp. 325–339.

[74]   Garcia, J. C. R., et al., *Optimized Object State Checkpointing Using Compile-Time Reflection*, LAAS Report 98173, 1998.

[75]   Rafnel, B. A., "A Transaction Approach to Error Handling," *Hewlett-Packard Journal*, June 1993, pp. 71–77.

[76]   Lee, P. A., and T. Anderson, *Fault Tolerance: Principles and Practice*, 2nd ed., New York: Springer-Verlag, 1990.

[77]   Lomet, D. B., "Process Structuring, Synchronization and Recovery Using Atomic Actions," *ACM SIGPLAN Notices*, Vol. 12, No. 3, 1977, pp. 128–137.

[78]   Liskov, B., and R. Scheifler, "Guardians and Actions: Linguistic Support for Robust Distributed Programs," *ACM TOPLAS*, Vol. 5, No. 3, 1983, pp. 381–404.

[79]   Reed, D. P., "Implementing Atomic Actions on Decentralized Data," *ACM TOCS*, Vol. 1, No. 1, 1975, pp. 3–23.

[80]   Campbell, R. H., and B. Randell, "Error Recovery in Asynchronous Systems," *IEEE Transactions on Software Engineering*, Vol. SE-12, No. 8, 1986, pp. 811–826.

[81]   Moss, J. E. B., *An Introduction to Nested Transactions*, Technical Report 86-41, Amherst, MA: University of Amherst Massachusetts, 1986.

[82]   Burns, A., and A. J. Wellings, *Real-Time Systems and Their Programming Languages*, Reading, MA: Addison-Wesley, 1990.

[83]   Wellings, A. J., and A. Burns, "Implementing Atomic Actions in Ada 95," *IEEE Transactions on Software Engineering*, Vol. 23, No. 2, 1997, pp. 107–123.

[84]   Detlefs, D., M. P. Herlihy, and J. M. Wing, "Inheritance of Synchronization and Recovery Properties in Avalon/C++," *IEEE Computer*, Vol. 21, No. 2, 1988, pp. 57–69.

[85]   Shrivastava, S. K., G. D. Dixon, and G. D. Parrington, "An Overview of the Arjuna Distributed Programming System," *IEEE Software*, Vol. 8, No. 1, 1991, pp. 66–73.

[86]   Laprie, J. -C., et al., "Definition and Analysis of Hardware-and-Software Fault-Tolerant Architectures," in B. Randell et al. (eds.), *Predictably Dependable Computing Systems*, New York: Springer, 1995, pp. 103–122.

[87]   Pullum, L. L., *Software Fault Tolerance Design Assistant (SWFTDA) User's Manual*, Quality Research Associates Technical Report, QRA-SWFTDA-SUM, 1997.

[88]   Avizienis, A., "Building Dependable Systems: How to Keep Up with Complexity," *Proceedings of FTCS-25—Special Issue*, Pasadena, CA, 1995, pp. 4–14.

[89]   Laprie, J. -C., "Dependability of Computer Systems: from Concepts to Limits," *1998 IFIP International Workshop on Dependable Computing and Its Applications (DCIA98)*, Johannesburg, South Africa, 1998, pp. 108–126.

[90]   Laprie, J. -C., "Software-Based Critical Systems," *Proceedings of the 15th International Conference on Computer Safety, Reliability and Security (SAFECOMP'96)*, Vienna, Austria, 1996, pp. 157–170.

[91]   Kaaniche, M., J. -P. Blanquart, and J. -C. Laprie, *A Dependability-Explicit Development Model,* LAAS Report 98341, 1998.

[92]   Kaaniche, M., J. -C. Laprie and J. -P. Blanquart, "A Dependability-Explicit Model for the Development of Computing Systems," *19th International Conference on Computer Safety, Reliability and Security (SAFECOMP-2000),* Rotterdam, NL, 2000, pp. 109–116.

[93]   Lyu, M. R., "A Design Paradigm for Multi-Version Software," Ph. D. dissertation, University of California in Los Angeles, 1988.

[94]   Lyu, M. R., and A. Avizienis, "Assuring Design Diversity in N-Version Software: A Design Paradigm for N-Version Programming," in J. F. Meyer and R. D. Schlichting (eds.), *Dependable Computing for Critical Applications 2,* New York: Springer-Verlag, 1992, pp. 197–218.

[95]   Lyu, M. R., and Y. -T. He, "Improving the N-Version Programming Process Through the Evolution of a Design Paradigm," *IEEE Transactions on Reliability,* Vol. 42, No. 2, 1993, pp. 179–189.

[96]   Avizienis, A., "The Methodology of N-Version Programming," in M. R. Lyu (ed.), *Software Fault Tolerance,* New York: John Wiley and Sons, 1995, pp. 23–46.

4

Design Diverse Software Fault Tolerance Techniques

Design diverse software fault tolerance techniques are based on several key principles. The overriding principle is that design diversity is implemented using redundant software components called variants (also known as versions or modules). By using design diversity, the designer assumes that coincident component failure is rare and that, if it does occur, the results are different enough to enable error detection and to distinguish a correct result or "best" answer. The philosophy behind design diversity is to increase the probability that the variants fail on disjoint subsets of the input space when they do fail, so as to decrease the probability of occurrence of coincident failure.

It is interesting to note some early observations and how they relate to design diversity. Dionysius Lardner stated in 1834 [1] that

> The most certain and effectual check upon errors which arise in the process of computation, is to cause the same computations to be made by separate and independent computers; and this check is rendered still more decisive if they make their computations by different methods.

When Lardner uses the term "computer" above, he is referring to the person performing the computation, not to the calculating engine or machine. Charles Babbage, in 1837 [2] stated that

When the formula to be computed is very complicated, it may be algebraically arranged for computation in two or more totally distinct ways, and two or more sets of cards may be made. If the same constants are now employed with each set, and if under these circumstances the results agree, we may then be quite secure of the accuracy of them all.

The design diverse techniques discussed in this chapter use these principles to detect and tolerate software faults. This chapter covers the original and basic design diverse software fault tolerance techniques—recovery blocks (RcB) and N-version programming (NVP). The results of research and application of these techniques have highlighted several issues regarding these techniques. Modifications and new techniques have been proposed to overcome the weaknesses in the original RcB and NVP techniques, while attempting to maintain the strengths of these foundational techniques. The additional techniques described in this chapter are distributed recovery blocks (DRB), N self-checking programming (NSCP), consensus recovery blocks (CRB), and acceptance voting (AV). All the techniques have advantages and disadvantages that will be discussed in this chapter, along with the techniques' operations.

A significant amount of material is presented in this chapter for each technique, broadly divided into operation, example, and issues. The first figure shown for each technique describes its operation. For those wanting a brief introduction to the technique, this operational figure is a good place to start. Operational details are provided via scenarios and an example. Issues related to each technique are summarized in a table in the third subsection for each technique. A similar format for discussion of each technique is followed in this chapter and in Chapters 5 and 6.

4.1   Recovery Blocks

The basic RcB scheme is one of the two original design diverse software fault tolerance techniques. It was introduced in 1974 by Horning, et al. [3], with early implementations developed by Randell [4] in 1975 and Hecht [5] in 1981. In addition to being a design diverse technique, the RcB is further categorized as a dynamic technique. In dynamic software fault tolerance techniques, the selection of a variant result to forward as the adjudicated output is made during program execution based on the result of the acceptance test (AT). This will be clarified when we examine the operation of the technique below. The hardware fault-tolerant architecture related to the RcB scheme is stand-by sparing or passive dynamic redundancy.

RcB uses an AT (see Section 7.2) and backward recovery (see Section 1.4.1) to accomplish fault tolerance. We know that most program functions can be performed in more than one way, using different algorithms and designs. These differently implemented function variants have varying degrees of efficiency in terms of memory management and utilization, execution time, reliability, and other criteria. RcB incorporates these variants such that the most efficient module is located first in the series, and is termed the primary alternate or primary try block. The less efficient variant(s) are placed serially after the primary try block and are referred to as (secondary) alternates or alternate try blocks. Thus, the resulting rank of the variants reflects the graceful degradation in the performance of the variants.

The operation of RcB is described in 4.1.1, with an example provided in 4.1.2. The advantages and disadvantages of RcB are presented in 4.1.3.

4.1.1 Recovery Block Operation

The basic RcB scheme consists of an executive, an acceptance test, and primary and alternate try blocks (variants). Many implementations of RcB, especially for real-time applications, include a watchdog timer (WDT) [6]. The executive orchestrates the operation of the RcB technique, which has the general syntax:

```
ensure              Acceptance Test
by                  Primary Alternate
else by             Alternate 2
else by             Alternate 3
...
else by             Alternate n
else failure exception
```

The RcB syntax above states that the technique will first attempt to ensure the AT (e.g., pass a test on the acceptability of a result of an alternate) by using the primary alternate (or try block). If the primary algorithm's result does not pass the AT, then n-1 alternates will be attempted until an alternate's results pass the AT. If no alternates are successful, an error occurs.

Figure 4.1 illustrates the structure and operation of the basic RcB technique with a WDT. We examine several scenarios to describe RcB operation:

- Failure-free operation;

- Exception or time-out in primary alternate execution;

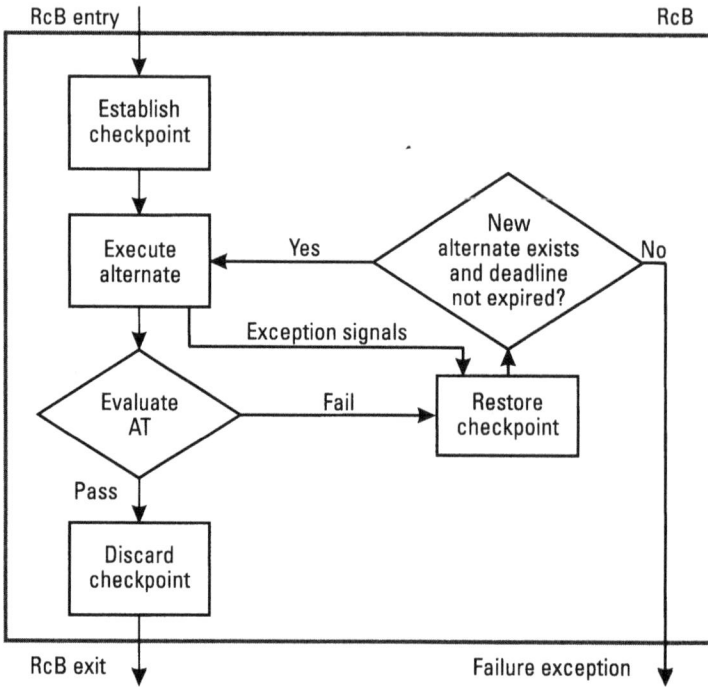

Figure 4.1 Recovery block structure and operation.

- Primary's results are on time, but fail AT; successful alternate execution;
- All alternates exhausted without success.

In examining these scenarios, we use the following abbreviations:

A	Alternate (when there is a single alternate other than P);
A_i	Alternate i (when there are multiple alternates other than P);
A_iOK	Global flag indicating whether or not A_i has failed;
AOK	Global flag indicating whether or not A has failed;
AT	Acceptance test;
P	Primary algorithm/alternate/try block;
POK	Global flag indicating whether or not P has failed;
RcB	Recovery block;
WDT	Watchdog timer.

4.1.1.1 Failure-Free Operation

We first examine the operation of the RcB technique when no failure or exception occurs.

- Upon entry to the RcB, the executive performs the following: a checkpoint (or recovery point) is established, calls to P and A are formatted, and the WDT is set for the expected maximum run time of P.

- P is executed. No exception or time-out occurs during execution of P.

- The results of P are submitted to the acceptance test, AT.

- P's results are on time and pass the AT.

- Control returns to the executive.

- The executive discards the checkpoint, resets the WDT with an appropriate time interval for the next operation, the results are passed outside the RcB, and the RcB is exited.

4.1.1.2 Exception or Time-Out in Primary Alternate Execution

Next let's examine the operation of the RcB technique when an exception occurs in P or P's results fail the AT. Differences between this scenario and the failure-free scenario are in gray type.

- Upon entry to the RcB, the executive performs the following: a checkpoint (or recovery point) is established, calls to P and A are formatted, and the WDT is set for the expected maximum run time of P.

- P is executed. An exception or time-out (via the WDT) occurs during execution of P.

- Control returns to the executive. The executive sets POK to indicate failure of P, checks to ensure the deadline for acceptable results has not expired (it has not in this scenario), resets the WDT to the expected maximum run time of A, and restores the checkpoint.

- A is executed. No exception or time-out occurs during execution of A.

- The results of A are submitted to the AT.

- A's results are on time and pass the AT.

- Control returns to the executive.

- The executive discards the checkpoint, resets the WDT with an appropriate time interval for the next operation, the results are passed outside the RcB, and the RcB is exited.

4.1.1.3 Primary's Results Are On-Time, but Fail Acceptance Test; Successful Alternate Execution

Now let's look at what happens if P executes without exception and its results are sent to the AT, but they do not pass the AT. If the deadline for acceptable results has not expired and a new alternate try block is available, the new alternate is executed. Differences between this scenario and the failure-free scenario are in gray type.

- Upon entry to the RcB, the executive performs the following: a checkpoint (or recovery point) is established, calls to P and A are formatted, and the WDT is set for the expected maximum run time of P.

- P is executed. No exception or time-out occurs during execution of P.

- The results of P are submitted to the AT.

- P's results fail the AT.

- Control returns to the executive. The executive sets POK to indicate failure of P, checks to ensure the deadline for acceptable results has not expired (it has not in this scenario), resets the WDT to the expected maximum run time of A_1, and restores the checkpoint.

- A_1 is executed. No exception or time-out occurs during execution of A_1.

- The results of A_1 are submitted to the AT.

- A_1's results are on time, but fail the AT.

- Control returns to the executive. The executive sets A_1OK to indicate failure of A_1, checks to ensure the deadline for acceptable results has not expired (it has not in this scenario), resets the WDT to the expected maximum run time of A_2, and restores the checkpoint.

- A_2 is executed. No exception or time-out occurs during execution of A_2.

- The results of A_2 are submitted to the AT.

- A_2's results are on time and pass the AT.

- Control returns to the executive.

- The executive discards the checkpoint, resets the WDT with an appropriate time interval for the next operation, the results are passed outside the RcB, and the RcB is exited.

4.1.1.4   All Alternates Exhausted Without Success

This scenario examines the case in which the deadline expires without an acceptable result or when all alternates fail. This may occur if alternates take too long to execute in total (versus individual algorithm time-outs) or when alternates are executed and their results continue to fail the AT. If there are no alternates available and no result has been accepted, a failure exception is raised and the RcB is exited. Differences between this scenario and the failure-free scenario are in gray type.

- Upon entry to the RcB, the executive performs the following: a checkpoint (or recovery point) is established, calls to P and A are formatted, and the WDT is set for the expected maximum run time of P.

- P is executed. No exception or time-out occurs during execution of P.

- The results of P are submitted to the AT.

- P's results fail the AT.

- Control returns to the executive. The executive sets POK to indicate failure of P, checks to ensure the deadline for acceptable results has not expired (it has not in this scenario), resets the WDT to the expected maximum run time of A_1, and restores the checkpoint.

- A_1 is executed. No exception or time-out occurs during execution of A_1.

- The results of A_1 are submitted to the AT.

- A_1's results are on time, but fail the AT.

- Control returns to the executive. The executive sets A_1OK to indicate failure of A_1, checks to ensure the deadline for acceptable results has not expired (it has not in this scenario), resets the WDT to the expected maximum run time of A_2, and restores the checkpoint.

- A_2 is executed. No exception or time-out occurs during execution of A_2.

- The results of A_2 are submitted to the AT.

- A_2's results are on time, but fail the AT.

- Control returns to the executive. The executive sets A_2OK to indicate failure of A_2, checks to ensure the deadline for acceptable results has not expired (it has not in this scenario), checks to see if another alternate is available to try (there is not—all alternates have been attempted on this data set).

- The executive discards the checkpoint, resets the WDT with an appropriate time interval for the next operation, a failure exception is raised, and the RcB is exited.

4.1.1.5   Augmentations to the Recovery Block Basic Technique

We have seen in these scenarios that RcB operation continues until acceptable results are produced, there are no new alternates to try, or the deadline expires without an acceptable result.

Several augmentations to the basic RcB technique have been suggested. One, of course, is the addition of a WDT, which we examined above. Another augmentation is to use an *alternate routine execution counter*. This counter is used when the primary fails and execution is switched to an alternate. The counter indicates the number of times to execute the alternate (on this and subsequent entries to the RcB) before reverting to executing the primary. The counter is incremented once the primary fails and prior to each execution of the alternate(s). The benefit of using the alternate routine execution counter is that it provides the ability to take the primary out of service for repair and/or replacement while the alternate continues the algorithm execution tasks.

The basic RcB technique may also be augmented by the use of a more detailed AT comprised of several tests. One AT is invoked before the primary routine execution and checks the format and parameters of the call. If either of these fails this AT, the alternate is called instead of the primary. Another AT executed before the call to the primary alternate tests the validity of the input data. If the input data fails this AT, then neither the primary nor secondary alternates are called. In this case, default or backup data may be used or the RcB can be further augmented with an alternate source for input data. The final AT of this AT set is the one commonly used with RcB—the AT that checks the results of the primary or alternate try blocks.

4.1.2 Recovery Block Example

Let's look at an example for the RcB technique. Suppose we have software that incrementally sorts a list of integers (see Figure 4.2). Also suppose the input is the list (8, 7, 13, −4, 17, 44). If the software operates correctly, we expect the result to be (−4, 7, 8, 13, 17, 44). However, unbeknownst to us, our sort algorithm implementation produces incorrect results if one or more of the inputs is negative. How can we protect our system against faults arising from this error?

A first thought may well be to test the software more thoroughly or to use other fault prevention techniques. This would be appropriate, especially with such a simple problem to solve. Of course, sound software engineering practice must be used in developing fault-tolerant software as it is (or should be) with non-fault-tolerant software. However, most software algorithms used in real applications are not likely to be as simple and well documented as the sort problem. The more complex the system—the algorithm, data, operating environment, and so on—the less able we are (with current technology) to thoroughly test the program or prove its correctness. Another thought likely to arise with regards to the example used is to question why it is so simple and unrepresentative of the actual software one might incorporate with software fault tolerance techniques. We use a simple algorithm to illustrate this and other techniques so that the illustration of the technique's operation is not obscured by the complexities of the algorithm. Now, on with the example.

Figure 4.3 illustrates an approach to using recovery blocks with the sort problem. Note the *additional* components needed for RcB technique implementation—an executive that handles checkpointing and orchestrating

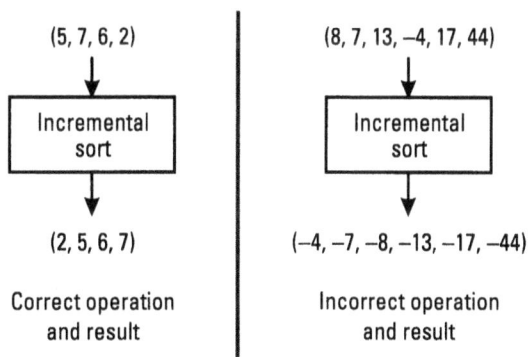

Figure 4.2 Example of original sort algorithm implementation.

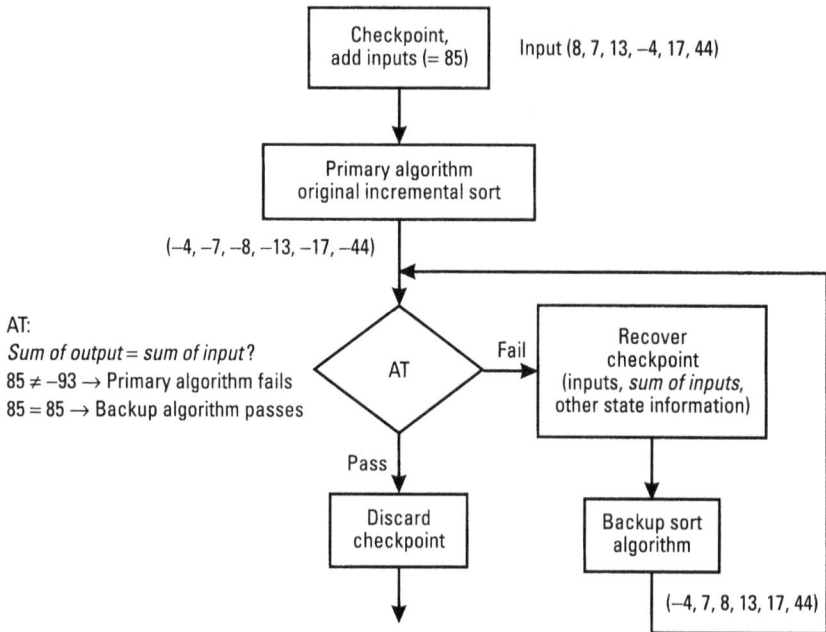

Figure 4.3 Example of recovery block implementation.

the technique, an alternate or backup sort algorithm, and an AT. In this example, no WDT is used.

Also note the design of the AT. How can we determine if a sort algorithm is correct without performing an entire other sort to check it against? In this example, we test if the sum of the inputs is equal to the sum of the outputs. This test will not determine if the items in the input list were sorted correctly, but it will indicate if something blatantly incorrect has resulted from the sort. To use this AT, the executive sums the inputs upon entry to the RcB and sums the results of the alternates (primary or secondary) upon arrival at the AT.

Now, let's step through the example.

- Prior to entering the RcB, a status module checks the primary module status. Since the primary has not yet failed, the RcB's operation proceeds.

- Upon entry to the RcB, the executive performs the following: a checkpoint is established, calls to the primary and backup (alternate) routines are formatted, and the inputs (8, 7, 13, −4, 17, 44) are summed. The *sum of input* = 85.

- The primary sort algorithm is executed. The results are (−4, −7, −8, −13, −17, −44).

- The results are submitted to the AT. The AT sums the items in the result vector. The *sum of output* = −93. The AT tests if the *sum of input* equals the *sum of output*. 85 ≠ −93, so the results of the primary sort algorithm fail the AT.

- Control returns to the executive. The executive sets the flag indicating failure of the primary algorithm and restores the checkpoint.

- The backup sort algorithm is executed using the same input vector. The results are (−4, 7, 8, 13, 17, 44).

- The results of the backup sort algorithm are submitted to the AT. The AT sums the items in the result vector. The *sum of output* = 85. The AT tests if the *sum of input* equals the *sum of output*. 85 = 85, so the results of the backup sort algorithm pass the AT.

- Control returns to the executive.

- The executive discards the checkpoint, the results are passed outside the RcB, and the RcB is exited.

4.1.3   Recovery Block Issues and Discussion

This section presents the advantages, disadvantages, and issues related to the RcB technique. In general, software fault tolerance techniques provide protection against errors in translating requirements and functionality into code, but do not provide explicit protection against errors in specifying requirements. This is true for all of the techniques described in this book. Being a design diverse, backward recovery technique, the RcB subsumes design diversity's and backward recovery's advantages and disadvantages, too. These are discussed in Sections 2.2 and 1.4.1, respectively. While designing software fault tolerance into a system, many considerations have to be taken into account. These are discussed in Chapter 3. Issues related to several software fault tolerance techniques (e.g., similar errors, coincident failures, overhead, cost, redundancy, and so on) and the programming practices used to implement the techniques are described in Chapter 3. Issues related to implementing acceptance tests are discussed in Section 7.2.

There are a few issues to note specifically for the RcB technique. The technique runs in a sequential (uniprocessor) environment. When the results of the primary try block or alternate pass the AT, the overhead incurred (beyond that of running the primary alone, as in non-fault-tolerant software) includes setting the checkpoint and executing the AT. If, however, the primary's results fail the AT, then the time overhead also includes the time for recovering the checkpointed information, execution times for each alternate run until one passes the AT (or until all fail the AT), and run-time of the AT each time an alternate's results are checked. It is assumed that most of the time, the primary's results will pass the AT, so the expected time overhead is that of setting the checkpoint and executing the AT. This is little beyond the primary's execution time (unless an unusually large amount of information is being checkpointed). In the worst case, however, the recovery block's execution time is the sum of all the module executions mentioned above (in the case where the primary's results fail the AT). This wide variation in execution time exposes the technique to timing errors that are likely unacceptable in real-time applications. One solution to the overhead problem is the DRB (see Section 4.3) in which the modules and AT are executed in parallel.

In RcB operation, when executing nonprimary alternates, the service that the module is to provide is interrupted during the recovery. This interruption may be unacceptable in applications that require high availability.

One advantage of the technique is that it is naturally applicable to software modules, as opposed to whole systems. It is natural to apply RcB to specific critical modules or processes in the system without incurring the cost and complexity of supporting fault tolerance for an entire system.

For the technique to be effective, a highly effective AT is required. Success of the RcB technique depends on all the error detection mechanisms used (including exception handling and others), not just on the AT. A simple, effective AT can be difficult to develop and depends heavily on the specification (see Section 7.2). If an error is not detected by the AT (or by the other error detection mechanisms), then that error is passed along to the module that receives the technique's results. This undetected error does not, of course, trigger any recovery mechanisms and may cause system failure.

A potential problem with the RcB technique is the domino effect (Section 3.1.3), in which cascaded rollbacks can push all processes back to their beginnings. This occurs if recovery and communication operations are not coordinated, especially in the case of nested recovery blocks. Section 4.1.3.1 below presents the conversation scheme, which was proposed as a means to avoid the domino effect.

To implement the RcB technique, the developer can use the programming techniques (such as assertions, checkpointing, atomic actions, idealized components) described in Chapter 3. Also needed for implementation and further examination of the technique is information on the underlying architecture and performance. These are discussed in Sections 4.1.3.2 and 4.1.3.3, respectively. Table 4.1 lists several issues related to the RcB technique, indicates whether or not they are an advantage or disadvantage (if applicable), and points to where in the book the reader may find additional information.

The indication that an issue in Table 4.1 can be a positive or negative (+/−) influence on the technique or on its effectiveness further indicates that the issue may be a disadvantage in general (e.g., cost is higher than non-fault-tolerant software) but an advantage in relation to another technique (e.g., the average cost of a two-try block RcB implementation is less than that

Table 4.1
Recovery Block Issue Summary

Issue	Advantage (+)/ Disadvantage (−)	Where Discussed
Provides protection against errors in translating requirements and functionality into code (true for software fault tolerance techniques in general)	+	Chapter 1
Does not provide explicit protection against errors in specifying requirements (true for software fault tolerance techniques in general)	−	Chapter 1
General backward recovery advantages	+	Section 1.4.1
General backward recovery disadvantages	−	Section 1.4.1
General design diversity advantages	+	Section 2.2
General design diversity disadvantages	−	Section 2.2
Similar errors or common residual design errors (RcB is affected to a lesser degree than forward recovery, voting techniques.)	−	Section 3.1.1
Coincident and correlated failures	−	Section 3.1.1
Domino effect	−	Section 3.1.3
Overhead for tolerating a single fault	+/−	Section 3.1.4
Cost (Table 3.3)	+/−	Section 3.1.4
Space and time redundancy	+/−	Section 3.1.4
Dependability studies	+/−	Section 4.1.3.3
Acceptance tests and discussions related to specific types of ATs	+/−	Section 7.2

for NVP with $n = 3$). In these cases, the reader is referred to the discussion of the issue (versus duplicating the discussion here).

4.1.3.1 Conversation Scheme

The conversation scheme is a means to avoid the domino effect. It is essentially a concurrent extension of the RcB technique in which a group of processes can interact safely. Each process entering a conversation is checkpointed. To prevent spreading data that has not been validated, processes within the conversation can communicate only with other processes that are in the conversation. When all processes have completed their operations, a global AT occurs. If it fails, all processes roll back and execute their next alternates. If the AT is satisfied, all processes discard their checkpoints and exit synchronously from the conversation. See [7, 8] for details on the operation and performance of the conversation scheme.

The conversation scheme spans two or more processes and creates a boundary that process interactions may not cross. The boundary of a conversation consists of a recovery line, a test line, and two side walls defining the membership of the conversation. The basic program-structuring rules of the conversation scheme are the following [8].

1. A conversation defines a recovery line as a line that processes in rollback cannot cross.

2. Processes enter a conversation asynchronously.

3. A conversation contains one or more interacting processes whose goal is to obtain the same or similar computational results.

4. A conversation test line is an acceptability criterion for the results of interacting processes, acting as a single global acceptance test—a conversation acceptance test.

5. Processes cooperate in error detection, regardless of where the error originates.

6. The processes participating in the conversation must neither obtain information from, nor leak information to, a process not participating in the conversation. The conversation's side walls define the process membership relationship.

Limitations of the conversation scheme include the following [9].

- It burdens the designer with the responsibility of establishing the coordinated recovery points.

- Process desertion may occur when there are timing deadlines to meet. Desertion is the failure of a process to start a conversation or arrive at the AT when it is expected by other processes.

- The conversation scheme may involve a long time delay for synchronization.

- The goal requirement of the group of processes is combined with those of the individual participants in the AT.

Several adaptations and extensions to the conversation scheme have been proposed to overcome some of the above limitations. These include programmer transparent coordination [10–12], the look-ahead approach [13], the exchange scheme [14], and a linguistic approach [15].

4.1.3.2 Architecture

We mentioned in Sections 1.3.1.2 and 2.5 that structuring is required if we are to handle system complexity, especially when fault tolerance is involved [16–18]. This includes defining the organization of software modules onto the hardware elements on which they run.

The recovery block approach is typically uniprocessor implemented, with the executive and all components residing on a single hardware unit. All communications between the software components is done through function calls or method invocations in this architecture. Distributing the RcB technique is discussed later in this chapter. Laprie, et al. [19] provide illustrations and discussion of distributed architectures for recovery blocks tolerating one fault and that for tolerating two consecutive faults.

4.1.3.3 Performance

There have been numerous investigations into the performance of software fault tolerance techniques in general (e.g., in the effectiveness of software diversity, discussed in Chapters 2 and 3) and the dependability of specific techniques themselves. Table 4.2 provides a briefly noted list of references for these dependability investigations. This list is by no means exhaustive, however, it does provide a good sampling of the types of analyses that have been performed and ample background for analyzing software fault tolerance dependability. The reader is encouraged to examine the references for details on assumptions made by the researchers, experiment design, and results interpretation. A comparative discussion of the techniques is provided in Section 4.7.

Table 4.2
Software Fault Tolerance Dependability Investigations

Comment	References
Analysis of software fault tolerance	[20–25]
Combined analysis of hardware and software fault tolerance	[26–29]
RcB, NVP, and NSCP stochastic reward net models	[30]
Reliability and safety models of RcB, NVP, NSCP, and DRB	[29, 31]
Modeling and evaluation of software fault tolerance dependability measures	[20, 21, 26, 32–36]
Dependability of fault-tolerant software executed iteratively, such as in process control applications	[37]
Reliability model (Markov) for RcB and NVP	[38, 54, 55]
Analyses that incorporate interversion failure correlation	[19, 21, 29, 39–45, 50, 52]
Modeling and analyses based on time domain characteristics	[19, 21, 42, 43, 46–49, 51, 53]
Analyses that incorporate coincident failures	[19, 29, 39, 41]

One experiment's results will be mentioned here, with others noted above and in the comparative analysis of the techniques in Section 4.7. The University of Newcastle upon Tyne conducted an experiment on the effectiveness of the RcB technique in improving operational software reliability [56] using a medium-scale naval command and control system. Through the project's three phases, the experiment illustrated an increasing effectiveness of the fault tolerance provisions evaluated. Table 4.3 notes the results of the final phase of the project.

4.2 *N*-Version Programming

The NVP and RcB techniques are the original design diverse software fault tolerance techniques. NVP was suggested by Elmendorf in 1972 [57] and developed by Avizienis and Chen [58, 59] in 1977–1978. NVP is a design diverse technique, and is further categorized as a static technique. In static software fault tolerance techniques, a task is executed by several processes or programs and a result is accepted only if it is adjudicated as an acceptable result, usually via a majority vote (see Section 7.1.1). The technique is called

Table 4.3
Overview of a Recovery Block Experiment's Results

Event Type	Percent Occurrence
Abnormal events correctly recovered	78%
Recovery failed	3%
Incorrect recovery, but no program failure	15%
Unnecessary recovery with no program failure	3%

"static" because the various programs executing the task will execute in the same manner, regardless of which result(s) was determined acceptable by the DM. This will be made clear in the discussion below on the operation of the NVP technique. The hardware fault tolerance architecture related to the NVP is N-modular or static redundancy. The processes can run concurrently on different computers or sequentially on a single computer. In practice, they are typically run concurrently.

The NVP technique uses a decision mechanism (DM) (see Section 7.1) and forward recovery (see Section 1.4.2) to accomplish fault tolerance. The technique uses at least two independently designed, functionally equivalent versions (variants) of a program developed from the same specification. The variants are run in parallel and a DM examines the results and selects the "best" result, if one exists. There are many alternative decision mechanisms available for use with NVP.

NVP is also helpful during back-to-back testing. This involves pairwise comparison of the responses from all the versions. When a difference is observed, the problem is investigated for all cases in which answers differ.

NVP operation is described in 4.2.1, with an example provided in 4.2.2. The advantages and disadvantages of NVP are presented in 4.2.3.

4.2.1 *N*-Version Programming Operation

The basic NVP technique consists of an executive, n variants (versions), and a DM. The executive orchestrates the NVP technique operation, which has the general syntax:

```
run Version 1, Version 2, ..., Version n
if (Decision Mechanism (Result 1, Result 2, ..., Result n))
    return Result
else failure exception
```

The NVP syntax above states that the technique executes the *n* versions concurrently. The results of these executions are provided to the DM, which operates upon them to determine if a correct result can be adjudicated. If one can (i.e., the Decision Mechanism statement above evaluates to TRUE), then it is returned. If a correct result cannot be determined, then an error occurs.

Figure 4.4 illustrates the structure and operation of the NVP technique. Both fault-free and failure scenarios (one in which a correct result cannot be found and one that fails prior to reaching the DM) for the NVP are described. In examining these scenarios, the following abbreviations will be used:

V_i	Version *i*;
n	The number of versions;
NVP	*N*-version programming;
DM	Decision mechanism;
R_i	Result of V_i.

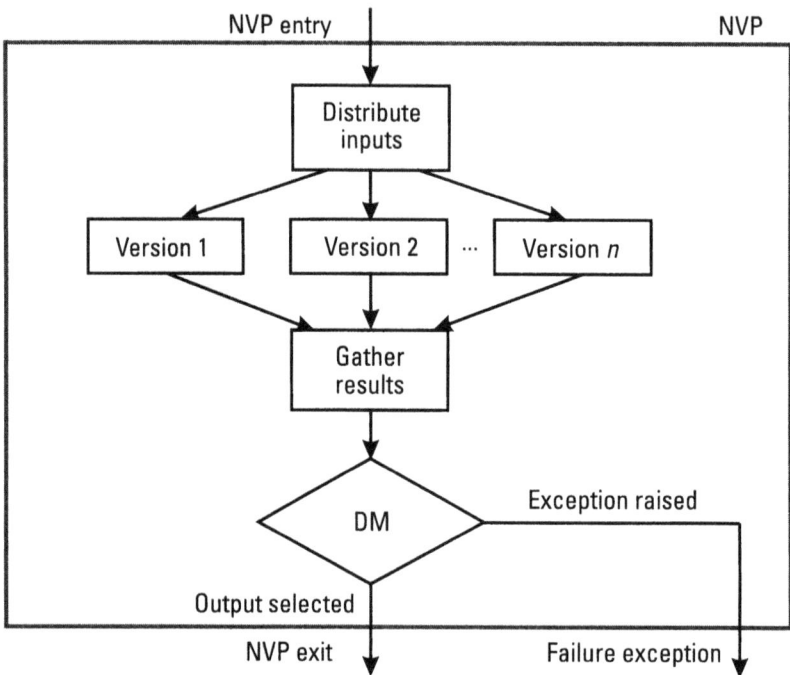

Figure 4.4 *N*-version programming structure and operation.

4.2.1.1   Failure-Free Operation

This scenario describes the operation of NVP when no failure or exception occurs.

- Upon entry to NVP, the executive performs the following: formats calls to the n versions and through those calls distributes the input(s) to the versions.
- Each version, V_i, executes. No failures occur during their execution.
- The results of the version executions (R_i, $i = 1, ..., n$) are gathered by the executive and submitted to the DM.
- The R_i are equal to one another, so the DM selects R_2 (randomly, since the results are equal), as the correct result.
- Control returns to the executive.
- The executive passes the correct result outside the NVP, and the NVP module is exited.

4.2.1.2   Failure Scenario—Incorrect Results

This scenario describes the operation of NVP when the DM cannot determine a correct result. Differences between this scenario and the failure-free scenario are in gray type.

- Upon entry to NVP, the executive performs the following: formats calls to the n versions and through those calls distributes the input(s) to the versions.
- Each version, V_i, executes.
- The results of the version executions (R_i, $i = 1, ..., n$) are gathered by the executive and submitted to the DM.
- The R_i differ significantly from one another. The DM cannot determine a correct result, and it sets a flag indicating this fact.
- Control returns to the executive.
- The executive raises an exception and the NVP module is exited.

4.2.1.3   Failure Scenario—Version Does Not Execute

This scenario describes the operation of NVP when at least one version does not complete its execution. Differences between this scenario and the failure-free scenario are in gray type.

- Upon entry to NVP, the executive performs the following: formats calls to the *n* versions and through those calls distributes the input(s) to the versions.

- The versions, V_i, begin execution. One or more versions do not complete execution for some reason (e.g., stuck in an endless loop).

- The executive cannot retrieve all version results in a timely manner. The executive submits the results it does have to the DM.

- The DM expects *n* results, but receives *n*-1 results (or *n*-2, etc., depending on the number of failed versions). The basic majority voter cannot handle fewer than *n* results and sets a flag indicating its failure to select a correct result. [Note: If the DM is not equipped to recognize this failure, it may fail and the executive would have to recognize the DM failure.]

- Control returns to the executive.

- The executive raises an exception and the NVP module is exited.

4.2.1.4   Augmentations to *N*-Version Programming Operation

We have seen in these scenarios that NVP operation continues until the DM adjudicates a correct result, the DM cannot select a correct result, or the DM fails.

Several augmentations to the basic NVP have been suggested. Many of these simply involve using a different decision mechanism than the basic majority voter. Chapter 7 describes several alternative decision mechanisms. One optional DM is the dynamic voter (Section 7.1.6). Its ability to handle a variable number of result inputs could tolerate the failure experienced in the scenario described in Section 4.2.1.3.

Another augmentation to the basic NVP involves voting upon the results as each version completes execution (as opposed to waiting on all versions to complete). Once two results are available, the DM can compare them and if they agree, complete that NVP cycle. If the first two results do not match, the DM performs a majority vote on three results when it receives the third version's results, and continues voting through the *n*th version execution, until it finds an acceptable result. When an acceptable result is found, it is passed outside the NVP, any remaining version executions are terminated, and the NVP module is exited. This scheme provides results more quickly than the basic NVP, assuming the versions have different expected execution times.

Other augmentations, enhancements, and combinations have been made to the NVP (and RcB) techniques. These are typically given an entirely new technique name rather than being called an extension to the NVP technique. Some of these techniques are described later in this chapter, and in the following two chapters.

4.2.2 *N*-Version Programming Example

This section provides an example implementation of the NVP technique. Recall the sort algorithm used in the RcB example (Section 4.1.2 and Figure 4.2). Our implementation produces incorrect results if one or more of the inputs is negative. How can we protect our system against faults arising from this error?

Figure 4.5 illustrates an NVP implementation of fault tolerance for this example. Note the additional components needed for NVP implementation:

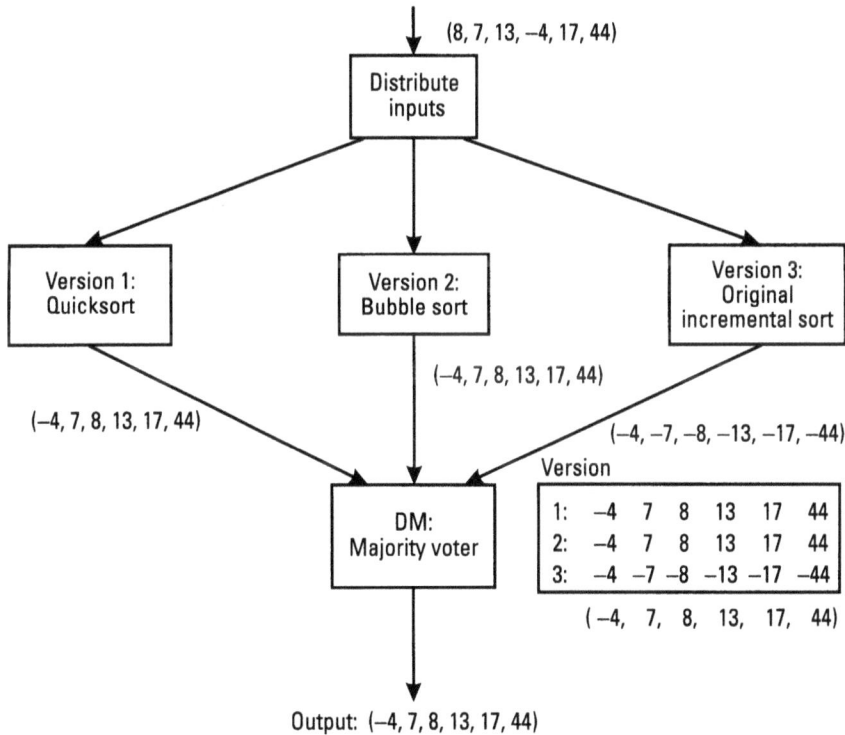

Figure 4.5 Example of *N*-version programming implementation.

an executive that handles orchestrating and synchronizing the technique (e.g., distributing the inputs, as shown), one or more additional variants (versions) of the algorithm/program, and a DM. The versions are different variants providing an incremental sort. For versions 1 and 2, a quick-sort and bubble sort are used, respectively. Version 3 is the original incre-mental sort.

Also note the design of the DM. It is straightforward to compare result values if those values are individual numbers or strings (or other basic types). How do we compare a list of values? Must all entries in all or a majority of the lists be the same for success? Or can we compare each entry in the result lists separately? Since the result of our sort is an ordered list, we can check each entry against the entries in the same position in the other result lists. If we designate the result in this example as r_{ij} where $i = 1, 2, 3$ (up to $n = 3$ ver-sions) and $j = 1, 2, ..., 6$ (up to $k = 6$ items in the result set), then our DM performs the following tests:

$$r_{1j} = r_{2j} = r_{3j} \quad \text{where } j = 1, ..., k$$

If the r_{ij} are equal for a specific j, then the result for that entry in the list is r_{1j} (randomly selected since they are all equal). If they are not all equal for a spe-cific j, do any two entries for a specific j match? That is, does

$$r_{1j} = r_{2j} \text{ OR } r_{1j} = r_{3j} \text{ OR } r_{2j} = r_{3j} \quad \text{where } j = 1, ..., k$$

If a match is found, the matching value is selected as the result for that posi-tion in the list. If there is no match, that is, $r_{1j} \neq r_{2j} \neq r_{3j,}$ then there is no correct result for that entry, designated by $\emptyset$.

Now, let's step through the example.

- Upon entry to NVP, the executive performs the following: it for-mats calls to the $n = 3$ versions and through those calls distributes the inputs to the versions. The input set is $(8, 7, 13, -4, 17, 44)$.

- Each version, V_i ($i = 1, 2, 3$), executes.

- The results of the version executions (r_{ij}, $i = 1, ..., n$; $j = 1, ..., k$) are gathered by the executive and submitted to the DM.

- The DM examines the results as follows (shading indicates matching results):

j	r_{1j}	r_{2j}	r_{3j}	**Result**
1	−4	−4	−4	−4
2	7	7	−7	7
3	8	8	−8	8
4	13	13	−13	13
5	17	17	−17	17
6	44	44	−44	44

- The adjudicated result is (−4, 7, 8, 13, 17, 44).

- Control returns to the executive.

- The executive passes the correct result, (−4, 7, 8, 13, 17, 44), outside the NVP, and the NVP module is exited.

4.2.3 *N*-Version Programming Issues and Discussion

This section presents the advantages, disadvantages, and issues related to NVP. As stated earlier in this chapter, software fault tolerance techniques generally provide protection against errors in translating requirements and functionality into code, but do not provide explicit protection against errors in specifying requirements. This is true for all of the techniques described in this book. Being a design diverse, forward recovery technique, NVP subsumes design diversity's and forward recovery's advantages and disadvantages, too. These are discussed in Sections 2.2 and 1.4.2, respectively. While designing software fault tolerance into a system, many considerations have to be taken into account. These are discussed in Chapter 3. Issues related to several software fault tolerance techniques (such as similar errors, coincident failures, overhead, cost, redundancy, etc.) and the programming practices used to implement the techniques are described in Chapter 3. Issues related to implementing voters are discussed in Section 7.1.

There are a few issues to note specifically for the NVP technique. NVP runs in a multiprocessor environment, although it could be executed sequentially in a uniprocessor environment. The overhead incurred (beyond that of running a single version, as in non-fault-tolerant software) includes additional memory for the second through the nth variants, executive, and DM; additional execution time for the executive and the DM; and synchronization overhead. The time overhead for the NVP technique is always dependent upon the slowest variant, since all variant results must be available for the voter to operate (for the basic majority voter). One solution to the synchronization time overhead is to use a DM performing an algorithm that operates on two or more results as they become available. (See the self-configuring optimal programming (SCOP) technique discussion in Section 6.4.)

In NVP operation, it is rarely necessary to interrupt the module's service during voting. This continuity of service is attractive for applications that require high availability.

To implement NVP, the developer can use the programming techniques (such as assertions, atomic actions, idealized components) described in Chapter 3. It is advised that the developer use the NVP paradigm described in Section 3.3.3 to maximize the effectiveness of NVP by minimizing the chances of introducing related faults. There are three elements to the NVP approach to software fault tolerance: the *process* of initial specification and NVP, the *product* of that process—the *N*-version software (NVS)—and the *environment* that supports execution of NVS and provides decision algorithms—the *N*-version executive (NVX).

The purpose of the NVP design paradigm [60, 5] (see Section 3.3.3) is to integrate NVP requirements and the software development methodology. The objectives of the design paradigm are to (a) reduce the possibility of oversights, mistakes, and inconsistencies in software development and testing; (b) eliminate the most perceivable causes of remaining design faults; and (c) minimize the probability that two or more variants produce similar erroneous results during the same decision action. Not only must the design and development be independent, but maintenance of the *n* variants must be performed by separate maintenance entities or organizations to maintain independence.

It is critical that the initial specification for the variants used in NVP be free of flaws. If the specification is flawed and the *n* programming teams use that specification, then the variants are likely to produce indistinguishable results. The success of NVP depends on the residual faults in each variant being distinguishable, that is, that they cause disagreement in the decision algorithm. Common mode failures or undetected similar errors among a majority of the variants can cause an incorrect decision to be made by the DM. Related faults among the variants and the DM also have to be minimized. The similar error problem is the core issue in design diversity [61] and has led to much research, some of it controversial (see [62]).

Also indistinguishable to voting-type decision algorithms are multiple correct results (MCR) (see Section 3.1.1). Hence, NVP in general, and voting-type decision algorithms in particular, are not appropriate for situations in which MCR may occur, such as in algorithms to find routes between cities or finding the roots of an equation.

Using NVP to improve testing (e.g., in back-to-back testing) will likely result in bugs being found that might otherwise not be found in single version software [63]. However, testing the variants against one another with comparison testing may cause the variants to compute progressively more similar functions, thereby reducing the opportunity for NVP to tolerate remaining faults [64].

Even though NVP utilizes the design diversity principle, it cannot be guaranteed that the variants have no common residual design faults. If this occurs, the purpose of NVP is defeated. The DM may also contain residual design faults. If it does, then the DM may accept incorrect results or reject correct results.

NVP does provide design diversity, but does not provide redundancy or diversity in the data or data structures used. Independent design teams may design data structures within each variant differently, but those structures global to NVP remain fixed [16]. This may limit the programmers' ability to diversify the variants.

Another issue in applying diverse, redundant software (this holds for NVP and other design diverse software approaches) is determination of the level at which the approach should be applied. The technique application level influences the size of the resulting modules, and there are advantages and disadvantages to both small and large modules. Stringini and Avizienis [65] detail these as follows. Small modules imply:

- Frequent invocations of the error detection mechanisms, resulting in low error latency but high overhead;

- Less computation must be redone in case of rollback, or less data must be corrected by a vote (i.e., in NVP), but more temporary data needs to be saved in checkpoints or voted upon;

- The specifications common to the diverse implementations must be similar to a higher level of detail. (Instead of specifying only what a large module should do, and which variables must compose the state of the computation outside that module, one needs to specify how that large module is decomposed into smaller modules, what each of the smaller modules does, and how it shall present its results to the DM.)

Also needed for implementation and further examination of the technique is information on the underlying architecture and technique performance. These are discussed in Sections 4.2.3.1 and 4.2.3.2, respectively. Table 4.4 lists several NVP issues, indicates whether or not they are an advantage or disadvantage (if applicable), and points to where in the book the reader may find additional information.

The indication that an issue in Table 4.4 can be a positive or negative (+/−) influence on the technique or on its effectiveness further indicates

Table 4.4
N-Version Programming Issue Summary

Issue	Advantage (+)/ Disadvantage (−)	Where Discussed
Provides protection against errors in translating requirements and functionality into code (true for software fault tolerance techniques in general)	+	Chapter 1
Does not provide explicit protection against errors in specifying requirements (true for software fault tolerance techniques in general)	−	Chapter 1
General forward recovery advantages	+	Section 1.3.1.2
General forward recovery disadvantages	−	Section 1.3.1.2
General design diversity advantages	+	Section 2.2
General design diversity disadvantages	−	Section 2.2
Similar errors or common residual design errors	−	Section 3.1.1
Coincident and correlated failures	−	Section 3.1.1
MCR and identical and wrong results	−	Section 3.1.1
Consistent comparison problem (CCP)	−	Section 3.1.2
Overhead for tolerating a single fault	+/−	Section 3.1.4
Cost (Table 3.3)	+/−	Section 3.1.4
Space and time redundancy	+/−	Section 3.1.4
Design considerations	+	Section 3.3.1
Dependable system development model	+	Section 3.3.2
NVS design paradigm	+	Section 3.3.3
Dependability studies	+/−	Section 4.1.3.3
Voters and discussions related to specific types of voters	+/−	Section 7.1

that the issue may be a disadvantage in general (e.g., cost is higher than non-fault-tolerant software) but an advantage in relation to another technique. In these cases, the reader is referred to the noted section for discussion of the issue.

4.2.3.1 Architecture

We mentioned in Sections 1.3.1.2 and 2.5 that structuring is required if we are to handle system complexity, especially when fault tolerance is involved [16–18]. This includes defining the organization of software modules onto the hardware elements on which they run.

NVP is typically multiprocessor implemented with components residing on *n* hardware units and the executive residing on one of the processors. Communications between the software components is done through remote function calls or method invocations. Laprie and colleagues [19] provide illustrations and discussion of architectures for NVP tolerating one fault and that for tolerating two consecutive faults.

4.2.3.2 Performance

There have been numerous investigations into the performance of software fault tolerance techniques in general (e.g., in the effectiveness of software diversity, discussed in Chapters 2 and 3) and the dependability of specific techniques themselves. Table 4.2 (in Section 4.1.3.3) provides a list of references for these dependability investigations. This list, although not exhaustive, provides a good sampling of the types of analyses that have been performed and substantial background for analyzing software fault tolerance dependability. The reader is encouraged to examine the references for details on assumptions made by the researchers, experiment design, and results interpretation. Laprie and colleagues [19] provide the derivation and formulation of an equation for the probability of failure for NVP. A comparative discussion of the techniques is provided in Section 4.7.

One way to improve the performance of NVP is to use a DM that is appropriate for the problem solution domain. CV (see Section 7.1.4) is one such alternative to majority voting. Consensus voting has the advantage of being more stable than majority voting. The reliability of CV is at least equivalent to majority voting. It performs better than majority voting when average *N*-tuple reliability is low, or the average decision space in which voters work is not binary [53]. Also, when *n* is greater than 3, consensus voting can make plurality decisions, that is, in situations where there is no majority (the majority voter fails), the consensus voter selects as the correct result the value of a unique maximum of identical outputs. A disadvantage of consensus voting is the added complexity of the decision algorithm. However, this may be overcome, at least in part, by pre-approved DM components [66].

4.3   Distributed Recovery Blocks

The DRB technique (developed by Kane Kim [10, 67, 68]) is a combination of distributed and/or parallel processing and recovery blocks that provides both hardware and software fault tolerance. The DRB scheme has been steadily expanded and supported by testbed demonstrations. Emphasis in the development of the technique has been placed on real-time target applications, distributed and parallel computing systems, and handling both hardware and software faults. Although DRB uses recovery blocks, it implements a forward recovery scheme, consistent with its emphasis on real-time applications.

The technique's architecture consists of a pair of self-checking processing nodes (PSP). The PSP scheme uses two copies of a self-checking computing component that are structured as a primary-shadow pair [69], resident on two or more networked nodes. In the PSP scheme, each computing component iterates through computation cycles and each of these cycles is two-phase structured. A two-phase structured cycle consists of an input acquisition phase and an output phase. During the input acquisition phase, input actions and computation actions may take place, but not output actions. Similarly, during the output phase, only output actions may take place. This facilitates parallel replicated execution of real-time tasks without incurring excessive overhead related to synchronization of the two partner nodes in the same primary-shadow structured computing station.

The structure and operation of the DRB are described in 4.3.1, with an example provided in 4.3.2. Advantages, limitations, and issues related to the DRB are presented in 4.3.3.

4.3.1   Distributed Recovery Block Operation

As shown in Figure 4.6, the basic DRB technique consists of a primary node and a shadow node, each cooperating and each running an RcB scheme. An input buffer at each node holds incoming data, released upon the next cycle. The logic and time AT is an acceptance test and WDT combination that checks its local processing. The time AT is a WDT that checks the other node in the pair. The same primary try blocks, alternate try blocks, and ATs

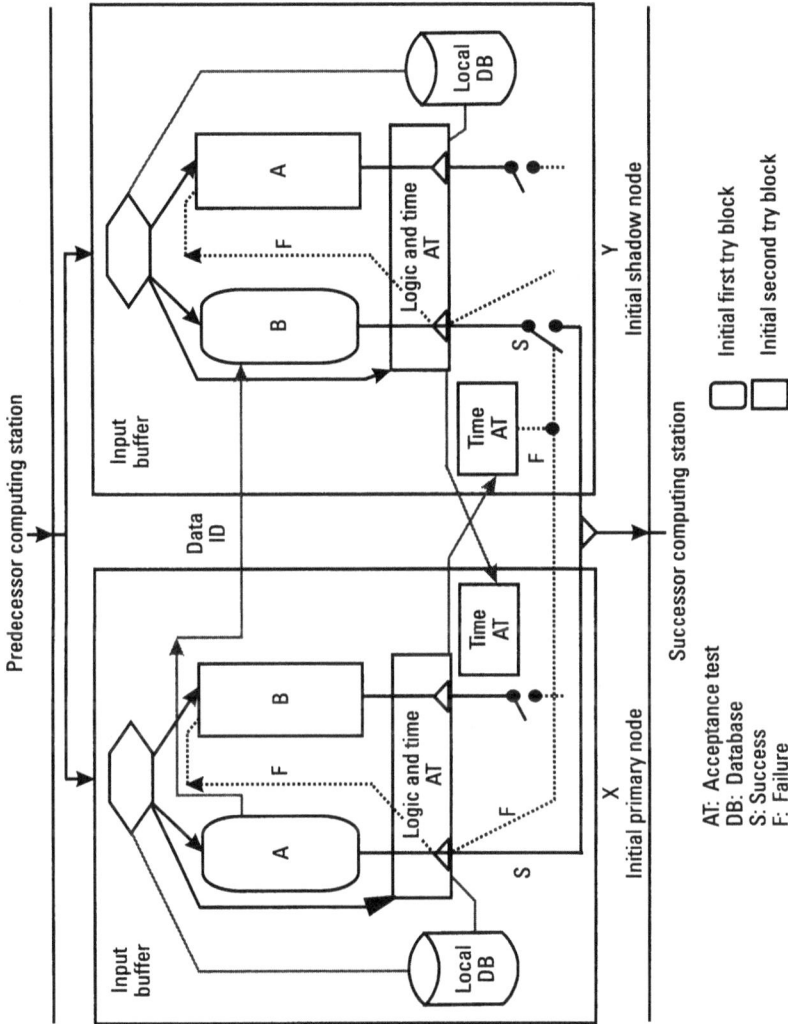

Figure 4.6 Distributed recovery block structure. (*From:* [67], © 1989, IEEE. Reprinted with permission.)

are used on both nodes. The local DB (database) holds the current local result. The DRB technique operation has the following much-simplified, single cycle, general syntax.

```
run      RB1 on Node 1 (Initial Primary),
             RB2 on Node 2 (Initial Shadow)
ensure   AT on Node 1 or Node 2
by       Primary on Node 1 or Alternate on Node 2
else by  Alternate on Node 1 or Primary on Node 2
else failure exception
```

The DRB single cycle syntax above states that the technique executes the recovery blocks on both nodes concurrently, with one node (the initial primary node) executing the primary algorithm first and the other (the initial shadow node) executing the alternate. The technique first attempts to ensure the AT (i.e., produce a result that passes the AT) with the primary algorithm on node 1's results. If this result fails the AT, then the DRB tries the result from the alternate algorithm on node 2. If neither passes the AT, then backward recovery is used to execute the alternate on Node 1 and the primary on Node 2. The results of these executions are checked to ensure the AT. If neither of these results passes the AT, then an error occurs. If any of the results are successful, the result is passed on to the successor computing station.

Both fault-free and failure scenarios for the DRB are described below. During this discussion of the DRB operation, keep in mind the following. The governing rule of the DRB technique is that the primary node tries to execute the primary alternate whenever possible and the shadow node tries to execute the alternate try block whenever possible. In examining these scenarios, the following abbreviations and notations are used:

AT   Acceptance test;

Check-1   Check the AT result of the partner node with the WDT on;

Check-1*   Check the progress of and/or AT status of the partner node;

Check-2   Check the delivery success of the partner node with the WDT on;

Status-1   Inform other node of pickup of new input;

Status-2   Inform other node of AT result;

Status-3   Inform that output was delivered to successor computing station successfully.

The *Check* and *Status* notations above were defined in [70].

4.3.1.1 Failure-Free Operation

Table 4.5 describes the operation of the DRB technique when no failure or exception occurs.

4.3.1.2 Failure Scenario—Primary Fails AT, Alternate Passes on Backup Node

Table 4.6 outlines the operation of the DRB technique when the primary try block (on the primary node) fails its AT and the alternate try block (on the backup node) is successful. Differences between this scenario and the failure-free scenario are in gray type.

Table 4.5
Distributed Recovery Block Without Failure or Exception

Primary Node	Backup Node
Begin the computing cycle (Cycle).	Begin the computing cycle (Cycle).
Receive input data from predecessor computing station (Input).	Receive input data from predecessor computing station (Input).
Start the recovery block (Ensure).	Start the recovery block (Ensure).
Inform the backup node of pickup of new input (Status-1 message).	Inform the primary node of pickup of new input (Status-1 message).
Run the primary try block (Try).	Run the alternate try block (Try).
Test the primary try block's results (AT). The results pass the AT.	Test the alternate try block's results (AT). The results pass the AT.
Inform backup node of AT success (Status-2 message).	Inform primary node of AT success (Status-2 message).
Check if backup node is up and operating correctly. Has it taken Status-2 actions during a preset maximum number of data processing cycles? (Check-1* Message) Yes, backup is OK.	Check AT result of primary node (Check-1 message). It passed and was placed in the buffer.
Deliver result to successor computing station (SEND) and update local database with result.	Check to make sure the primary successfully delivered result (Check-2 message).
—	[Wait]
Tell backup node that result was delivered (Status-3 message).	Primary was successful in delivering result (No Timeout).
End this processing cycle.	End this processing cycle.

Table 4.6
Operation of Distributed Recovery Block When the Primary Fails and the Alternate Is Successful

Primary Node	Backup Node
Begin the computing cycle (`Cycle`).	Begin the computing cycle (`Cycle`).
Receive input data from predecessor computing station (`Input`).	Receive input data from predecessor computing station (`Input`).
Start the recovery block (`Ensure`).	Start the recovery block (`Ensure`).
Inform the backup node of pickup of new input (`Status-1` message).	Inform the primary node of pickup of new input (`Status-1` message).
Run the primary try block (`Try`).	Run the alternate try block (`Try`).
Test the primary try block's results (`AT`). The results fail the AT.	Test the alternate try block's results (`AT`). The results pass the AT.
Inform backup node of AT failure (`Status-2` message).	Inform primary node of AT success (`Status-2` message).
Attempt to become the backup— rollback and retry using alternate try block (on primary node) using same data on which primary try block failed (to keep the state consistent or local database up-to-date). Assume the role of backup node.	Check AT result of primary node (`Check-1` message). The primary node failed. Assume the role of primary node.
	Deliver result to successor computing station (`SEND`) and update local database with result.
Test the alternate try block's results (`AT`). The results pass the AT.	Tell primary node that result was delivered (`Status-3` message).
Inform backup node of AT success (`Status-2` message).	—
Check AT result of backup node (`Check-1` message). It passed and was placed in the buffer.	—
Check to make sure the backup node successfully delivered result (`Check-2` message).	—
Backup was successful in delivering result (No `Timeout`).	—
End this processing cycle.	End this processing cycle.

4.3.1.3   Failure Scenario—Primary Node Stops Processing

This scenario is briefly described because it greatly resembles the previous scenario with few exceptions. If the primary node stops processing entirely, then no update message (`Status-2`) can be sent to the backup. The backup node detects the crash with the expiration of a local timer associated with the Check-1 message. The backup node operates as if the primary failed its AT (as shown in the right-hand column in Table 4.6). If the backup node had stopped instead, there would be no need to change processing in the primary node, since it would simply retain the role of primary.

4.3.1.4 Failure Scenario—Both Fail

Table 4.7 outlines the operation of the DRB technique when the primary try block (on the primary node) fails its AT and the alternate try block (on the backup node) also fails its AT. Differences between this scenario and the failure-free scenario are in gray type.

In this scenario, the primary and back-up nodes did not switch roles. When both fail their AT, there are two (or more) alternatives for resumption of roles: (1) retain the original roles (primary as primary, backup as backup) or (2) the first node to successfully pass its AT assumes the primary role. Option one is less complex to implement, but option two can result in faster recovery when the retry of the initial primary node takes significantly longer than that of the initial backup.

4.3.2 Distributed Recovery Block Example

This section provides an example implementation of the DRB technique. Recall the sort algorithm used in the RcB technique example (Section 4.1.2 and Figure 4.2). The implementation produces incorrect results if one or more of the inputs is negative. In a DRB implementation of fault tolerance for this example, upon each node resides a recovery block consisting of the original sort algorithm implementation as primary and a different algorithm implemented for the alternate try block. The AT is the *sum of inputs and outputs* AT used in the RcB technique example, with a WDT. See Section 4.1.2 for a description of the AT. Look at Figure 4.6 for the following description of the DRB components for this example:

- Initial primary node X:
  - Input buffer;
  - Primary A: Original sort algorithm implementation;
  - Alternate B: Alternate sort algorithm implementation;
  - Logic and time AT: Sum of inputs and outputs AT with WDT;
  - Local database;
  - Time AT;

Table 4.7
Operation of Distributed Recovery Block When Both the Primary and Alternate Try Blocks Fail

Primary Node	Backup Node
Begin the computing cycle (`Cycle`).	Begin the computing cycle (`Cycle`).
Receive input data from predecessor computing station (`Input`).	Receive input data from predecessor computing station (`Input`).
Start the recovery block (`Ensure`).	Start the recovery block (`Ensure`).
Inform the backup node of pickup of new input (`Status-1` message).	Inform the primary node of pickup of new input (`Status-1` message).
Run the primary try block (`Try`).	Run the alternate try block (`Try`).
Test the primary try block's results (`AT`). The results fail the AT.	Test the alternate try block's results (`AT`). The results fail the AT.
Inform backup node of AT failure (`Status-2` message).	Inform primary node of AT failure (`Status-2` message).
Rollback and retry using alternate try block (on primary node) using same data on which primary try block failed (to keep the state consistent or local database up-to-date).	Rollback and retry using primary try block (on backup node) using same data on which alternate try block failed (to keep the state consistent or local database up-to-date).
Test the alternate try block's results (`AT`). The results pass the AT.	Test the primary try block's results (`AT`). The results pass the AT.
Inform backup node of AT success (`Status-2` message).	Inform primary node of AT success (`Status-2` message).
Check if backup node is up and operating correctly. Has it taken Status-2 actions during a preset maximum number of data processing cycles? (`Check-1*` Message) Yes, backup is OK.	Check AT result of primary node (`Check-1` message). It passed and was placed in the buffer.
Deliver result to successor computing station (`SEND`) and update local database with result.	Check to make sure the primary node successfully delivered result (`Check-2` message).
Tell backup node that result was delivered (`Status-3` message).	Primary was successful in delivering result (No `Timeout`).
End this processing cycle.	End this processing cycle.

- Initial shadow node Y:
  - Input buffer;
  - Primary A: Alternate sort algorithm implementation;

- Alternate B: Original sort algorithm implementation;

- Logic and time AT: Sum of inputs and outputs AT with WDT;

- Local database;

- Time AT.

Table 4.8 describes the events occurring on both nodes during the concurrent DRB execution.

4.3.3 Distributed Recovery Block Issues and Discussion

This section presents the advantages, disadvantages, and issues related to the DRB technique. In general, software fault tolerance techniques provide protection against errors in translating requirements and functionality into code but do not provide explicit protection against errors in specifying requirements. This is true for all of the techniques described in this book. Being a design diverse, forward recovery technique, the DRB subsumes design diversity's and forward recovery's advantages and disadvantages, too. These are discussed in Sections 2.2 and 1.4.2, respectively. While designing software fault tolerance into a system, many considerations have to be taken into account. These are discussed in Chapter 3. Issues related to several software fault tolerance techniques (such as similar errors, coincident failures, overhead, cost, redundancy, etc.) and the programming practices used to implement the techniques are described in Chapter 3. Issues related to implementing ATs are discussed in Section 7.2.

There are a few issues to note specifically for the DRB technique. The DRB runs in a multiprocessor environment. When the results of the initial primary node's primary try block pass the AT, the overhead incurred (beyond that of running the primary alone, as in non-fault-tolerant software) includes running the alternate on the shadow node, setting the checkpoints for both nodes, and executing the ATs on both nodes. When recovery is required, the time overhead is minimal because maximum concurrency is exploited in DRB execution.

The DRB's relatively low run-time overhead makes it a candidate for use in real-time systems. The DRB was originally developed for systems such as command and control in which data from one pair of processors is output to another pair of processors. The extended DRB implements changes to the DRB for application to real-time process control [71, 72]. Extensions and modifications to the original DRB scheme have also been developed

Table 4.8
Concurrent Events in an Example Distributed Recovery Block Execution

Primary Node	Backup Node
Begin the computing cycle.	Begin the computing cycle.
Receive input data from predecessor computing station. Input is (8, 7, 13, −4, 17, 44). Sum the inputs for later use by AT. (*Sum of inputs* = 85.)	Receive input data from predecessor computing station. Input is (8, 7, 13, −4, 17, 44). Sum the inputs for later use by AT. (*Sum of inputs* = 85.)
Start the recovery block.	Start the recovery block.
Inform the backup node of pickup of new input.	Inform the primary node of pickup of new input.
Run the primary try block (original sort algorithm). Result = (−4, −7, −8, −13, −17, −44).	Run the alternate try block (backup sort algorithm). Result = (−4, 7, 8, 13, 17, 44).
Test the primary try block's results. *Sum of inputs* was 85; sum of results = −93, not equal. The results fail the AT.	Test the alternate try block's results. *Sum of inputs* was 85; sum of results = 85, equal. The results pass the AT.
Inform backup node of AT failure.	Inform primary node of AT success.
Attempt to become the backup—rollback and retry using alternate algorithm (on primary node) using same data on which original sort algorithm failed. Result = (−4, 7, 8, 13, 17, 44).	Check AT result of primary node. The primary node failed. Assume the role of primary node.
Test the alternate try block's (backup sort algorithm) results. *Sum of inputs* was 85; sum of results = 85, equal. The results pass the AT.	Deliver result to successor computing station and update local database with result.
Inform backup node of AT success.	Tell primary node that result was delivered.
Check AT result of backup node. It passed and was placed in the buffer.	—
Check to make sure the backup node successfully delivered result.	—
Backup was successful in delivering result.	—
End this processing cycle.	End this processing cycle.

for a repairable DRB [70] and for use in a load-sharing multiprocessing scheme [67].

As with the RcB technique, an advantage of the DRB is that it is naturally applicable to software modules, versus whole systems. It is natural to apply the DRB to specific critical modules or processes in the system without incurring the cost and complexity of supporting fault tolerance for an entire system.

Also similar to the RcB technique, effective DRB operation requires simple, highly effective ATs. A simple, effective AT can be difficult to develop and depends heavily on the specification (see Section 7.2). Timing tests are essential parts of the ATs for DRB use in real-time systems.

The DRB technique can provide real-time recovery from processing node omission failures and can prevent the follow-on nodes from processing faulty values to the extent determined by the AT's detection coverage. The following DRB station node omission failures are tolerated: those caused by (a) a fault in the internal hardware of a DRB station, (b) a design defect in the operating system running on internal processing nodes of a DRB station, or (c) a design defect in some application software modules used within a DRB station [68].

Kim [68] lists the following major useful characteristics of the DRB technique.

- Forward recovery can be accomplished in the same manner regardless of whether a node fails due to hardware faults or software faults.

- The recovery time is minimal since maximum concurrency is exploited between the primary and the shadow nodes.

- The increase in the processing turnaround time is minimal because the primary node does not wait for any status message from the shadow node.

- The cost-effectiveness and the flexibility of the DRB technique is high because:

    - A DRB computing station can operate with just two try blocks and two processing nodes;

    - The two try blocks are not required to produce identical results and the second try block need not be as sophisticated as the first try block.

However, the DRB technique does impose some restrictions on the use of RcB. To be used in DRB, a recovery block should be two-phase structured (see the DRB operational description earlier in Section 4.3). This restriction is necessary to prevent the establishment of interdependency, for recovery, among the various DRB stations.

To implement the DRB technique, the developer can use the programming techniques (such as assertions, checkpointing, atomic actions, idealized components) described in Chapter 3. Implementation techniques for the DRB are discussed by Kim in [68]. Also needed for implementation and further examination of the technique is information on the underlying architecture and performance. These are discussed in Sections 4.3.3.1 and 4.3.3.2, respectively. Table 4.9 lists several DRB issues, indicates whether or not they are an advantage or disadvantage (if applicable), and points to where in the book the reader may find additional information.

The indication that an issue in Table 4.9 can be a positive or negative (+/−) influence on the technique or on its effectiveness further indicates that the issue may be a disadvantage in general but an advantage in relation to

Table 4.9
Distributed Recovery Block Issue Summary

Issue	Advantage (+)/ Disadvantage (−)	Where Discussed
Provides protection against errors in translating requirements and functionality into code (true for software fault tolerance techniques in general)	+	Chapter 1
Does not provide explicit protection against errors in specifying requirements (true for software fault tolerance techniques in general)	−	Chapter 1
General forward recovery advantages	+	Section 1.4.2
General forward recovery disadvantages	−	Section 1.4.2
General design diversity advantages	+	Section 2.2
General design diversity disadvantages	−	Section 2.2
Similar errors or common residual design errors (The DRB is affected to a lesser degree than other forward recovery techniques.)	−	Section 3.1.1
Coincident and correlated failures	−	Section 3.1.1
Domino effect	−	Section 3.1.3
Overhead for tolerating a single fault	+/−	Section 3.1.4
Cost (Table 3.3)	+/−	Section 3.1.4
Space and time redundancy	+/−	Section 3.1.4
Dependability studies	+/−	Section 4.1.3.3
ATs and discussions related to specific types of ATs	+/−	Section 7.2

another technique. In these cases, the reader is referred to the discussion of the issue (versus repeating the discussion here).

4.3.3.1 Architecture

We mentioned in Sections 1.3.1.2 and 2.5 that structuring is required if we are to handle system complexity, especially when fault tolerance is involved [16–18]. This includes defining the organization of software modules onto the hardware elements on which they run.

The DRB uses multiple processors with the recovery block components and executive residing on distributed hardware units. Communications between the software components is done through remote function calls or method invocations. Laprie and colleagues [19] provide illustrations and discussion of distributed architectures for recovery blocks tolerating one fault and those for tolerating two consecutive faults.

4.3.3.2 Performance

There have been numerous investigations into the performance of software fault tolerance techniques in general (e.g., in the effectiveness of software diversity, discussed in Chapters 2 and 3) and the dependability of specific techniques themselves. Table 4.2 (in Section 4.1.3.3) provides a list of references for these dependability investigations. This list, although not exhaustive, provides a good sampling of the types of analyses that have been performed and substantial background for analyzing software fault tolerance dependability. The reader is encouraged to examine the references for details on assumptions made by the researchers, experiment design, and results interpretation. A comparative discussion of the techniques is provided in Section 4.7. Laprie and colleagues [19] provide the derivation and formulation of an equation for the probability of failure for the DRB technique.

One DRB experiment will be mentioned here, with others noted in Table 4.2 and in the comparative analysis of the techniques provided in Section 4.7. Kim and Welch [67] demonstrated the feasibility of the DRB using a radar tracking application. The most important results of the demonstration include the following.

- The increase in the average response time went from 1.8 to 2.6 milliseconds (this is small in relation to the maximum response time of 40 milliseconds for the application).

- The average processor utilization for the AT was 8%.

- Backup processing was not a significant portion of the total workload.

4.4 *N* Self-Checking Programming

NSCP is a design diverse technique developed by Laprie, et al. [73, 19]. The hardware fault tolerance architecture related to NSCP is active dynamic redundancy. Self-checking programming is not a new concept, having been introduced in 1975 [74]. A self-checking program uses program redundancy to check its own behavior during execution. It results from either the application of an AT to a variant's results or from the application of a comparator to the results of two variants. Self-checking software was used as the basis of the Airbus A-300, A-310, and A-320 [75] flight control systems and the Swedish railways interlocking system.

The NSCP hardware architecture consists of four components grouped in two pairs in hot standby redundancy, in which each hardware component supports one software variant. NSCP software includes two variants and a comparison algorithm or one variant and an AT on each hardware pair. When the NSCP executes, one of the self-checking components is the "active" component. The other components are "hot spares." When the active component fails, one of the spares is switched to for delivery of the service. When a spare fails, the active component continues to deliver the service as it did before the spare failed. This is called *result switching*.

The *N* in NSCP is typically even, with the NSCP modules executed in pairs. (*N* can be odd, for instance, in the case where one variant is used in both pairs. In this case, if there are four hardware components, $N = 3$.) Since the pairs are executed concurrently, there is an executive or consistency mechanism that controls any required synchronization of inputs and outputs. The self-checking group results are compared or otherwise assessed for correction. If there is no agreement, then the pair results are discarded. If there is agreement, then the pair results are compared with the other pair's results. NSCP failure occurs if both pairs disagree or the pairs agree but produce different results. NSCP is thus vulnerable to related faults between the variants.

NSCP operation is described in 4.4.1, with an example provided in 4.4.2. The advantages and disadvantages of NSCP are presented in 4.4.3.

4.4.1 *N* Self-Checking Programming Operation

The NSCP technique consists of an executive, *n* variants, and comparison algorithm(s). The executive orchestrates the NSCP technique operation, which has the general syntax (for $n = 4$):

```
run Variants 1 and 2 on Hardware Pair 1,
    Variants 3 and 4 on Hardware Pair 2
compare Results 1 and 2         compare Results 3 and 4
if not (match)                  if not (match)
    set NoMatch1                    set NoMatch2
else set Result Pair 1          else set Result Pair 2
if NoMatch1 and not NoMatch2, Result = Result Pair 2
else if NoMatch2 and not NoMatch1, Result = Result Pair 1
else if NoMatch1 and NoMatch2, raise exception
else if not NoMatch1 and not NoMatch2
    then compare Result Pair 1 and 2
    if not (match), raise exception
    if (match), Result = Result Pair 1 or 2
return Result
```

The NSCP syntax above states that the technique executes the *n* variants concurrently, on *n*/2 hardware pairs. The results of the paired variants are compared (e.g., variant 1 and 2 results are compared, variant 3 and 4 results are compared). If any pair's results do not match, a flag is set indicating pair failure. If a single pair failure has occurred, then the nonfailing pair's results are returned as the NSCP result. If both pairs failed to match, then an exception is raised. If pair results match (i.e., result 1 = result 2 and result 3 = result 4) then the results of the pairs are compared. If they match (i.e., result 1 = result 2 = result 3 = result 4), then the result is set as one of the matching values and returned as the NSCP result. If the result of the pair matches does not match, then an exception is raised.

NSCP operation is illustrated in Figure 4.7. The NSCP block is entered and the inputs are distributed to the variants. Each variant executes on the inputs and the pairs' results are gathered. Perhaps the above verbal description of the NSCP result selection clouds the fairly simple concept. Another way of illustrating the result selection process follows in Figure 4.8.

4.4.2   *N* Self-Checking Programming Example

This section provides an example implementation of the NSCP technique. Recall the sort algorithm used in the RcB example (Section 4.1.2 and Figure 4.2). Our original sort implementation produces incorrect results if one or more of the inputs are negative. Let's look at how the NSCP might be used to protect our system against faults arising from this error.

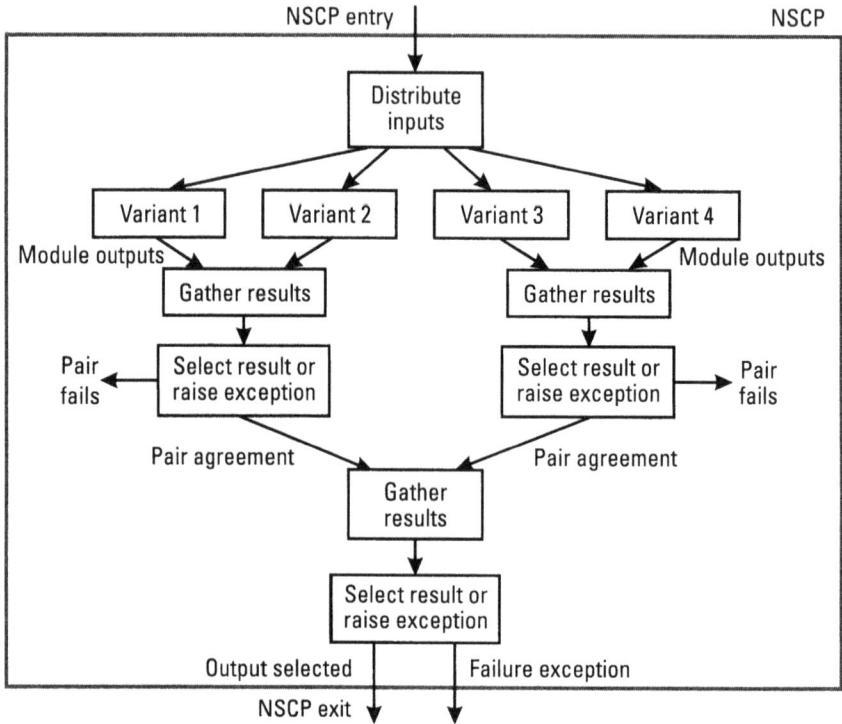

Figure 4.7 *N* self-checking programming structure and operation.

Figure 4.9 illustrates an NSCP implementation of fault tolerance for this example. Note the additional components needed for NSCP implementation: an executive that handles orchestrating and synchronizing the technique, $n = 4$ variants of incremental sort functionality, and comparators. Variant 1 is the original incremental sort; variant 2 uses the quicksort algorithm; variant 3 uses a bubble sort algorithm; and variant 4 uses heapsort. The comparators simply test if the values of its inputs (the variant results) are equal.

Now, let's step through the example.

- Upon entry to the NSCP, the executive formats calls to the $n = 4$ variants and through those calls distributes the inputs to the variants. The input set is (8, 7, 13, −4, 17, 44).

- Each variant, $V_i (i = 1, 2, 3, 4)$, executes.

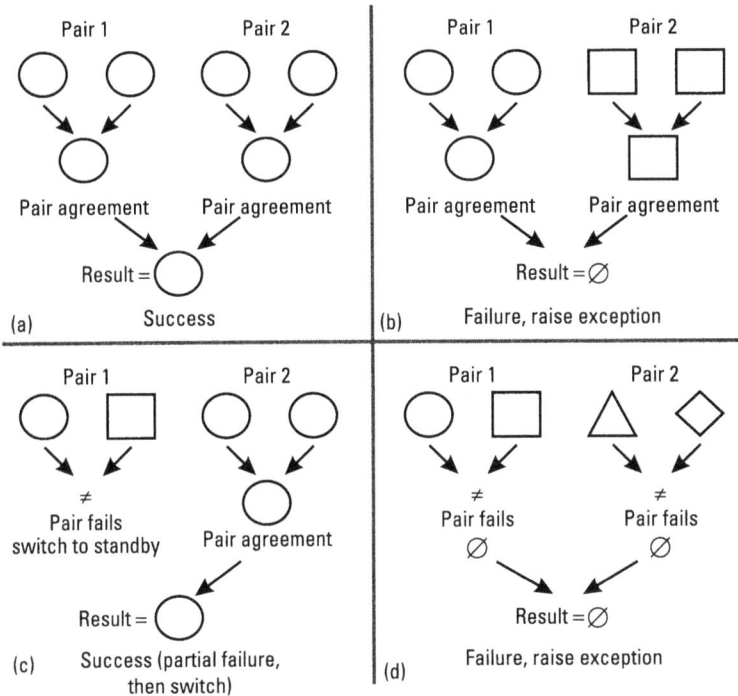

Figure 4.8 *N* self-checking programming result selection process examples (a) success, (b) failure, (c) partial failure, and (d) failure.

- The results of variants 1 and 2 executions are gathered and submitted to the comparator.

- The comparator examines the results as follows:

$R_1 = (-4, -7, -8, -13, -17, -44)$

$R_2 = (-4, 7, 8, 13, 17, 44)$

$R_1 \neq R_2$

Pair failure. Set NoMatch1 (to use the other pair's results).

- The results of variants 3 and 4 executions are gathered and submitted to the comparator.

- The comparator examines the results as follows:

$R_3 = (-4, 7, 8, 13, 17, 44)$

$R_4 = (-4, 7, 8, 13, 17, 44)$

$R_3 = R_4$

Pair agreement.

Pair result = $(-4, 7, 8, 13, 17, 44)$.

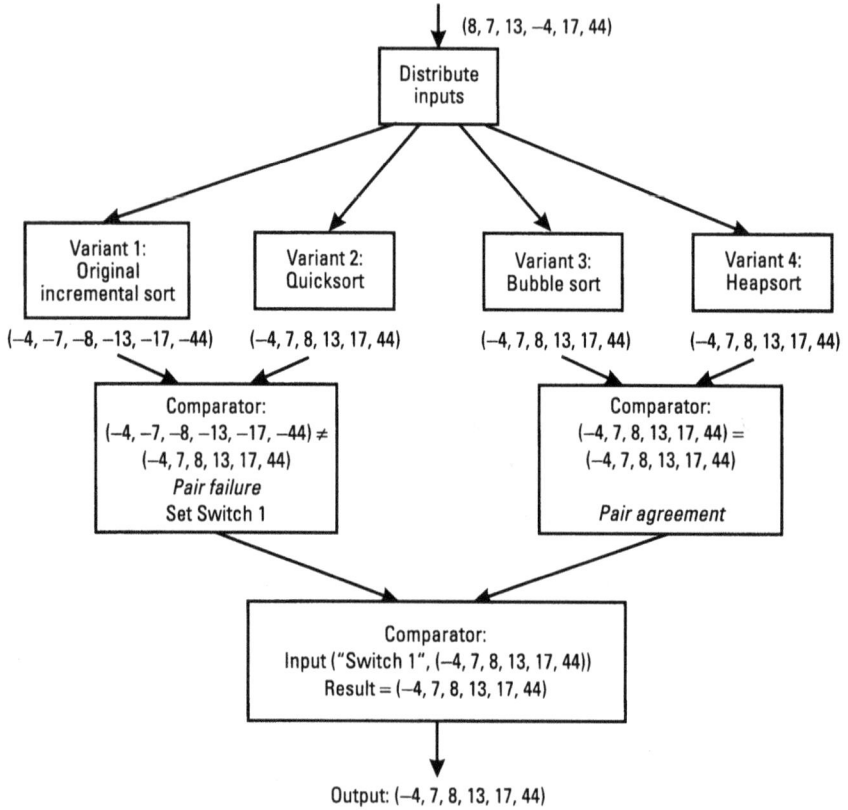

Figure 4.9 Example of *N* self-checking programming implementation.

- The pair results, the NoMatch1 flag, and (−4, 7, 8, 13, 17, 44) are gathered and submitted to another comparator.

- The comparator examines the results as follows:

  If (NoMatch1 AND NOT NoMatch2) use pair 2's results:

  The adjudicated result is (−4, 7, 8, 13, 17, 44).

- Control returns to the executive.

- The executive passes the correct result, (−4, 7, 8, 13, 17, 44), outside the NSCP, and the NSCP module is exited.

4.4.3 *N* Self-Checking Programming Issues and Discussion

This section presents the advantages, disadvantages, and issues related to NSCP. As stated earlier in this chapter, software fault tolerance techniques generally provide protection against errors in translating requirements and functionality into code, but do not provide explicit protection against errors in specifying requirements. This is true for all of the techniques described in this book. Being a design diverse, forward recovery technique, NSCP subsumes design diversity's and forward recovery's advantages and disadvantages, too. These are discussed in Sections 2.2 and 1.4.2, respectively. While designing software fault tolerance into a system, many considerations have to be taken into account. These are discussed in Chapter 3. Issues related to several software fault tolerance techniques (e.g., similar errors, coincident failures, overhead, cost, and redundancy) and the programming practices used to implement the techniques are described in Chapter 3.

There are a few issues to note specifically for the NSCP technique. NSCP runs in a multiprocessor environment. The overhead incurred (beyond that of running a single non-fault-tolerant component) includes additional memory for the second through the nth variants, executive, and DM (comparators); additional execution time for the executive and the DMs; and synchronization (input consistency) overhead.

The NSCP delays results only for comparison and result switching and rarely requires interruption of the module's service during the comparisons or result switching. This continuity of service is attractive for applications that require high availability.

In NVP, the variants cooperate via the voting DM to deliver a correct result. In NSCP though, each variant is responsible for delivering an acceptable result.

To implement NSCP, the developer can use the programming techniques (such as assertions, atomic actions, and idealized components) described in Chapter 3. The developer may use relevant aspects of the NVP paradigm described in Section 3.3.3 to minimize the chances of introducing related faults.

As in NVP and other design diverse techniques, it is critical that the initial specification for the variants used in NSCP be free of flaws. Common mode failures or undetected similar errors among the variants can cause an incorrect decision to be made by the comparators. Related faults among the variants and the comparators also have to be minimized.

Another issue in applying diverse, redundant software (i.e., this holds for NSCP and other design diverse software fault tolerance approaches) is determination of the level at which the approach should be applied. The technique application level influences the size of the resulting modules, and there are advantages and disadvantages to both small and large modules (see Section 4.2.3 for a discussion).

NSCP is made up of self-checking components executing the same functionality. Combined with its error compensation capability, this gives the NSCP the important benefit of clearly defined error containment areas. The transformation from an erroneous to a potentially error-free state consists of simply switching to the nonfailed "hot spare" pair.

Also needed for implementation and further examination of the technique is information on the underlying architecture and technique performance. These are discussed in Sections 4.4.3.1 and 4.4.3.2, respectively. Table 4.10 lists several NSCP issues, indicates whether or not they are an advantage or disadvantage (if applicable), and points to where in the book the reader may find additional information.

The indication that an issue in Table 4.10 can be a positive or negative (+/−) influence on the technique or on its effectiveness further indicates that the issue may be a disadvantage in general but an advantage in relation to another technique. In these cases, the reader is referred to the noted section for discussion of the issue.

4.4.3.1 Architecture

We mentioned in Sections 1.3.1.2 and 2.5 that structuring is required if we are to handle system complexity, especially when fault tolerance is involved [16–18]. This includes defining the organization of software modules onto the hardware elements on which they run.

As stated earlier, the NSCP hardware architecture consists of four components grouped in two pairs in hot standby redundancy, in which each hardware component supports one software variant. NSCP software includes two variants and a comparison algorithm or one variant and an AT on each hardware pair. The executive also resides on one of the hardware components. If the production of four variants is cost-prohibitive, then three variants can be distributed across the two hardware pairs with a single variant duplicated across the pairs. Communications between the software components is done through remote function calls or method invocations. Laprie and colleagues [19] provide illustrations and discussion of architectures for NSCP tolerating one fault and that for tolerating two consecutive faults.

4.4.3.2 Performance

There have been numerous investigations into the performance of software fault tolerance techniques in general (e.g., in the effectiveness of

Table 4.10
N Self-Checking Programming Issue Summary

Issue	Advantage (+)/ Disadvantage (−)	Where Discussed
Provides protection against errors in translating requirements and functionality into code (true for software fault tolerance techniques in general)	+	Chapter 1
Does not provide explicit protection against errors in specifying requirements (true for software fault tolerance techniques in general)	−	Chapter 1
General forward recovery advantages	+	Section 1.4.2
General forward recovery disadvantages	−	Section 1.4.2
General design diversity advantages	+	Section 2.2
General design diversity disadvantages	−	Section 2.2
Similar errors or common residual design errors	−	Section 3.1.1
Coincident and correlated failures	−	Section 3.1.1
CCP	−	Section 3.1.2
Overhead for tolerating a single fault	+/−	Section 3.1.4
Cost (Table 3.3)	+/−	Section 3.1.4
Space and time redundancy	+/−	Section 3.1.4
Design considerations	+	Section 3.3.1
Dependable system development model	+	Section 3.3.2
NVS design paradigm	+	Section 3.3.3
Dependability studies	+/−	Section 4.1.3.3

software diversity, discussed in Chapters 2 and 3) and the dependability of specific techniques themselves. Table 4.2 (in Section 4.1.3.3) provides a list of references for these dependability investigations. This list, although not exhaustive, provides a good sampling of the types of analyses that have been performed and substantial background for analyzing software fault tolerance dependability. The reader is encouraged to examine the references for details on assumptions made by the researchers, experiment design, and results interpretation. Laprie and colleagues [19] provide the determination and formulation of an equation for the probability of failure for NSCP. A comparative discussion of the techniques is provided in Section 4.7.

4.5   Consensus Recovery Block

The CRB technique, suggested by Scott, Gault, and McAllister [76, 77, 20], combines RcB and NVP implementation techniques. It is claimed that the CRB technique reduces the importance of the AT used in the RcB and is able to handle cases where NVP would not be appropriate because of MCR. CRB uses *n* variants that are ranked, as in RcB, in order of their service and reliability. The *n* variants are first run concurrently in NVP fashion, and their results are checked by a voter. If the voter does not determine a correct result (typically using a majority decision algorithm), then the results of the highest ranked variant are submitted to the AT. If that variant's results fail the AT, then the next highest ranked variant's results are sent to the AT, and so on, until an acceptable result passes the AT or no variants are left. In the RcB part of the CRB technique, the existing results of variant execution, that is, the ones that just failed to result in a majority decision, can be run through the AT, or, if a transient failure is likely, the variants can be run again prior to submitting their results to the AT. The system fails if both the NVP and the RcB portions of the technique fail to come up with a correct result.

CRB operation is described in 4.5.1, with an example provided in 4.5.2. The advantages and disadvantages of CRB are presented in 4.5.3.

4.5.1   Consensus Recovery Block Operation

A CRB consists of an executive, *n* ranked variants, a voter-type DM, and an AT. The executive orchestrates the CRB technique operation, which has the general syntax:

```
run Ranked Variant 1, Ranked Variant 2, ..., Ranked Variant n
if (Decision Mechanism (Result 1, Result 2, ..., Result n))
    return Result
else
    ensure              Acceptance Test
    by                  Ranked Variant 1 [Result]
    else by             Ranked Variant 2 [Result]
    ...
    else by             Ranked Variant n [Result]
    else raise failure exception
return Result
```

The CRB syntax above states that the technique executes the *n* ranked variants concurrently, as in NVP. The results of these executions are provided to the decision mechanism, which operates upon them to determine if a correct result can be adjudicated. If one can (i.e., the Decision Mechanism statement above evaluates to TRUE), then it is returned. If a correct result cannot be determined, then the AT is attempted with the ranked variants' results until an acceptable result is found. The brackets "[ ]" around the term Result above indicate that the variant results may be used in the AT with or without re-executing the variants. If no variant results pass the AT, an error occurs.

Figure 4.10 illustrates the operation of the CRB. Fault-free, partial failure, and failure scenarios for the CRB technique are described below. In examining these scenarios, the following abbreviations are used:

AT	Acceptance test;
CRB	Consensus recovery block;
DM	Decision mechanism;
n	The number of variants;
NVP	*N*-version programming;
R_i	Result of V_i;
V_i	Variant i, where $i = 1, 2, \ldots, n$ and indicates the variant rank order with V_1 being the highest ranked variant.

4.5.1.1 Failure-Free Operation

This scenario describes the operation of the CRB technique when no failure or exception occurs.

- Upon entry to the CRB, the executive performs the following: formats calls to the n ranked variants and through those calls distributes the input(s) to the variants.
- Each variant, V_i, executes. No failures occur during their execution.
- The results of the variant executions (R_i, $i = 1, \ldots, n$) are gathered by the executive and submitted to the DM, which is a voter in this part of the technique.

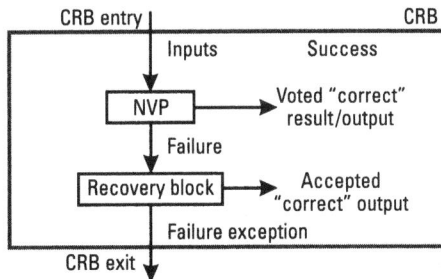

Figure 4.10 Consensus recovery block structure and operation.

- The R_i are equal to one another, so the DM selects R_2 (randomly, since the results are equal), as the correct result.
- Control returns to the executive.
- The executive passes the correct result outside the CRB, and the CRB is exited.

4.5.1.2 Partial Failure Scenario—Voter Cannot Determine Correct Result, but Acceptance Test Does

This scenario describes the operation of the CRB technique when partial failure occurs, that is, when the DM cannot determine a correct result, but the AT finds one of the variant results acceptable. Differences between this scenario and the failure-free scenario are in gray type.

- Upon entry to the CRB, the executive performs the following: formats calls to the n variants and through those calls distributes the input(s) to the variants.
- Each variant, V_i, executes.
- The results of the variant executions (R_i, $i = 1, ..., n$) are gathered by the executive and submitted to the DM, which is a voter in this part of the technique.
- The R_i differ significantly from one another. The DM cannot determine a correct result, and it sets a flag indicating this fact.
- Control returns to the executive.
- The results of the highest ranked variant, V_1, are submitted to the AT.
- V_1's results fail the AT.
- Control returns to the executive.
- The results of the next highest ranked variant, V_2, are submitted to the AT.
- V_2's results pass the AT.
- Control returns to the executive.
- The executive passes the results outside the CRB, and the CRB is exited.

4.5.1.3 Failure Scenario—Neither Voter nor Acceptance Test Can Determine Correct Result

This scenario describes the failure operation of the CRB, that is, when neither the DM nor the AT can determine a correct result. Suppose in this case that $n = 3$. Differences between this scenario and the failure-free scenario are in gray type.

- Upon entry to the CRB, the executive performs the following: formats calls to the n variants and through those calls distributes the input(s) to the variants.

- Each variant, V_i, executes.

- The results of the variant executions (R_i, $i = 1, \ldots, n$) are gathered by the executive and submitted to the DM, which is a voter in this part of the technique.

- The R_i differ significantly from one another. The DM cannot determine a correct result, and it sets a flag indicating this fact.

- Control returns to the executive.

- The results of the highest ranked variant, V_1, are submitted to the AT.

- V_1's results fail the AT.

- Control returns to the executive.

- The results of the next highest ranked variant, V_2, are submitted to the AT.

- V_2's results fail the AT.

- The results of the next highest ranked variant, V_3, are submitted to the AT.

- V_3's results fail the AT.

- Control returns to the executive.

- The executive raises an exception and the CRB is exited.

4.5.2 Consensus Recovery Block Example

This section provides an example implementation of the CRB technique. We use a different example for this technique. Suppose we want to find the fastest round-trip route between a set of four cities. This is a nondeterministic problem that can yield more than one correct answer. That is, there may be multiple combinations of cities that can be traveled in the same amount of

(City A, City B, City C, City D)

Distribute
inputs

Variant 1   Variant 2   Variant 3

[(City A, City B, City C,
City D, City D), 125]

[(City A, City C, City B,
City D, City A), 4]

[(City A, City D, City C,
City B, City A), 57]

DM:
Majority voter

Voter fails to find match

AT: a) Round trip?
     b) All cites?   Fail
     c) Trip time > 7? V_1, V_2

Pass

V_3 passes, result is:
[(City A, City D, City C, City B, City A), 57]

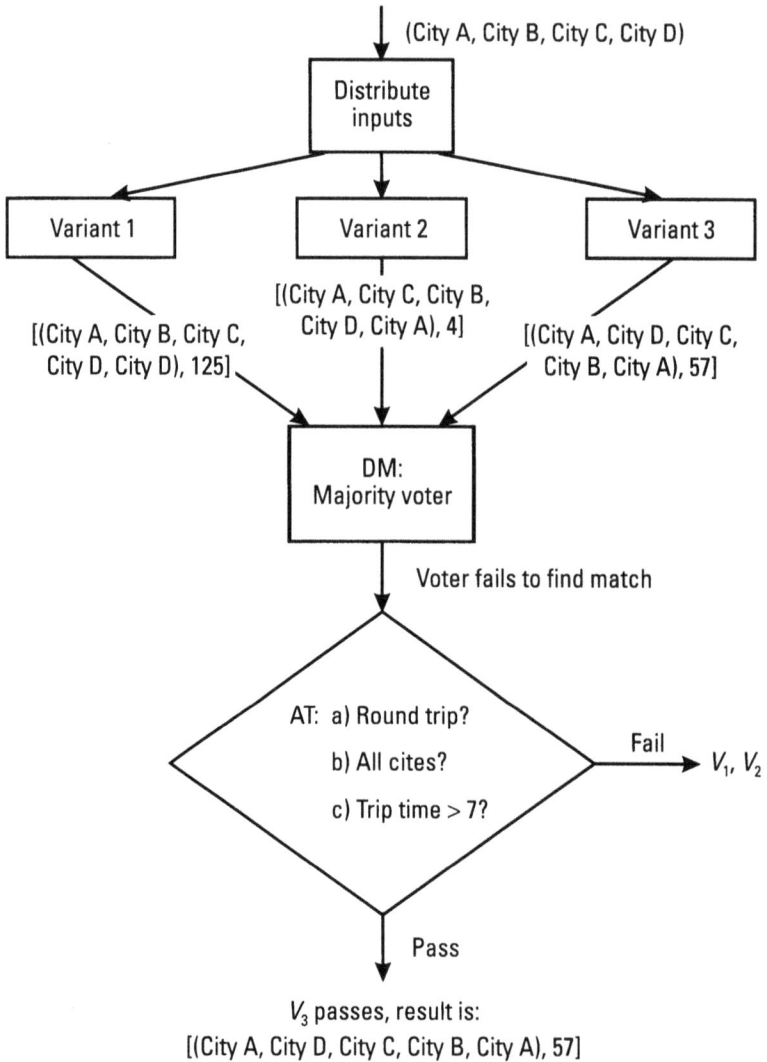

Figure 4.11 Example of consensus recovery block implementation.

time. Hence, we have the possibility of MCR occurring. How can the CRB technique be used to protect our system against the MCR problem?

Figure 4.11 illustrates a CRB implementation of fault tolerance for this example. Note the additional components needed for CRB implementation: an executive that handles orchestrating and synchronizing the technique, one or more additional variants of the route finder algorithm/program, a DM, and an AT. Each variant uses a different shortest-route-finding algorithm and along with the route provides the amount of time it takes to traverse that route.

Also note the design of the voter DM. Since the result of our algorithm is an ordered list, we can check each entry against the entries in the same position in the other result lists. If we designate the result in this example as r_{ij} where $i = 1, 2, 3$ (up to $n = 3$ variants) and $j = 1, 2, ..., 5$ (up to $k = 4$ cities in the result set, with the starting and ending city listed first and last in the set if the algorithm performs correctly), then our DM performs the following tests:

$$r_{1j} = r_{2j} \quad \text{for } j = 1, ..., k$$
$$r_{1j} = r_{3j} \quad \text{for } j = 1, ..., k$$
$$r_{2j} = r_{3j} \quad \text{for } j = 1, ..., k$$

If the r_{ij} in any of the above tests are equal for all j, then the resultant set for either i in the equality is selected as the correct result. That is, if $r_{1j} = r_{2j}$ for $j = 1, ..., k$, then either r_{1j} or r_{2j} can be the correct result (i.e., they are the same route), and one of them is selected randomly and passed on as the correct result. If none of the above tests are equal for all j, then the voter cannot select a correct result.

Suppose the AT checks the following: (a) that all cities in the original set of cities are in the resultant set, (b) that the starting and ending cities are the same, and (c) that the time it takes to traverse the set of cities is within a set of reasonable bounds. (Note: If the system had available time, the AT could examine all resulting times and select the route with the lowest round-trip time that also met the other criteria.)

Now, let's step through the example.

- Upon entry to the CRB, the executive performs the following: formats calls to the $n = 3$ variants and through those calls distributes the inputs to the variants. The input set is (City A, City B, City C, City D).

- Each variant, V_i ($i = 1, 2, 3$), executes.

- The results of the variant executions (r_{ij}, $i = 1, ..., n; j = 1, ..., k$) are gathered by the executive and submitted to the voter DM.

- The DM examines the results as follows:

j	r_{1j}	r_{2j}	r_{3j}	Result
1	City A	City A	City A	
2	City B	City C	City D	
3	City C	City B	City C	Multiple correct or incorrect results
4	City D	City D	City B	
5	City D	City A	City A	
Time	125	4	57	

No correct result could be found. There are either multiple correct or multiple incorrect results.

- Control returns to the executive.
- The results of the highest ranked variant, V_1, are submitted to the AT. The AT checks whether the first and last cities in the route are the same (the round-trip test). They are not, so the results of V_1 fail the AT.
- Control returns to the executive.
- The results of V_2 are submitted to the AT. The AT performs the round-trip test and the results pass. The AT checks that all input cities are in the result route. They are. Last, the AT sees that the time to take this route is calculated as 4 time units. Knowing that the shortest time between any of the cities is 7 time units (a lower-bound test), the AT rejects V_2's results.
- Control returns to the executive.
- The results of V_3 are submitted to the AT. The AT performs the round-trip test and the results pass. The AT checks that all input cities are in the result route and they are. Last, the AT sees that the time to take this route is calculated as 57 time units and checks that against the lower bound of 7 time units. V_3's results pass the AT.
- Control returns to the executive.
- The executive passes the results outside the CRB, and the CRB is exited.

4.5.3 Consensus Recovery Block Issues and Discussion

This section presents the advantages, disadvantages, and issues related to the CRB technique. As stated earlier in this chapter, software fault tolerance techniques generally provide protection against errors in translating requirements and functionality into code, but do not provide explicit protection against errors in specifying requirements. This is true for all of the techniques described in this book. Being a design diverse, forward recovery technique, the CRB subsumes design diversity's and forward recovery's advantages and disadvantages, too. These are discussed in Sections 2.2 and 1.4.2, respectively. While designing software fault tolerance into a system, many considerations have to be taken into account. These are discussed in Chapter 3. Issues related to several software fault tolerance techniques (such as similar errors, coincident failures, overhead, cost, redundancy, etc.) and the programming practices used to implement the techniques are described in Chapter 3.

There are a few issues to note specifically for the CRB technique. CRB runs in a multiprocessor environment. The overhead incurred (beyond that of running a single non-fault-tolerant component) includes additional memory for the second through the nth variants, executive, and DMs (voting-type and AT); additional execution time for the executive and the DMs; and synchronization (input consistency) overhead.

The CRB delays results only for voting and acceptance testing (if necessary) and rarely requires interruption of the module's service during the decision making. This continuity of service is attractive for applications that require high availability.

To implement the CRB technique, the developer can use the programming techniques (such as assertions, atomic actions, idealized components) described in Chapter 3. The developer may use relevant aspects of the NVP paradigm described in Section 3.3.3 to minimize the chances of introducing related faults.

As in NVP and other design diverse techniques, it is critical that the initial specification for the variants used in CRB be free of flaws. Common mode failures or undetected similar errors among the variants can cause an incorrect decision to be made by the DMs. Related faults among the variants and the DMs also have to be minimized.

Another issue in applying diverse, redundant software (i.e., this holds for the CRB and other design diverse software fault tolerance approaches) is determination of the level at which the approach should be applied. The technique application level influences the size of the resulting modules, and there are advantages and disadvantages to both small and large modules (see Section 4.2.3 for a discussion).

A general disadvantage of all hybrid strategies such as the CRB is an increased complexity of the fault-tolerance mechanism, which is accompanied by an increase in the probability of existence of design or implementation errors. The increased complexity does not, however, necessarily imply an increase in costs [78].

The anticipated increase in effectiveness of the CRB technique over NVP, for example, is largely based on the assumption that there are no common faults between the variants. We discussed common faults and correlated failures (see Section 3.1.1 and [79–81, 24, 25]) and know that this is generally not the case. Scott, Gault, and McAllister [20] developed reliability models for RcB, NVP, and CRB and showed that CRB was superior to NVP and RcB. However, if the CRB voter finds a match or a majority, the matching result is not submitted to the AT, thus bypassing the possible test for erroneous results caused by a correlated failure in two or more variants (or between the variants and the voter).

Information on the underlying architecture and technique performance is needed for implementation and further examination of the CRB technique. These are discussed in Sections 4.5.3.1 and 4.5.3.2, respectively. Table 4.11 lists several general issues related to the CRB technique, indicates whether or not they are an advantage or disadvantage (if applicable), and points to where in the book the reader may find additional information.

The indication that an issue in Table 4.11 can be a positive or negative (+/−) influence on the technique or on its effectiveness further indicates that the issue may be a disadvantage in general, but an advantage in relation to another technique. In these cases, the reader is referred to the noted section for discussion of the issue.

4.5.3.1   Architecture

We mentioned in Sections 1.3.1.2 and 2.5 that structuring is required if we are to handle system complexity, especially when fault tolerance is involved [16–18]. This includes defining the organization of software modules onto the hardware elements on which they run.

The CRB technique's architecture is very similar to that of NVP. It is typically multiprocessor implemented with components residing on n (the number of variants in the CRB) hardware units and an executive residing on one of the hardware components. The primary difference, in terms of component types, between the NVP and CRB techniques is that CRB employs the addition of AT(s). The most likely residence of a single AT used with CRB is on the same hardware component as the voting DM.

Table 4.11
Consensus Recovery Block Issue Summary

Issue	Advantage (+)/ Disadvantage (−)	Where Discussed
Provides protection against errors in translating requirements and functionality into code (true for software fault tolerance techniques in general)	+	Chapter 1
Does not provide explicit protection against errors in specifying requirements (true for software fault tolerance techniques in general)	−	Chapter 1
General forward recovery advantages	+	Section 1.4.2
General forward recovery disadvantages	−	Section 1.4.2
General design diversity advantages	+	Section 2.2
General design diversity disadvantages	−	Section 2.2
Similar errors or common residual design errors	−	Section 3.1.1
Coincident and correlated failures	−	Section 3.1.1
CCP	−	Section 3.1.2
Space and time redundancy	+/−	Section 3.1.4
Design considerations	+	Section 3.3.1
Dependable system development model	+	Section 3.3.2
NVS design paradigm	+	Section 3.3.3
Dependability studies	+/−	Section 4.1.3.3

Communications between the software components is done through remote function calls or method invocations.

4.5.3.2 Performance

There have been numerous investigations into the performance of software fault tolerance techniques in general (e.g., in the effectiveness of software diversity, discussed in Chapters 2 and 3) and the dependability of specific techniques themselves. Table 4.2 (in Section 4.1.3.3) provides a list of references for these dependability investigations. This list, although not exhaustive, provides a good sampling of the types of analyses that have been performed and substantial background for analyzing software fault tolerance dependability. The reader is encouraged to examine the references for details on assumptions made by the researchers, experiment design, and results interpretation. Belli and Jedrzejowicz [82] provide a determination and formulation of an equation for the probability of failure for CRB. A comparative discussion of the techniques is provided in Section 4.7.

4.6   Acceptance Voting

The AV technique was proposed by Athavale [83] and evaluated by Belli and Jedrzejowicz [84] and Gantenbeim, et al. [85]. The AV technique uses both an AT (see Section 7.2) and a voting-type DM (see Section 7.1), along with forward recovery (see Section 1.4.2) to accomplish fault tolerance. In AV, all variants can execute in parallel. The variant results are evaluated by an AT, and only accepted results are sent to the voter. Since the DM may see anywhere from 1 to n (where n is the number of variants) results, the technique requires a dynamic voting algorithm (see Section 7.1.6). The dynamic voter is able to process a varying number of results upon each invocation. That is, if two results pass the AT, they are compared. If five results pass, they are voted upon, and so on. If no results pass the AT, then the system fails. It also fails if the dynamic voter cannot select a correct result.

The operation of the AV technique is described in 4.6.1, and an example is provided in 4.6.2. Advantages, limitations, and issues related to the AV technique are presented in 4.6.3.

4.6.1   Acceptance Voting Operation

The AV technique consists of an executive, n variants, ATs, and a dynamic voter DM. The executive orchestrates the AV technique operation, which has the general syntax:

```
run Variant 1, Variant 2, ..., Variant n
    ensure    Acceptance Test 1 by Variant 1
    ensure    Acceptance Test 2 by Variant 2
    ...
    ensure    Acceptance Test n by Variant n
[Result i, Result j, ..., Result m pass the AT]
if (Decision Mechanism (Result i, Result j,
            ..., Result m))
    return Result
else
    return failure exception
```

The AV syntax above states that the technique executes the n variants concurrently as in NVP. The results of each of these executions are provided to ATs. A different AT may be used with each variant; however, in practice, a single AT algorithm is used. All results that pass their AT are passed to the DM. The DM selects the majority, if one exists, and outputs it. If no results pass their ATs or if there is no majority (or matching result if $k = 2$) result, then an exception is raised. If only one output passes its AT, the voter assumes it is correct and outputs that result.

Figure 4.12 illustrates the operation of the AV technique. Fault-free, partial failure, and failure scenarios for the AV technique are described below. In examining these scenarios, the following abbreviations are used:

A_j	Accepted result $j, j = 1, \ldots, m$;
AT_i	Acceptance test associated with variant i;
AV	Acceptance voting;
DM	Decision mechanism;
m	The number of accepted variant results;
n	The number of variants;

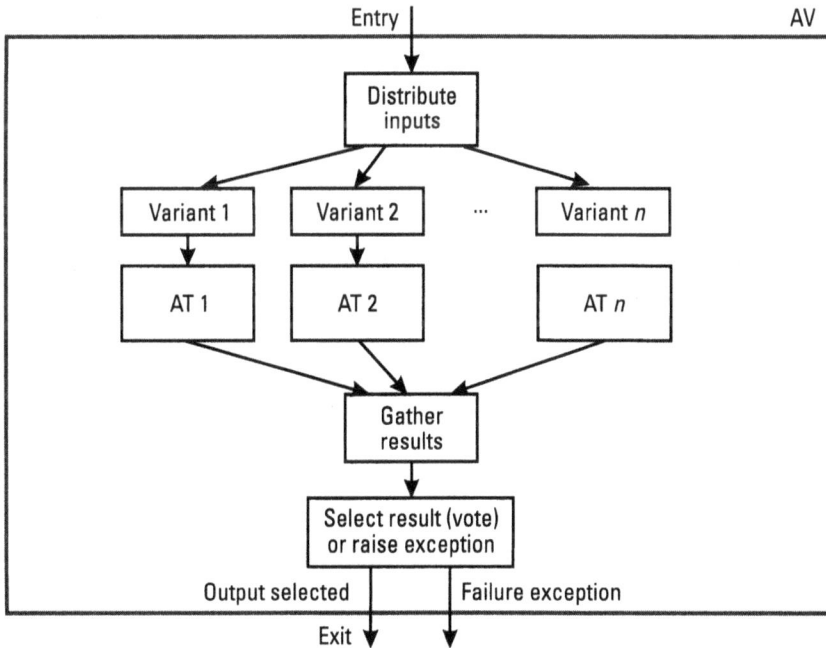

Figure 4.12 Acceptance voting technique structure and operation.

R_i Result of V_i;

V_i Variant i, where $i = 1, 2, \ldots, n$.

4.6.1.1   Failure-Free Operation

This scenario describes the operation of the AV technique when no failure or exception occurs.

- Upon entry to the AV block, the executive performs the following: formats calls to the n variants and through those calls distributes the input(s) to the variants.

- Each variant, V_i, executes. No failures occur during their execution.

- The results of the variant executions (R_i, $i = 1, \ldots, n$) are submitted to an AT.

- Each result passes its AT.

- The accepted results of the AT executions (A_j, $j = 1, \ldots, m$) are gathered by the executive and submitted to the DM, which is a dynamic voter in this part of the technique.

- The A_j are equal to one another, so the DM selects A_2 (randomly, since the results are equal), as the correct result.

- Control returns to the executive.

- The executive passes the correct result outside the AV block, and the AV block is exited.

4.6.1.2   Partial Failure Scenario—Some Results Fail Acceptance Test, but Voter Can Select a Correct Result from the $k \geq 1$ Accepted Results

This scenario describes the operation of the AV technique when partial failure occurs, that is, when only some k ($1 \leq k < n$) results pass the AT, but the DM can still select a correct result. Differences between this scenario and the failure-free scenario are in gray type.

- Upon entry to the AV block, the executive performs the following: formats calls to the n variants and through those calls distributes the input(s) to the variants.

- Each variant, V_i, executes.

- The results of the variant executions (R_i, $i = 1, \ldots, n$) are submitted to an AT.

- Some results pass their AT, some fail their AT.
- The accepted results of the AT executions (A_j, $j = 1, \ldots, m$) are gathered by the executive and submitted to the DM, which is a dynamic voter in this part of the technique.
- A majority of the A_j are equal to one another, so the DM selects one of the majority results as the correct result.
- Control returns to the executive.
- The executive passes the correct result outside the AV block, and the AV block is exited.

4.6.1.3   Failure Scenario—Results Passing Acceptance Test Fail Decision Mechanism

This scenario describes one failure scenario of the AV technique, that is, when some k ($1 \leq k < n$) results pass their AT, but the DM cannot determine a correct result. Differences between this scenario and the failure-free scenario are in gray type.

- Upon entry to the AV block, the executive performs the following: formats calls to the n variants and through those calls distributes the input(s) to the variants.
- Each variant, V_i, executes.
- The results of the variant executions (R_i, $i = 1, \ldots, n$) are submitted to an AT.
- Some results pass their AT, some fail their AT.
- The accepted results of the AT executions (A_j, $j = 1, \ldots, m$) are gathered by the executive and submitted to the DM, which is a dynamic voter in this part of the technique.
- The A_j differ significantly from one another. The DM cannot determine a correct result, and it sets a flag indicating this fact.
- Control returns to the executive.
- The executive raises an exception and the CRB module is exited.

4.6.1.4   Failure Scenario—No Variant Results Pass Acceptance Test

This scenario describes another failure scenario for the AV technique, that is, when none of the variant results pass their AT. Differences between this scenario and the failure-free scenario are in gray type.

- Upon entry to the AV block, the executive performs the following: formats calls to the *n* variants and through those calls distributes the input(s) to the variants.

- Each variant, V_i, executes.

- The results of the variant executions ($R_i i = 1, ..., n$) are submitted to an AT.

- None of the results pass their AT.

- Control returns to the executive.

- The executive raises an exception and the AV block is exited.

4.6.2   Acceptance Voting Example

This section provides an example implementation of the AV technique. We use the same example for this technique as we did for the CRB—finding the fastest round-trip route between a set of four cities. Recall that this problem has the possibility of resulting in MCR. How can the AV technique be used to provide fault tolerance for this system?

Figure 4.13 illustrates an AV implementation of fault tolerance for this example. Note the additional components needed for AV implementation: an executive that handles orchestrating and synchronizing the technique, one or more additional variants of the route finder algorithm/program, an AT, and a DM. Each variant uses a different shortest-route-finding algorithm and along with the route provides the amount of time it takes to traverse that route.

We use the same AT as that used in the CRB example. The AT checks the following: (a) that all cities in the original set of cities are in the resultant set, (b) that the starting and ending cities are the same, and (c) that the time it takes to traverse the set of cities is within a set of reasonable bounds. The same AT will be used for each variant.

Also note the design of the dynamic voter DM. If no results pass their ATs, the executive can either bypass the voter and raise an exception itself or send zero results to the voter. If the executive sends the voter zero results to process, the voter can set a flag indicating to the executive that the voter has failed to select a correct result. Then the executive can raise the exception. The voter could also issue the exception itself. The manner of implementation depends on whether consistent operation is desired. By consistent operation, we mean the dynamic voter operation in each case of 0, 1, 2, or $j \geq 3$ results follows a consistent process. That is:

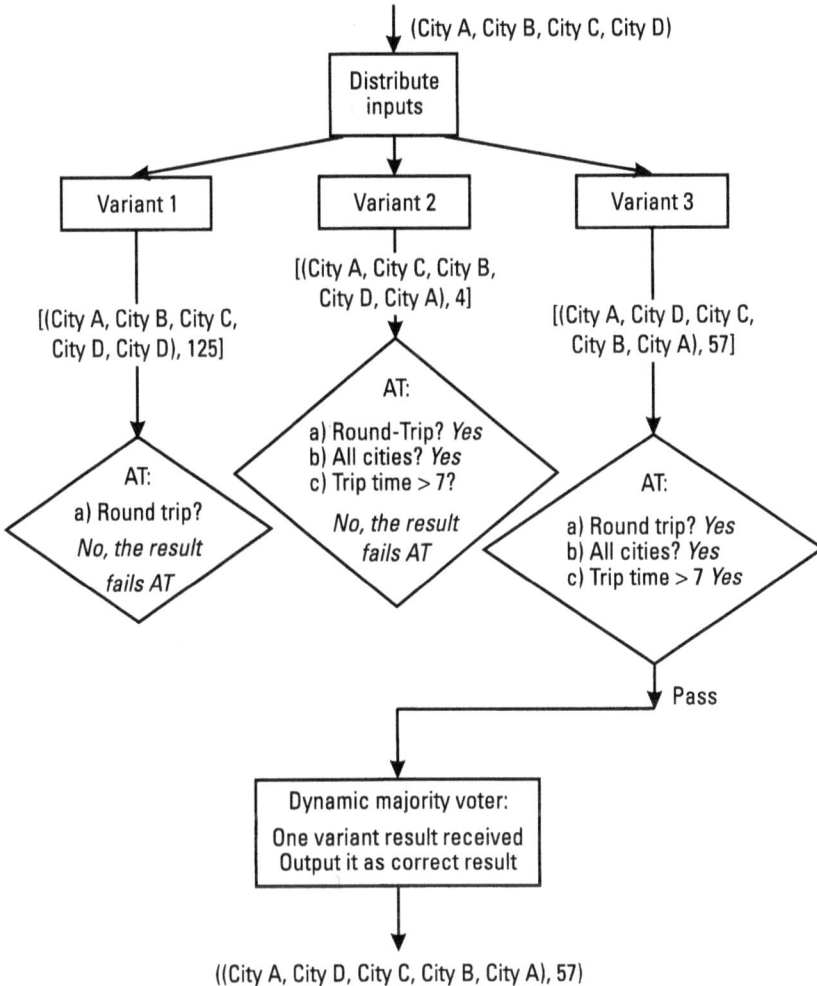

Figure 4.13 Example of acceptance voting implementation.

- Executive retrieves results from ATs;
- Executive passes results to voter;
- Voter determines number of results in the input set and determines whether or not a "correct" result can be adjudicated;
- Voter returns indicator of success and result;
- Executive retrieves voter findings and either raises an exception or passes on the adjudicated result.

Our executive works in the manner described above.

Table 4.12 indicates the voter operation based on the number of results it receives as input. The comparison and voting algorithm for the voter used in this example is described in Section 4.5.2.

Now, let's step through the example.

- Upon entry to the AV the executive performs the following: formats calls to the $n = 3$ variants and through those calls distributes the inputs to the variants. The input set is (City A, City B, City C, City D).
- Each variant, V_i ($i = 1, 2, 3$), executes.
- The results of the variant executions are submitted to an AT. The results of the AT checks are as follows:

Variant	Variant Result	AT Result
1	[(City A, City B, City C, City D, City D), 125]	a) Round-trip?
		No—result fails the AT
2	[(City A, City C, City B, City D, City A), 4]	a) Round-trip? *Yes*
		b) All cities visited? *Yes*
		c) Trip time > 7?
		No—result fails the AT
3	[(City A, City D, City C, City B, City A), 57]	a) Round-trip? *Yes*
		b) All cities visited? *Yes*
		c) Trip time > 7? *Yes*
		Result passes the AT

Table 4.12

Acceptance Voting Technique Voter Operation

Number of Inputs	Operation
0	Raise exception
1	Return single input as correct result
2	Compare inputs
≥3	Vote

- Control returns to the executive.

- The results of the acceptable variant executions (R_3) are gathered by the executive and submitted to the dynamic voter DM.

- The DM examines the results:

Number of Inputs	Input	Procedure	Result
1	[(City A, City D, City C, City B, City A), 57]	Single accepted result—output as adjudicated/correct result	[(City A, City D, City C, City B, City A), 57]

- Control returns to the executive.

- The executive passes the results outside the AV, and the AV is exited.

4.6.3 Acceptance Voting Issues and Discussion

This section presents the advantages, disadvantages, and issues related to the AV technique. In general, software fault tolerance techniques provide protection against errors in translating requirements and functionality into code but do not provide explicit protection against errors in specifying requirements. This is true for all of the techniques described in this book. Being a design diverse, forward recovery technique, AV subsumes design diversity's and forward recovery's advantages and disadvantages, too. These are discussed in Sections 2.2 and 1.4.2, respectively. While designing software fault tolerance into a system, many considerations have to be taken into account. These are discussed in Chapter 3. Issues related to several software fault tolerance techniques (such as similar errors, coincident failures, overhead, cost, redundancy, etc.) and the programming practices used to implement the techniques are described in Chapter 3. Issues related to implementing ATs and DMs are discussed in Sections 7.2 and 7.1, respectively.

There are a few issues to note specifically for the AV technique. The AV technique runs in a multiprocessor environment. The overhead incurred (beyond that of running a single non-fault-tolerant component) includes additional memory for the second through nth variants, executive, and DMs (ATs and voting type); additional execution time for the executive and the DMs; and synchronization overhead.

The AV technique delays results only for acceptance testing and voting and rarely requires interruption of the module's service during the decision making. This continuity of service is attractive for applications that require high availability.

To implement the AV technique, the developer can use the programming techniques (such as assertions, atomic actions, and idealized components) described in Chapter 3. The developer may use relevant aspects of the NVP paradigm described in Section 3.3.3 to minimize the chances of introducing related faults.

As in NVP and other design diverse techniques, it is critical that the initial specification for the variants used in AV be free of flaws. Common mode failures or undetected similar errors among the variants can cause an incorrect decision to be made by the DMs. Related faults among the variants and the DMs also have to be minimized.

Another issue in applying diverse, redundant software (i.e., this holds for the AV technique and other design diverse software fault tolerance approaches) is determination of the level at which the approach should be applied. The technique application level influences the size of the resulting modules, and there are advantages and disadvantages to both small and large modules (see Section 4.2.3 for a discussion).

A general disadvantage of all hybrid strategies such as the AV technique is an increased complexity of the fault tolerance mechanism, which is accompanied by an increase in the probability of existence of design or implementation errors. The AV technique is very dependent on the reliability of its AT. If it allows erroneous results to be accepted, then the advantage of catching potential related faults prior to being assessed by the voter-type DM is minimal at best.

The AV technique is very similar to the combined RcB and NVP technique [82] and the multiversion software (MVS) technique [62]. It is suggested (in [82]) that this structure be used when the testing modules within the traditional RcB are unreliable, for example, due to being overly simple or to difficulties in evaluating functional module performance.

Also needed for implementation and further examination of the technique is information on the underlying architecture and performance. These are discussed in Sections 4.6.3.1 and 4.6.3.2, respectively. Table 4.7 in Section 4.5.3 lists several issues for the CRB technique that are also relevant to the AV technique. An additional pointer, beyond those in the table, should be provided for the AV technique—the dynamic voter. It is discussed in Section 7.1.6.

4.6.3.1 Architecture

We mentioned in Sections 1.3.1.2 and 2.5 that structuring is required if we are to handle system complexity, especially when fault tolerance is involved [16–18]. This includes defining the organization of software modules onto the hardware elements on which they run.

The AV technique's architecture is very similar to that of NVP. It is typically multiprocessor implemented with components residing on n (the number of variants in AV) hardware units. The primary difference, in terms of component types, between the NVP and AV techniques is that AV employs the addition of AT(s). An AT tests each variant's result prior to allowing the result to be submitted to the voting DM. A single AT could reside on the same hardware component as the voter, but this may add unnecessary communications overhead between the variants and the AT. One example architecture consists of three hardware nodes, with a single variant on each node, the AT replicated on each node, and the executive and a voter on one of the nodes. (There could also be a different AT for each variant.) This configuration would decrease communications overhead when any variant (other than the one on the same processor as the voter) fails. Communication between the software components is done through remote function calls or method invocations.

4.6.3.2 Performance

There have been numerous investigations into the performance of software fault tolerance techniques in general (e.g., in the effectiveness of software diversity, discussed in Chapters 2 and 3) and the dependability of specific techniques themselves. Table 4.2 (in Section 4.1.3.3) provides a list of references for these dependability investigations. This list, although not exhaustive, provides a good sampling of the types of analyses that have been performed and substantial background for analyzing software fault tolerance dependability. The reader is encouraged to examine the references for details on assumptions made by the researchers, experiment design, and results interpretation. Belli and Jedrzejowicz [82] provide a determination and formulation of an equation for the probability of failure for AV (or the combined RcB and NVP approach). A comparative discussion of the techniques is provided in Section 4.7.

The addition of an AT to each of the n variants increases the performance and coverage of the decision function. This AT excludes clearly erroneous results from the decision function. These ATs need not be as vigorous as those used in RcB because of the presence of the voting DM. They are to serve as coarse filters so that clearly erroneous results are not presented to the DM and so that the DM does not wait for a result that will not arrive. After the voter has determined an output, the result can be used as feedback to the error-producing modules, which may, in turn, use the result to correct their internal state.

4.7 Technique Comparisons

There have been many experiments and analytical studies of software fault tolerance techniques. The results of some of these studies have been described elsewhere in this book (Chapter 3 for instance). The study results presented here provide insight into the performance of the techniques themselves. Since each study has different underlying assumptions, it is difficult to compare the results across experiments. The fault assumptions used in the experiments and studies are important and if changed or ignored can alter the interpretation of the results. In this section, we have grouped the work within subsections based on the techniques analyzed. Within that categorization, the results of experiments are presented. Most existing research has been performed on the two basic techniques—the RcB and NVP. These findings are described in Section 4.7.1. Other research on technique comparisons are presented for:

- RcB and DRB in Section 4.7.2;

- CRB, RcB, and NVP in Section 4.7.3;

- AV, CRB, RcB, and NVP in Section 4.7.4.

Before continuing, we present the following tables that summarize the techniques described in this chapter. Table 4.13 presents the main characteristics of the design diverse software fault tolerance techniques described. The structure of the table and the entries for the RcB, NVP, and NSCP techniques were developed by Laprie and colleagues [19]. Entries for the DRB, CRB, and AV techniques have been added for this summary. Table 4.14 presents the main sources of overhead for the techniques in tolerating a single fault (versus non-fault-tolerant software). Again, the structure of the table and the entries for the RcB, NVP, and NSCP techniques were developed by Laprie and colleagues [19], with entries for the DRB, CRB, and AV techniques added by this author for the summary.

Table 4.13
Main Characteristics of the Design Diverse Software Fault Tolerance Techniques (*After:* [19].)

Method	Error Processing Technique		Judgement on Result Acceptability	Variant Execution Scheme	Consistency of Input Data	Suspension of Service Delivery During Error Processing	Number of Variants for Tolerance of Sequential Faults
RcB	Error detection by AT and backward recovery		Absolute, with respect to specification	Sequential	Implicit, from backward recovery principle	Yes, duration necessary for executing one or more variants	$f+1$
NSCP	Error detection and result switching	Detection by AT(s)	Relative, on variant results	Parallel	Explicit, by dedicated mechanisms	Yes, duration necessary for result switching	$2(f+1)$
		Detection by comparison					
NVP	Vote					No	$f+2$
DRB	Error detection by AT and forward recovery		Absolute, with respect to specification	Parallel	Implicit, from internal backward recovery principle and explicit from two-phase commit principle	No	$f+1$

Table 4.13 (continued)

Method	Error Processing Technique	Judgement on Result Acceptability	Variant Execution Scheme	Consistency of Input Data	Suspension of Service Delivery During Error Processing	Number of Variants for Tolerance of Sequential Faults
CRB	Vote, then AT	Both relative on variant results with result selected by voter and absolute, with respect to specification when AT used	Parallel	Explicit, by dedicated mechanisms	No	$f + 1$
AV	AT, then vote	Both absolute, with respect to specification when AT used and relative on variant results with result selected by voter	Parallel	Explicit, by dedicated mechanisms	No	$f + 1$

Table 4.14
Software Fault Tolerance Technique Overheads for Tolerance of One Fault (with Respect to Non-Fault-Tolerant Software) (*After:* [19].)

Method Name		Structural Overhead		Operational Time Overhead		
		Diversified Software Layer	Mechanisms (Layers Supporting the Diversified Software Layer)	Systematic		On Error Occurrence
				Decider	Variants Execution	
RcB		One variant and one AT	Recovery cache	AT execution	Accesses to recovery cache	One variant and AT execution
NSCP	Error detection by ATs	One variant and two ATs	Result switching		Input data consistency and variants execution synchronization	Possible result switching
	Error detection by comparison	Three variants	Comparators and result switching	Comparison execution		
NVP		Two variants	Voters	Vote execution		Usually neglectable
DRB		2X(one variant, one AT)	Recovery cache, WDT	AT execution	Accesses to recovery cache	Usually neglectable
CRB		Two variants and one AT	Voter	Vote execution and AT execution	Input data consistency and variants execution synchronization	Usually neglectable
AV		Two variants and one AT	Voter	AT execution and vote execution	Input data consistency and variants execution synchronization	Usually neglectable

4.7.1   *N*-Version Programming and Recovery Block Technique Comparisons

Before looking at comparisons of NVP and RcB, we briefly examine the reliability of NVP compared with that of a single non-fault-tolerant component. McAllister, Vouk, and colleagues [52, 53, 86] provide this analysis from both data and time domain perspectives. From the data domain perspective, they found that majority voting increases the reliability over a single component only if the reliability of the variants is larger than 0.5 and the voter is perfect. Specifically, if (a) the output space has cardinality ρ, (b) all components fail independently, (c) the components have the same reliability r, (d) correct outputs are unique, and (e) the voter is perfect, then NVP will result in a system that is more reliable than a single component only if $r > 1/\rho$ [86]. The basic majority voting approach has a binary output space, and hence its boundary variant reliability is $1/\rho = 0.5$. The variant reliability must be larger than the boundary variant reliability to improve the performance of the system when more variants are added [53]. Let the system reliability be bounded by R. If $R \leq r$, then one should invest software development time on a single component rather than develop a three-version NVP system.

From the time domain perspective, reliability can be defined as the probability that a system will complete its mission, or operate through a certain period of time, without failing. Suppose we use the simplest time-dependent failure model for this analysis. It assumes that failures arrive randomly with an exponentially distributed interarrival time, with expected value λ. λ is the failure or hazard rate and is constant. For $t \leq t_0$ ($t_0 = \ln2/\lambda \approx 0.7\lambda$), the three-variant NVP system (NVP3) is more reliable than a single component. However, during longer missions, $t > t_0$, NVP3 fault tolerance may actually degrade system reliability [53].

Now that we have an idea of when it would be appropriate to develop an NVP system from a reliability perspective, let's turn our attention to comparing the NVP and RcB techniques. We know from the earlier discussion on RcB that its AT must be more reliable than the alternates. We also know that, in NVP, related faults among the variants and between the variants and the DM must be minimized. The basic NVP DM is fairly generic, basing its decision on a relative basis among the variant results. The RcB technique AT, however, is specific to each application, providing an absolute decision for each alternate's result against the specification. Armed with this information, let's compare the way related faults affect these techniques.

- The probabilities of activation of an independent fault in the DM and of related faults between the variants and the DM are likely to be greater for RcB than for NVP [49].

- NVP is far more sensitive to the removal of independent faults than RcB because of the parallel nature of the NVP execution and decision making [43, 50].

- If similar or related faults are present, they are likely to have a larger impact on RcB technique performance. Therefore, the removal of similar or related faults and of faults in decision nodes will likely produce more substantial reliability gains for RcB than for NVP [53].

- If one could develop a perfect AT and a perfect voter and if we assume failure independence, then an RcB system with three alternates (RcB3) is a better solution than the NVP3 system. (The requirements for and difficulty of producing an AT is discussed in Chapter 7.)

Tai and colleagues have done extensive investigation into the performability of NVP and RcB (see [42, 87, 88]). Tai defines *performability* as a unification of performance and dependability, that is, a system's ability to perform (serve its users) in the presence of fault-caused errors and failures [42]. The major results of their investigations follow.

- *Effectiveness for a 10-hour mission:* RcB is more effective than NVP throughout the considered domain of related-fault probabilities.

- *Relative dependability:* As shown in other studies, for both RcB and NVP, the probability of a catastrophic failure is dominated by the probability of a related fault between the components. In RcB, an error due to a related fault in the primary and secondary alternates cannot result in catastrophic failure. Also, in RcB, an error due to a related fault in the secondary alternate and the AT can result in a catastrophic failure only if the AT rejects the primary's results. In NVP, the probability of a related fault between any two variants contributes directly to the probability of catastrophic failure. The occurrence of a catastrophic failure (during a single iteration) for NVP is approximately three times more likely than that for RcB.

- *Performability:* RcB has a performability advantage over NVP. This is due, in part, to distinctions in strict performance of the techniques. The mean iteration time for RcB is dominated by the mean combined execution time of the primary and the AT. However, NVP's mean iteration time is lengthened because variant synchronization requires the system to wait for the slowest variant. If variant execution times are assumed to be exponentially distributed, variant synchronization results in a relatively severe penalty on NVP performance.

- *Difference in effectiveness:* When the mean execution times of the components are identical, the effectiveness of NVP is slightly better than that of RcB in the very low related-fault probability domain. The difference between RcB and NVP effectiveness becomes greater as the probability of a related fault increases. If the probability of a related fault is low, the difference in the effectiveness of RcB and NVP is due mainly to the performance penalty imposed by variant synchronization. As the probability of related faults increases, this difference in effectiveness is amplified since NVP is more vulnerable to a catastrophic failure caused by a related fault between two variants.

- *Summary:* Tai and colleagues surmise that NVP is inferior to RcB for the following reasons: (1) from the *performance* perspective, NVP iteration time suffers a severe performance penalty due to variant synchronization (when variant execution time is exponentially distributed); (2) from the *dependability* perspective, the basic NVP technique is more vulnerable to undetected errors caused by related faults between variants.

4.7.1.1 *N*-Version Programming Improvements

Based on the analysis noted above, Tai [42] suggests two modifications that could enhance the effectiveness of the basic NVP technique, for example, (1) enhancing performance by modifying the use of the computational redundancy in an operational context, and (2) enhancing dependability by applying an AT before the decision function delivers a result. The first modification results in an NVP variation that incorporates a variant synchronization strategy consisting of three variants and two decision functions. When the fastest two variants complete execution, their results are compared. If they match, the result is output. If they do not match, the slowest variant's result is used as a tie-breaker (TB). The second DM tries to determine a majority from all three variant results and operates like the basic NVP voter. This technique is referred to as NVP with a tie-breaker (NVP-TB). Performability analysis results for NVP-TB are provided below [88].

- *Synchronization penalty:* In a mission of 10 hours, the performance penalty due to variant synchronization was significantly reduced in NVP-TB. With this modification, the iteration time is dominated by the two faster variants instead of the slowest one.

- *Related faults:* If the probability of related faults increases such that dependability is sufficiently reduced, the NVP-TB becomes less effective than the RcB and basic NVP techniques.

Hence, it was shown that an improvement in performance alone does not assure improved performability and that the system dependability is a factor in determining whether strict performance improvements will be beneficial. So, to reduce the probability of an erroneous result from a consensus decision, Tai and colleagues modified the basic NVP technique by adding an AT of the type employed by RcB. In this new technique, NVP-AT, when the decision function reaches a consensus decision, it passes the majority result to an AT, which decides whether the result is correct. They found that the use of an AT reduces the probability of an undetected error (catastrophic failure). However, the probability of suppressing a result during an iteration became greater. Performability analysis results for NVP-AT are provided below [88].

- *Low probability of related faults:* When the probability of a related fault between two variants is low, the effectiveness of NVP-AT is less than that of the basic NVP. So, when dependability is already relatively high, the AT fails to compensate for the performance penalties it imposes.

- *Moderate to high probability of related faults:* When the probability of a related fault is moderate to high, NVP-AT is more effective than the basic NVP. The dependability enhancement provided by the AT now helps the overall system performability. The amount of improvement increases as the original system becomes less dependable.

From this analysis, it was found that a design modification based strictly on either performance or dependability considerations can have negative effects on the overall effectiveness of a fault-tolerant software system.

Since, as a function of the probability of related faults, the effectiveness of the two modified techniques complemented one another, a combined technique was designed. The combined technique, referred to as the NVP-TB-AT, incorporates both a tie-breaker and an AT. The AT is only applied when the second decision function reaches a consensus decision. When the probability of related faults is low, the efficient synchronization provided by the TB mechanism compensates for the performance reduction caused by the AT. When the probability of related faults is high, the additional error detection provided by the AT reduces the likelihood (due to the high execution rate of NVP-TB) of an undetected error [88].

4.7.2   Recovery Block and Distributed Recovery Block Technique Comparisons

Tai and colleagues examined the performability of the RcB and DRB techniques [42, 87, 88]. (Performability was defined in the previous section.) The analysis examined the probability of occurrence of several events for the techniques and resulted in the following key observations:

- *Risk related to hardware error:* In the DRB technique, a hardware error kills a task only if it is combined with certain other error conditions. In the RcB, a single hardware error can corrupt a task.

- *Risk related to timing error:* For the DRB, a timing error causes a task loss only if a timing error in the execution of the secondary followed by the AT occurs in coincidence with other error conditions (i.e., a timing error of primary followed by the AT, a software error in the primary and AT, or a hardware error in the processor accommodating the primary and AT). On the other hand, in the RcB technique, the excessive execution time for the primary followed by the AT alone can cause an unrecoverable timing error. Therefore, in general, P(the event that a task is lost due to timing error, given that it is executed in RcB) > P(the event that a task is lost due to timing error, given that it is executed in the DRB).

- *Risk related to software error:* For DRB, the event that a software error (ultimately) kills a task can be triggered by other error conditions (i.e., a timing error of primary followed by the AT and a hardware error in the processor accommodating the same). However, these error conditions would not trigger a software error in the RcB since they directly kill a task by themselves. In other words, in RcB, a potential software error could be masked by other types of errors. Therefore, P(the event that a task is lost due to software error, given that it is executed in RcB) $< P$(the event that a task is lost due to software error, given that it is executed in DRB), in general. The difference between the probabilities of failure due to a software error in the two techniques is less significant than that between the probabilities of failure due to a hardware error in the two techniques and that between the probabilities of failure due to a timing error in the two techniques (which may differ by orders of magnitude).

- *Risk related to system being full:* DRB task execution results in a higher P(the event that a task is lost due to the system being full), so as the DRB continues to execute tasks, P(the event that a task is lost due to hardware error) and P(the event that a task is lost due to timing error) decrease and P(the event that a task is lost due to software error) and P(the event that a task is lost due to the system being full) increase.

4.7.3 Consensus Recovery Block, Recovery Block Technique, and *N*-Version Programming Comparisons

The CRB technique has been found (as reported in [52, 53]) to be surprisingly robust in the presence of high interversion correlation. However, it is important to note that the models used did not include correlation effects. Although these statements appear contradictory in nature, the example results below should clarify the particular situations in which the CRB technique performs well. In general, when the AT is not of very high quality, CRB tends to outperform NVP and to perform competitively with the RcB technique. The following results of CRB performance are from the experiments and studies reported in [52, 53], unless otherwise referenced.

- When there is failure independence between variants and a zero probability of identical and wrong (IAW) answers, CRB is always superior to NVP (given the same variant reliability and the same voting strategy) and to RcB (given the same variant and AT reliability) [20, 82].

- When there is a very high failure correlation between variants, CRB is expected to outperform NVP (given the same voting strategy) only when the variants that do fail coincidentally return different results. (The CRB-AT would then be invoked.)

- When the probability of IAW results is very high, CRB is not superior to NVP. (The CRB-AT would be invoked infrequently because the majority voter would select one of the identically incorrect results as the "correct" answer.) The NVP does not perform well either in this situation.

- For $n = 3$, CRB with majority voting has reliability equal to or better than the reliability of NVP with majority voting (using the same variants).

- For $n = 5$, with a lower n-tuple reliability, NVP with consensus voting performs almost as well as CRB.

- Most of the time, CRB with consensus voting is more reliable than NVP with consensus voting.

- NVP with consensus voting may be marginally more reliable than CRB with consensus voting when the AT reliability is low, or when AT and program failures produce IAW results. This situation was observed with low frequency [52].

So, in general, we have the following conclusions.

- CRB with majority voting is more stable and is at least as reliable as NVP with majority voting.

- The advantage of using CRB may be marginal in high failure correlation situations or where the AT is of poor quality.

- CRB performs poorly in all situations where the voter is likely to select a set of IAW responses as the correct answer.

- It is noted (by Vouk and McAllister [52, 53]) that, given a sufficiently reliable AT or binary output space or very high interversion failure correlation, all schemes that vote may have difficulty competing with RcB technique.

4.7.4   Acceptance Voting, Consensus Recovery Block, Recovery Block Technique, and N-Version Programming Comparisons

The AV technique's performance is very dependent on the reliability of its AT. In general, the technique provides lower reliability than the CRB, RcB, and NVP techniques. However, in the following situations, the AV technique can outperform (i.e., be more reliable than) the CRB, RcB, NVP, or any other voting-based approach. (These results are from [53].)

- *AV and CRB:* When there is a large probability that the CRB voter would return a wrong answer, and simultaneously the AT (in AV) is reliable enough to eliminate most of the incorrect responses before voting, AV reliability can be greater than that of CRB. This may happen when the voter decision space is small.

- *AV and RcB:* When the AT is sufficiently reliable, the AV technique can be more reliable than the RcB technique.

References

[1]   Lardner, D., "Babbage's Calculating Engine," *Edinburgh Review*, July 1834. Reprinted in P. Morrison and E. Morrison (eds.), *Charles Babbage and His Calculating Engines*, New York: Dover, 1961, p. 177.

[2]   Babbage, C., "On the Mathematical Powers of the Calculating Machine," Dec. 1837, (Unpublished Manuscript) Buxton MS7, Museum of the History of Science, Oxford, and in B. Randell (ed.), *The Origins of Digital Computers: Selected Papers*, New York: Springer-Verlag, 1972, pp. 17–52.

[3]   Horning, J. J., et al., "A Program Structure for Error Detection and Recovery," in E. Gelenbe and C. Kaiser (eds.), *Lecture Notes in Computer Science*, Vol. 16, New York: Springer-Verlag, 1974, pp. 171–187.

[4]   Randell, B., "System Structure for Software Fault Tolerance," *IEEE Transactions on Software Engineering*, Vol. SE-1, No. 2, 1975, pp. 220–232.

[5]   Hecht, M., and H. Hecht, "Fault Tolerant Software Modules for SIFT," SoHaR, Inc. Report TR-81-04, April 1981.

[6]   Hecht, H., "Fault Tolerant Software for Real-Time Applications," *ACM Computing Surveys*, Vol. 8, No. 4, 1976, pp. 391–407.

[7]   Kim, K. H., "Approaches to Mechanization of the Conversation Scheme Based on Monitors," *IEEE Transactions on Software Engineering*, Vol. 8, No. 3, 1982, pp. 189–197.

[8]   Kim, K. H., S. Heu, and S. M. Yang, "Performance Analysis of Fault-Tolerant Systems in Parallel Execution of Conversations," *IEEE Transactions on Reliability*, Vol. 38, No. 2, 1989, pp. 96–101.

[9]   Goel, A. L., and N. Mansour, "Software Engineering for Fault Tolerant Systems," Air Force Rome Laboratory, Technical Report RL-TR-91-15, 1991.

[10] Kim, K. H., "Distributed Execution of Recovery Blocks: An Approach to Uniform Treatment of Hardware and Software Faults," *Proceedings Fourth International Conference on Distributed Computing Systems*, 1984, pp. 526–532.

[11] Kim, K. H., "An Approach to Programmer-Transparent Coordination of Recovering Parallel Processes and Its Efficient Implementation Rules," *Proceedings IEEE Computer Society International Conference on Parallel Processing*, 1978, pp. 58–68.

[12] Kim, K. H., "Programmer Transparent Coordination of Recovering Concurrent Processes: Philosophy and Rules of Efficient Implementation," *IEEE Transactions on Software Engineering*, Vol. SE-14, No. 6, 1988, pp. 810–821.

[13] Kim, K. H., and S. M. Yang, "Performance Impact of Look-Ahead Execution in the Conversation Scheme," *IEEE Transactions on Computers*, Vol. 38, No. 8, 1989, pp. 1188–1202.

[14] Anderson, T., and J. C. Knight, "A Framework for Software Fault Tolerance in Real-Time Systems," *IEEE Transactions on Software Engineering*, Vol. SE-9, No. 5, 1983, pp. 355–364.

[15] Gregory, S. T., and J. C. Knight, "A New Linguistic Approach to Backward Error Recovery," *Proceedings of FTCS-15*, Ann Arbor, MI, 1985, pp. 404–409.

[16] Anderson, T., and P. A. Lee, "Software Fault Tolerance," in *Fault Tolerance: Principles and Practice*, Englewood Cliffs, NJ: Prentice-Hall, 1981, pp. 249–291.

[17] Randell, B., "Fault Tolerance and System Structuring," *Proceedings 4th Jerusalem Conference on Information Technology*, Jerusalem, 1984, pp. 182–191.

[18] Neumann, P. G., "On Hierarchical Design of Computer Systems for Critical Applications," *IEEE Transactions on Software Engineering*, Vol. 12, No. 9, 1986, pp. 905–920.

[19] Laprie, J. -C., et al., "Definition and Analysis of Hardware- and Software-Fault-Tolerant Architectures," *IEEE Computer*, Vol. 23, No. 7, 1990, pp. 39–51.

[20] Scott, R. K., J. W. Gault, and D. F. McAllister, "Fault Tolerant Software Reliability Modeling," *IEEE Transactions on Software Engineering*, Vol. 13, No. 5, 1987, pp. 582–592.

[21] Grnarov, A., J. Arlat, and A. Avizienis, "On the Performance of Software Fault Tolerance Strategies," *Proceedings of FTCS-10*, Kyoto, Japan, 1980, pp. 251–253.

[22] Shin, K. G., and Y. Lee, "Evaluation of Error Recovery Blocks Used for Cooperating Processes," *IEEE Transactions on Software Engineering*, Vol. 10, No. 6, 1984, pp. 692–700.

[23] Ciardo, G., J. Muppala, and K. Trivedi, "Analyzing Concurrent and Fault-Tolerant Software Using Stochastic Reward Nets," *Journal of Parallel and Distributed Computing*, Vol. 15, 1992, pp. 255–269.

[24] Scott, R. K., et al., "Experimental Validation of Six Fault Tolerant Software Reliability Models," *Proceedings of FTCS-14*, 1984, pp. 102–107.

[25] Scott, R. K., et al., "Investigating Version Dependence in Fault Tolerant Software," *AGARD 361*, 1984, pp. 21.1–21.10.

[26] Laprie, J. -C., "Dependability Evaluation of Software Systems in Operation," *IEEE Transactions on Software Engineering*, Vol. SE-10, No. 6, 1984, pp. 701–714.

[27] Stark, G. E., "Dependability Evaluation of Integrated Hardware/Software Systems," *IEEE Transactions on Reliability*, Vol. R-36, No. 4, 1987, pp. 440–444.

[28] Laprie, J. -C., and K. Kanoun, "X-ware Reliability and Availability Modeling," *IEEE Transactions on Software Engineering*, Vol. 18, No. 2, 1992, pp. 130–147.

[29] Dugan, J. B., and M. R. Lyu, "Dependability Modeling for Fault-Tolerant Software and Systems," in M. Lyu (ed.), *Software Fault Tolerance*, New York: John Wiley & Sons, 1995, pp. 109–138.

[30] Tomek, L. A., and K. S. Trivedi, "Analyses Using Stochastic Reward Nets," in M. Lyu (ed.), *Software Fault Tolerance*, New York: John Wiley & Sons, 1995, pp. 139–165.

[31] Arlat, J., K. Kanoun, and J. -C. Laprie, "Dependability Modeling and Evaluation of Software Fault-Tolerant Systems," in B. Randell, et al. (eds.), *Predictably Dependable Computing Systems*, New York: Springer-Verlag, 1995, pp. 441–457.

[32] Hecht, H., "Fault-Tolerant Software," *IEEE Transactions on Reliability*, Vol. R-28, No. 4, 1979, pp. 227–232.

[33] Mulazzani, M., "Reliability Versus Safety," *Proceedings 4th IFAC Workshop on Safety of Computer Control Systems (SAFECOMP '85)*, W. J. Quirk (ed.), Como, Italy, 1985, pp. 141–146.

[34] Cha, S. D., "A Recovery Block Model and Its Analysis," *Proceedings IFAC Workshop on Safety of Computer Control Systems (SAFECOMP '86)*, W. J. Quirk (ed.), Sarlat, France, 1986, pp. 21–26.

[35] Tso, K. S., A. Avizienis, and J. P. J. Kelly, "Error Recovery in Multi-Version Software," *Proceedings IFAC SAFECOMP '86*, Sarlat, France, 1986, pp. 35–41.

[36] Csenski, A., "Recovery Block Reliability Analysis with Failure Clustering," in A. Avizienis and J. -C. Laprie, (eds.), *Dependable Computing for Critical Applications (Proceedings 1st IFIP International Working Conference on Dependable Computing for Critical Applications: DCCA-1, Santa Barbara, CA, 1989)*, A. Avizienis, H. Kopetz, and J.-C. Laprie (eds.) *Dependable Computing and Fault-Tolerant Systems*, Vol. 4, Vienna, Austria: Springer-Verlag, 1991, pp. 75–103.

[37] Bondavalli, A., et al., "Dependability Analysis of Iterative Fault-Tolerant Software Considering Correlation," in B. Randell, et al. (eds.), *Predictably Dependable Computing Systems*, New York: Springer-Verlag, 1995, pp. 460–472.

[38] Mainini, M. T., "Reliability Evaluation," in M. Kersken and F. Saglietti (eds.), *Software Fault Tolerance: Achievement and Assessment Strategies*, New York: Springer-Verlag, 1992, pp. 177–197.

[39] Eckhardt, D. E., Jr., and L. D. Lee, "A Theoretical Basis for the Analysis of Multiversion Software Subject to Coincident Errors," *IEEE Transactions on Software Engineering*, Vol. SE-11, No. 12, 1985, pp. 1511–1517.

[40] Littlewood, B., and D. R. Miller, "Conceptual Modeling of Coincident Failures in Multiversion Software," *IEEE Transactions on Software Engineering*, Vol. 15, No. 12, 1989, pp. 1596–1614.

[41] Nicola, V. F., and A. Goyal, "Modeling of Correlated Failures and Community Error Recovery in Multi-Version Software," *IEEE Transactions on Software Engineering*, Vol. 16, No. 3, 1990.

[42] Tai, A. T., J. F. Meyer, and A. Avizienis, "Performability Enhancement of Fault-Tolerant Software," *IEEE Transactions on Reliability*, Vol. 42, No. 2, 1993, pp. 227–237.

[43] Kanoun, K., et al., "Reliability Growth of Fault-Tolerant Software," *IEEE Transactions on Reliability*, Vol. 42, No. 2, 1993, pp. 205–219.

[44] Tomek, L. A., J. K. Muppala, and K. S. Trivedi, "Modeling Correlation in Software Recovery Blocks," *IEEE Transactions on Software Engineering*, Vol. 19, No. 11, 1993, pp. 1071–1086.

[45] Lyu, M. R. (ed.), *Software Fault Tolerance*, New York: John Wiley & Sons, 1995.

[46] Trivedi, T. S., *Probability and Statistics with Reliability, Queuing, and Computer Science Applications*, Englewood Cliffs, NJ: Prentice-Hall, 1982.

[47] Deb, A. K., and A. L. Goel, "Model for Execution Time Behavior of a Recovery Block," *Proceedings COMPSAC '86*, Chicago, IL, 1986, pp. 497–502.

[48] Deb, A. K., "Stochastic Modeling for Execution Time and Reliability of Fault-Tolerant Programs Using Recovery Block and N-Version Schemes," Ph.D. thesis, Syracuse University, 1988.

[49] Arlat, J., K. Kanoun, and J. -C. Laprie, "Dependability Evaluation of Software Fault-Tolerance," *IEEE Transactions on Computers*, Vol. 39, No. 4, 1990, pp. 504–513.

[50] Laprie, J. -C., et al., "The Transformation Approach to the Modeling and Evaluation of the Reliability and Availability Growth," *Proceedings of FTCS-20*, Newcastle upon Tyne, U.K., 1990, pp. 364–371.

[51] Siewiorek, D. P., and R. S. Swarz, *Reliable Computer Systems—Design and Evaluation*, 2nd ed., Bedford, MA: Digital Press, 1992.

[52] Vouk, M., et al., "An Empirical Evaluation of Consensus Voting and Consensus Recovery Block Reliability in the Presence of Failure Correlation," *Journal of Computer and Software Engineering*, Vol. 1, No. 4, 1993, pp. 367–388.

[53] McAllister, D. F., and M. A. Vouk, "Fault-Tolerant Software Reliability Engineering," in M. R. Lyu (ed.), *Handbook of Software Reliability Engineering*, New York: IEEE Computer Society Press, 1996.

[54] Pucci, G., "On the Modeling and Testing of Recovery Block Structures," *Proceedings of FTCS-20*, Newcastle upon Tyne, U.K., 1990, pp. 356–363.

[55] Pucci, G., "A New Approach to the Modeling of Recovery Block Structures," *IEEE Transactions on Software Engineering*, Vol. SE-18, No. 2, 1992, pp. 356–363.

[56] Anderson, T., et al., "Software Fault Tolerance: An Evaluation," *IEEE Transactions on Software Engineering*, Vol. SE-11, No. 12, 1985, pp. 1502–1510.

[57] Elmendorf, W. R., "Fault-Tolerant Programming," *Proceedings of FTCS-2*, Newton, MA, 1972, pp. 79–83.

[58] Avizienis, A., "On the Implementation of N-Version Programming for Software Fault-Tolerance During Execution," *COMPSAC '77*, Chicago, IL, 1977, pp. 149–155.

[59] Chen, L., and A. Avizienis, "N-Version Programming: A Fault-Tolerance Approach to Reliability of Software Operation," *Proceedings of FTCS-8*, Toulouse, France, 1978, pp. 3–9.

[60] Lyu, M. R., "A Design Paradigm for Multi-Version Software," Ph.D. dissertation, UCLA, Computer Science Department, 1988.

[61] Kelly, J. P. J., T. I. McVittie, and W. I. Yamamoto, "Implementing Design Diversity to Achieve Fault Tolerance," *IEEE Software*, July 1991, pp. 61–71.

[62] Kelly, J. P. J., and S. Murphy, "Achieving Dependability Throughout the Development Process: A Distributed Software Experiment," *IEEE Transactions on Software Engineering*, Vol. SE-16, No. 2, 1990, pp. 153–165.

[63] Abbott, R. J., "Resourceful Systems for Fault Tolerance, Reliability, and Safety," *ACM Computing Surveys*, Vol. 22, No. 3, 1990, pp. 35–68.

[64] Knight, J. C., and P. E. Ammann, "Issues Influencing the Use of N-Version Programming," in G. X. Ritter (ed.), *Information Processing 89*, North-Holland, 1989, pp. 217–222.

[65] Stringini, L., and A. Avizienis, "Software Fault Tolerance and Design Diversity: Past Experience and Future Evolution," *SAFECOMP '85*, 1985, pp. 167–172.

[66] Duncan, R. V., Jr., and L. L. Pullum, "Object-Oriented Executives and Components for Fault Tolerance," *IEEE Aerospace Conference*, Big Sky, MT, 2001.

[67] Kim, K. H., and H. O. Welch, "Distributed Execution of Recovery Blocks: An Approach for Uniform Treatment of Hardware and Software Faults in Real-Time Applications," *IEEE Transactions on Computers*, Vol. 38, No. 5, 1989, pp. 626–636.

[68] Kim, K. H., "The Distributed Recovery Block Scheme," in M. R. Lyu (ed.), *Software Fault Tolerance*, New York: John Wiley & Sons, 1995, pp. 189–209.

[69] Kim, K. H., "Structuring DRB Computing Stations in Highly Decentralized Systems," *Proceedings International Symposium on Autonomous Decentralized Systems*, Kawasaki, 1993, pp. 305–314.

[70] Kim, K. H., and J. C. Yoon, "Approaches to Implementation of a Repairable Distributed Recovery Block Scheme," *Proceedings of FTCS-18*, Tokyo, Japan, 1988, pp. 50–55.

[71] Hecht, M., et al., "A Distributed Fault Tolerant Architecture for Nuclear Reactor and Other Critical Process Control Applications," *Proceedings of FTCS-21*, Montreal, Canada, 1991, pp. 462–469.

[72] Hecht, M., J. Agron, and H. Hecht, "A New Low Cost Distributed Fault Tolerant Architecture for Process Control Applications," *Proceedings Southeastcon*, Vol. 1, Birmingham, AL, 1991.

[73] Laprie, J. -C., et al., "Hardware and Software Fault Tolerance: Definition and Analysis of Architectural Solutions," *Proceedings of FTCS-17*, Pittsburgh, PA, 1987, pp. 116–121.

[74] Yau, S. S., and R. C. Cheung, "Design of Self-Checking Software," *Proceedings International Conference on Reliable Software*, Los Angeles, CA, 1975, pp. 450–457.

[75] Traverse, P., "AIRBUS and ATR System Architecture and Specification," in U. Voges (ed.), *Software Diversity in Computerized Control Systems*, New York: Springer-Verlag, 1988, pp. 95–104.

[76] Scott, R. K., J. W. Gault, and D. F. McAllister, "The Consensus Recovery Block," *Proceedings of the Total Systems Reliability Symposium*, Gaithersburg, MD, 1983, pp. 3–9.

[77] Scott, R. K., J. W. Gault, and D. F. McAllister, "The Consensus Recovery Block," *Proceedings of the Total Systems Reliability Symposium*, 1985, pp. 74–85.

[78] McAllister, D. F., and R. K. Scott, "Cost Models for Fault-Tolerant Software," *Journal of Information and Software Technology*, Vol. 33, No. 8, 1991, pp. 594–603.

[79] Knight, J. C., N. G. Leveson, and L. D. St. Jean, "A Large Scale Experiment in N-Version Programming," *Proceedings of FTCS-15*, Ann Arbor, MI, 1985, pp. 135–139.

[80] Knight, J. C., and N. G. Leveson, "An Empirical Study of Failure Probabilities in Multi-Version Software," *Proceedings of FTCS-16*, Vienna, Austria, 1986, pp. 165–170.

[81] Knight, J. C., and N. G. Leveson, "An Experimental Evaluation of the Assumption of Independence in Multiversion Programming," *IEEE Transactions on Software Engineering*, Vol. SE-12, No. 1, 1986, pp. 96–109.

[82] Belli, F., and P. Jedrzejowicz, "Fault Tolerant Programs and their Reliability," *IEEE Transactions on Reliability*, Vol. 39, No. 3, 1990, pp. 182–192.

[83] Athavale, A., "Performance Evaluation of Hybrid Voting Schemes," M.S. thesis, North Carolina State University, Department of Computer Science, 1989.

[84] Belli, F., and P. Jedrzejowicz, "Comparative Analysis of Concurrent Fault-Tolerance Techniques for Real-Time Applications," *Proceedings of the Second International Symposium on Software Reliability Engineering*, Austin, TX, 1991.

[85] Gantenbein, R. E., S. Y. Shin, and J. R. Cowles, "Evaluation of Combined Approaches to Distributed Software-Based Fault Tolerance," *Pacific Rim International Symposium on Fault Tolerant Systems*, 1991, pp. 70–75.

[86] McAllister, D. F., C. E. Sun, and M. A. Vouk, "Reliability of Voting in Fault-Tolerant Software Systems for Small Output Spaces," *IEEE Transactions on Reliability*, Vol. R-39, No. 5, 1990, pp. 524–534.

[87] Tai, A. T., A. Avizienis, and J. F. Meyer, "Evaluation of Fault-Tolerant Software: A Performability Modeling Approach," in C. E. Landweh, B. Randell, and L. Simoncini (eds.), *Dependable Computing for Critical Applications 3*, Vienna, Austria: Springer-Verlag, 1993, pp. 113–135.

[88] Tai, A. T., J. F. Meyer, and A. Avizienis, *Software Performability: From Concepts to Applications*, Norwell, MA: Kluwer Academic Publishers, 1996.

5

Data Diverse Software Fault Tolerance Techniques

Ammann and Knight [1–3] proposed the use of data diversity as a software fault tolerance strategy to complement design diversity by compensating for design diversity's limitations. Data diversity involves obtaining a related set of points in the program data space, executing the same software on those points, and then using a decision algorithm to determine the resulting output. Data diversity is based on a generalization of the works of [4-6], which utilize data diverse approaches relying on circumstantial changes in execution conditions. These execution conditions can be changed deliberately to produce data diversity [3]. This is done using data re-expression. Data diverse techniques use data re-expression algorithms (DRA) to obtain their input data. Through a pilot study on data diversity [1–3], the N-copy programming (NCP) and retry block (RtB) data diverse software fault tolerance structures were developed. In addition, Pullum introduced two-pass adjudicators (TPA) as a combination technique using both design and data diverse techniques [7–9].

The data diverse techniques discussed in this chapter use the principle of redundancy and diversifying input data to detect and tolerate software faults. This chapter covers the original data diverse software fault tolerance techniques—RtB and NCP. New techniques and combinations of data and design diverse techniques have been proposed to attack different problem domains, while attempting to maintain the strengths of these foundational techniques. An additional technique described in this chapter is the set of techniques called the TPA. The techniques' operations, advantages, and disadvantages are discussed in this chapter.

A significant amount of material is presented in this chapter for each technique, broadly divided into operation, example, and issues. The first figure shown for each technique describes its operation. For those wanting a brief introduction to the technique, this operational figure is a good place to start. Operational details are provided via scenarios and an example. Issues related to each technique are summarized in a table in the third subsection (issues) for each technique. A similar format for discussion of each technique is followed in this chapter and in Chapters 4 and 6.

5.1   Retry Blocks

The basic RtB technique is one of the two original data diverse software fault tolerance techniques developed by Ammann and Knight [1–3]. In addition to being a data diverse technique, the RtB technique is also categorized as a dynamic technique (described in Section 4.1). The hardware fault tolerance architecture related to the RtB technique is stand-by sparing or passive dynamic redundancy. The RtB technique is the data diverse complement of the recovery block (RcB) scheme (see Section 4.1).

The RtB technique uses acceptance tests (AT) (see Section 7.2) and backward recovery (see Section 3.1) to accomplish fault tolerance. The technique typically uses one DRA (see Sections 2.3.1 through 2.3.3) and one algorithm. A watchdog timer (WDT) is also used and triggers execution of a backup algorithm if the original algorithm does not produce an acceptable result within a specified period of time. The algorithm is executed using the original system input. The primary algorithm's results are examined by an AT that has the same form and purpose as the AT used in the RcB. If the algorithm results pass the AT, then the RtB is complete. However, if the results are not acceptable, then the input is re-expressed and the same primary algorithm runs again using the new, re-expressed, input data. This continues until the AT finds an acceptable result or the WDT deadline is violated. If the deadline expires, a backup algorithm may be invoked to execute on the original input data.

The operation of the RtB technique is described in 5.1.1, with an example provided in 5.1.2. The advantages and disadvantages of the RtB technique are presented in 5.1.3.

5.1.1 Retry Block Operation

The RtB technique consists of an executive, an AT, a DRA, a WDT, and primary and backup algorithms. The executive orchestrates the operation of the RtB, which has the general syntax:

```
ensure               Acceptance Test
by                   Primary Algorithm(Original Input)
else by              Primary Algorithm(Re-expressed Input)
else by              Primary Algorithm(Re-expressed Input)
...
...                  [Deadline Expires]
else by              Backup Algorithm(Original Input)
else failure exception
```

The RtB syntax above states that the technique will first attempt to ensure the AT (e.g., pass a test on the acceptability of a result of the algorithm) by using the primary algorithm. If the primary algorithm's result does not pass the AT, then the input data will be re-expressed and the same algorithm attempted until a result passes the AT or the WDT deadline expires. If the deadline expires, the backup algorithm is invoked with the original inputs. If this backup algorithm is not successful, an error occurs. Note that if more than one additional attempt using re-expressed inputs is to be tried (say n attempts with re-expression), then either n ($n \geq 2$) DRA are required or a single DRA using a re-expression algorithm based on random values is required.

Figure 5.1 illustrates the structure and operation of the basic RtB with a WDT. We examine several scenarios to describe RtB operation:

- Failure-free operation;

- Exception in primary algorithm execution;

- Primary's results are on time, but fail AT; successful execution with re-expressed input;

- All DRA options are used without success; successful backup execution;

- All DRA options are used without success; backup executes, but fails the AT.

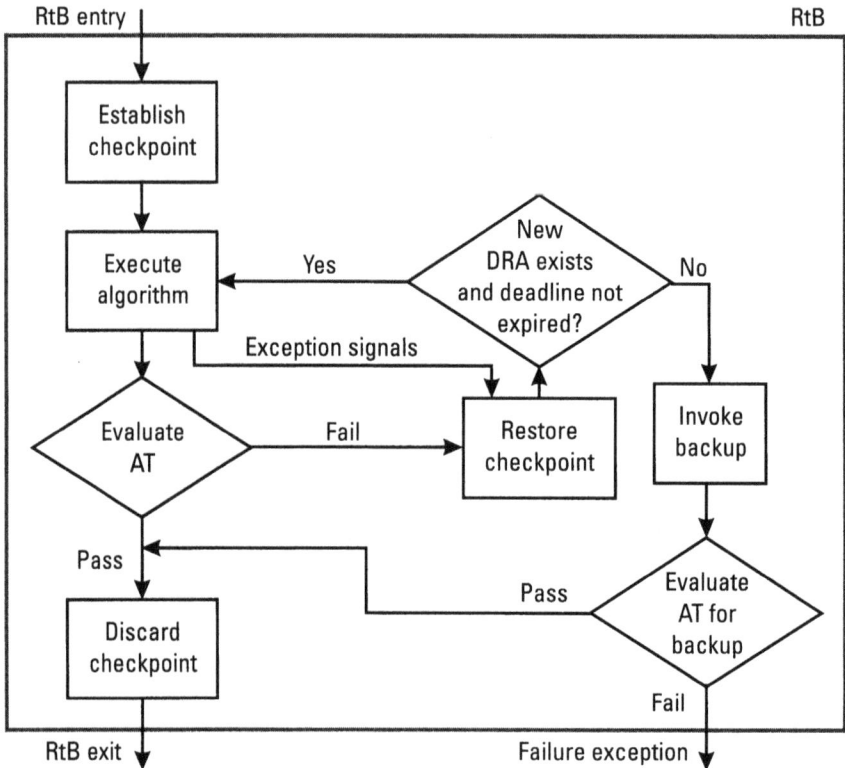

Figure 5.1 Retry block structure and operation.

In examining these scenarios, we use the following abbreviations:

AT   Acceptance test;

ATB   Acceptance test for the backup (may be the same as AT);

B   Backup algorithm;

DRA$_i$ Data re-expression algorithm i (when there are multiple DRA, or the ith re-expression of the input if a single DRA is used);

P   Primary algorithm;

RtB   Retry block;

WDT   Watchdog timer;

WP   Expected maximum wait time for an acceptable result from P.

5.1.1.1   Failure-Free Operation

We first examine the operation of the RtB technique when no failure or exception occurs.

- Upon entry to the RtB, the executive performs the following: a checkpoint (or recovery point) is established, a call to P is formatted, and the WDT is set to WP.

- P is executed. No exception or time-out occurs during execution of P.

- The results of P are submitted to the AT.

- P's results are on time and pass the AT.

- Control returns to the executive.

- The executive discards the checkpoint, clears the WDT, the results are passed outside the RtB, and the RtB is exited.

5.1.1.2   Exception in Primary Algorithm Execution

Next let's examine the operation of RtB technique when an exception occurs in P. Differences between this scenario and the failure-free scenario are in gray type.

- Upon entry to the RtB, the executive performs the following: a checkpoint (or recovery point) is established, a call to P is formatted, and the WDT is set to WP.

- P is executed. An exception occurs during execution of P.

- Control returns to the executive. The executive checks to ensure the deadline for acceptable results has not expired (it has not in this scenario) and checks if there is a(nother) DRA option available that has not been attempted on this input (there is one available).

- The executive restores the checkpoint, then calls the DRA with the original input data as its argument.

- The executive formats a call to P using the re-expressed input.

- P is executed. No exception or time-out occurs during execution of P with the re-expressed input.

- The results of P are submitted to the AT.

- P's results are on time and pass the AT.

- Control returns to the executive.

- The executive discards the checkpoint and clears the WDT; the results are passed outside the RtB, and the RtB is exited.

5.1.1.3   Primary's Results Are On Time, but Fail Acceptance Test; Successful Execution with Re-Expressed Inputs

Now let's look at what happens if P executes without exception and its results are sent to the AT, but they do not pass the AT. If the deadline for acceptable results has not expired and a new DRA option is available, the inputs are re-expressed and the primary is executed with the new input data. Differences between this scenario and the failure-free scenario are in gray type. This scenario is similar to the previous scenario, except for the cause of P's initial failure.

- Upon entry to the RtB, the executive performs the following: a checkpoint (or recovery point) is established, a call to P is formatted, and the WDT is set to WP.

- P is executed. No exception or time-out occurs during execution of P.

- The results of P are submitted to the AT.

- P's results fail the AT.

- Control returns to the executive. The executive checks to ensure the deadline for acceptable results has not expired (it has not in this scenario) and checks if there is a(nother) DRA option available that has not been attempted on this input (there is one available).

- The executive restores the checkpoint, then calls the DRA with the original input data as its argument.

- The executive formats a call to P using the re-expressed input.

- P is executed. No exception or time-out occurs during execution of P with the re-expressed input.

- The results of P are submitted to the AT.

- P's results are on time and pass the AT.

- Control returns to the executive.

- The executive discards the checkpoint and clears the WDT; the results are passed outside the RtB, and the RtB is exited.

5.1.1.4   All Data Re-Expression Algorithm Options Are Used Without Success; Successful Backup Execution

This scenario examines the case when the deadline expires without an acceptable result or when all DRA options fail. This may occur if the combined execution time of the $P(DRA_i(x))$, $i = 1, 2, \ldots$ *number of DRA*, is too long (versus individual algorithm time-outs) or when the DRA results are input to P and executed, and their results continue to fail the AT. If there are no DRA options remaining and no primary algorithm result has been accepted, the backup algorithm is invoked and, in this scenario, passes its AT (i.e., ATB). Differences between this scenario and the failure-free scenario are in gray type.

- Upon entry to the RtB, the executive performs the following: a checkpoint (or recovery point) is established, a call to P is formatted, and the WDT is set to WP.

- P is executed. No exception or time-out occurs during execution of P.

- The results of P are submitted to the AT.

- P's results fail the AT.

- Control returns to the executive. The executive checks to ensure the deadline for acceptable results has not expired (it has not) and checks if there is a(nother) DRA option available that has not been attempted on this input (there is one available).

- The executive restores the checkpoint, then calls DRA_1 with the original input data as its argument.

- The executive formats a call to P using the re-expressed input.

- P is executed. No exception or time-out occurs during execution of P with this re-expressed input.

- The results of P are submitted to the AT.

- P's results are on time, but fail the AT.

- Control returns to the executive. The executive checks to ensure the deadline for acceptable results has not expired (it has not) and checks if there is a(nother) DRA option available that has not been attempted on this input (there is one available).

- The executive restores the checkpoint, then calls DRA_2 with the original input data as its argument.

- The executive formats a call to P using the re-expressed input.

- P is executed. No exception or time-out occurs during execution of P with this re-expressed input.

- The results of P are submitted to the AT.

- P's results are on time, but fail the AT.

- Control returns to the executive. The executive checks to ensure the deadline for acceptable results has not expired (it has not) and checks if there is a(nother) DRA option available that has not been attempted on this input (there are no additional DRA options available).

- The executive restores the checkpoint, formats a call to the backup, B, using the original inputs, and invokes B.

- B is executed. No exception occurs during execution of B.

- The results of B are submitted to the ATB.

- B's results are on time and pass the ATB.

- Control returns to the executive.

- The executive discards the checkpoint, clears the WDT, the results are passed outside the RtB, and the RtB is exited.

5.1.1.5   All Data Re-Expression Algorithm Options Are Used Without Success; Backup Executes, but Fails Backup Acceptance Test

This scenario examines the case when the deadline expires without an acceptable result or when all DRA options fail. This may occur if the combined execution time of the $P(DRA_i(x))$, $i = 1, 2, \ldots$ *number of DRA* is too long (versus individual algorithm time-outs) or when the DRA results are input to P and executed and their results continue to fail the AT. If there are no DRA options remaining and no primary algorithm result has been accepted, the backup algorithm is invoked. In this scenario, the backup fails its AT (the ATB). A failure exception is raised and the RtB is exited. Differences between this scenario and the failure-free scenario are in gray type.

- Upon entry to the RtB, the executive performs the following: a checkpoint (or recovery point) is established, a call to P is formatted, and the WDT is set to WP.

- P is executed. No exception or time-out occurs during execution of P.

- The results of P are submitted to the AT.

- P's results fail the AT.

- Control returns to the executive. The executive checks to ensure the deadline for acceptable results has not expired (it has not) and checks if there is a(nother) DRA option available that has not been attempted on this input (there is one available).

- The executive restores the checkpoint, then calls DRA_1 with the original input data as its argument.

- The executive formats a call to P using the re-expressed input.

- P is executed. No exception or time-out occurs during execution of P with this re-expressed input.

- The results of P are submitted to the AT.

- P's results are on time, but fail the AT.

- Control returns to the executive. The executive checks to ensure the deadline for acceptable results has not expired (it has not) and checks if there is a(nother) DRA option available that has not been attempted on this input (there is one available).

- The executive restores the checkpoint, then calls DRA_2 with the original input data as its argument.

- The executive formats a call to P using the re-expressed input.

- P is executed. No exception or time-out occurs during execution of P with this re-expressed input.

- The results of P are submitted to the AT.

- P's results are on time, but fail the AT.

- Control returns to the executive. The executive checks to ensure the deadline for acceptable results has not expired (it has not) and checks if there is a(nother) DRA option available that has not been attempted on this input (there are no additional DRA options available).

- The executive restores the checkpoint, formats a call to the backup, B, using the original inputs, and invokes B.

- B is executed. No exception occurs during execution of B.

- The results of B are submitted to the ATB.

- B's results are on time, but fail the ATB.

- Control returns to the executive.

- The executive discards the checkpoint and clears the WDT; a failure exception is raised, and the RtB is exited.

5.1.1.6   Augmentations to Retry Block Technique Operation

We have seen in these scenarios that the RtB operation continues until acceptable results are produced, there are no new DRA options to try and the backup fails, or the deadline expires without an acceptable result from either the primary or the backup.

Several augmentations to the RtB can be imagined. One is to use a *DRA execution counter.* This counter is used when the primary fails on the original input and primary execution is attempted with re-expressed inputs. This counter indicates the maximum number of times to execute the primary with different re-expressed inputs. The counter is incremented once the primary fails and prior to each execution with re-expressed input. The benefit of using the DRA execution counter is that it provides the ability to have a means of imposing a deadline without using a timer. However, the counter cannot detect execution failure or infinite loops within the primary. This type of failure can be detected by a watchdog type of augmentation timer (recall Section 4.1 for its use with the RcB technique).

The RtB technique may also be augmented by the use of a more detailed AT comprised of several tests, as described in Section 4.1.1.5 in conjunction with the RcB technique. Also, notice in the scenarios that we denoted a different AT for the backup algorithm, ATB. If the backup algorithm is significantly different from the primary or if its functionality includes additional measures to ensure graceful degradation, for example, it may be necessary to use a different AT than that of the primary. However, if the primary and backup are developed based on the same specification and required functionality, then the same AT can be used for both variants.

We also indicated in the scenarios that there is at least one DRA and perhaps multiple DRA *options.* This possibly awkward wording was used because there can either be a single DRA that can re-express an input in multiple ways or multiple DRAs to use. This is illustrated in Figure 5.2.

With the multiple DRA, a different algorithm is used in each case: $DRA_i(x)_j$, where

$i =$ the DRA algorithm number;

$j =$ number of the pass within the RtB technique.

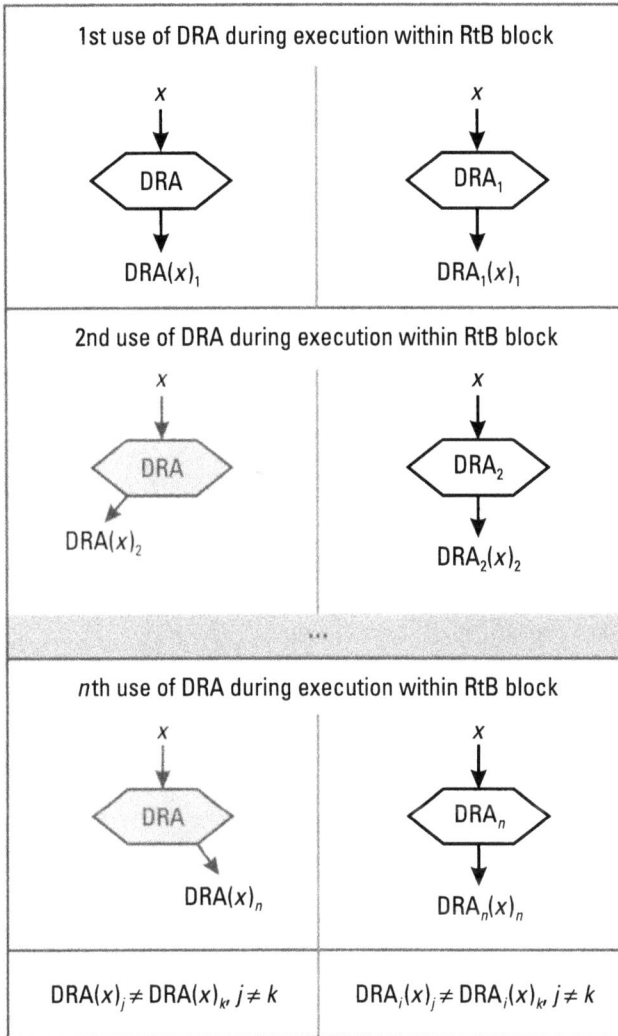

Figure 5.2 Multiuse single versus multiple data re-expression algorithms.

Note that with the single DRA, something within the DRA must result in a different re-expression of the input on each use of the algorithm. This could be implemented using a random number generator, a conditional switch implementing a different algorithm or by providing a different algorithm parameter (other than the input x), and so on.

5.1.2   Retry Block Example

Let's look at an example for the RtB technique. Suppose the original program uses inputs x and y, where x and y are measured by sensors with a tolerance of ±0.02. Also, suppose the original algorithm should not receive an input of $x = 0.0$ because of the nature of the algorithm. However, the values of x can be very close to zero (see Figure 5.3 illustrating $f(x, y)$). For example, if the program receives the input (1.5, 1.2), it operates correctly and produces a correct result. However, suppose that if it receives input close to $x = 0.0$, such as $(1e^{-10}, 2.2)$, lack of precision in the data type used causes storage of the x value to be zero, and causes a divide-by-zero error in the program.

Figure 5.4 illustrates an approach to using retry blocks with this problem. Note the additional components needed for RtB technique implementation: an executive that handles checkpointing and orchestrating the technique, a DRA, a backup sort algorithm, and an AT. In this example, no WDT is used. The AT in this example is a simple bounds test; that is, the result is accepted if $f(x, y) \geq 100.0$.

Now, let's step through the example.

- Upon entry to the RtB, the executive establishes a checkpoint and formats calls to the primary and backup routines. The input is $(1e^{-10}, 2.2)$.

- The primary algorithm, $f(x, y)$, is executed and results in a divide-by-zero error.

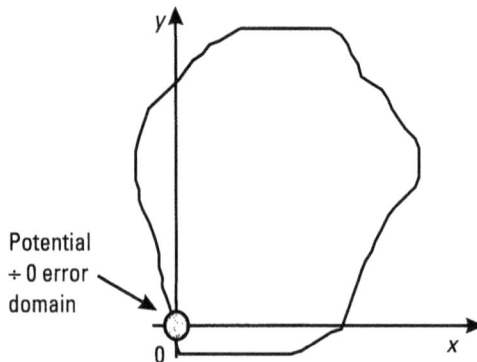

Figure 5.3 Example input space.

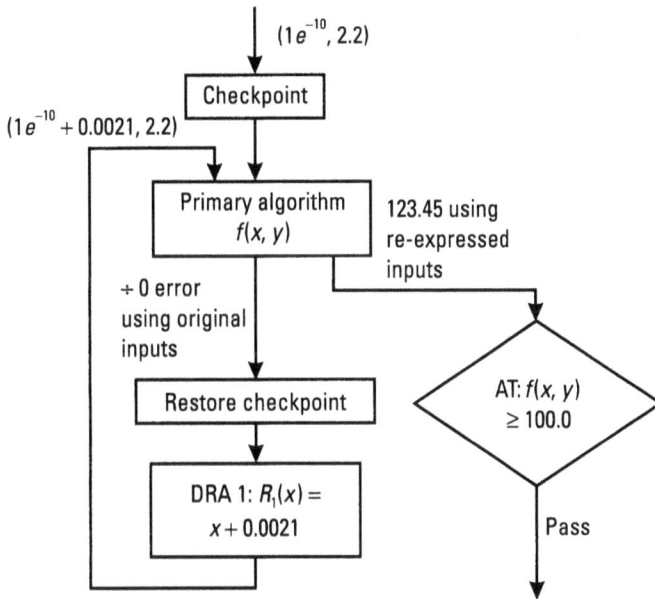

Figure 5.4 Example of retry block implementation.

- An exception is raised and is handled by the RtB executive. The executive sets a flag indicating failure of the primary algorithm using the original inputs and restores the checkpoint.
- The executive formats a call to the DRA to re-express the original inputs.
- The DRA, $R(x) = x + 0.0021$, modifies the x input parameter within x's limits of accuracy.
- The executive formats a call to the primary algorithm with the re-expressed inputs.
- The primary algorithm executes and returns the result 123.45.
- The result is submitted to the AT. The result is greater than or equal to 100.0, so the result of the primary algorithm using re-expressed inputs passes the AT.
- Control returns to the executive.
- The executive discards the checkpoint, the results are passed outside the RtB, and the RtB is exited.

5.1.3   Retry Block Issues and Discussion

This section presents the advantages, disadvantages, and issues related to the RtB technique. In general, software fault tolerance techniques provide protection against errors in translating requirements and functionality into code, but do not provide explicit protection against errors in specifying requirements. This is true for all of the techniques described in this book. Being a data diverse, backward recovery technique, the RtB technique subsumes data diversity's and backward recovery's advantages and disadvantages, too. These are discussed in Sections 2.3 and 1.4.1, respectively. While designing software fault tolerance into a system, many considerations have to be taken into account. These are discussed in Chapter 3. Issues related to several software fault tolerance techniques (such as similar errors, coincident failures, overhead, cost, redundancy, etc.) and the programming practices used to implement the techniques are described in Chapter 3. Issues related to implementing ATs are discussed in Section 7.2.

There are a few issues to note specifically for the RtB technique. The RtB technique runs in a sequential (uniprocessor) environment. When the results of the primary with original inputs pass the AT, the overhead incurred (beyond that of running the primary alone, as in non-fault-tolerant software) includes setting the checkpoint and executing the AT. If, however, these results fail the AT, then the time overhead also includes the time for recovering the checkpointed information, execution time for each DRA (or each pass through a single DRA), execution times for each time the primary is run with re-expressed inputs until one passes the AT (or until all attempts fail the AT), and run-time of the AT each time results are checked. It is assumed that most of the time the primary's first-execution results will pass the AT, so the expected time overhead is that of setting the checkpoint and executing the AT. This is little beyond the primary's execution time (unless an unusually large amount of information is being checkpointed). In the worst case, however, the RtB technique's execution time is the sum of all the module executions mentioned above (in the case where the primary's results fail the AT). This wide variation in execution time exposes the RtB to timing errors that may be unacceptable for real-time applications. One solution to the overhead problem is the distributed recovery block (DRB) (see Section 4.3) in which the modules and AT are executed in parallel, modified for use with data diverse program elements.

In RtB operation, when executing DRAs and re-executing the primary, the service that the module is to provide is interrupted during the recovery.

This interruption may be unacceptable in applications that require high availability.

One advantage of the RtB technique is that it is naturally applicable to software modules, as opposed to whole systems. It is natural to apply RtB to specific critical modules or processes in the system without incurring the cost and complexity of supporting fault tolerance for an entire system.

Simple, highly effective DRAs and ATs are required for effective RtB technique operation. The success of data diverse software fault tolerance techniques depends on the performance of the re-expression algorithm used. Several ways to perform data re-expression and insight on actual re-expression algorithms and their use are presented in Sections 2.3.1 through 2.3.3. DRAs are very application dependent, with their development requiring in-depth knowledge of the algorithm. Development of DRAs also requires a careful analysis of the type and magnitude of re-expression appropriate for each candidate datum [3]. There is no general rule for the derivation of DRAs for all applications; however, this can be done for some special cases [10] and they do exist for a fairly wide range of applications [11]. A simple DRA is more desirable than a complex one because the simpler algorithm is less likely to contain design faults.

A simple, effective AT can also be difficult to develop and depends heavily on the specification (see Section 7.2). If an error is not detected by the AT (or by the other error detection mechanisms), then that error is passed along to the module that receives the retry block's results and will not trigger any recovery mechanisms.

Both RcB and RtB techniques can suffer the domino effect (Section 3.1.3), in which cascaded rollbacks can push all processes back to their beginnings. This occurs if recovery and communication operations are not coordinated, especially in the case of nested recovery or retry blocks.

Not all applications can employ data diversity; however, many real-time control systems and other applications can use DRAs. For example, sensors typically provide noisy and imprecise data, so small modifications to that data would not adversely affect the application [1] and can yield a means of implementing fault tolerance. The performance of the DRA itself is much more important to program dependability than the technique structure (such as NCP, RtB, and others) in which it is embedded [12].

The RtB technique provides data diversity, but not design diversity. This may limit the technique's ability to tolerate some fault types. The use of combination design and data diverse techniques (see Section 5.3 for example) may assist in overcoming this limitation, but more research and experimentation is required.

To implement the RtB technique, the developer can use the programming techniques (such as assertions, checkpointing, atomic actions) described in Chapter 3. Also needed for implementation and further examination of the technique is information on the underlying architecture and performance. These are discussed in Sections 5.1.3.1 and 5.1.3.2, respectively. Table 5.1 lists several RtB technique issues, indicates whether or not they are an advantage or disadvantage (if applicable), and points to where in the book the reader may find additional information.

The indication that an issue in the above table can be a positive or negative (+/−) influence on the technique or on its effectiveness further indicates that the issue may be a disadvantage in general (e.g., cost is higher than non-fault-tolerant software) but an advantage in relation to another technique. In these cases, the reader is referred to the discussion of the issue.

Table 5.1
Retry Block Issue Summary

Issue	Advantage (+)/ Disadvantage (−)	Where Discussed
Provides protection against errors in translating requirements and functionality into code (true for software fault tolerance techniques in general)	+	Chapter 1
Does not provide explicit protection against errors in specifying requirements (true for software fault tolerance techniques in general)	−	Chapter 1
General backward recovery advantages	+	Section 1.4.1
General backward recovery disadvantages	−	Section 1.4.1
General data diversity advantages	+	Section 2.3
General data diversity disadvantages	−	Section 2.3
DRA	+/−	Sections 2.3.1–2.3.3
Similar errors or common residual design errors	−	Section 3.1.1
Coincident and correlated failures	−	Section 3.1.1
Domino effect	−	Section 3.1.3
Space and time redundancy	+/−	Section 3.1.4
Dependability studies	+/−	Section 4.1.3.3
ATs and discussions related to specific types of ATs	+/−	Section 7.2

5.1.3.1 Architecture

We mentioned in Sections 1.3.1.2 and 2.5 that structuring is required if we are to handle system complexity, especially when fault tolerance is involved [13–15]. This includes defining the organization of software modules onto the hardware elements on which they run. The RtB approach is typically uniprocessor, with all components residing on a single hardware unit. All communications between the software components is done through function calls or method invocations in this architecture.

5.1.3.2 Performance

There have been numerous investigations into the performance of software fault tolerance techniques in general (discussed in Chapters 2 and 3) and the dependability of specific techniques themselves. Table 4.2 (Section 4.1.3.3) provides a list of references for these dependability investigations. This list, although not exhaustive, provides a good sampling of the types of analyses that have been performed and substantial background for analyzing software fault tolerance dependability. Ammann and Knight provide a model to determine the success of an RtB system in [3]. The reader is encouraged to examine all references (in Table 4.2 and otherwise) for details on assumptions made by the researchers, experiment design, and results interpretation.

The fault tolerance of a system employing data diversity depends upon the ability of the DRA to produce data points outside of a failure region, given an initial data point that is within a failure region. The program executes correctly on re-expressed data points only if they are outside a failure region. If the failure region has a small cross section in some dimensions, then re-expression should have a high probability of translating the data point out of the failure region.

5.2 *N*-Copy Programming

NCP, also developed by Ammann and Knight [1–3], is the other (along with RtB) original data diverse software fault tolerance technique. NCP is a data diverse technique, and is further categorized as a static technique (described in Section 4.2). The hardware fault tolerance architecture related to the NCP is *N*-modular or static redundancy. The processes can run concurrently on different computers or sequentially on a single computer, but in practice, they are typically run concurrently. NCP is the data diverse complement of *N*-version programming (NVP).

The NCP technique uses a decision mechanism (DM) (see Section 7.1) and forward recovery (see Section 1.4.2) to accomplish fault tolerance. The technique uses one or more DRAs (see Sections 2.3.1 through 2.3.3) and at least two copies of a program. The system inputs are run through the DRA(s) to re-express the inputs. The copies execute in parallel using the re-expressed data as input (each input is different, one of which may be the original input value). A DM examines the results of the copy executions and selects the "best" result, if one exists. There are many alternative DMs available for use with NCP.

NCP operation is described in 5.2.1, with an example provided in 5.2.2. The advantages and disadvantages of the NCP technique are presented in 5.2.3.

5.2.1 *N*-Copy Programming Operation

The basic NCP technique consists of an executive, 1 to *n* DRA, *n* copies of the program or function, and a DM. The executive orchestrates the NCP technique operation, which has the general syntax:

```
run DRA 1, DRA 2, ..., DRA n
run Copy 1(result of DRA 1),
    Copy 2(result of DRA 2), ...,
    Copy n(result of DRA n)
if (Decision Mechanism (Result 1, Result 2, ...,
                        Result n))
    return Result
else failure exception
```

The NCP syntax above states that the technique first runs the DRA concurrently to re-express the input data, then executes the *n* copies concurrently. The results of the copy executions are provided to the DM, which operates upon the results to determine if a correct result can be adjudicated. If one can (i.e., the Decision Mechanism statement above evaluates to TRUE), then it is returned. If a correct result cannot be determined, then an error occurs.

Figure 5.5 illustrates the structure and operation of the NCP technique. As shown, *n* copies of a program execute in parallel, each on a different set of re-expressed data. If the re-expression algorithm used is exact (that is, all copies should generate identical outputs), then a conventional majority voter can be used. If an approximate re-expression algorithm is used, the *n* copies could produce different but acceptable outputs, and an enhanced DM

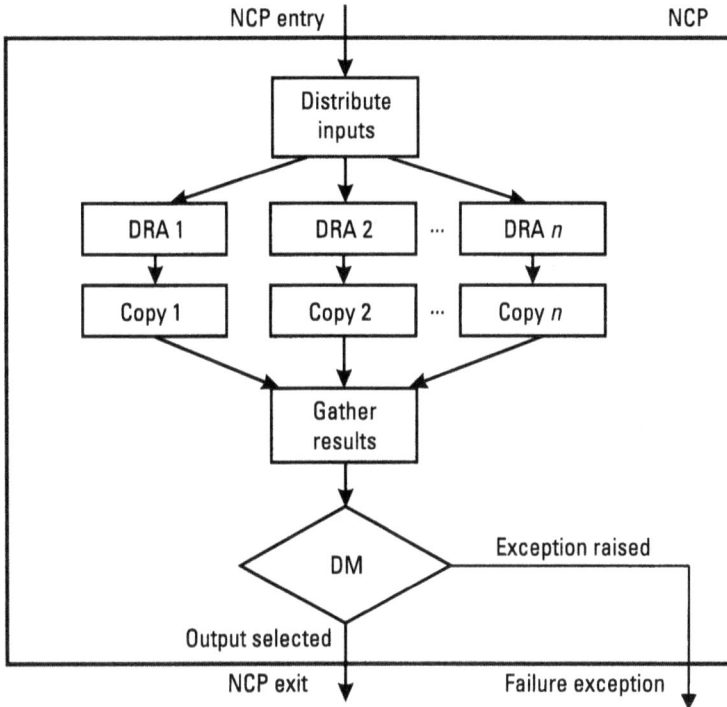

Figure 5.5 *N*-copy programming structure and operation.

(such as the formal majority voter, Section 7.1.5) is needed. (Exact and approximate re-expression algorithms are defined in Section 2.3.2.)

Both fault-free and failure scenarios (one in which a correct result cannot be found and one that fails prior to reaching the DM) for the NCP are described below. In examining these scenarios, the following abbreviations will be used:

C_i	Copy i;
DM	Decision mechanism;
DRA_i	Data re-expression algorithm i;
n	The number of copies;
NCP	*N*-copy programming;
R_i	Result of C_i;
x	Original input;
y_i	Re-expressed input, $y_i = DRA_i(x)$, $i = 1, \ldots, n$.

5.2.1.1   Failure-Free Operation

This scenario describes the operation of NCP when no failure or exception occurs.

- Upon entry to NCP, the executive sends the input, x, to the n DRA to be re-expressed.

- The DRA run their re-expression algorithms (exact DRA, in this example) on x, yielding the re-expressed inputs $y_i = DRA_i(x)$.

- The executive gathers the re-expressed input, formats calls to the n copies and through those calls distributes the re-expressed inputs to the copies.

- Each copy, C_i, executes. No failures occur during their execution.

- The results of the copy executions (R_i, $i = 1, ..., n$) are gathered by the executive and submitted to the exact majority DM.

- The R_i are equal to one another, so the DM selects R_2 (randomly, since the results are equal), as the correct result.

- Control returns to the executive.

- The executive passes the correct result outside the NCP, and the NCP module is exited.

5.2.1.2   Failure Scenario—Incorrect Results

This scenario describes the operation of NCP when the DM cannot determine a correct result. Differences between this scenario and the failure-free scenario are in gray type.

- Upon entry to NCP, the executive sends the input, x, to the n DRA to be re-expressed.

- The DRA run their re-expression algorithms (exact DRA, in this example) on x, yielding the re-expressed inputs $y_i = DRA_i(x)$.

- The executive gathers the re-expressed input, formats calls to the n copies and through those calls distributes the re-expressed inputs to the copies.

- Each copy, C_i, executes.

- The results of the copy executions (R_i, $i = 1, ..., n$) are gathered by the executive and submitted to the exact majority DM.

- None of the R_i are equal. The DM cannot determine a correct result, and it sets a flag indicating this fact.
- Control returns to the executive.
- The executive raises an exception and the NCP module is exited.

5.2.1.3 Failure Scenario—Copy Does Not Execute

This scenario describes the operation of NCP when at least one copy does not complete its execution. Differences between this scenario and the failure-free scenario are in gray type.

- Upon entry to NCP, the executive sends the input, x, to the n DRA to be re-expressed.
- The DRA run their re-expression algorithms (exact DRA here) on x, yielding the re-expressed inputs $y_i = DRA_i(x)$.
- The executive gathers the re-expressed input, formats calls to the n copies, and through those calls distributes the re-expressed inputs to the copies.
- The copies, C_i, begin execution. One or more copies do not complete execution for some reason (e.g., stuck in an endless loop).
- The executive cannot retrieve all copy results in a timely manner. The executive submits the results it does have to the DM.
- The DM expects n results, but receives n-1 (or n-2, etc., depending on the number of failed copies) results. The basic exact majority voter cannot handle fewer than n results and sets a flag indicating its failure to select a correct result. (Note: If the DM is not equipped to recognize this failure, it may fail, and the executive would have to recognize the DM failure.)
- Control returns to the executive.
- The executive raises an exception and the NCP module is exited.

5.2.1.4 Augmentations to N-Copy Programming Operation

We have seen in these scenarios that NCP operation continues until the DM adjudicates a correct result, the DM cannot select a correct result, or the DM itself fails. It is also evident how similar the operations are of the NVP and NCP techniques.

Augmentations to the basic NCP can involve using a different DM than the basic majority voter. Chapter 7 describes several alternatives. One optional DM is the dynamic voter (Section 7.1.6). Its ability to handle a variable number of result inputs could tolerate the failure experienced in the last scenario above.

Another augmentation to basic NCP involves voting on the results as each copy completes execution (as opposed to waiting on all copies to complete). Once two results are available, the DM can compare them and, if they agree, complete that NCP cycle. If the first two results do not match, the DM performs a majority vote on three results when it receives the third copy's results, and continues voting through the nth copy execution, until it finds an acceptable result. When an acceptable result is found, it is passed outside the NCP, any remaining copy executions are terminated, and the NCP module is exited. This scheme provides results more quickly than the basic NCP only if it is possible that one or more copies have different execution times based on the input received.

The DRA used with the NCP technique are application dependent, but there is room for variety in their design. Several example DRA are described in Section 2.3.3.

Another augmentation, this one via combination with other techniques, has been made to the NCP technique. This is the TPA described later in this chapter.

5.2.2 *N*-Copy Programming Example

This section provides an example implementation of the NCP technique. Suppose the original program uses inputs x and y, where x and y are measured by sensors with a tolerance of ±0.02. Also, suppose the original algorithm should not receive an input of $x = 0.0$ because of the nature of the algorithm. However, the values of x can be very close to zero (see Figure 5.3 in Section 5.1.2 illustrating $f(x, y)$). For example, if the program receives the input (1.5, −1.2), it operates correctly and produces a correct result. However, suppose that if it receives input close to $x = 0.0$, such as $(1e^{-10}, 2.2)$, lack of precision in the data type used causes storage of the x value to be zero, and causes a divide-by-zero error in the program.

Figure 5.6 illustrates an example NCP implementation of the example problem. Note the additional components needed for NCP implementation—an executive that handles orchestrating and synchronizing the technique, one or more DRA, one or more additional copies of the algorithm/program, and a DM. In this example, three DRAs are used: a

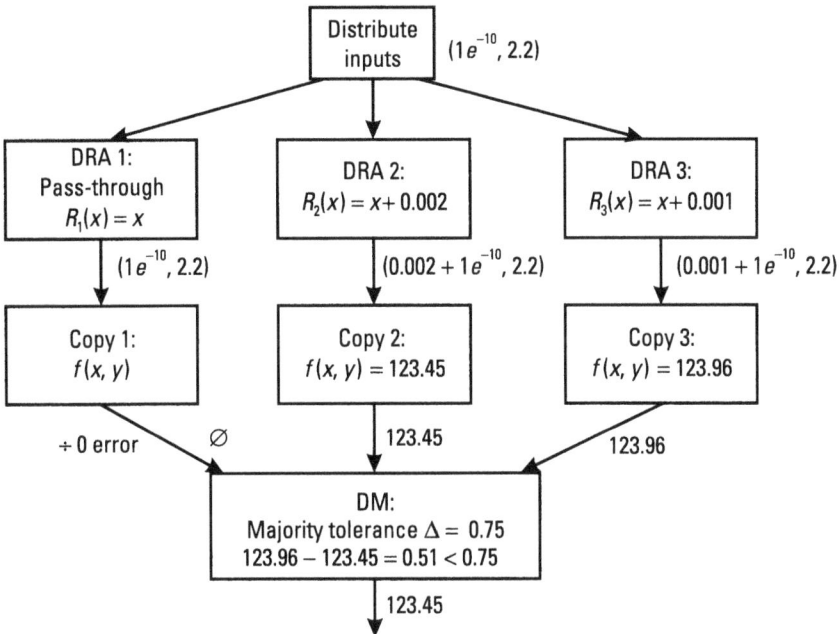

Figure 5.6 Example of *N*-copy programming implementation.

pass-through DRA, which simply forwards the original inputs without modification; a DRA that adds 0.002 (recall the tolerance for x) to the input; and
a DRA that adds 0.001 to the input. These re-expressed inputs are sent to the
algorithm copies. The copies perform their functions on the inputs and the
voter determines the correct result. In this case, a majority voter using tolerances is applied. (Note that the voter tolerance is a different entity than the
input's tolerance.) As suspected, the original input produces a divide-by-zero
error. But the other DRA/copy pairs produce results that are equal within a
tolerance of 0.75 and pass the voter. (See Chapter 7 for more information on
tolerance voters.)

Now, let's step through the example.

- Upon entry to NCP, the executive sends the input, $(1e^{-10}, 2.2)$, to
  the three DRAs to be re-expressed.

- The DRAs run their re-expression algorithms on the input yielding
  the following re-expressed inputs:

$$\text{DRA}_1(1e^{-10}, 2.2) = (1e^{-10}, 2.2) \qquad \text{Pass-through DRA}$$

$$DRA_2(1e^{-10}, 2.2) = (0.002 + 1e^{-10}, 2.2)$$
$$DRA_3(1e^{-10}, 2.2) = (0.001 + 1e^{-10}, 2.2)$$

- The executive gathers the re-expressed inputs, formats calls to the $n = 3$ copies and through those calls distributes the re-expressed inputs to the copies.
- Each copy, C_i ($i = 1, 2, 3$), executes.
- The results of the copy executions (r_i, $i = 1, ..., n$) are gathered by the executive and submitted to the DM.
- The DM examines the results:

Copy	r_i	Decision Mechanism Algorithm
1	∅ (divide-by-zero error)	—
2	123.45	| 123.45 − 123.96 | = 0.51 < 0.75 (where 0.75 is
3	123.96	the DM tolerance)

The adjudicated result is 123.45 (randomly selected from those copy results matching within the tolerance).

- Control returns to the executive.
- The executive passes the correct result, 123.45, outside the NCP, and the NCP module is exited.

5.2.3   *N*-Copy Programming Issues and Discussion

This section presents the advantages, disadvantages, and issues related to NCP. As stated earlier, software fault tolerance techniques generally provide protection against errors in translating requirements and functionality into code, but do not provide explicit protection against errors in specifying requirements. This is true for all of the techniques described in this book. Being a data diverse, forward recovery technique, NCP subsumes data diversity's and forward recovery's advantages and disadvantages, too. These are discussed in Sections 2.3 and 1.4.2, respectively. While designing software fault tolerance into a system, many considerations have to be taken into account. These are discussed in Chapter 3. Issues related to several software fault tolerance techniques (such as, similar errors, overhead, cost, redundancy, etc.) and the programming practices (e.g., assertions, atomic actions, and idealized components) used to implement the techniques are described in Chapter 3. Issues related to implementing voters are discussed in Section 7.1.

There are some issues to note specifically for the NCP technique. NCP runs in a multiprocessor environment, although it could be executed sequentially in a uniprocessor environment. The overhead incurred (beyond that of running a single copy, as in non-fault-tolerant software) includes additional memory for the second through the nth copies, DRA, executive, and DM; additional execution time for the executive, DRA, and DM; and synchronization overhead. If the copy execution times vary significantly based on input value, the time overhead for the NCP technique will be dependent upon the slowest copy, since all copy results must be available for the voter to operate (for the basic majority voter). One solution to this synchronization time overhead is to use a DM performing an algorithm that uses two or more results as they become available. (See the self-configuring optimal programming (SCOP) technique discussion in Chapter 6.)

In NCP operation, it is rarely necessary to interrupt the module's service during voting. This continuity of service is attractive for applications that require high availability.

It is critical that the initial specification for the NCP copies be free of flaws. If the specification is flawed, then the copies will simply repeat the error and may produce indistinguishably incorrect results. Common mode failures between the copies and the DM can also cause the technique to fail. However, the relative independence of the copies and the DM lessens the likelihood of this threat. The DM may also contain residual design faults. If it does, then the DM may accept incorrect results or reject correct results.

The success of data diverse software fault tolerance techniques depends on the performance of the re-expression algorithm used. Several ways to perform data re-expression and insight on actual re-expression algorithms and their use are presented in Sections 2.3.1 through 2.3.3. DRAs are very application dependent. Development of a DRA also requires a careful analysis of the type and magnitude of re-expression appropriate for each candidate datum [3]. There is no general rule for the derivation of DRAs for all applications; however, this can be done for some special cases [10], and they do exist for a fairly wide range of applications [11]. Of course, a simple DRA is more desirable than a complex one because the simpler algorithm is less likely to contain design faults.

Not all applications can employ data diversity; however, many real-time control systems and other applications can use DRAs. For example, sensors typically provide noisy and imprecise data, so small modifications to those data would not adversely affect the application [1] and can yield a means of implementing fault tolerance. The performance of the DRA itself is much more important to program dependability than the technique structure (such as NCP and RtB) in which it is embedded [12].

NCP provides data diversity, but not design diversity. This may limit the technique's ability to tolerate some fault types. The use of combination design and data diverse techniques may assist in overcoming this limitation, but more research and experimentation is required.

Also needed for implementation and further examination of the technique is information on the underlying architecture and technique performance. These are discussed in Sections 5.2.3.1 and 5.2.3.2, respectively. Table 5.2 lists several NCP issues, indicates whether or not they are an

Table 5.2
N-Copy Programming Issue Summary

Issue	Advantage (+)/ Disadvantage (−)	Where Discussed
Provides protection against errors in translating requirements and functionality into code (true for software fault tolerance techniques in general)	+	Chapter 1
Does not provide explicit protection against errors in specifying requirements (true for software fault tolerance techniques in general)	−	Chapter 1
General forward recovery advantages	+	Section 1.4.2
General forward recovery disadvantages	−	Section 1.4.2
General data diversity advantages	+	Section 2.3
General data diversity disadvantages	−	Section 2.3
DRA	+/−	Section 2.3.1 - 2.3.3
Similar errors or common residual design errors	−	Section 3.1.1
Coincident and correlated failures	−	Section 3.1.1
Consistent comparison problem (CCP)	−	Section 3.1.2
Space and time redundancy	+/−	Section 3.1.4
Design considerations	+	Section 3.3.1
Dependable system development model	+	Section 3.3.2
Dependability studies	+/−	Section 4.1.3.3
Voters and discussions related to specific types of voters	+/−	Section 7.1

advantage or disadvantage (if applicable), and points to where in the book the reader may find additional information.

The indication that an issue in Table 5.2 can be a positive or negative (+/−) influence on the technique or on its effectiveness further indicates that the issue may be a disadvantage in general (e.g., cost is higher than non-fault-tolerant software) but an advantage in relation to another technique. In these cases, the reader is referred to the noted section for discussion of the issue.

5.2.3.1 Architecture

We mentioned in Sections 1.3.1.2 and 2.5 that structuring is required if we are to handle system complexity, especially when fault tolerance is involved [13–15]. This includes defining the organization of software modules onto the hardware elements on which they run. NCP is typically multiprocessor, with components residing on *n* hardware units and the executive residing on one of the processors. Communications between the software components is done through remote function calls or method invocations.

5.2.3.2 Performance

There have been numerous investigations into the performance of software fault tolerance techniques in general (discussed in Chapters 2 and 3) and the dependability of specific techniques themselves. Table 4.2 (in Section 4.1.3.3) provides a list of references for these dependability investigations. This list, although not exhaustive, provides a good sampling of the types of analyses that have been performed and substantial background for analyzing software fault tolerance dependability. To determine the performance of an NCP system, Ammann and Knight [3] analyze a three-copy system and compare it to a single version. The reader is encouraged to examine the original references for dependability studies for details on assumptions made by the researchers, experiment design, and results interpretation.

The fault tolerance of a system employing data diversity depends upon the ability of the DRA to produce data points outside of a failure region, given an initial data point that is within a failure region. The program executes correctly on re-expressed data points only if they are outside a failure region. If the failure region has a small cross section in some dimensions, then re-expression should have a high probability of translating the data point out of the failure region.

One way to improve the performance of NCP is to use DMs that are appropriate for the problem solution domain. Consensus voting (see Section 7.1.4) is one such alternative to majority voting. Consensus voting has the advantage of being more stable than majority voting. The reliability of consensus voting is at least equivalent to majority voting. It performs better than majority voting when average *N*-tuple reliability is low, or the average decision space in which voters work is not binary [16]. Also, when *n* is greater than 3, consensus voting can make plurality decisions; that is, in situations where there is no majority (the majority voter fails), the consensus voter selects as the correct result the value of a unique maximum of identical outputs. A disadvantage of consensus voting is the added complexity of the decision algorithm. However, this may be overcome at least in part by preapproved DM components [17].

5.3   Two-Pass Adjudicators

The TPA technique developed by Pullum [7–9], is a set of combination data and design diverse software fault tolerance techniques. TPA is also a combination static and dynamic technique (described in Section 4.2), based on the recovery technique required. The hardware fault tolerance architecture related to the technique is *N*-modular redundancy. The processes can run concurrently on different computers or sequentially on a single computer, but are designed to run concurrently.

The TPA technique uses a DM (see Section 7.1) and both forward and backward recovery (see Sections 1.4.1 and 1.4.2) to accomplish fault tolerance. The technique uses one or more DRA (see Sections 2.3.1 through 2.3.3) and at least two variants of a program. The system operates like NVP (Section 4.2) unless and until the DM cannot determine a correct result given the variant results. If this occurs, then the inputs are run through the DRA(s) to be re-expressed. The variants reexecute using the re-expressed data as input (each input is different, one of which may be the original input value). A DM examines the results of the variant executions of this second pass and selects the "best" result, if one exists. There are a number of alternative detection and selection mechanisms available for use with TPA. These are discussed in Section 5.3.1.

Basic TPA operation is described in 5.3.1, with an example provided in 5.3.2. TPA advantages, disadvantages, and issues are presented in 5.3.3.

5.3.1   Two-Pass Adjudicator Operation

The basic TPA technique consists of an executive, 1 to *n* DRA, *n* variants of the program or function, and a DM. The executive orchestrates the TPA technique operation, which has the general syntax:

```
Pass 1:   run Variant 1(original input),
              Variant 2(original input),...,
              Variant n(original input)
      if (Decision Mechanism
              (Result(Pass 1, Variant 1),
              Result(Pass 1, Variant 2), ...,
              Result(Pass 1, Variant n)))
              return Result
      else
Pass 2:   run DRA 1, DRA 2, ..., DRA n
              run Variant 1(result of DRA 1),
              Variant 2(result of DRA 2),...,
              Variant n(result of DRA n)
      if (Decision Mechanism
              (Result(Pass 2, Variant 1),
              Result(Pass 2, Variant 2),...,
              Result(Pass 2, Variant n)))
              return Result
      else failure exception
```

The TPA syntax above states that the technique first runs the n variants using the original inputs as parameters. The results of the variant executions are provided to the DM to determine if a correct result can be adjudicated. If one can (i.e., the first Decision Mechanism statement above evaluates to TRUE), then it is returned. If a correct result cannot be determined, then Pass 2 is initiated by concurrently re-expressing the original inputs via the DRA(s). The n variants are reexecuted using the re-expressed inputs as parameters. The results of the reexecutions are provided to the DM to determine if a correct result can be adjudicated. If one can (i.e., the second Decision Mechanism statement above evaluates to TRUE), then it is returned. If a correct result cannot be determined, then an error occurs.

Figure 5.7 illustrates the structure and operation of the basic TPA technique. As shown, n variants of a program initially execute in parallel on the original input as in the NVP technique. The technique continues operation as described above.

Both fault-free and failure scenarios for the TPA are described below. In examining these scenarios, the following abbreviations will be used:

V_i Variant i, $i = 1, ..., n$;

DM   Decision mechanism;

DRA_i Data re-expression algorithm i, $i = 1, ..., n$;

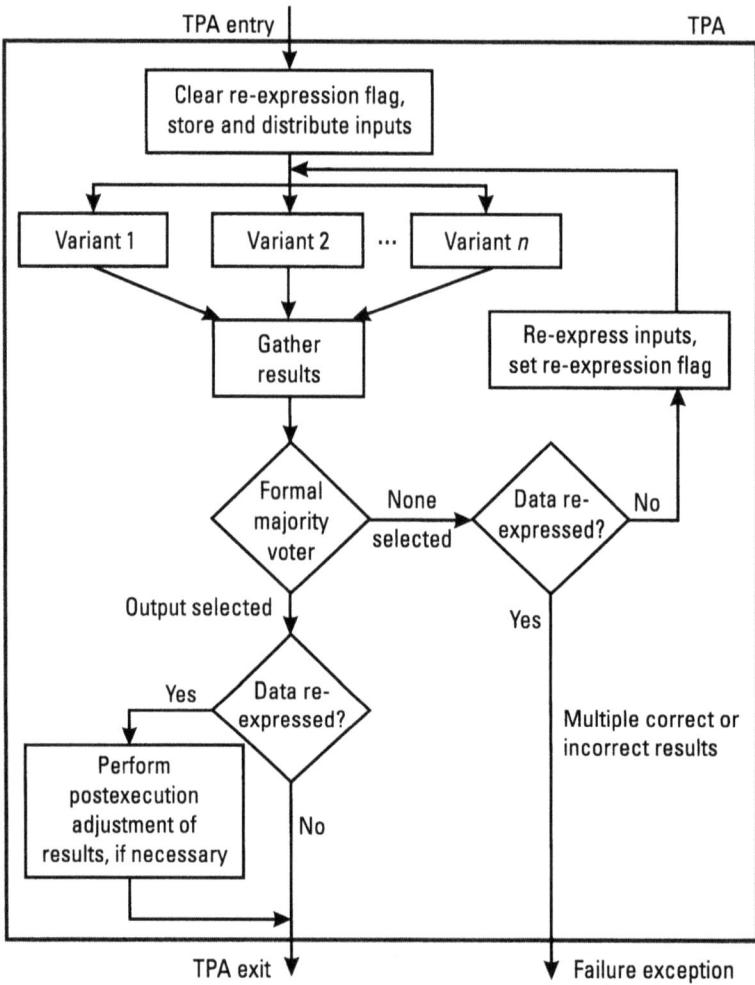

Figure 5.7 Two-pass adjudicator structure and operation. (*After:* [7].)

n	The number of variants;
TPA	Two-pass adjudicator;
R_{ki}	Result of V_i for Pass k, $i = 1, ..., n$; $k = 1, 2$;
x	Original input;
y_i	Re-expressed input, $y_i = DRA_i(x)$, $i = 1, ..., n$.

5.3.1.1 Failure-Free Operation

This scenario describes the operation of the TPA technique when no failure or exception occurs.

- Upon entry to the TPA, the executive sets the re-expression flag to 0 (indicating that these inputs are original), stores the original inputs, formats calls to the *n* variants, and through those calls distributes the inputs.
- Each variant, V_i, executes. No failures occur during their execution.
- The results of the Pass 1 variant executions (R_{1i}, $i = 1, \ldots, n$) are gathered by the executive and submitted to the tolerance DM.
- The R_{1i} are equal to one another, so the DM selects R_{12} (randomly, since the results are equal), as the correct result.
- Control returns to the executive.
- The executive passes the correct result outside the TPA, and the TPA module is exited.

5.3.1.2 Partial Failure Scenario—Incorrect Results on First Pass

This scenario describes the operation of TPA when the DM cannot determine a correct result on the first pass, that is, with the results of the variants operating on the original inputs. Differences between this scenario and the failure-free scenario are in gray type.

- Upon entry to the TPA, the executive sets the re-expression flag to 0 (indicating that these inputs are original), stores the original inputs, formats calls to the *n* variants, and through those calls distributes the inputs.
- Each variant, V_i, executes.
- The results of the Pass 1 variant executions (R_{1i}, $i = 1, \ldots, n$) are gathered by the executive and submitted to the tolerance DM.
- The R_{1i} differ significantly from one another. The DM cannot determine a correct result, and it sets a flag indicating this fact.
- Control returns to the executive. The executive checks the re-expression flag to see if the inputs have been re-expressed. They have not.

- The executive retrieves the stored input, x, sends it to the n DRA to be re-expressed (via an exact DRA), and sets the re-expression flag to 1 (indicating the input has been re-expressed).

- The DRA run their re-expression algorithms on x, yielding the re-expressed inputs $y_i = DRA_i(x)$.

- The executive gathers the re-expressed input, formats calls to the n variants and through those calls distributes the re-expressed inputs to the variants.

- Each variant, V_i, executes.

- The results of the Pass 2 variant executions (R_{2i}, $i = 1, \ldots, n$) are gathered by the executive and submitted to the DM.

- The R_{2i} are equal within a tolerance of one another, so the DM selects R_{23} (randomly, since the results are equal), as the correct result.

- Control returns to the executive.

- The executive passes the correct result outside the TPA, and the TPA module is exited.

5.3.1.3 Failure Scenario—Incorrect Results on Both Passes

This scenario describes the operation of TPA when the DM cannot determine a correct result on the first or second pass, that is, with the results of the variants operating on the original inputs and on the re-expressed inputs. Differences between this scenario and the failure-free scenario are in gray type.

- Upon entry to the TPA, the executive sets the re-expression flag to 0 (indicating that these inputs are original), stores the original inputs, formats calls to the n variants, and through those calls distributes the inputs.

- Each variant, V_i, executes.

- The results of the Pass 1 variant executions (R_{1i}, $i = 1, \ldots, n$) are gathered by the executive and submitted to the tolerance DM.

- The R_{1i} differ significantly from one another. The DM cannot determine a correct result, and it sets a flag indicating this fact.

- Control returns to the executive. The executive checks the re-expression flag to see if the inputs have been re-expressed. They not.

- The executive retrieves the stored input, x, sends it to the n DRA to be re-expressed (via an exact DRA), and sets the re-expression flag to 1 (indicating the input has been re-expressed).

- The DRA run their re-expression algorithms on x, yielding the re-expressed inputs $y_i = DRA_i(x)$.

- The executive gathers the re-expressed input, formats calls to the n variants and through those calls distributes the re-expressed inputs to the variants.

- Each variant, V_i, executes.

- The results of the Pass 2 variant executions (R_{2i}, i = 1, ..., n) are gathered by the executive and submitted to the DM.

- The R_{2i} differ significantly from one another. The DM cannot determine a correct result, and it sets a flag indicating this fact.

- Control returns to the executive. The executive checks the re-expression flag to see if the inputs have been re-expressed. They have been.

- The executive raises an exception and the TPA module is exited.

5.3.2 Two-Pass Adjudicators and Multiple Correct Results

We have seen in these scenarios that TPA operation continues until the DM adjudicates a correct result on the first or second pass or the DM cannot select a correct result on either pass. It is also evident that the failure-free operation of the TPA is the same as that of the NVP technique (other than setting the re-expression flag).

Pullum [7–9] originally developed the TPA technique to handle multiple correct results (MCR). Limitations to the usefulness of any software fault tolerance technique can arise from difficulties with the technique's DM. If a single correct result exists for an execution cycle, equality comparison by the majority voting scheme is easily performed and agreed upon when variants yield integer or character results. Difficulties arise when the variants manipulate and yield floating-point values or when MCR occur. Both design and data diverse software fault tolerance techniques suffer from the inability to use variants that yield MCR.

Research into the problem of MCR reveals that there are three conditions from which MCR arise: (1) applications correctly resulting in multiple solutions, (2) use of finite-precision arithmetic, and (3) the existence of the CCP. No information is currently available on the general frequency of occurrence of the MCR event.

To address and propose solutions to the MCR event, the problem was separated into nine MCR system categories based on the type of system (with or without history, with or without convergent states) and the situation causing the MCR (a correctly multiple application, finite-precision arithmetic, or CCP). The TPA solutions have varying degrees of complexity in the selection process based on the type of system in which the technique is used and, thus, are based on the amount of information available upon which to base a decision.

Any technique proposed to improve upon the NVP-with-majority-voter should not perform worse than that technique under the most common operational case, that is, when the application results form a majority under majority voting rules (or under those of a finite-precision arithmetic-related DM). TPA performs exactly like NVP with a majority voter in this case. No additional operational time is required when Pass 1 results in a majority. Only when there is no decision on the first pass does TPA require more time to determine the correct result(s) (unless the two passes are run concurrently).

The TPA technique's set of solutions (1) provides a solution to the MCR problem, (2) yields a higher probability than the NVP majority voter of detecting and selecting correct results including MCR, and (3) is relatively simple and easy to understand and implement. The solutions were purposefully kept as simple as possible in order to apply to more applications and so that the fault tolerance technique implementation would be less prone to the introduction of additional design faults. Given a specific application type, TPA can be enhanced and extended, primarily in the result selection process.

Solutions to the MCR problem were categorized according to the MCR-causal situation and the system type as shown in the MCR categorization matrix of Table 5.3. Solutions to each of the categories were developed [7]. Details of the category I solution are presented in this chapter. The remaining TPA solution techniques may be found in [7].

5.3.2.1 Type I Solution

Certain types of applications may correctly result in more than one solution. Systems with no history compute their outputs for a given frame, or set of inputs, using only constants and the inputs for that frame. Category I MCR

Table 5.3
Multiple Correct Results Solution Category Matrix (*From:* [7], © 1992, Laura L. Pullum.)

	System Type		
		With History	
MCR Case	**Without History**	With Nonconvergent States	With Convergent States
Application has MCR	I	II	III
Finite-precision arithmetic	IV	V	VI
CCP	VII	VIII	IX

are those arising from problems that can correctly yield more than one result existing in systems with no history. Examples of this type problem are shortest-path-through-a-network computations and traveling-salesman-type problems.

Detection

A simple majority voter can detect a lack of consensus among results. However, this lack of consensus can be either multiple correct or multiple incorrect results. There are several cases that need to be considered for detection. These cases are derived from whether the system is embedded or stand-alone and whether or not the multiple results are close to one another. These cases are listed in Table 5.4.

In two of the cases of Table 5.4, techniques used for finite-precision arithmetic MCR (system categories IV, V, and VI) can be used for the detection of, and selection among, MCR. These are cases in which the results are "close" to one another, regardless of whether the system is embedded or stand-alone.

In embedded systems, if no consensus (or majority) is reached for one set or frame of inputs, and if the inputs are changing (as in a control system), then it is extremely unlikely that the lack of consensus will last for more than a short time. After a brief interval, the inputs should leave the region of difficulty and subsequent computations will be unaffected by the current MCR. In this case, the effects of category I MCR are transient. Hence, the results for the current frame can be ignored, and there is little need to distinguish between multiple correct and multiple incorrect results.

Table 5.4
Category I MCR Case Matrix (*From:* [7], © 1992, Laura L. Pullum.)

System	Results	
	Close	Not Close/Distinct
Embedded	Use finite-precision detection techniques.	Ignore the current frame. No need to distinguish.
Stand-alone	Use finite-precision detection techniques.	Need to distinguish. Use data diverse technique.

In the last case, the application or system is stand-alone (e.g., calculator-like in nature—one in which each problem is solved and valued for itself), and no consensus is reached. The solution in this case is a fault avoidance technique that uses data re-expression and a variant of NCP. This technique (the category I MCR detection technique) is the basic TPA, shown in Figure 5.7 and illustrated in the scenarios above.

Using the strictest sense of the term "no history," the solution to category I MCR cannot include any information outside the current frame or set of inputs. Hence, re-expression of data is used to avoid those areas of the input domain that may have caused a lack of consensus in the first pass. Since the re-expressed inputs are essentially treated as an additional or new frame, no comparison is allowed between Pass 1 and Pass 2 results. Then, if both passes yield multiple different results, it will not be possible, based solely on current frame data, to determine whether the results of a nonmajority case in Pass 2 are correct or incorrect. The additional pass and use of data re-expression decreases the probability of failure, while increasing the required amount of code and adding additional time required to execute the second pass when required.

Selection

A majority (tolerance) voter is used to select the adjudicated result in the cases where either Pass 1 or 2 results in a majority. This assumes no other category MCR is likely to occur. If this is not the case, combinations of the selection techniques discussed below may be used. There is only one case that results in multiple correct or incorrect results, that is when both passes result in no majority. If the results are supplied in real-time to the user, the user may be able to aid in the selection process by stating a preference for a particular result or by rejecting all multiple results. If selected, the preferred result can then be output to the user or passed to the next module in the application.

If the user is not in-the-loop with the system or application under consideration, then only *a priori* preference, utility, or other (such as range check) information can be used in the system with no history. *A priori* information is known before execution of the system or is information that remains constant throughout the operation of the application. If there is no *a priori* information on any of the results, or if it is highly likely that MCR exists and no preference exists for any of the correct results so that one must be selected, then random selection among the *m* correct results is an acceptable solution. If there is *a priori* preference or constraint information, it can be indicated using utility functions, a rule-base of preference information and system/application knowledge, or constraint (e.g., range) checks.

5.3.3 Two-Pass Adjudicator Example

This section provides an example implementation of the TPA detection and selection techniques for category I MCR. Suppose we have a network of cities, all of which must be visited, starting at city node 1. The network of airline flights and flight durations is shown in Figure 5.8. No revisiting of cities is allowed. The objective is to determine the route (or routes) that satisfies the requirements in the least amount of time. Table 5.5 provides the list of all possible routes meeting the requirements.

Suppose a program is implemented using TPA solution category I to solve this type of problem. Let the inputs (the flight network information) defining the specific problem be those shown in Figure 5.8. The output of

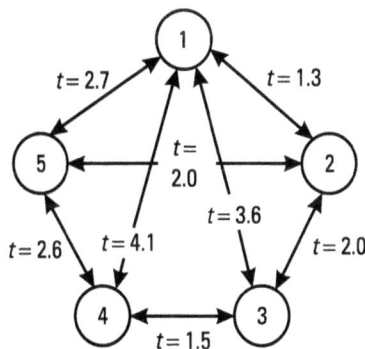

Figure 5.8 Example problem network. (*From:* [7], © 1992, Laura L. Pullum.)

Table 5.5
Routes Meeting Problem Requirements (*From:* [7], © 1992, Laura L. Pullum.)

Route	Cities Visited (in Order)	Total Time	Comment
A	1-2-3-4-5	7.4	MCR
B	1-2-5-4-3	7.4	MCR
C	1-3-5-4-2	9.7	—
D	1-3-2-5-4	10.2	—
E	1-4-5-2-3	10.7	—
F	1-4-3-2-5	9.6	—
G	1-5-2-3-4	8.2	—
H	1-5-4-3-2	8.8	—

the variant operation is the route letter or the list of cities. If all variants are operating correctly, a majority vote will yield either route A or route B as the correct answer (because, in this example, there are two correct answers and three correctly operating variants for this input domain). Consider the case in which one of the variants fails for this input domain and the resulting decision vector is (A, B, C). A majority voter would raise an exception in this case, even though two of the answers are correct.

Now, suppose the TPA category I detection technique is used. When a consensus is not reached on Pass 1 (because it operates like NVP with a majority voter on Pass 1), then the inputs are re-expressed. One means of re-expressing the data is to multiply the flight times by 10 (yielding flight times expressed as integers). If the data re-expression yields an input domain outside the failure region of variant 3 (the previously failed version), and assuming it is outside the failure region of variants 1 and 2, then a majority is found on one of the correct results when the outputs of Pass 2 are voted upon.

Suppose the data re-expression does not yield a correct result and the result vector is (A, B, D). In this case, no majority occurs, and since this is a system with no history, there is no further information available for the voter to automatically select a result. Now, look at the selection process for this case. If the user is in-the-loop, the results of each pass in the detection process are output to the user as follows:

Pass 1 results: (A, B, C);
Pass 2 results: (A, B, D).

The user can see that it is likely that A and B are multiply correct and can select one or both or reject all the results.

If the user is not in the loop, then a time-range check on preferred maximum travel time can be used. The user can input this value with the problem inputs or it can be preset to eliminate obviously erroneous results or eliminate nonpreferred results. Using the same result vectors for Pass 1 and 2 above and a time constraint of *tflight* $\leq$ 9 hours would result in multiple correct results, A and B. Care must be taken, however, so that the constraints are not too strict, yielding no valid-range results and, conversely, not too lenient, yielding all results for every execution of the program. Range checks must be carefully set to be effective.

Another means of selecting among MCR is the use of *a priori* preference or utility information. Suppose the traveler prefers to visit two of the cities in a particular order, say city 5 to city 4, because of the customers in those cities. Perhaps a purchase by the customer in city 5 can influence a purchase by the customer in city 4. This *a priori* information can be included in the selection technique and result in route A (correct result) or C (incorrect, but within range and preference constraints). Weights can also be added to the set of actions based on the value of the expected consequences of the actions, and hence, a utility function can be used in the selection process.

5.3.4   Two-Pass Adjudicator Issues and Discussion

This section presents the advantages, disadvantages, and issues related to the TPA. As stated earlier, software fault tolerance techniques generally provide protection against errors in translating requirements and functionality into code, but do not provide explicit protection against errors in specifying requirements. This is true for all of the techniques described in this book. Being a combined design and data diverse, backward and forward recovery technique, TPA subsumes the advantages and disadvantages of these attributes, too. These are discussed in Sections 2.2, 2.3, 1.4.1, and 1.4.2, respectively. While designing software fault tolerance into a system, many considerations have to be taken into account. These are discussed in Chapter 3. Issues related to several software fault tolerance techniques (such as similar errors, overhead, cost, redundancy, etc.) and the programming practices (e.g., assertions, atomic actions, and idealized components) used to implement the techniques are described in Chapter 3. Issues related to implementing voters are discussed in Section 7.1.

There are some issues to note specifically for the TPA technique. TPA runs in a multiprocessor environment, although it could be executed sequentially in a uniprocessor environment. The overhead incurred (beyond that of running a single variant, as in non-fault-tolerant software) includes additional memory for the second through the nth variants, DRA, executive, and DM; additional execution time for the executive, DRA on Pass 2, and DM; and synchronization overhead on both passes and the execution of Pass 2. One solution to the synchronization time overhead is to use a DM performing an algorithm that uses two or more results as they become available. (See the SCOP technique discussion in Chapter 6.)

In TPA operation, the second pass may interrupt the module's service. This is a detriment to TPA's use in real-time applications that require high availability.

It is critical that the initial specification for the TPA variants be free of flaws. If the specification is flawed, then the variants may produce indistinguishable incorrect results. Common mode failures between the variants themselves and between the variants and the DM can also cause the technique to fail. However, the relative independence of the variants and the DM lessens the likelihood of this part of the common mode failure threat. The DM may also contain residual design faults. If it does, then the DM may accept incorrect results or reject correct results.

The success of the data diverse pass of this technique depends on the performance of the re-expression algorithm used. Several ways to perform data re-expression and insight on actual re-expression algorithms and their use are presented in Sections 2.3.1 through 2.3.3. DRA are very application dependent. Development of a DRA also requires a careful analysis of the type and magnitude of re-expression appropriate for each data that is a candidate for re-expression [3]. There is no general rule for the derivation of DRAs for all applications; however, this can be done for some special cases [10], and they do exist for a fairly wide range of applications [11]. Of course, a simple DRA is more desirable than a complex one because the simpler algorithm is less likely to contain design faults.

Not all applications can employ data diversity; however, many real-time control systems and other applications can use DRAs. For example, sensors typically provide noisy and imprecise data, so small modifications to the data would not adversely affect the application [1] and can yield a means of implementing fault tolerance. The performance of the DRA itself is much more important to program dependability than the technique structure (such as TPA, NCP, or RtB) in which it is embedded [12].

Also needed for implementation and further examination of the technique is information on the underlying architecture and technique performance. These are discussed in Sections 5.3.4.1 and 5.3.4.2, respectively.

Table 5.6 lists several TPA issues, indicates whether or not they are an advantage or disadvantage (if applicable), and points to where in the book the reader may find additional information. Some analysis has been performed on the TPA set of techniques (see the performance section below), but more research and experimentation is required before they can be used with confidence.

The indication that an issue in Table 5.6 can be a positive or negative (+/−) influence on the technique or on its effectiveness further indicates that the issue may be a disadvantage in general (e.g., cost is higher than non-fault-tolerant software) but an advantage in relation to another technique. In

Table 5.6
Two-Pass Adjudicator Issue Summary

Issue	Advantage (+)/ Disadvantage (−)	Where Discussed
Provides protection against errors in translating requirements and functionality into code (true for software fault tolerance techniques in general)	+	Chapter 1
Does not provide explicit protection against errors in specifying requirements (true for software fault tolerance techniques in general)	−	Chapter 1
General backward and forward recovery advantages	+	Sections 1.4.1, 1.4.2
General backward and forward recovery disadvantages	−	Sections 1.4.1, 1.4.2
General design and data diversity advantages	+	Sections 2.2, 2.3
General design and data diversity disadvantages	−	Sections 2.2, 2.3
DRA	+/−	Sections 2.3.1–2.3.3
Similar errors or common residual design errors	−	Section 3.1.1
Coincident and correlated failures	−	Section 3.1.1
CCP	−	Section 3.1.2
Space and time redundancy	+/−	Section 3.1.4
Design considerations	+	Section 3.3.1
Dependable system development model	+	Section 3.3.2
Dependability studies	+/−	Section 4.1.3.3
Voters and discussions related to specific types of voters	+/−	Section 7.1

these cases, the reader is referred to the noted section for discussion of the issue.

5.3.4.1 Architecture

We mentioned in Sections 1.3.1.2 and 2.5 that structuring is required if we are to handle system complexity, especially when fault tolerance is involved [13–15]. This includes defining the organization of software modules onto the hardware elements on which they run. The TPA is typically multi-processor, with components residing on n hardware units and the executive residing on one of the processors. Communications between the software components is done through remote function calls or method invocations.

5.3.4.2 Performance

There have been numerous investigations into the performance of software fault tolerance techniques in general (discussed in Chapters 2 and 3) and the dependability of specific techniques themselves. Table 4.2 (in Section 4.1.3.3) provides a list of references for these dependability investigations. This list, although not exhaustive, provides a good sampling of the types of analyses that have been performed and substantial background for analyzing software fault tolerance dependability. The reader is encouraged to examine the references for details on assumptions made by the researchers, experiment design, and results interpretation.

The fault tolerance of a system employing data diversity depends upon the ability of the DRA to produce data points that lie outside of a failure region, given an initial data point that lies within a failure region. The program executes correctly on re-expressed data points only if they lie outside a failure region. If the failure region has a small cross section in some dimensions, then re-expression should have a high probability of translating the data point out of the failure region.

Pullum [7] provides a formulation for determination of the probabilities that each TPA solution has of producing a correct adjudged result. Expected execution times and additional performance details are provided by the author in [7].

5.4   Summary

This chapter presented the two original data diverse techniques, NCP and RtB, and a spin-off, TPA. The data diverse techniques are offered as a complement to the battery of design diverse techniques and are not meant to replace them. RtB are similar in structure to the RcB, as NCP is similar to NVP. The primary difference in operation is the attribute diversified. The TPA technique uses both data and design diversity to avoid and handle MCR. For each technique, its operation, an example, and issues were presented. Pointers to the original source and to extended examinations of the techniques were provided for the reader's additional study, if desired.

The following chapter examines several "other" techniques—those not easily categorized as design or data diverse and those different enough to warrant belonging to this separate grouping. These techniques are discussed in much the same manner as were those in this chapter and the techniques in Chapter 4.

References

[1] Ammann, P. E., "Data Diversity: An Approach to Software Fault Tolerance," *Proceedings of FTCS-17*, Pittsburgh, PA, 1987, pp. 122–126.

[2] Ammann, P. E., "Data Diversity: An Approach to Software Fault Tolerance," Ph.D. dissertation, University of Virginia, 1988.

[3] Ammann, P. E., and J. C. Knight, "Data Diversity: An Approach to Software Fault Tolerance," *IEEE Transactions on Computers*, Vol. 37, No. 4, 1988, pp. 418–425.

[4] Gray, J., *Why Do Computers Stop and What Can Be Done About It?* Tandem, Technical Report 85.7, 1985.

[5] Martin, D. J., "Dissimilar Software in High Integrity Applications in Flight Control," *Software for Avionics, AGARD Conference Proceedings*, 1982, pp. 36-1–36-13.

[6] Morris, M. A., "An Approach to the Design of Fault Tolerant Software," M.Sc. thesis, Cranfield Institute of Technology, 1981.

[7] Pullum, L. L., "Fault Tolerant Software Decision-Making Under the Occurrence of Multiple Correct Results," Doctoral dissertation, Southeastern Institute of Technology, 1992.

[8] Pullum, L. L., "A New Adjudicator for Fault Tolerant Software Applications Correctly Resulting in Multiple Solutions," Quality Research Associates, Technical Report QRA-TR-92-01, 1992.

[9] Pullum, L. L., "A New Adjudicator for Fault Tolerant Software Applications Correctly Resulting in Multiple Solutions," *Proceedings: 12th Digital Avionics Systems Conference*, Fort Worth, TX, 1993.

[10] Ammann, P. E., D. L. Lukes, and J. C. Knight, *Applying Data Diversity to Differential Equation Solvers." in "Software Fault Tolerance Using Data Diversity*, University of Virginia Technical Report, Report No. UVA/528344/CS92/101, for NASA Langley Research Center, Grant No. NAG-1-1123, 1991.

[11]   Ammann, P. E., and J. C. Knight, *Data Re-expression Techniques for Fault Tolerant Systems*, Technical Report, Report No. TR90-32, Department of Computer Science, University of Virginia, 1990.

[12]   Ammann, P. E., "Data Redundancy for the Detection and Tolerance of Software Faults," *Proceedings: Interface '90*, East Lansing, MI, 1990.

[13]   Anderson, T., and P. A. Lee, "Software Fault Tolerance," in *Fault Tolerance: Principles and Practice*, Englewood Cliffs, NJ: Prentice-Hall, 1981, pp. 249–291.

[14]   Randell, B., "Fault Tolerance and System Structuring," *Proceedings 4th Jerusalem Conference on Information Technology*, Jerusalem, 1984, pp. 182–191.

[15]   Neumann, P. G., "On Hierarchical Design of Computer Systems for Critical Applications," *IEEE Transactions on Software Engineering*, Vol. 12, No. 9, 1986, pp. 905–920.

[16]   McAllister, D. F., and M. A. Vouk, "Fault-Tolerant Software Reliability Engineering," in M. R. Lyu (ed.), *Handbook of Software Reliability Engineering*, New York: IEEE Computer Society Press, 1996, pp. 567–614.

[17]   Duncan, R. V., Jr., and L. L. Pullum, "Object-Oriented Executives and Components for Fault Tolerance," *IEEE Aerospace Conference*, Big Sky, MT, 2001.

6

Other Software Fault Tolerance Techniques

New techniques are often proposed to overcome the limitations associated with previous techniques, to provide fault tolerance for specific problem domains, or to apply new technologies to the needs of software fault tolerance, while attempting to maintain the strengths of the foundational techniques. This chapter covers some of these "other" software fault tolerance techniques, those that do not necessarily fit nicely into either the design or data diverse categories—variants of the N-version programming (NVP) technique, resourceful systems, the data-driven dependability assurance scheme, self-configuring optimal programming (SCOP), and other software fault tolerance techniques.

6.1 N-Version Programming Variants

Numerous variations on the basic NVP technique have been proposed. These NVP variants range from simple use of a decision mechanism (DM) other than the basic majority voter (see Section 7.1 for some alternatives) to combinations with other techniques (see, for example, the consensus recovery block (CRB) and acceptance voting (AV) techniques described in Sections 4.5 and 4.6, respectively) to those that appear to be an entirely new technique (for example, the two-pass adjudicators (TPA), Section 5.3). As stated above, many of these techniques arise from a real or perceived deficiency in the original technique.

In this section, we will examine one such NVP variant, the NVP-TB-AT (*N*-version programming with a tie-breaker and an acceptance test (AT)) technique, developed by Ann Tai and colleagues [1–3]. The technique was developed to illustrate performability modeling and making design modifications to enhance performability. Tai defines performability as a unification of performance and dependability, that is, a system's ability to perform (serve its users) in the presence of fault-caused errors and failures [1]. See Section 4.7.1 for an overview of the performability investigation for the NVP and recovery block (RcB) techniques. (Also see [1–3] for a more detailed discussion.)

The NVP-TB-AT technique was developed by combining the performability advantages of two modified NVP techniques, the NVP-TB (NVP with a tie-breaker) and NVP-AT (NVP with an AT). Hence, NVP-TB-AT incorporates both a tie-breaker and an AT. When the probability of related faults is low, the efficient synchronization provided by the tie-breaker mechanism compensates for the performance reduction caused by the AT. The AT is applied only when the second DM reaches a consensus decision. When the probability of related faults is high, the additional error detection provided by the AT reduces the likelihood (due to the high execution rate of NVP-TB) of an undetected error [3].

NVP-TB-AT is a design diverse, forward recovery (see Section 1.4.2) technique. The technique uses multiple variants of a program, which run concurrently on different computers. The results of the first two variants to finish their execution are gathered and compared. If the results match, they are output as the correct result. If the results do not match, the technique waits for the third variant to finish. When it does, a majority voter-type DM is used on all three results. If a majority is found, the matching result must pass the AT before being output as the correct result.

NVP-TB-AT operation is described in Section 6.1.1 An example is provided in Section 6.1.2. The technique's performance was discussed in Section 4.7.1.

6.1.1 *N*-Version Programming with Tie-Breaker and Acceptance Test Operation

The NVP-TB-AT technique consists of an executive, *n* variants (three variants are used in this discussion) of the program or function, and several DMs: a comparator, a majority voter, and an AT. The executive orchestrates the NVP-TB-AT technique operation, which has the general syntax:

```
run Variant 1, Variant 2, Variant 3
if (Comparator (Fastest Result 1,
            Fastest Result 2))
    return Result
else Wait (Last Result)
    if (Voter (Fastest Result 1,
            Fastest Result 2,
            Last Result))
        if (Acceptance Test (Result))
            return Result
else error
```

The NVP-TB-AT syntax above states that the technique executes the three variants concurrently. The results of the two fastest running of these executions are provided to the comparator, which compares the results to determine if they are equal. If they are, then the result is returned as the presumed correct result. If they are not equal, then the technique waits for the slowest variant to produce a result. Given results from all variants, the majority voter DM determines if a majority of the results are equal. If a majority is found, then that result is tested by an AT. If the result is acceptable, it is output as the presumed correct result. Otherwise, an error exception is raised. Figure 6.1 illustrates the structure and operation of the NVP-TB-AT technique.

Both fault-free and failure scenarios for NVP-TB-AT are described below. The following abbreviations are used:

AT	Acceptance test;
V_i	Variant i;
n	The number of versions ($n = 3$);
NVP-TB-AT	*N*-version programming with tie-breaker and acceptance test;
R_i	Result occurring in the ith order; that is, R_1 is the fastest, R_3 is the slowest;
R	Result of NVP-TB-AT.

6.1.1.1 Failure-Free Operation

This scenario describes the operation of NVP-TB-AT when no failure or exception occurs.

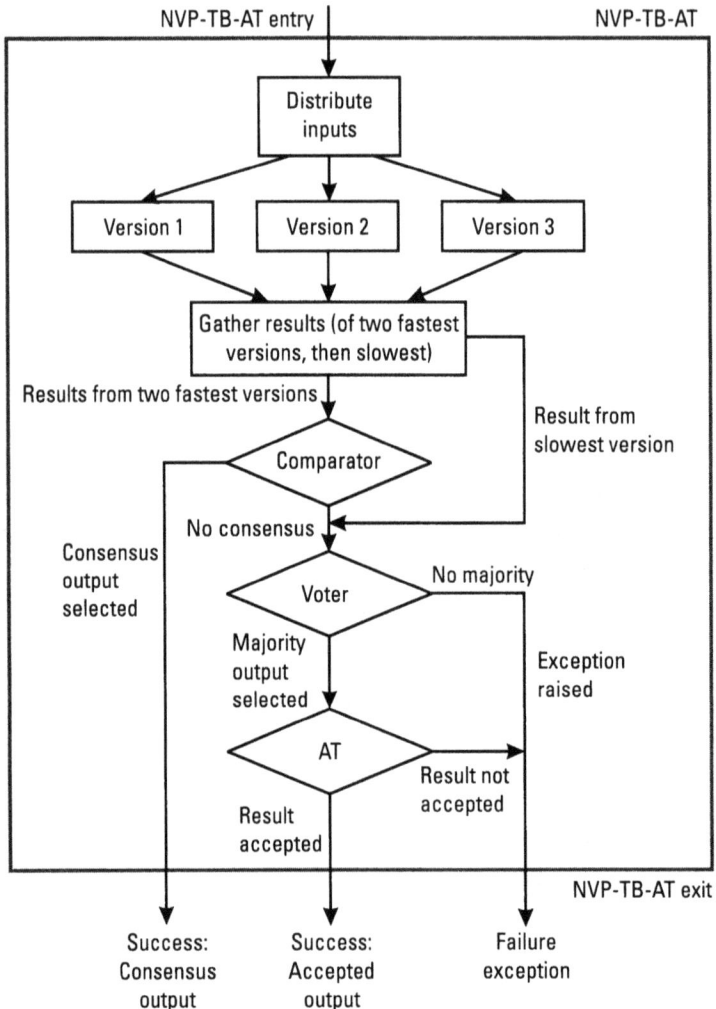

Figure 6.1 *N*-version programming with tie-breaker and acceptance test structure and operation.

- Upon entry to the NVP-TB-AT, the executive performs the following: formats calls to the three variants and through those calls distributes the input(s) to the variants.

- Each variant, V_i, executes. No failures occur during their execution.

- The results of the two fastest variant executions (R_1 and R_2) are gathered by the executive and submitted to the comparator.

- $R_1 = R_2$, so the comparator sets $R = R_1 = R_2$, as the correct result.

- Control returns to the executive.

- The executive passes the correct result outside the NVP-TB-AT, and the NVP-TB-AT module is exited.

6.1.1.2 Partial Failure Scenario—Results Fail Comparator, Pass Voter, Pass Acceptance Test

This scenario describes the operation of NVP-TB-AT when the comparator cannot determine a correct result, but the result from the slowest variant forms a majority with one of the other results and that majority result passes the AT. Differences between this scenario and the failure-free scenario are in gray type.

- Upon entry to the NVP-TB-AT, the executive performs the following: formats calls to the three variants and through those calls distributes the input(s) to the variants.

- Each variant, V_i, executes. No failures occur during their execution.

- The results of the two fastest variant executions (R_1 and R_2) are gathered by the executive and submitted to the comparator.

- $R_1 \neq R_2$, so the comparator cannot determine a correct result.

- Control returns to the executive, which waits for the result from the slowest executing variant.

- The slowest executing variant completes execution.

- The result from the slowest variant, R_3, is gathered by the executive, and along with R_1 and R_2, is submitted to the majority voter.

- $R_3 = R_2$, so the majority voter sets $R = R_2 = R_3$ as the correct result.

- Control returns to the executive.

- The executive submits the majority result, R, to the AT.

- The AT determines that R is an acceptable result.

- Control returns to the executive.

- The executive passes the correct result outside the NVP-TB-AT, and the NVP-TB-AT module is exited.

6.1.1.3 Failure Scenario—Results Fail Comparator, Pass Voter, Fail Acceptance Test

This scenario describes the operation of NVP-TB-AT when the comparator cannot determine a correct result, but the result from the slowest variant forms a majority with one of the other results; however that majority result does not pass the AT. Differences between this scenario and the failure-free scenario are in gray type.

- Upon entry to the NVP-TB-AT, the executive performs the following: formats calls to the three variants and through those calls distributes the input(s) to the variants.

- Each variant, V_i, executes. No failures occur during their execution.

- The results of the two fastest variant executions (R_1 and R_2) are gathered by the executive and submitted to the comparator.

- $R_1 \neq R_2$, so the comparator cannot determine a correct result.

- Control returns to the executive, which waits for the result from the slowest executing variant.

- The slowest executing variant completes execution.

- The result from the slowest variant, R_3, is gathered by the executive, and along with R_1 and R_2, is submitted to the majority voter.

- $R_3 = R_2$, so the majority voter sets $R = R_2 = R_3$ as the correct result.

- Control returns to the executive.

- The executive submits the majority result, R, to the AT.

- R fails the AT.

- Control returns to the executive.

- The executive raises an exception and the NVP-TB-AT module is exited.

6.1.1.4 Failure Scenario—Results Fail Comparator, Fail Voter

This scenario describes the operation of NVP-TB-AT when the comparator cannot determine a correct result and the result from the slowest variant does not form a majority with one of the other results. Differences between this scenario and the failure-free scenario are in gray type.

- Upon entry to the NVP-TB-AT, the executive performs the following: formats calls to the three variants and through those calls distributes the input(s) to the variants.

- Each variant, V_i, executes. No failures occur during their execution.

- The results of the two fastest variant executions (R_1 and R_2) are gathered by the executive and submitted to the comparator.

- $R_1 \neq R_2$, so the comparator cannot determine a correct result.

- Control returns to the executive, which waits for the result from the slowest executing variant.

- The slowest executing variant completes execution.

- The result from the slowest variant, R_3, is gathered by the executive, and along with R_1 and R_2, is submitted to the majority voter.

- $R_1 \neq R_2 \neq R_3$, so the majority voter cannot determine a correct result.

- Control returns to the executive.

- The executive raises an exception and the NVP-TB-AT module is exited.

An additional scenario will be mentioned, but not examined in detail, as done above. That is, it is also possible that one of the variants fails to produce any result because of an endless loop (or possible hardware malfunction). This "failure to produce a result" event is handled by NVP-TB-AT with a time-out and the return of a null result.

6.1.1.5 Architecture

We mentioned in Sections 1.3.1.2 and 2.5 that structuring is required if we are to handle system complexity, especially when fault tolerance is involved [4–6]. This includes defining the organization of software modules onto the hardware elements on which they run. NVP-TB-AT is a multiprocessor technique with software components residing on $n = 3$ hardware units and the executive residing on one of the processors. Communications between the software components is done through remote function calls or method invocations.

6.1.2 *N*-Version Programming with Tie-Breaker and Acceptance Test Example

This section provides an example implementation of the NVP-TB-AT technique. Recall the sort algorithm used in the RcB and NVP examples (see

Sections 4.1.2 and 4.2.2, and Figure 4.2). The original sort implementation produces incorrect results if one or more of the inputs are negative. The following describes how NVP-TB-AT can be used to protect the system against faults arising from this error.

Figure 6.2 illustrates an NVP-TB-AT implementation of fault tolerance for this example. Note the additional components needed for NVP-TB-AT implementation: an executive that handles orchestrating and synchronizing the technique, two additional variants (versions) of the algorithm/program, a comparator, a voter, and an AT. The versions are different variants providing an incremental sort. For variants 1 and 2, a bubble sort and quicksort are used, respectively. Variant 3 is the original incremental sort.

Now, let's step through the example.

- Upon entry to NVP-TB-AT, the executive performs the following: formats calls to the $n = 3$ variants and through those calls distributes the inputs to the variants. The input set is (8, 7, 13, −4, 17, 44). The executive also sums the items in the input set for use in the AT. *Sum of input* = 85.
- Each variant, V_i ($i = 1, 2, 3$), executes.
- The results of the two fastest variant executions (R_{ij}, $i = 2, 3$; $j = 1$, ..., k) are gathered by the executive and submitted to the comparator.
- The comparator examines the results as follows (shading indicates matching results):

j	R_{2j}	R_{3j}	Result
1	−4	−4	−4
2	7	−7	Ø
3	8	−8	Ø
4	13	−13	Ø
5	17	−17	Ø
6	44	−44	Ø

The results do not match.

- The executive now waits for the result of the slowest variant to complete execution.

(8, 7, 13, −4, 17, 44)

Sum of inputs = 85,
distribute inputs

Variant 1:
Bubble sort

Variant 2:
Quicksort

Variant 3:
Original
incremental sort

(−4, 7, 8, 13, 17, 44)

(−4, 7, 8, 13, 17, 44)

(−4, −7, −8, −13, −17, −44)

Comparator:
Result = no
match

R_{2j}: −4 7 8 13 17 44
R_{3j}: −4 −7 −8 −13 −17 −44

Majority
voter: Result =
R_{1j} and R_{2j} match

R_{1j}: −4 7 8 13 17 44
R_{2j}: −4 7 8 13 17 44
R_{3j}: −4 −7 −8 −13 −17 −44

$R = (−4, 7, 8, 13, 17, 44)$

AT: Sum of inputs = 85
= sum of outputs

Output: (−4, 7, 8, 13, 17, 44)

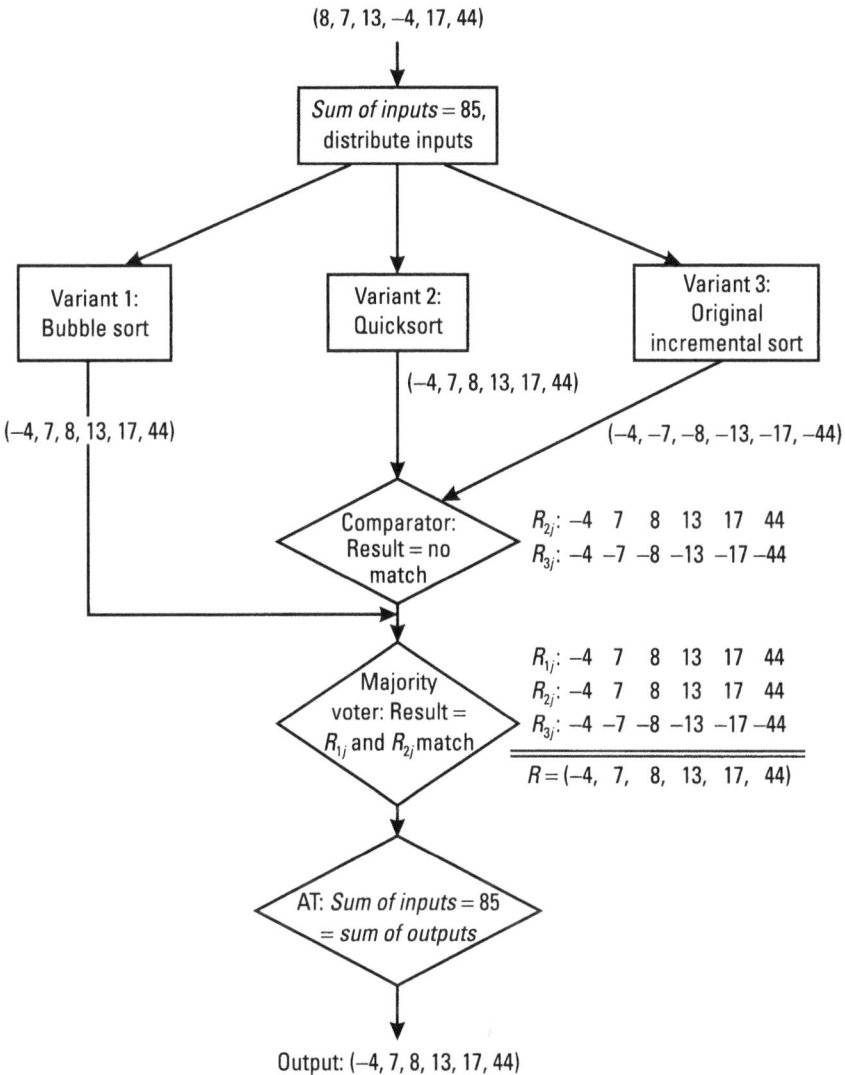

Figure 6.2 Example of *N*-version programming with tie-breaker and acceptance test implementation.

- The slowest variant, V_1, completes execution.

- The result from the slowest variant, R_1, is gathered by the executive and, along with R_2 and R_3, is submitted to the majority voter.

- The majority voter examines the results as follows (shading indicates matching results):

j	R_{1j}	R_{2j}	R_{3j}	Result
1	−4	−4	−4	−4
2	7	7	−7	7
3	8	8	−8	8
4	13	13	−13	13
5	17	17	−17	17
6	44	44	−44	44

R_1 and R_2 match, so the majority result is (−4, 7, 8, 13, 17, 44).

- Control returns to the executive.
- The executive submits the majority result to the AT.
- The AT sums the items in the output set. *Sum of output* = 85. The AT tests if the *sum of input* equals the *sum of output*. 85 = 85, so the majority result passes the AT.
- Control returns to the executive.
- The executive passes the presumed correct result, (−4, 7, 8, 13, 17, 44), outside the NVP-TB-AT, and the NVP-TB-AT module is exited.

6.2 Resourceful Systems

Resourceful systems were proposed by Abbott [7, 8] as an approach to software fault tolerance. It is an artificial intelligence approach, sometimes called functional diversity, that exploits diversity in the functional space available in some applications. The resourceful systems approach is based on self-protective and self-checking components, and is derived from an approach to fault tolerance in which system goals are made explicit. It was evolved from the efforts of Taylor and Black [9] and Bastani and Yen [10], and work in planning and robotics. Taylor and Black's aim in [9] was to make goals explicit for the sake of protecting the system from disaster, rather than for reliability. Bastani and Yen's work [10] focused on decentralized control, rather than on system goals. Resourceful systems marry these ideas and a planning component, yielding an extended RcB framework.

The resourceful system approach requires that system goals be made explicit and that the system have the ability to achieve its goals in multiple ways. A resourceful system, like a system using RcB, has the ability to determine whether it has achieved a goal (the goal must be testable) and, if it has failed, to develop and carry out alternative plans for achieving the goal [8]. In an RcB, the alternatives are available prior to execution; however, in the resourceful system the new ways to reach the goal may be generated during execution. Hence, resourceful systems may generate new code dynamically. (Obviously, dynamic code generation raises additional questions as to whether the autogenerated code is safe (in the systems context) and whether the code generator itself is dependable. These issues require additional investigation.) The resourceful system approach is based on the premise that, although the system may fail to achieve the final goal in its primary or initial way, the system may be able to achieve the goal in another way by modifying plans and operations (see Figure 6.3). Associated with the goal may be constraints such as "within x time units" or "within k iterations."

Systems using RcB may be viewed as a limited form of resourcefulness, and resourceful systems may be viewed as a generalization of the RcB approach [8].

Abbott, in [8], provides the following properties a resourceful system must possess.

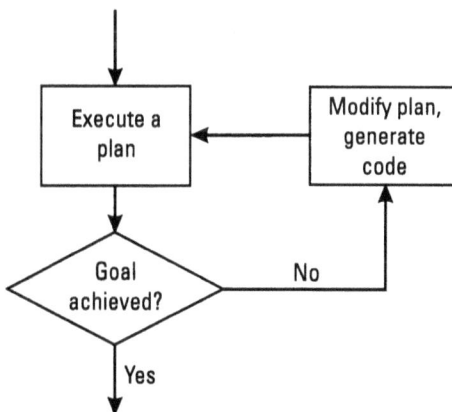

Figure 6.3 General concept of a resourceful system.

- *Functional richness:* The required redundancy is in the end results; it is only necessary that it be possible to achieve the same end results in a number of different ways. Functional richness is a property of a system in the context of the environment in which it is functioning, not of the system in isolation.

- *Explicitly testable goals:* The system must be able to determine whether or not it has achieved its goals. This is similar to the need for ATs in an RcB technique.

- *An ability to develop and carry out plans for achieving its goals:* The system must be able to reason about its goals well enough to make use of its functional richness. The required reasoning ability must complement the system's functionality. The system must be able to decompose its goals into subgoals in ways that correspond to the ways it has of achieving those goals.

What is desired for a resourceful system is a broad set of basic functions along with the ability to combine those functions into programs or plans. In other words, one wants a system organized into levels of abstraction, where each level provides the functional richness needed by the potential programs on the next higher level of abstraction. The system itself does the programming, that is, the planning and reacting, to deal with contingencies as they arise [8].

Abbott contends that resourceful systems would be affordable because functional richness grows out of a levels-of-abstraction object-oriented (OO) approach to system design [8]. He adds that OO designs do not appear to impose a significant cost penalty and may result in less expensive systems in the long run.

Artificial intelligence techniques are used by the system to reason about its goals, to devise methods of accomplishing the task, and to develop and carry out plans for achieving its goals. The resourceful system approach tends to change the way one views the relationships among a system, its environment, and the goals the system is intended to achieve. These altered views are presented by Abbott [8] as follows.

- The boundary between the system and the environment is less distinct.

- The system's goals become that of guiding the system and environment as an ensemble to assume a desired state, rather than to perform a function in, on, or to the environment.

- System component failures are seen more as additional obstacles to be overcome than as losses in functionality.

The following are important features for any language used for programs that control the operation of resourceful systems [8], but not necessarily the language in which the system itself is implemented.

- Components;

- Ability to express the information to be checked;

- Error reporting mechanism;

- Planning capability;

- Ability to generate and execute new code dynamically.

Abbott asserts (in [8]) that the technology needed for providing a dynamic debugging (i.e., automatic detection and correction of bugs) capability is essentially the same as that of program verification and that in 1990 the technology was not suitable for general application. This is still the case today. It is also asserted [8] that logic programming (e.g., using the Prolog language) offers the best available language resources for developing fault-tolerant software. The application areas in which resourcefulness has been most fully developed are robotics and game playing systems. Intelligent agent technology may hold promise for implementing resourceful systems [11]. The resourceful system approach to software fault tolerance still suffers the same problems as all new approaches, that is, lack of testing, experimental evaluation, implementation, and independent analysis.

6.3 Data-Driven Dependability Assurance Scheme

The data-driven dependability assurance scheme was developed by Parhami [12, 13]. This approach is based on attaching dependability tags (d-tag) to data objects and updating the d-tags as computation progresses. A *d-tag* is an indicator of the probability of correctness of a data object. For software fault tolerance use, the d-tag value for a particular data object can be used to determine the acceptability of that data object or can be used in more complex decision-making functions.

Let a data object, D, and its d-tag comprise the composite object, $\langle D, d \rangle$. The d-tag, d, assumes values from a finite set of dependability indicators, $d \in \{0, 1, ..., \delta - 1\}$, where δ is an application-dependent constant. Each d-tag value, d, has the constants, π_δ and π'_δ, associated with it such that the probability that the data object, D, is correct is bounded by these constants:

$$\pi_\delta \leq \text{prob}[D \text{ is correct}] \leq \pi'_\delta$$

The d-tag values are arranged so that a larger d-tag value implies higher confidence in the correctness of the associated data object. The d-tag values are obtained from knowledge of the data and the application. We let the upper bound, $\pi'_j = \pi_{\delta-1} = 1$, that is, a perfect value, and the lower bound, π_0 be 0, a hopelessly incorrect value.

The π_j values are not required to conform to any particular rule or pattern. In practice, though, it is desirable to have a capability for greater discrimination at the high end of dependability values [12]. The reasoning for this is that correctness probabilities 0.99 and 0.999 are significantly different, while the values 0.4 and 0.5 are not, because they both represent practically useless data values. The following example illustrates 8-valued d-tags ($\delta = 8$) [12]:

j:	0	1	2	3	4	5	6	7
π_j:	0	0.75	0.883	0.9612	0.9894	0.9973	0.9999	1

The d-tags can be associated with data objects at any level; however, practical considerations (e.g., data storage redundancy, and computational overhead) will likely restrict their use to high-level data objects with complex structures and operations.

The d-tags are manipulated, as the computation progresses, to indicate the dependability of the data object. Normal operations on data objects (such as multiplication, division, addition, subtraction, etc.) tend to lower the value of the d-tag. If it can be reasonably assumed that the operations themselves are perfectly dependable, then the dependability of each result of an operation is a function of the operands' dependabilities. With a unary operator then, the dependability of the result would be the same as that of the single operand. Parhami [13] extends this to the development of a dependability evaluation function for binary operators, such that the dependability of the result is never more than the smallest d-tag value involved in the operation.

If the final computation results have acceptable d-tag values, then nothing further is required. However, if the resultant d-tags are below a required minimum (e.g., using a bounds AT), then something must be done to increase the dependability of the data object. These dependability-raising operations are involved only as needed during or at the end of computation.

Results that are obtained in more than one way (e.g., using hardware, software, or temporal redundancy) increase the value of the d-tag. That is, they increase the probability of correctness of the data object. Parhami [13] provides detailed derivation of the correctness probability of a data object D obtained in two different ways. In general, it can be concluded from the derivation that dependability improvement is likely as a result of matching values of D as long as the associated d-tag values are sufficiently high [13].

The results are extended and generalized to n variant results. If all the results are different, then the data object with the highest d-tag value can be selected as the final result. This is illustrated in the top third of Figure 6.4. If all of the data object values are the same, then the output is set to one of them with a d-tag value functionally comprised of all the variant results' d-tag values (see middle portion of Figure 6.4). In the other case, if the data objects can be partitioned into classes of identical objects, then a result can be determined as follows. For each class of identical objects, a d-tag value is computed. The class with the largest computed d-tag determines the resultant output data value. This case is illustrated in the bottom section of Figure 6.4.

The last case, in which some (but not a majority of) data objects are identical, is perhaps best explained by an example. Suppose we have seven variants (v_i, $i = 1, 2, \ldots, 7$), and these variants produce the data objects and associated d-tags shown in Table 6.1.

There is no majority of identical data objects. However, there are classes (subsets) of identical objects. The members of these classes are:

Class 1: $\langle D_1, d_1 \rangle, \langle D_6, d_6 \rangle$;

Class 2: $(D_2, d_2), \langle D_4, d_4 \rangle, \langle D_5, d_5 \rangle$;

Class 3: $\langle D_3, d_3 \rangle$;

Class 4: $\langle D_4, d_4 \rangle$.

To determine which result to use, class 1's data object value 10.7, class 2's 11.1, class 3's 42.9, or class 4's -3.6, a d-tag value must be determined for

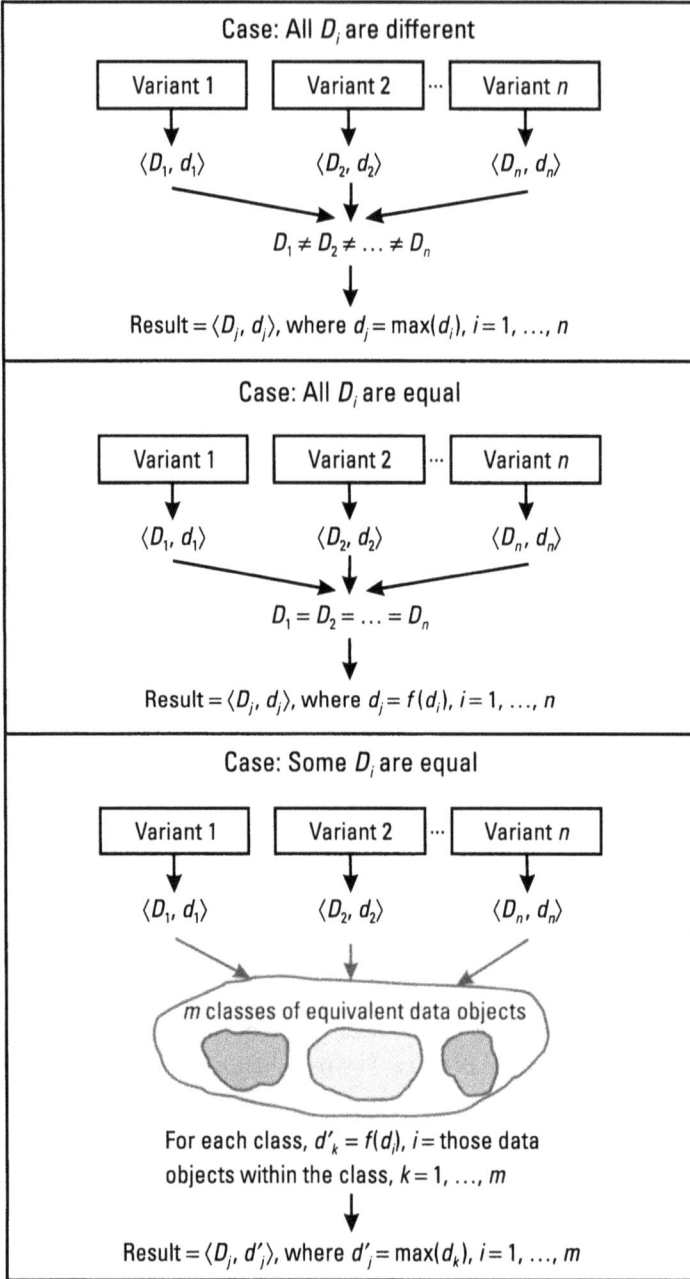

Figure 6.4 Using d-tags with *n* variants to determine result.

Table 6.1

Example Data Object and d-tag Values

Variant, i	Data Object, D_i	d-tag, d_i
1	10.7	0.9886
2	11.1	0.9984
3	42.9	0.2111
4	11.1	0.9946
5	11.1	0.9986
6	10.7	0.9940
7	−3.6	0.1234

each class. Suppose the class d-tag values are simply the average of the d-tag values associated with the data objects in each class. The class d-tag values are provided below.

Class 1's d-tag value: $d'_1 = \text{avg}(0.9886, 0.9940) = 0.9913$

Class 2's d-tag value: $d'_2 = \text{avg}(0.9984, 0.9946, 0.9986) = 0.9972$

Class 3's d-tag value: $d'_3 = \text{avg}(0.2111) = 0.2111$

Class 4's d-tag value: $d'_4 = \text{avg}(0.1234) = 0.1234$

The result, in this example, will be the data object value of the class with the maximum associated d-tag value.

$$\max(d'_i) = d'_2, \ i = 1, 2, \ldots, 7$$

So, the data object value associated with class 2, 11.1, is output as the presumed correct result.

There are several issues related to d-tags.

- *d-tag values:* Determining the number and values of d-tags to use is nontrivial. The number of d-tag intervals affects the storage and processing overheads. The optimal number will be application dependent. To effectively perform the trade-off analyses to determine these numbers, the concept of d-tags and their associated direct and indirect costs must be formalized and further refined [13].

- *Erroneous d-tags:* The d-tags themselves may be incorrect and, hence, lower or higher than the correct value. If the d-tag is lower than correct, then this error is "safe" because it can lead to the following events [13]:

  - A correct result will have an erroneously low, but acceptable, d-tag value and will be trusted and used;

  - A correct result will have an unacceptably low d-tag value and will be either discarded or used cautiously;

  - Or, an incorrect result will have a correct d-tag and will be either discarded or used with appropriate care.

  Hence, it is sufficient to guard against erroneously high d-tag values. These positive d-tag errors have three causes:

  - Incorrect storage and/or transmission of d-tag values;

  - Error(s) during dependability-lowering operations;

  - Error(s) during dependability-raising operations.

  Several means of combating these causes, including use of error codes, exploiting asymmetry in the application, arithmetic error codes, table look-up error codes, and self-checking circuits, are provided by Parhami [13].

- *Imperfect operations:* Operators (e.g., +, −, /, *) may be erroneous, comparison and voting operations may be erroneous, and operators may incorrectly operate on composite data objects.

Earlier in this section, we showed how to use d-tags with n variants (design diversity) to determine the correct result. It is also possible to use d-tags with data diverse techniques to determine the correct result. For example, they can be added to the operation of the RtB technique and used in voting on the result if the original computation and computation with re-expressed inputs fail to pass the AT. In addition, d-tags can be added, along with ATs and stepwise comparison, to the N-copy programming (NCP) technique. Furthermore, d-tags can also be used with combined design and data diverse techniques to aid in decision making and selective use of redundancy (see [13] for details).

6.4 Self-Configuring Optimal Programming

SCOP, developed by Bondavalli, Di Giandomenico, and Xu [14–17], is a scheme for handling dependability and efficiency. SCOP attempts to reduce the cost of fault-tolerant software in terms of space and time redundancy by providing a flexible redundancy architecture. Within this architecture, dependability and efficiency can be dynamically adjusted at run time.

The SCOP technique uses n software variants, a DM (Section 7.1), a controller or executive, and forward recovery (Section 1.4.2) to accomplish fault tolerance. The main characteristics of SCOP are dynamic use of redundancy, growing syndrome space (collection of information to support result selection), flexibility and efficiency, and generality. These characteristics will be described in the SCOP operation discussion.

SCOP operation is described in Section 6.4.1, with an example provided in Section 6.4.2. Some issues and SCOP evaluation are presented in Section 6.4.3.

6.4.1 Self-Configuring Optimal Programming Operation

The SCOP technique consists of an executive or controller, n variants of the program or function, and a DM. The controller orchestrates the SCOP technique operation, which follows the algorithm below.

```
Index_of_Current_Phase = 0
Current_State = non_end_state
Syndrome = empty
Delivery_Condition = one of {Possible_Delivery_Conditions}
Max_Number_Phases = f[Time_Constraints]
while ((Current_State ≠ non_end_state) AND
      (Index_of_Current_Phase < Max_Number_Phases))
      begin
      Index_of_Current_Phase = Index_of_Current_Phase + 1
      construct Currently_Active_Set_of_Variants
      execute (Currently_Active_Set_of_Variants,
            New_Syndrome)
      adjudicate (Currently_Active_Set_of_Variants,
            All_Syndromes, New_State, Result)
      Current_State = New_State
      end
if (Current_State = end_state)
      then deliver(Result)
      else signal(failure)
```

The SCOP control algorithm [17] above states that first some initializations take place: the current phase number is set to 0, the current state is set to a non-end state (which is also a nonfailure state), and the information syndrome is cleared. In the SCOP technique, an information syndrome contains the variant results and an indication of each result's correctness. The delivery condition is set next. SCOP provides different levels of dependability based on the selected delivery condition. Different delivery conditions usually have different fault coverages and can be chosen, statically or dynamically, based on the application criticality or system degradation, for example. The maximum number of phases is determined next. Its value is based on time constraints and the expected time per phase.

The first phase is initiated. Additional phases will be performed as long as the maximum number of phases is not exceeded and the current state of the system is not an end state. Upon starting the phase, the phase counter is incremented. The initial currently active set (CAS) of variants, V_1, is constructed according to the selected delivery condition and the given application environment. In subsequent phases, the CAS set V_i ($i > 1$) is constructed based on the syndrome S_{i-1} collected in the $(i-1)$th phase and the information on phases [17]. The variants in V_i are selected from the variants that have not been used in any of the previous phases; that is, V_i is a subset of $V - (V_1 \cup V_2 \cup \ldots \cup V_{i-1})$. If the ith phase is the last, V_i would contain all the remaining spare variants [17].

The execute procedure manages the execution of the CAS variants and generates the syndrome S_i (where S_0 is an empty set and S_{i-1} is a subset of S_i). The adjudication function is based on the selected delivery condition. The adjudicator receives the syndrome S_i, then, based on its result, sets the new state and selects the result if one exists. When the current state is the end state, the selected result is delivered or a failure notification is signaled.

Figure 6.5 (based on information in [17]) illustrates the structure and operation of the SCOP technique in a multiprocessor environment. In the description of the figure and the operation of SCOP below, the following variables are used:

C	Delivery condition;
CAS	Currently active set (of variants);
i	Phase number;
N_p	Maximum number of software variants that can be executed in parallel on hardware resources currently allocated to the given application;

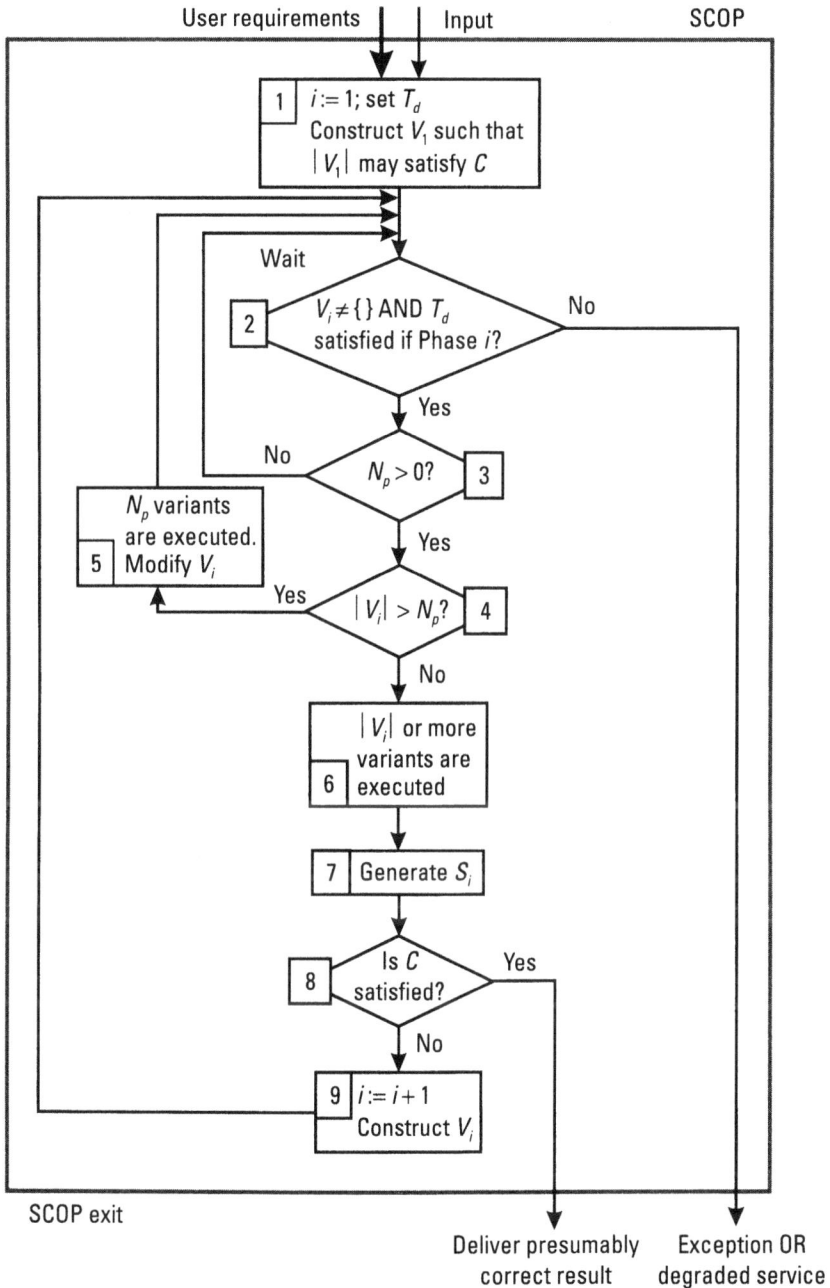

Figure 6.5 Self-configuring optimal programming structure and operation. (*After:* [17], © 1995 Springer-Verlag, Figure 2, p. 161.)

S_i Syndrome i;

T_d Time deadline that indicates the maximum response delay
               permitted for the application;

V_i Variant i.

The steps below (*source:* [17], p. 162, with permission) describe the dynamic behavior of SCOP in a multiprocessor environment. Note that the step number corresponds to a number in Figure 6.5.

1. For a given application, SCOP first establishes the delivery condition C (or several delivery conditions that permit different levels of dependability), according to the user's requirements, and then configures the CAS set, V_1, from V, that includes the minimum number of variants needed to be executed to generate a result satisfying the condition C in the absence of faults. The timing constraint, T_d, is also determined based on the response requirement.

2. Check whether the time deadline T_d will be missed when the ith phase is initiated for the execution of V_i ($i = 1, 2, 3, ...$) and whether V_i is an empty set. If T_d allows for no new phase or $V_i = \{\}$, an exception will be raised to signal to the user that a timely result satisfying the required condition C cannot be provided. In this case, a degraded service may be considered.

3. Check whether $N_p > 0$. $N_p = 0$ means that no variant can be executed at this moment due to the limitation of available resources in the system. Wait and go back to step 2 to check T_d.

4. Check whether $| V_i | > N_p$. If $| V_i | > N_p$, only some of the variants in V_i can be carried out within the current phase and thus additional time is needed for the execution of V_i.

5. N_p software variants in V_i are executed and V_i is modified so that V_i excludes the variants that have been executed. Back to step 2.

6. Since $| V_i | \le N_p$, $| V_i |$ variants are executed and completed within the current phase. If the scheduler used by the supporting system allocates $N_p > | V_i |$ processors to SCOP during the ith phase, it is possible to consider the execution of N_p variants (more than $| V_i |$). This avoids wasting the resources that would be left idle otherwise, and requires the ability to select the additional variants among those not yet used.

7. Syndrome S_i is generated based on all the information collected up to this point.

8. Check whether a result exists that satisfies the delivery condition C. If so, deliver the result to the user; otherwise step 9.

9. Set $i = i + 1$ and construct a new CAS set, V_i, from the spare variants according to the information about the syndrome, the deadline, and the resources available. If no sufficient spare variants are available, set V_i empty.

Since the SCOP control algorithm and adjudicator operation can be complex, their complexity can cause design errors. A design methodology for SCOP has been developed to avoid such problems. It is described in detail in [17]. Here, we simply note the SCOP component design parameters to take into consideration [17]: the number N of available variants, an estimate of reliability of each variant, and an estimate of the execution time of each variant; a timing constraint that the SCOP instance may be given for producing timely results; and the delivery condition(s) and the degree of flexibility in delivering results.

6.4.2 Self-Configuring Optimal Programming Example

This section provides an example implementation of the SCOP technique. Recall the sort algorithm used in the RcB and NVP examples (see Sections 4.1.2 and 4.2.2 and Figure 4.2). The original sort implementation produces incorrect results if one or more of the inputs are negative. This section describes how SCOP can be used to protect the system against faults arising from this error.

The following hardware and software component information is provided for the example.

- Three processors are available; they can execute a total of up to three software variants concurrently.

- The SCOP technique controller is available.

- There are seven software variants of the incremental sort function.

- The adjudicator requires at least three results to agree and the results can be from consecutive phases having the same input (i.e., it uses cumulative syndrome information). This is the delivery condition.

The maximum time delay for this example is three phases.
   Now, let's step through the example.

- Upon entering the SCOP block, the following initializations are made. The `Index_of_Current_Phase` is set to 0. The `Current_State` is set to a non-end-state. The syndrome is set to empty. The delivery condition is set to three matching results across consecutive phases having the same input. The `Max_Number_Phases` is set to 3.

- The input set is $(8, 7, 13, -4, 17, 44)$.

- The CAS set, V_1, from V, is configured as $\{v_1, v_2, v_3\}$. Note that this is the minimum number of variants needed to be executed to generate a result satisfying the condition C in the absence of faults.

  - Increment the phase count to 1.
  - Set the timing constraint, T_d.

- Check whether the time deadline T_d will be missed when the *first* phase is initiated for the execution of V_1 (it will not be missed in Phase 1) and whether V_1 is an empty set ($V_1 \neq \{\}$).

- Check whether $N_p > 0$. $N_p = 3$ processors available, which is greater than 0, so continue.

- Check whether $|V_1| > N_p$. $|V_1| = 3$ variants $= N_p$, so continue. Three variants can run on three processors.

- The software variants v_1, v_2, v_3 are executed and V_1 is modified so that V_1 excludes the variants that have been executed. $V_1 = \{v_4, v_5, v_6, v_7\}$ now.

- Let r_i be the result from v_i. The results are

$$r_1 = (8, 7, 13, -4, 17, 44)$$
$$r_2 = (-4, 7, 8, 13, 17, 44)$$
$$r_3 = (-4, 7, 44)$$

Syndrome S_1 is generated based on all the information collected up to this point. The results are summarized below. In the syndrome column, bold indicates erroneous, disagreeing results and italics indicate correct results.

Phase	V_i	Spare Variants	Syndrome	Judgment & Result
1	$\{v_1, v_2, v_3\}$	$\{v_4, v_5, v_6, v_7\}$	r_1, r_2, r_3	Non-end state (i.e., no result, but not complete)

- The results do not satisfy the delivery condition.

- Increment the phase number to 2 and construct a new CAS set, V_2, from the spare variants. $V_2 = \{v_4, v_5\}$. Only two additional variants are needed to possibly satisfy the delivery conditions since one of the three results from the first phase may be correct.

- Check whether the time deadline T_d will be missed when the *second* phase is initiated for the execution of V_2 (it will not be missed in Phase 2) and whether V_2 is an empty set ($V_2 \neq \{\,\}$).

- Check whether $N_p > 0$. $N_p = 3$ processors available, which is greater than 0, so continue.

- Check whether $|V_2| > N_p$. $|V_2| = 2$ variants $> N_p$, so continue. Two variants can run on three processors.

- The software variants v_4 and v_5 are executed and V_2 is modified so that V_2 excludes the variants that have been executed. $V_2 = \{v_6, v_7\}$ now.

- The results are

$$r_4 = (-4, 7, 8, 13, 17, 44)$$
$$r_5 = (-4, 7, 8, 13, 17, 44)$$

Syndrome S_2 is generated. The results from both phases are summarized below.

Phase	V_i	Spare Variants	Syndrome	Judgment & Result
1	$\{v_1, v_2, v_3\}$	$\{v_4, v_5, v_6, v_7\}$	r_1, r_2, r_3	Non-end state (i.e., no result, but not complete)
2	$\{v_4, v_5\}$	$\{v_6, v_7\}$	r_1, r_2, r_3, r_4, r_5	End-state, r_2

- The results do satisfy the delivery condition. Deliver r_2 to the user as the presumably correct result.

6.4.3   Self-Configuring Optimal Programming Issues and Discussion

This section presents the advantages, disadvantages, and issues related to SCOP. As stated in Chapter 4, software fault tolerance techniques generally provide protection against errors in translating requirements and functionality into code but do not provide explicit protection against errors in specifying requirements. This is true for all of the techniques described in this book. SCOP is a design diverse (although includes the flexibility to be implemented as a data diverse), forward recovery technique, and, as such, subsumes design diversity's and forward recovery's advantages and disadvantages, too. These are discussed in Sections 2.2 and 1.4.2, respectively. While designing software fault tolerance into a system, many considerations have to be taken into account. These are discussed in Chapter 3. Issues related to several software fault tolerance techniques (such as similar errors, overhead, cost, redundancy, etc.) and the programming practices (e.g., assertions, atomic actions, idealized components) used to implement the techniques are described in Chapter 3. Issues related to implementing voters are discussed in Section 7.1.

There are some issues to note specifically for the SCOP technique. SCOP runs in a multiprocessor environment, although it could be executed sequentially in a uniprocessor environment. The overhead incurred (beyond that of running a single variant, as in non-fault-tolerant software) includes additional memory for the second through the nth variants, the controller, and DM and additional execution time for the controller, DM, and additional phases.

It is critical that the initial specification for the variants used in SCOP be free of flaws. If the specification is flawed, then the variants are likely to produce indistinguishable results. Common mode failures or undetected similar errors among a majority of the variants can cause the adjudicator to be unable to select a correct result. Related faults among the variants and the DM also have to be minimized. Multiple correct results (MCR) (see Section 3.1.1) will also degrade the performance of the SCOP technique.

Also needed for implementation and further examination of the technique is information on the underlying architecture and technique performance. These are discussed in Sections 6.4.3.1 and 6.4.3.2, respectively. Table 6.2 lists several SCOP issues, indicates whether or not they are an advantage or disadvantage (if applicable), and points to where in the book the reader may find additional information.

The indication that an issue in Table 6.2 can be a positive or negative (+/−) influence on the technique or on its effectiveness further indicates that

Table 6.2
Self-Configuring Optimal Programming Issue Summary

Issue	Advantage (+)/ Disadvantage (−)	Where Discussed
Provides protection against errors in translating requirements and functionality into code (true for software fault tolerance techniques in general)	+	Chapter 1
Does not provide explicit protection against errors in specifying requirements (true for software fault tolerance techniques in general)	−	Chapter 1
General forward recovery advantages	+	Section 1.4.2
General forward recovery disadvantages	−	Section 1.4.2
General design diversity advantages	+	Section 2.2
General design diversity disadvantages	−	Section 2.2
Similar errors or common residual design errors	−	Section 3.1.1
Coincident and correlated failures	−	Section 3.1.1
MCR and identical and wrong results	−	Section 3.1.1
Consistent comparison problem (CCP)	−	Section 3.1.2
Space and time redundancy	+	Section 3.1.4
Design considerations	+	Section 3.3.1, 6.4.1
Dependability studies	+/−	Section 4.1.3.3
Voters and discussions related to specific types of voters	+/−	Section 7.1

the issue may be a disadvantage in general but an advantage in relation to another technique. In these cases, the reader is referred to the noted section for discussion of the issue.

6.4.3.1 Architecture

We mentioned in Sections 1.3.1.2 and 2.5 that structuring is required if we are to handle system complexity, especially when fault tolerance is involved [4–6]. This includes defining the organization of software modules onto the hardware elements on which they run. SCOP is typically multiprocessor with $|V|$ variants residing on N_p hardware units, with the controller residing on one of the processors. Communication between the software components is conducted through remote function calls or method invocations.

6.4.3.2 Performance

There have been numerous investigations into the performance of software fault tolerance techniques in general (discussed in Chapters 2 and 3) and the dependability of specific techniques themselves. Table 4.2 (in Section 4.1.3.3) provides a list of references for these dependability investigations. This list, although not exhaustive, provides a good sampling of the types of analyses that have been performed and substantial background for analyzing software fault tolerance dependability. The reader is encouraged to examine the references for details on assumptions made by the researchers, experiment design, and results interpretation.

Bondavalli, et al. [15] examined the reliability and safety of SCOP in comparison with NVP, RcB, and N-self-checking programming (NSCP). In terms of dependability (derived by examining the probability of software failure and the probability of undetected failure), SCOP and NVP were shown to have similar levels of dependability for benign and catastrophic failures. Both NVP and SCOP adjudicators are significant factors in the dependability equations for these techniques. Per [15], RcB appears to be the best (dependability-wise), but the influence on the dependability of the application-dependent AT can vary significantly. Related faults affected all techniques, including the NSCP. In terms of resource consumption (and not considering timing constraints), RcB again seems to be better, with SCOP ranking more efficient than NVP and NSCP.

The SCOP technique attempts to attack the complexity problem caused by its highly dynamic behavior by introducing a design methodology. This methodology simplifies the on-line process by making the off-line design process more complex but systematic and thorough. With the SCOP control framework, multivariant software (design diversity), diversity in the data space (data diversity or robust data), and simple copies (software redundancy or data diversity) can be selected depending on cost effectiveness and application-dependent factors. Different result delivery conditions can also be used to increase fault coverage or to provide graceful degradation as faults occur. Explicit use of SCOP had not been documented to the date of this writing; however, four-version software and two-variant hardware were combined in a dynamically reconfigurable architecture for pitch control support in the A320 aircraft [18]. This could be considered a simplified form of SCOP [17].

Table 6.3
Some of the Other Software Fault Tolerance Techniques

Technique Name	Description	Reference
Algorithmic fault tolerance	Algorithmic fault tolerance describes a set of techniques in which the fault tolerance technique is specifically tailored to the algorithm to be performed. Examples of algorithmic fault tolerance include techniques for matrix operations [19] and redundantly linked lists [20, 21].	[19–21]
Certification trails (CT)	The central idea of the CT scheme is to execute an algorithm so that it leaves behind a trail of data (the certification trail) and, using this data, execute another algorithm for solving the same problem more quickly and/or more simply than the first algorithm. The outputs of the two executions are then compared. They are considered correct if they agree; otherwise, other algorithms are executed to determine the solution. This technique requires time redundancy. Care must be taken in designing use of CT to avoid data dependency (error propagation from the first algorithm to the second algorithm, possibly resulting in erroneous output). Although it may be of limited applicability, CT does provide an alternative to the recovery block scheme.	[22–24]
Community error recovery (CER)	CER is an error recovery algorithm for multivariant software. It consists of two levels: (1) the crosscheck point level, responsible for local error recovery, and (2) the recovery point level, responsible for global error recovery. CER uses consensus data values to help recover failed variants, and thus assumes that at any given time, there is a majority of variants that can supply correct information to recover a failed variant.	[25, 26]
Concurrent error-detection (CED)	CED is a broad category of techniques that detect errors during program execution using a watchdog. The watchdog can be a separate, concurrent process that monitors the main process and collects relevant data. An error is detected when the watchdog determines that a discrepancy between the anticipated behavior and actual execution behavior has occurred. Assertions are a typical means of error detection in CED.	[27]

Table 6.3 (continued)

Technique Name	Description	Reference
Correspondent computing-based software fault tolerance	Correspondent computing generates results that are *correspondent* to the results of an operation. For error detection, a comparative test is formulated using the precise relationship between the operation and its correspondent operations. The correspondent operations provide the redundancy required for forward error recovery, so that correspondent computing may be formulated as a software fault tolerance technique.	[28–30]
Hierarchical N-version programming (HNVP)	The HNVP method views a problem as a set of objects that can be hierarchically organized into several levels. NVP is then applied to the objects at different levels. An example of the levels that could be considered include: level 1—the whole program, level 2—module (e.g., an Ada package), level 3—procedure (e.g., an Ada procedure), and level 4—data structure. The HNVP technique is motivated by the fact that the reliability of the whole system depends on the reliability of the subsystems at each level [31].	[31]
$t/(n-1)$-Variant programming	The $t/(n-1)$-Variant programming software fault tolerance technique, $t/(n-1)$-VP, is based on $t/(n-1)$-diagnosability, a system-level diagnosis technique used in hardware. By applying the diagnosis algorithm to some of the results of n concurrently executed variants, it selects a presumably correct result as the output. The adjudication function used in this technique is based on result comparison. The technique can always identify one correct result from the subset of results of n variants if the number of faulty variants is less than or equal to t, that is, the technique can tolerate t software faults. A study comparison of the $t/(n-1)$-VP and NVP techniques showed that both techniques can tolerate some related faults between software variants and that, in general, $t/(n-1)$-VP has higher reliability, whereas NVP is better from a safety viewpoint [33].	[32, 33]

6.5　Other Techniques

Regardless of the size, comprehensiveness, and timeliness of a book of this nature, one is bound to have insufficient space and/or time to include significant discussion on all existing software fault tolerance techniques. In addition, new techniques are being developed as this book is being written. This section attempts to give brief information and references for some of the techniques in the former category. Table 6.3 provides the name of the technique, a short description, and reference(s) from which the reader may obtain additional information.

6.6 Summary

This chapter presented other software fault tolerance techniques—those not easily categorized as design or data diverse and those different enough from both to warrant belonging to this separate classification. Some of the techniques presented are the result of modifications to existing techniques to improve performance, for example, NVP-TB-AT. Other techniques take a new approach to software fault tolerance—resourceful system's use of a goal-oriented approach, the data-driven dependability assurance scheme's use of data dependability indicators, and SCOP's use of flexible redundancy.

In Chapters 4, 5, and 6, we presented quite a few techniques. All of these techniques must, at some point in their operation, decide whether or not the result at hand will be forwarded as the presumable correct result or be rejected. The decisions are handled by DMs or adjudicators, described in the next, and last, chapter.

References

[1] Tai, A. T., J. F. Meyer, and A. Avizienis, "Performability Enhancement of Fault-Tolerant Software," *IEEE Transactions on Reliability*, Vol. 42, No. 2, 1993, pp. 227–237.

[2] Tai, A. T., A. Avizienis, and J. F. Meyer, "Evaluation of Fault-Tolerant Software: A Performability Modeling Approach," in C. E. Landweh, B. Randell, and L. Simoncini (eds.), *Dependable Computing for Critical Applications 3*, Vienna, Austria: Springer-Verlag, 1993, pp. 113–135.

[3] Tai, A. T., J. F. Meyer, and A. Avizienis, *Software Performability: From Concepts to Applications*, Norwell, MA: Kluwer Academic Publishers, 1996.

[4] Anderson, T., and P. A. Lee, "Software Fault Tolerance," in *Fault Tolerance: Principles and Practice*, Englewood Cliffs, NJ: Prentice-Hall, 1981, pp. 249–291.

[5] Randell, B., "Fault Tolerance and System Structuring," *Proceedings 4th Jerusalem Conference on Information Technology*, Jerusalem, 1984, pp. 182–191.

[6]   Neumann, P. G., "On Hierarchical Design of Computer Systems for Critical Applications," *IEEE Transactions on Software Engineering*, Vol. 12, No. 9, 1986, pp. 905–920.

[7]   Abbott, R. J., "Resourceful Systems and Software Fault Tolerance," *Proceedings of the First International Conference on Industrial and Engineering Applications of Artificial Intelligence and Expert Systems*, Tullahoma, TN, 1988, pp. 992–1000.

[8]   Abbott, R. J., "Resourceful Systems for Fault Tolerance, Reliability, and Safety," *ACM Computing Surveys*, Vol. 22, No. 3, 1990, pp. 35–68.

[9]   Taylor, D. J., and J. P. Black, "Principles of Data Structure Error Correction," *IEEE Transactions on Computers*, Vol. C-31, No. 7, 1982, pp. 602–608.

[10] Bastani, F. B., and I. L. Yen, "Analysis of an Inherently Fault Tolerant Program," *Proceedings of COMPSAC 85*, Chicago, IL, 1985, pp. 428–436.

[11] Duncan, R. V., Jr., and L. L. Pullum, "Fault Tolerant Intelligent Agents—State Machine Design," Quality Research Associates, Inc. Technical Report, 1997.

[12] Parhami, B., "A New Paradigm for the Design of Dependable Systems," *International Symposium on Circuits and Systems*, Portland, OR, 1989, pp. 561–564.

[13] Parhami, B., "A Data-Driven Dependability Assurance Scheme with Applications to Data and Design Diversity," in A. Avizienis and J. -C. Laprie (eds.), *Dependable Computing for Critical Applications 4*, New York: Springer-Verlag, 1991, pp. 257–282.

[14] Bondavalli, A., F. Di Giandomenico, and J. Xu, "A Cost-Effective and Flexible Scheme for Software Fault Tolerance," Technical Report No. 372, University of Newcastle upon Tyne, 1992.

[15] Bondavalli, A., F. Di Giandomenico, and J. Xu, "Cost-Effective and Flexible Scheme for Software Fault Tolerance," *Journal of Computer System Science & Engineering*, Vol. 8, No. 4, 1993, pp. 234–244.

[16] Xu, J., A. Bondavalli, and F. Di Giandomenico, "Software Fault Tolerance: Dynamic Combination of Dependability and Efficiency," Technical Report No. 442, University of Newcastle upon Tyne, 1993.

[17] Xu, J., A. Bondavalli, and F. Di Giandomenico, "Dynamic Adjustment of Dependability and Efficiency in Fault-Tolerant Software," in B. Randell, et al. (eds.), *Predictably Dependable Computing Systems*, New York: Springer-Verlag, 1995, pp. 155–172.

[18] Traverse, P., "AIRBUS and ATR System Architecture and Specification," in U. Voges (ed.), *Software Diversity in Computerized Control Systems*, Vienna, Austria: Springer-Verlag, 1988, pp. 95–104.

[19] Huang, K. -H., and J. A. Abraham, "Algorithm-Based Fault Tolerance for Matrix Operations," *IEEE Transactions on Computers*, Vol. C-33, No. 6, 1984, pp. 518–528.

[20] Taylor, D. J., D. E. Morgan, and J. P. Black, "Redundancy in Data Structures: Improving Software Fault Tolerance," *IEEE Transactions on Software Engineering*, Vol. SE-6, No. 6, 1990, pp. 585–594.

[21]   Taylor, D. J., D. E. Morgan, and J. P. Black, "Redundancy in Data Structures: Some Theoretical Results," *IEEE Transactions on Software Engineering*, Vol. SE-6, No. 6, 1990, pp. 595-602.

[22]   Sullivan, G. F., and G. M. Masson, "Certification Trails for Data Structures," Technical Report JHU 90/17, Johns Hopkins University, Baltimore, MD, 1990.

[23]   Sullivan, G. F., and G. M. Masson, "Using Certification Trails to Achieve Software Fault Tolerance," *Proceedings: FTCS-20*, Newcastle Upon Tyne, UK, 1990, pp. 423–431.

[24]   Sullivan, G. F., and G. M. Masson, "Certification Trails for Data Structures," *Proceedings: FTCS-21*, Montreal, Canada, 1991, pp. 240–247.

[25]   Tso, K. S., A. Avizienis, and J. P. J. Kelly, "Error Recovery in Multi-Version Software," *Proc. IFAC SAFECOMP '86*, Sarlat, France, 1986, pp. 35–41.

[26]   Tso, K. S., and A. Avizienis, "Community Error Recovery in N-Version Software: A Design Study with Experimentation," *Digest of Papers: FTCS-17*, Pittsburgh, PA, 1987, pp. 127–133.

[27]   Mahmood, A., and E. J. McCluskey, "Concurrent Error Detection Using Watchdog Processors—A Survey," *IEEE Transactions on Computers*, Vol. 37, No. 2, 1988, pp. 160–174.

[28]   Lee, P. -N., A. Tamboli, and J. Blankenship, "Correspondent Computing Based Software Fault Tolerance," Allerton, 1988, pp. 378–387.

[29]   Lee, P. -N., and A. Tamboli, "Concurrent Correspondent Modules: A Fault Tolerant Ada Implementation," *Proceedings: Computers and Communications*, 1989, pp. 300–304.

[30]   Lee, P. -N., and J. Blankenship, "Correspondent Computing for Software Implementation Fault Tolerance," *Proceedings: Symposium on Applied Computing*, 1990, pp. 12–19.

[31]   Wu, J., "Software Fault Tolerance using Hierarchical N-Version Programming," *Southeastcon '91*, 1991, pp. 243–247.

[32]   Xu, J., "The $t/(n-1)$-Diagnosability and Its Applications to Fault Tolerance," *Proceedings: FTCS-21*, Montreal, Canada, 1991, pp. 496–503.

[33]   Xu, J., and B. Randell, "Software Fault Tolerance: $t/(n-1)$-Variant Programming," *IEEE Transactions on Reliability*, Vol. 46, No. 1, 1997, pp. 60–68.

7

Adjudicating the Results

Adjudicators determine if a "correct" result is produced by a technique, program, or method. Some type of adjudicator, or decision mechanism (DM), is used with every software fault tolerance technique. In discussing the operation of most of the techniques in Chapters 4, 5, and 6, when the variants, copies, try blocks, or alternates—the application-specific parts of the technique—finished executing, their results were eventually sent to an adjudicator. The adjudicator would run its decision-making algorithm on the results and determine which one (if any) to output as the presumably correct result. Just as we can imagine different specific criteria for determining the "best" item depending on what that item is, so we can use different criteria for selecting the "correct" or "best" result to output. So, in many cases, more than one type of adjudicator can be used with a software fault tolerance technique. For instance, the N-version programming (NVP) technique (Section 4.2) can use the exact majority voter, the mean or median adjudicators, the consensus voter, comparison tolerances, or a dynamic voter. The recovery block (RcB) technique (Section 4.1) could use any of the various acceptance test (AT) types described in Section 7.2. For these reasons, we can discuss the adjudicators separately—in many cases, they can be treated as "plug-and-play" components.

Adjudicators generally come in two flavors—voters and ATs (see Figure 7.1). Both voters and ATs are used with a variety of software fault tolerance techniques, including design and data diverse techniques and other techniques. Voters compare the results of two or more variants of a program to determine the correct result, if any. There are many voting algorithms

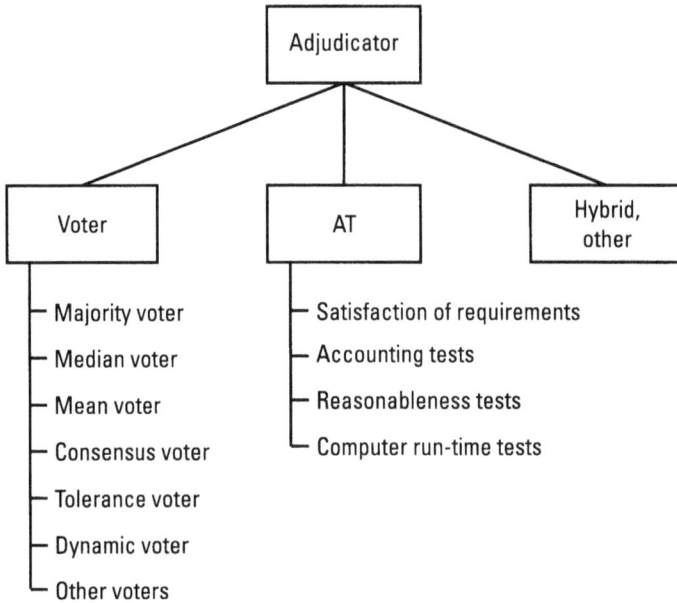

Figure 7.1 General taxonomy of adjudicators.

available and the most used of those are described in Section 7.1. ATs verify that the system behavior is "acceptable." There are several ways to check the acceptability, and those are covered in Section 7.2. As shown in Figure 7.1, there is another category of adjudicator—the hybrid. A hybrid adjudicator generally incorporates a combination of AT and voter characteristics. We discussed voters of this type with their associated technique (e.g., the N self-checking programming (NSCP) technique, in Section 4.4) since they are so closely associated with the technique and are not generally used in other techniques.

7.1 Voters

Voters compare the results from two or more variants. If there are two results to examine, the DM is called a "comparator." The voter decides the correct result, if one exists. There are many variations of voting algorithms, of which the exact majority voter is one of the more simple. Voters tend to be single points of failure for most software fault tolerance techniques, so they should be designed and developed to be highly reliable, effective, and efficient.

These qualities can be achieved in several ways. First, keep it simple. A highly complex voter adds to the possibility of its failure. A DM can be a reusable component, at least partially independent of the technique and application with which it is used. Thus, a second option is to reuse a validated DM component. Be certain to include the voter component in the test plans for the system. A third option is to perform the decision making itself in a fault-tolerant manner (e.g., vote at each node on which a variant resides). This can add significantly to the communications resources used and thus have a serious negative impact on the throughput of the system [1].

In general, all voters operate in a similar manner (see Figure 7.2). Once the voter is invoked, it initializes some variables or attributes. An indicator of the status of the voter is one that is generally set. Others will depend on the specific voter operation. The voter receives the variant results as input (or retrieves them) and applies an adjudication algorithm to determine the correct or adjudicated result. If the voter fails to determine a correct result, the status indicator will be set to indicate that fact. Otherwise, the status indicator will signal success. The correct result and the status indicator are then returned to the method that invoked the voter (or are retrieved by this or other methods). For each voter examined in this section, a diagram of its specific functionality is provided.

There are some issues that affect all voters, so they are discussed here: comparison granularity and frequency, and vote comparison issues. In implementing a technique that uses a voter, one must decide on the granularity and frequency of comparisons. In terms of voters, the term granularity refers

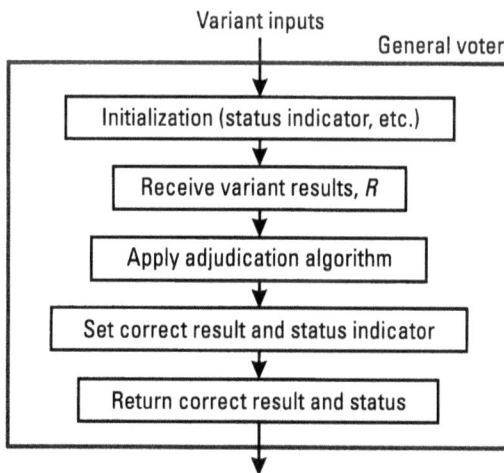

Figure 7.2 General voter functionality.

to the size of subsets of the outputs that are adjudicated and the frequency of adjudication. If the comparisons (votes) are performed infrequently or at the level of complex data types, then the granularity is termed "coarse." Granularity is "fine" if the adjudication is performed frequently or at a basic data type level. The use of coarse granularity can reduce overheads and increase the scope for diversity and variation among variants. But, the different versions will have more time to diverge between comparisons, which can make voting difficult to perform effectively. Fine granularity imposes high overheads and may decrease the scope for diversity and the range of possible algorithms that can be used in the variants. In practice, the granularity is primarily guided by the application such that an appropriate level of granularity for the voter must be designed. Saglietti [2] examines this issue and provides guidelines that help to define optimal adjudicators for different classes of application.

There are several issues that can make vote comparison itself difficult: floating-point arithmetic (FPA), result sensitivity, and multiple correct results (MCR). FPA is not exact and can differ from one machine or language to another. Voting on floating-point variant results may require tolerance or inexact voting. Also, outputs may be extremely sensitive to small variations in critical regions, such as threshold values. When close to such thresholds, the versions may provide results that vary wildly depending on which side of the threshold the version considers the system. Finally, some problems have MCR or solutions (e.g., square roots), which may confuse the adjudication algorithm.

The following sections describe several of the most used voters. For each voter, we describe how it works, provide an example, and discuss limitations or issues concerning the voter. Before discussing the individual voters, we introduce some notation to be used in the upcoming voter descriptions.

$r*$	Adjudged output or result.
syndrome	The input to the adjudicator function consisting of at least the variant outputs. A syndrome may contain a reduced set of information extracted from the variant outputs. This will become more clear as we use syndromes to develop adjudicator tables.
$\lceil a \rceil$	Ceiling function. $\lceil a \rceil = x$, where x is any value greater than a, $x \geq a$.

Adjudication table   A table used in the design and evaluation of adjudicators, where each row is a possible state of the fault-tolerant component. The rows, at minimum, contain an indication of the variant results and the result to be obtained by the adjudicator.

7.1.1 Exact Majority Voter

The exact majority voter [3, 4] selects the value of the majority of the variants as its adjudicated result. This voter is also called the m-out-of-n voter. The agreement number, m, is the number of versions required to match for system success [5–7]. The total number of variants, n, is rarely more than 3. m is equal to $\lceil (n + 1)/2 \rceil$, where $\lceil \; \rceil$ is the ceiling function. For example, if $n = 3$, then m is anything 2 or greater. In practice, the majority voter is generally seen as a 2-out-of-3 (or 2/3) voter.

7.1.1.1 Operation

The exact majority voter selects as the "correct" output, $r*$, the variant output occurring most frequently, if such a value exists. $r*$ is a correct value only if it is produced by a majority of correct variants. Table 7.1 provides a list of syndromes and shows the results of using the exact majority voter, given several sets of example inputs to the voter. The examples are provided for $n = 3$. r_i is the result of the ith variant. Table entries A, B, and C are numeric values, although they could be character strings or other results of execution of the variants. The symbol $\varnothing$ indicates that no result was produced by the corresponding variant. The symbol ε_i is a very small value relative to the value of A, B, or C. An exception is raised if a correct result cannot be determined by the adjudication function.

The exact majority voter functionality is illustrated in Figure 7.3. The variable Status indicates the state of the voter, for example, as follows:

Status = NIL   The voter has not completed examining the variant results. Status is initialized to this value. If the Status returned from the voter is NIL, then an error occurred during adjudication. Ignore the returned $r*$.

Status = NO MAJORITY   The voter did complete processing, but was not able to find a majority given the input variant results. Ignore the returned $r*$.

Table 7.1
Exact Majority Voter Syndromes, $n = 3$

Variant Results (r_1, r_2, r_3)	Voter Result, $r*$	Notes
(A, A, A)	A	—
(A, A, B)	A	—
(A, B, A)	A	—
(B, A, A)	A	—
(A, A, $\varnothing$)	Exception	With a dynamic voter (Section 7.1.6), $r* = A$. Also see discussion in Section 7.1.1.3.
Any combination including $\varnothing$, except one with 2 or 3 $\varnothing$.	Exception	See dynamic voter (Section 7.1.6) and discussion in Section 7.1.1.3.
(A, B, C)	Exception	Multiple correct or incorrect results. See discussion in Section 7.1.1.3.
(A, A + ε_1, A − ε_2)	Exception	With a tolerance voter (Section 7.1.5), $r* = A$ if tolerance $> \varepsilon_1$ or ε_2. Also see discussion in Section 7.1.1.3.
Other combinations with small variances between variant results.	Exception	See tolerance voter (Section 7.1.5) and discussion in Section 7.1.1.3.

Status = SUCCESS   The voter did complete processing and found a majority result, $r*$, the assumed correct, adjudicated result.

The following pseudocode illustrates the exact majority voter. Recall that $r*$ is the adjudicated or correct result. Values for Status are used as defined above.

```
ExactMajorityVoter (input_vector, r*)
//  This Decision Mechanism determines the correct or
//  adjudicated result (r*), given the input vector of
//  variant results (input_vector), via the Exact
//  Majority Voter adjudication function.

    Set Status = NIL, r* = NIL
    Receive Variant Results (input_vector)

    Was a Result Received from each Variant?
    No: Set Status = NO MAJORITY (Exception), Go To Out
    Yes: Continue
```

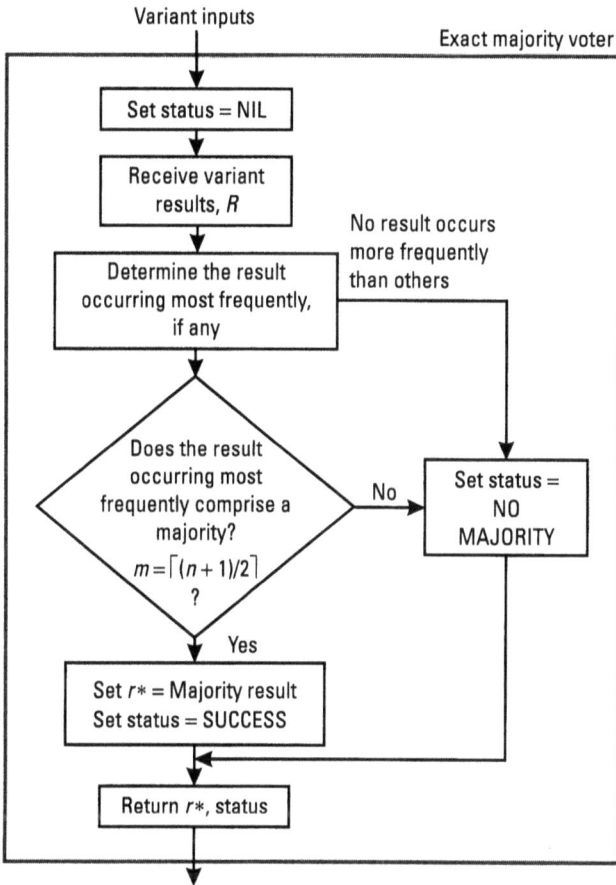

Figure 7.3 Exact majority voter operation.

```
Determine the Result (RMost), that Occurs Most
Frequently.
Is there an RMost?
No: Set Status = NO MAJORITY (Exception), Go To Out
Yes: Does the Number of Times RMost Occurs
     Comprise a Majority?  (M = ⌈(N+1)/2⌉?)
Yes: Set r* = RMost
     Set Status = SUCCESS
No: Set Status = NO MAJORITY (Exception)

Out  Return r*, Status
// ExactMajorityVoter
```

7.1.1.2   Example

An example of the exact majority voter operation is shown in Figure 7.4. Suppose we have a 2-out-of-3 voter ($m = 2$, $n = 3$). If the results of the variants are:

$$r_1 = 12;$$
$$r_2 = 11;$$
$$r_3 = 12;$$

then the input vector to the voter is (12, 11, 12). We see that the value 12 occurs most frequently, namely twice. The agreement number, m, is

$$m = \lceil (n+1)/2 \rceil = \lceil (2+1)/2 \rceil = \lceil 3/2 \rceil = \lceil 1.5 \rceil$$
$$m \in \{i \ni : i \geq 2\}.$$

Since the variant value 12 occurs most frequently, and it occurs twice, it meets the agreement number requirement of being 2 or greater. Hence, the exact majority voter's adjudicated result will be 12.

7.1.1.3   Discussion

The exact majority voter is most appropriately used to examine integer or binary results, but can be used on any type of input. However, if it is used on other data types, the designer must be wary of several factors that can drastically reduce the effectiveness of the voter. First, recall the problems

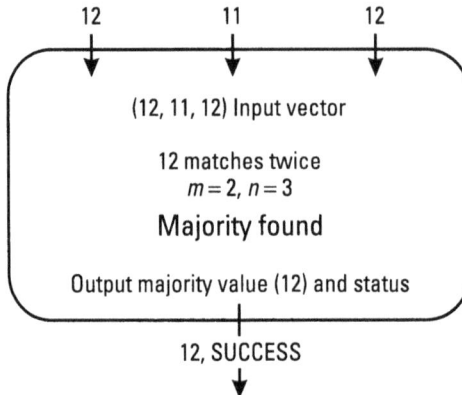

12   11   12

(12, 11, 12) Input vector

12 matches twice
$m = 2$, $n = 3$
Majority found

Output majority value (12) and status

12, SUCCESS

Figure 7.4 Example of exact majority voter.

(discussed in Chapter 3) of coincidental, correlated, and similar errors. These types of errors can defeat the exact majority voter and in general cause problems for most voters. Other issues related to the exact majority voter are discussed below.

The majority voter assumes one correct output for each function. Note that agreement or matching values is not the same as correctness. For example, the voter can receive identical, but wrong results, and be defeated.

The use of FPA and design diversity can yield versions outputting multiple correct, but different, results. When MCR occurs, the exact majority voting scheme results in an exception being raised; that is, the voting scheme will be defeated, finding no correct or adjudicated result. With FPA and MCR (discussed in Chapter 3), correct result values may be approximately (within a tolerance) the same, but not equal. (MCR can also result in vastly different correct result values.) Therefore, the exact majority voter will not recognize these results as correct. If these are the types of correct results expected for an application, it is more appropriate to use comparison tolerances in the voter (see Section 7.1.5).

There may be cases in which the correct result must be guessed by the voter. This occurs when less than a majority of variants is correct and is not handled by the exact majority voter. The consensus voter handles this situation.

The exact majority voter is also defeated when any variant fails to provide a result, since this voter expects a result from each variant. The dynamic voters (Section 7.1.6) were developed to handle this situation.

For data diverse techniques, if the data re-expression algorithm (DRA) is exact (that is, all copies should generate identical outputs), then the exact majority voter can be used with confidence. If, however, the DRA is approximate, the n copies will produce similar (not exact) acceptable results and an enhanced DM, such as the formal majority voter (Section 7.1.5) is needed.

In studies on the effectiveness of voting algorithms (e.g., [8]), it was shown that the majority voter has a high probability of selecting the correct result value when the probability of variant failure is less than 50% and the number of processes, n, is "large." (Blough and Sullivan [8] used $n = 7$ and $n = 15$ in the study.) However, when the probability of variant failure exceeds 50%, then the majority voter performs poorly. In another study, the majority voter was found to work well if, as sufficient conditions, no more than $n - m$ variants produce erroneous results and all correct results are identical [9]. Other investigations of the simple, exact majority voter as used in NVP are presented in [5, 9–27].

7.1.2   Median Voter

The median voter selects the median of the values input to the voter (i.e., the variant results, R) as its adjudicated result. A median voter can be defined for variant outputs consisting of a single value in an ordered space (e.g., real numbers). It uses a fast voting algorithm (the median of a list of values) and can be used on integer, float, double, or other numeric values. If it can be assumed that, for each input value, no incorrect result lies between two correct results, and that a majority of the replica outputs are correct, then this function produces a correct output.

7.1.2.1   Operation

The median voter selects as the "correct" output, $r*$, the median value among the list of variant results, R, it receives. Let n be the number of variants. The median is defined as the value whose position is central in the set R (if n is odd), otherwise the value in position $n/2$ or $(n/2 + 1)$ (if n is even). For example, if there are three items in the sorted list of results, the second item will be selected as $r*$. If there are four items in the list, the third item ($n/2 + 1 = 4/2 + 1 = 3$) will be selected as $r*$.

Table 7.2 provides a list of syndromes and shows the results of using the median voter, given several sets of example inputs to the voter. The examples are provided for $n = 3$. r_i is the result of the ith variant. Table entries A, B, and C are numeric values, where A < B < C. (They could be character strings or other results of execution of the variants if using the generalized median voter [28].) The symbol $\varnothing$ indicates that no result was produced by the corresponding variant. The symbol ε_i is a very small value relative to the value of A, B, or C. An exception is raised if a correct result cannot be determined by the adjudication function.

Note that a "Sorted Results" column has been included in the table. This column contains the result list sorted in ascending order, or a "0" if an error would occur in the basic median voter while sorting the results. The basic median voter expects a correct result from each variant. Note also that ascending or descending order can be used with no application-independent preference for either approach.

The median voter functionality is illustrated in Figure 7.5. The variable Status indicates the state of the voter, for example, as follows:

Status = NIL   The voter has not completed examining the variant results. Status is initialized to this value. If the Status returned from the voter is NIL, then an error occurred during adjudication. Ignore the returned $r*$.

Table 7.2

Median Voter Syndromes, $n = 3$

Variant Results (r_1, r_2, r_3)	Sorted Results	Voter Result, $r*$	Notes
(A, A, A)	(A, A, A)	A	—
(A, A, B)	(A, A, B)	A	—
(A, B, A)	(A, A, B)	A	—
(B, A, A)	(A, A, B)	A	—
(A, B, B)	(A, B, B)	B	—
(B, A, B)	(A, B, B)	B	—
(B, B, A)	(A, B, B)	B	—
(A, B, C)	(A, B, C)	B	—
(A, C, B)	(A, B, C)	B	—
(B, A, C)	(A, B, C)	B	—
(C, A, B)	(A, B, C)	B	—
(B, C, A)	(A, B, C)	B	—
(C, B, A)	(A, B, C)	B	—
(A, A, ∅)	0	Exception	With a dynamic voter (Section 7.1.6), $r* = A$. Also see discussion in Section 7.1.2.3.
Any combination including ∅.	0	Exception	See dynamic voter (Section 7.1.6) and discussion in Section 7.1.2.3.
(A, A + ε_1, A − ε_2)	(A − ε_2, A, A + ε_1)	A	—

Status = NO MEDIAN   The voter was not able to find a median given the input variant results. Ignore the returned $r*$.

Status = SUCCESS   The voter completed processing and found a median result, $r*$. Thus, $r*$ is the assumed correct, adjudicated result.

The following pseudocode illustrates the operation of the median voter. Recall that $r*$ is the adjudicated or correct result. Values for Status are used as defined above.

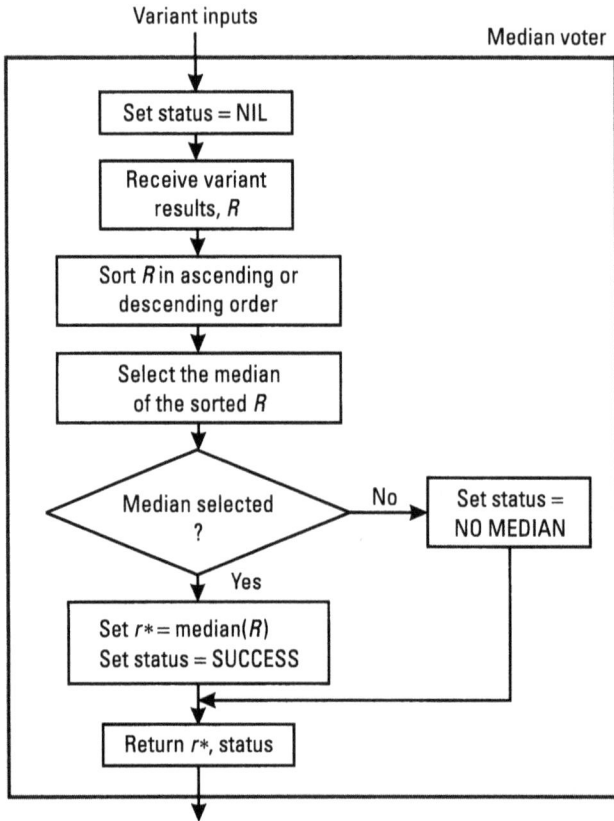

Figure 7.5 Median voter operation.

```
MedianVoter (input_vector, r*)
//   This Decision Mechanism determines the correct or
//   adjudicated result (r*), given the input vector
//   (input_vector) of variant results, via the Median
//   Voter adjudication function.

    Set Status = NIL, r* = NIL
    Receive Variant Results (input_vector)

    Was a Result Received from each Variant?
    No: Set Status = NO MEDIAN (Exception), Go To Out
    Yes: Continue

    Sort Replica Outputs in Ascending or Descending Order
```

```
Select the Median of the Sorted Replica Outputs
Was a Median Selected?
     No: Set Status = NO MEDIAN (Exception), Go To Out
     Yes: Set r* = Median(input_vector)
          Set Status = SUCCESS

Out Return r*, Status
// MedianVoter
```

7.1.2.2 Example

An example of the median voter operation is shown in Figure 7.6. Suppose we have a fault-tolerant component with three variants, $n = 3$. If the results of the variants are:

$r_1 = 17.5;$

$r_2 = 16.0;$

$r_3 = 18.1;$

then the input vector to the voter is (17.5, 16.0, 18.1). The sorted list of results is (16.0, 17.5, 18.1). We see that the value 17.5 is the median value. Hence, the median voter's adjudicated result will be 17.5.

7.1.2.3 Discussion

The median voter is a fast voting algorithm and is likely to select a result in the correct range. The median voting scheme is less biased (given a small output sample) than the averaging (or mean value) voting scheme. Another

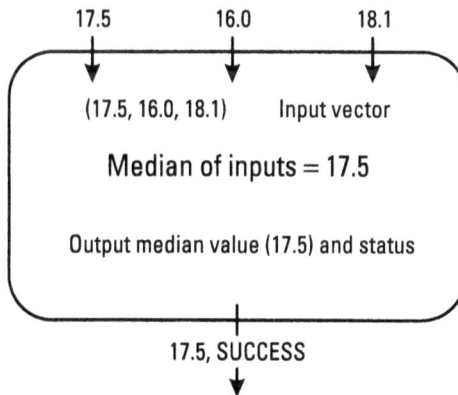

Figure 7.6 Example of median voter.

advantage of this voting scheme is that it is not defeated by MCR. The median voting scheme has been applied successfully in aerospace applications [29]. For data diverse software fault tolerance techniques, this type of DM can be useful when the DRA is approximate (causing the copies to produce similar, but not exact, acceptable results).

The median voter is defeated when any variant fails to provide a result, since this voter expects a result from each variant. The dynamic voters (Section 7.1.6) were developed to handle this situation.

In a study [8] on the effectiveness of voting algorithms, Blough states that the median voter is expected to perform better than the mean voting strategy and shows the overall superiority of the median strategy over the majority voting scheme. This study further shows that the median voter has a high probability of selecting the correct result value when the probability of variant failure is less than 50%. However, when the probability of variant failure exceeds 50%, then the median voter performs poorly.

7.1.3   Mean Voter

The mean voter [30] selects the mean or weighted average of the values input to the voter (i.e., the variant results, R) as the correct result. A mean voter can be defined for variant outputs consisting of a single value in an ordered space (e.g., real numbers). It uses a fast voting algorithm and can be used on integer, float, double, or other numeric values.

If using the weighted average variation on the mean voter, there are various ways to assign weights to the variant outputs using additional information related to the trustworthiness of the variants [31, 32]. This information is known *a priori* (and perhaps continually updated) or defined directly at invocation time (e.g., by assigning results' weights inversely proportional to the variant output's distance from all other results).

7.1.3.1   Operation

Using the mean adjudication function (or mean voter), $r*$ is selected as either the mean or as a weighted average of the variant outputs, R. The mean voter computes the mean of the variant output values as the adjudicated result, $r*$. The weighted average voter applies weights to the variant outputs, then computes the mean of the weighted outputs as the adjudicated result, $r*$.

Table 7.3 provides a list of syndromes and shows the results of using the mean voter, given several sets of example inputs to the voter. The examples are provided for $n = 3$. r_i is the result of the ith variant. Table entries A,

Table 7.3
Mean Voter Syndromes, $n = 3$

Variant Results (r_1, r_2, r_3)	Voter Result, $r*$	Notes
(A, A, A)	A	—
(A, A, B)	mean(A, A, B)	—
Any list of the results A, A, and B.	mean(A, A, B)	—
(A, B, B)	mean(A, B, B)	—
Any list of the results A, B, and B.	mean(A, B, B)	—
(A, B, C)	mean(A, B, C)	—
Any list of the results A, B, and C.	mean(A, B, C)	—
(A, A, ∅)	Exception	With a dynamic voter (Section 7.1.6), $r* = A$. Also see discussion in Section 7.1.3.3.
Any combination including ∅.	Exception	See dynamic voter (Section 7.1.6) and discussion in Section 7.1.3.3.
(A, A + ε_1, A − ε_2)	mean(A, A + ε_1, A − ε_2)	—

B, and C are numeric values. The symbol ∅ indicates that no result was produced by the corresponding variant. The symbol ε_i is a very small value relative to the value of A, B, or C. An exception is raised if a correct result cannot be determined by the adjudication function. The basic mean voter expects a correct result from each variant.

Table 7.4 lists syndromes and provides the results of using the weighted average voter, given several sets of example inputs to the voter. Note that a "Variant Weights" column has been added to the table. This column contains the weights assigned to the results associated with the various variants.

The functionality of the mean voter and of the weighted average voter is illustrated in Figure 7.7 and Figure 7.8, respectively. The variable Status indicates the state of the voter, for example, as follows:

Status = NIL   The voter has not completed examining the variant results. Status is initialized to this value. If the Status returned from the voter is NIL, then an error occurred during adjudication. Ignore the returned $r*$.

Table 7.4
Weighted Average Voter Syndromes, $n = 3$

Variant Results (r_1, r_2, r_3)	Variant Weights	Voter Result, $r*$
(A, A, A)	(w_1, w_2, w_3)	average(Aw_1, Aw_2, Aw_3)
(A, A, B)	(w_1, w_2, w_3)	average(Aw_1, Aw_2, Bw_3)
(A, B, A)	(w_1, w_2, w_3)	average(Aw_1, Bw_2, Aw_3)
(B, A, A)	(w_1, w_2, w_3)	average(Bw_1, Aw_2, Aw_3)
(A, B, B)	(w_1, w_2, w_3)	average(Aw_1, Bw_2, Bw_3)
(B, A, B)	(w_1, w_2, w_3)	average(Bw_1, Aw_2, Bw_3)
(B, B, A)	(w_1, w_2, w_3)	average(Bw_1, Bw_2, Aw_3)
(A, B, C)	(w_1, w_2, w_3)	average(Aw_1, Bw_2, Cw_3)
(A, C, B)	(w_1, w_2, w_3)	average(Aw_1, Cw_2, Bw_3)
(B, A, C)	(w_1, w_2, w_3)	average(Bw_1, Aw_2, Cw_3)
(C, A, B)	(w_1, w_2, w_3)	average(Cw_1, Aw_2, Bw_3)
(B, C, A)	(w_1, w_2, w_3)	average(Bw_1, Cw_2, Aw_3)
(C, B, A)	(w_1, w_2, w_3)	average(Cw_1, Bw_2, Aw_3)
(A, A, $\emptyset$)	(w_1, w_2, w_3)	Exception

With a dynamic voter (Section 7.1.6), $r* = $ average(Aw_1, Aw_2). Also see discussion in Section 7.1.3.3.

Any combination including $\emptyset$.	(w_1, w_2, w_3)	Exception

See dynamic voter (Section 7.1.6) and discussion in Section 7.1.3.3.

(A, A + ε_1, A − ε_2)	(w_1, w_2, w_3)	average(Aw_1, (A + ε_1)w_2, (A − ε_2)w_3)

Status = NO MEAN   The voter was not able to find a mean (or weighted average) given the input variant results. Ignore the returned $r*$.

Status = SUCCESS   The voter completed processing and found a mean (or weighted average) result, $r*$. $r*$ is the assumed correct, adjudicated result.

The following pseudocode segments illustrate the mean and weighted average voters. Recall that $r*$ is the adjudicated or correct result. Values for Status are used as defined above.

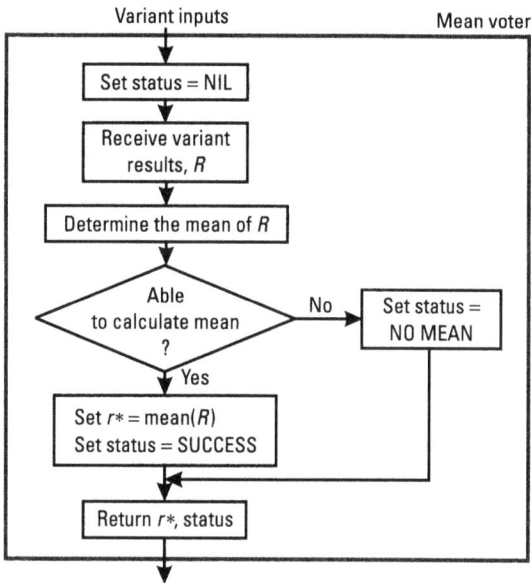

Figure 7.7 Mean voter operation.

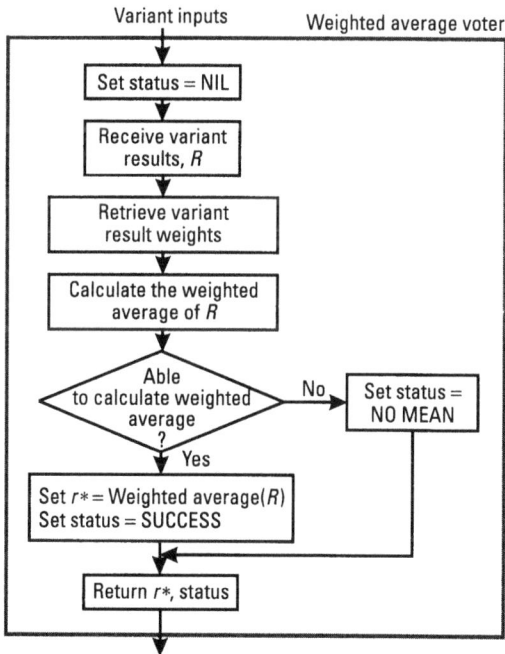

Figure 7.8 Weighted average voter operation.

```
MeanVoter (input_vector, r*)
//  This Decision Mechanism determines the correct or
//  adjudicated result (r*), given the input vector
//  (input_vector) of variant results, via the Mean
//  Voter adjudication function.

    Set Status = NIL, r* = NIL
    Receive Variant Results (input_vector)

    Was a Result Received from each Variant?
    No: Set Status = NO MEAN (Exception), Go To Out
    Yes: Continue
    Compute the Mean of the Variant Outputs
    Set r* = Mean(input_vector)
    Set Status = SUCCESS

Out  Return r*, Status
//  MeanVoter


WeightedAverageVoter (input_vector, weights, r*)
//  This Decision Mechanism determines the correct or
//  adjudicated result (r*), given the input vector
//  (input_vector) of variant results and weights, via
the
//  Weighted Average adjudication function.


    Set Status = NIL, r* = NIL
    Receive Variant Results (input_vector)
    Retrieve weights


    Was a Result Received from each Variant?
    No: Set Status = NO MEAN (Exception), Go To Out
    Yes: Continue
    Compute the Weighted Average of the Variant Outputs
    Set r* = Weighted_Average(input_vector, weights)
    Set Status = SUCCESS


Out  Return r*, Status
//  WeightedAverageVoter
```

7.1.3.2 Example

An example of the mean voter operation is shown in Figure 7.9. Suppose we have a fault-tolerant component with three variants, $n = 3$. If the results of the variants are:

$r_1 = 17.5;$

$r_2 = 16.0;$

$r_3 = 18.1;$

then the input vector to the voter is (17.5, 16.0, 18.1). Using the equation

$$\text{mean}(R) = \frac{\sum_{i=1}^{n} r_i}{n}$$

we calculate the mean, 17.2. Hence, the mean voter's adjudicated result will be 17.2.

Next, let's look at an example for the weighted average voter (see Figure 7.10). Using the system defined in the example above of the mean voter, we define weights for the variants and execute a weighted average voter. The input vector is (17.5, 16.0, 18.1). We define the variant weights for this example as their result's probability of correctness. (Note: It would be most appropriate to check that the weights in this case are above some

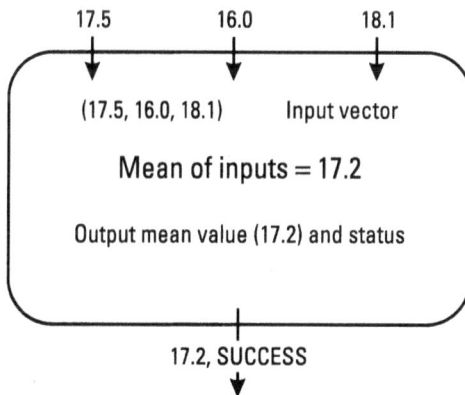

17.5   16.0   18.1

(17.5, 16.0, 18.1)   Input vector

Mean of inputs = 17.2

Output mean value (17.2) and status

17.2, SUCCESS

Figure 7.9 Example of mean voter.

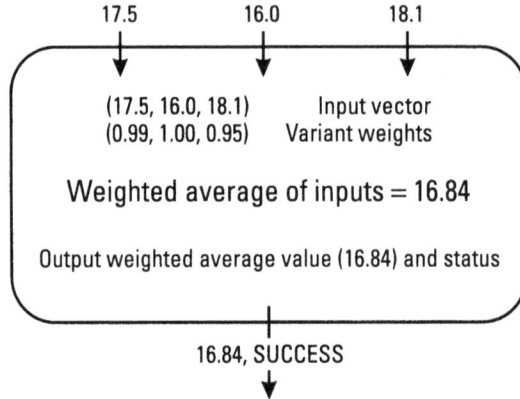

17.5   16.0   18.1

(17.5, 16.0, 18.1)   Input vector
(0.99, 1.00, 0.95)   Variant weights

Weighted average of inputs = 16.84

Output weighted average value (16.84) and status

16.84, SUCCESS

Figure 7.10 Example of weighted average voter.

threshold so that values with unacceptably low probabilities of correctness do not unduly skew the voter's final result. See Section 7.1.3.3.) Suppose the weights are:

$w_1 = 0.99$ for variant 1;

$w_2 = 1.00$ for variant 2;

$w_3 = 0.95$ for variant 3.

Using the equation

$$\text{weighted average}(R) = \frac{\sum_{i=1}^{n} r_i w_i}{n}$$

we calculate the weighted average, 16.84. Hence, the weighted average voter's adjudicated result will be 16.84.

7.1.3.3 Discussion

The mean and weighted average voters are defeated when any variant fails to provide a result, since these voters expect a result from each variant. Dynamic voters (Section 7.1.6) were developed to handle this situation. The mean adjudication algorithm seems well suited for situations where the probabilities of the values of the variant outputs decrease with increasing distances from the ideal result [9]. For data diverse software fault tolerance techniques, this type of DM (mean and weighted average) can be useful when the DRA is approximate (causing the copies to produce similar, but not exact, acceptable results).

In a study [8] on the effectiveness of voting algorithms, Blough states that the mean voter is expected to perform worse than the median voting strategy. This study further shows that the mean voter has a high probability of selecting the correct result value when the probability of variant failure is less than 50%. However, when the probability of variant failure exceeds 50%, then the mean voter performs poorly.

In the example for the weighted average voter, we define the variant weights based on the variant results' probabilities of correctness. When assigning such weights dynamically, it would be appropriate to ensure (by checking) that a variant's probability of failure is above some threshold (say, 50%, given the study noted above). If a variant's probability of failure is above the threshold, the adjudication algorithm could disregard that variant's result so as not to unduly skew the voter's final result toward a probably incorrect result.

7.1.4 Consensus Voter

The consensus voter [27, 33] is a generalization of the majority voter. A consensus is a set of matching variant results, not necessarily a majority. This voter allows the selection of a consensus of variant results as the adjudicated result if no majority exists. The consensus voter can be used to adjudicate the same types of variant outputs as the majority voter (or tolerance voter, if tolerances are used in the consensus voter).

7.1.4.1 Operation

The adjudication algorithm for the consensus voter is as follows. Let n be the number of variants. If there is majority agreement, (e.g., 2 out of 3), with $n > 1$, then use the majority as the correct result. If there is no majority agreement, then, if there is a unique maximum agreement (but the number of variants agreeing is less than the majority), then use the unique maximum agreement as the correct result. If there is no majority or unique maximum agreement, then if there is a tie in the maximum agreement number, (e.g., 2 out of 5 results match and another group of 2 out of 5 results match), the result depends on the technique being used. If using NVP, randomly choose a group and use its answer as the correct result. If using the consensus recovery block (CRB) technique, all groups of matching results are sent through the AT, which is used to select the correct result.

Table 7.5 provides brief examples to illustrate the consensus voter (also see Section 7.1.4.2).

Table 7.6 lists syndromes and provides the results of using the consensus voter, given several sets of example inputs to the voter. The examples are provided for $n = 5$. r_i is the result of the ith variant. Table entries A, B, C, D, and E are numeric values. The symbol $\varnothing$ indicates that no result was produced by the corresponding variant. The symbol ε_i is a very small value relative to the value of the variant result. An exception is raised if a correct result cannot be determined by the adjudication function. The basic consensus voter expects a correct result from each variant.

The consensus voter functionality is illustrated in Figure 7.11. The variable Status indicates the state of the voter, for example, as follows:

Status = NIL   The voter has not completed examining the variant results. Status is initialized to this value. If the Status returned from the voter is NIL, then an error occurred during adjudication. Ignore the returned $r*$.

Status = NO CONSENSUS   The voter was not able to find a consensus given the input variant results. Ignore the returned $r*$.

Status = SUCCESS   The voter completed processing and found a consensus result, $r*$. $r*$ is the assumed correct, adjudicated result.

Table 7.5
Example of Consensus Voter Results

Variant Results, *R*	Consensus Voter Result, *r*∗
(5.0, 3.0, 5.0, 5.0, 5.0)	$r* = 5.0$ Majority of values match.
(3.0, 3.0, 2.0, 5.0, 4.0)	$r* = 3.0$ No majority. Unique maximum agreement of values.
(1.0, 3.0, 5.0, 3.0, 5.0)	$r* = 3.0$ or 5.0 No majority. No unique maximum agreement. Tie in maximum agreement number. If using NVP, randomly choose either 3.0 or 5.0 as the correct result. If using CRB, use the AT to select between 3.0 and 5.0 as the correct result.
(1.0, 2.0, 3.0, 4.0, 5.0)	$r* = \varnothing$ (exception) No majority. Maximum agreement number $= 1$ (i.e., no variant results match).

Table 7.6

Consensus Voter Syndromes, $n = 5$

Variant Results (r_1, r_2, r_3, r_4, r_5)	Voter Result, $r*$	Notes
(A, A, A, A, A)	A	Majority match
(A, A, A, A, B)	A	Majority match
(A, A, A, B, B)	A	Majority match
Any **R** with a majority of values matching.	Majority(**R**)	Majority match
(A, A, B, C, D)	A	No majority, but a unique maximum agreement value.
Any **R** with no majority of values matching, but with a unique maximum agreement number greater than 1.	Unique maximum agreement value(**R**)	No majority, but a unique maximum agreement value.
(A, A, B, C, C)	A or C	No majority. Tie in maximum agreement number (not unique). If using NVP, randomly choose A or C. If using CRB, use an AT to select between A and C.
Any **R** with no majority of values matching, and a tie in the maximum agreement number (greater than 1).	Tie-broken maximum agreement value.	(see above)
(A, B, C, D, E)	Exception	No matches in **R**.
(A, A, A, B, ∅)	Exception	With a dynamic voter (Section 7.1.6), $r* = A$. Also see discussion in Section 7.1.4.3.
Any combination including ∅ with a majority or other consensus of remaining values.	Exception	See dynamic voter (Section 7.1.6) and discussion in Section 7.1.4.3.
(A, A + ε_1, B, C, A − ε_2)	Exception	See tolerance voter (Section 7.1.5) and discussion in Section 7.1.4.3.

The following pseudocode illustrates the consensus voter. Recall that $r*$ is the adjudicated or correct result. Values for Status are used as defined above.

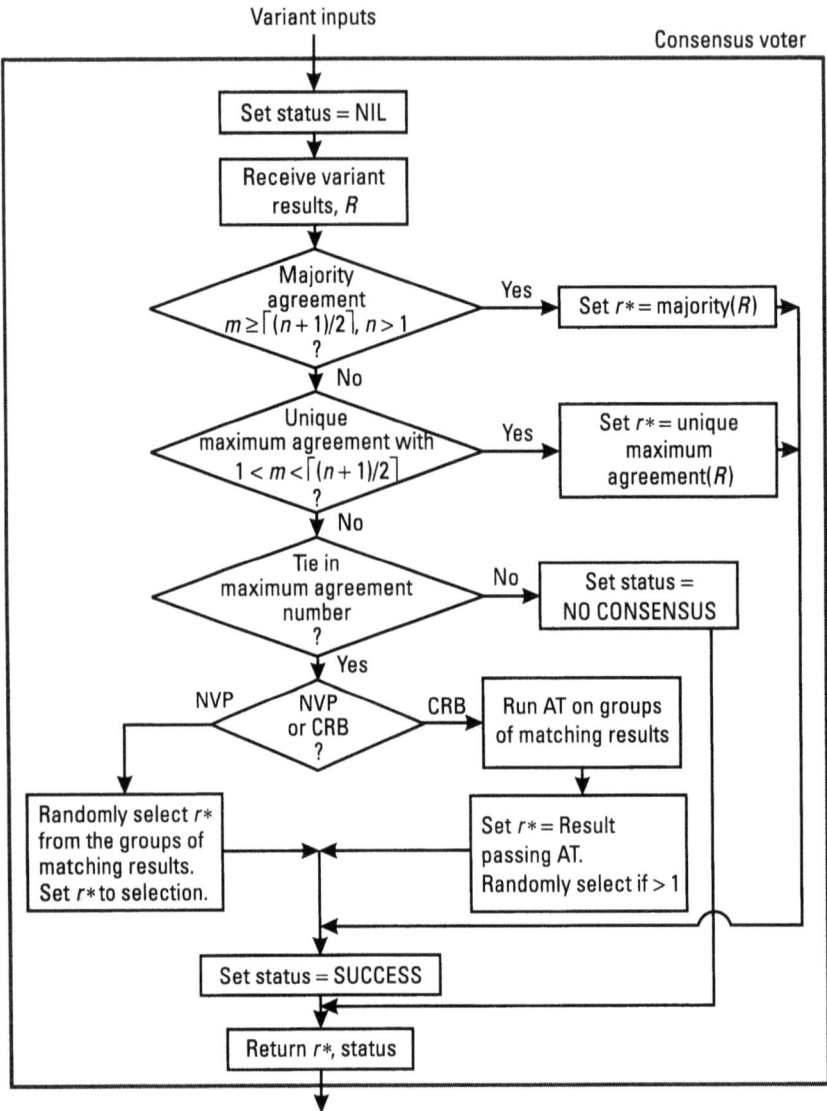

Figure 7.11 Consensus voter operation.

```
ConsensusVoter (input_vector, r*)
//  This Decision Mechanism determines the correct or
//  adjudicated result (r*), given the input vector
//  (input_vector) of variant results, via the
//  Consensus Voter adjudication function.
```

```
Set Status = NIL, r* = NIL
Receive Variant Results (input_vector)

Was a Result Received from each Variant?
No: Set Status = NO CONSENSUS (Exception), Go To Out
Yes: Continue

If Majority Agreement m ≥ ⌈(n + 1) / 2⌉, n > 1,
    then use Majority as Correct Result
Else, if a Unique Maximum Agreement, but Number of
    Versions Agreeing, m < ⌈(n + 1) / 2⌉,
    then use Unique Maximum as the Correct Result
Else, if Tie in Maximum Agreement Number
        (≥ 1 Group of Agreeing Outputs), then
    If NVP, Randomly Choose a Group & use
        its Answer as the Correct Result
    If Consensus Recovery Block, send all Groups
        through Acceptance Test to Select the
        Correct Result

Was a correct result selected?
    No: Set Status = NO CONSENSUS (Exception), Go To Out
    Yes: Set r* = Consensus (input_vector)
        Set Status = SUCCESS

Out Return r*, Status
// ConsensusVoter
```

7.1.4.2 Example

An example of the consensus voter operation is shown in Figure 7.12. Suppose we have a fault-tolerant component with five variants, $n = 5$. If the results of the variants are

$r_1 = 17.5;$

$r_2 = 16.0;$

$r_3 = 18.1;$

$r_4 = 17.5;$

$r_5 = 16.0;$

then the input vector to the voter is (17.5, 16.0, 18.1, 17.5, 16.0). We see there is no majority. But are there any matches? Yes, there are two groups of matching values, 16.0 and 17.5. Each group has two matches. That is,

```
   17.5    16.0    18.1    17.5    16.0
    |       |       |       |       |
    ▼       ▼       ▼       ▼       ▼

   (17.5, 16.0, 18.1, 17.5, 16.0)      Input vector

                    No majority
        No unique maximum agreement number
     two groups of matches with m > 1, 17.5 and 16.0

                  Technique: CRB
                  AT: 17.0 < rᵢ < 19.0
                     16.0 fails AT
                     17.5 passes AT

             Consensus value = 17.5

        Output consensus value (17.5) and status

                    17.5, SUCCESS
                       ▼
```

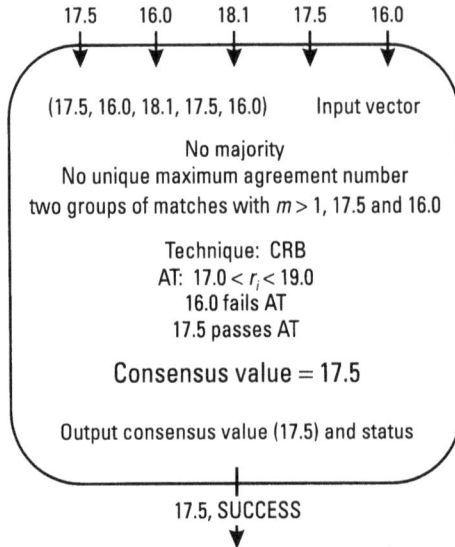

Figure 7.12 Example of consensus voter.

the agreement number for each group is 2. So, there is no *unique* maximum agreement, but there is a tie in the maximum agreement number.

Now, suppose we are using the CRB technique. This means the consensus voter attempts to resolve the tie using the CRB technique's AT. Let the AT for this example be to accept values between 17.0 and 19.0. The matching values 16.0 and 17.5 are sent to the AT. Value 16.0 fails the AT, but value 17.5 passes the AT. Hence, the consensus voter's adjudicated result will be 17.5.

7.1.4.3 Discussion

FPA and MCR (see Chapter 3) can yield different but approximately equal correct results. This can defeat any DM that attempts to find exact matches among variant results. If these are the types of correct results expected for an application, it is more appropriate to use comparison tolerances in the voter (see Section 7.1.5).

The consensus voter is also defeated when any variant fails to provide a result, since this voter expects a result from each variant. The dynamic consensus voter (Section 7.1.6) is an adaptation of the basic consensus voter that was developed to handle this situation.

The consensus voting scheme is particularly effective in small output spaces. For $m > 2$, majority voting is the upper bound on the probability of failing the system using consensus voting and 2-out-of-n is the lower bound [33]. For $m = 2$, consensus voting is the same as majority voting.

Consensus voting and CRB-based systems were found [27] to perform better, and more uniformly, than corresponding traditional strategies such as the RcB technique, and NVP with majority voting. Consensus voting is more stable than majority voting and always offers reliability at least equivalent to majority voting. This adjudicator performs better than majority voting when average N-tuple reliability is low, or the average decision space in which voters work is not binary [29]. In terms of implementation, the consensus voting algorithm is more complex than the majority voting algorithm, since the consensus voting algorithm requires multiple comparisons and random number generation.

7.1.5 Comparison Tolerances and the Formal Majority Voter

If the output space of the replicated or diverse software is a metric space, then the first likely addition to the information used by the adjudication function (beyond the variant results themselves) is a parameter, ε, indicating the maximum distance allowed between two correct output values for the same input (based on the specification function). (Unfortunately, the ε used in conjunction with tolerance rating is not the same ε used in the prior sections in this chapter.) In numerical algorithms, an alternative is the addition of the parameter d, indicating the maximum distance from a specified ideal output (then, ε would be equal to $2d$). DMs using this type of information rely on the (usually realistic) hypothesis that different correct implementations of the same specification function can produce results that are different, but quite close together [9].

The formal majority voter [28] uses this parameter (a comparison tolerance) to compare the differences between the variant results it evaluates. (Hence, it is sometimes called the tolerance voter or inexact voting [34].) Comparison tolerances are useful when comparing real numbers (floating points, doubles, etc.) and can be used to enhance many types of voters. To explain the use of comparison tolerances, let ε be the comparison tolerance value. The voter evaluates the variant results two at a time. For example, if x, y, and z are the variant results, the voter examines the following:

$$|x - y| = \delta_1$$
$$|x - z| = \delta_2$$
$$|y - z| = \delta_3$$

Given the results of this evaluation, the voter checks the differences between the variant results against the specified tolerance.

$$\delta_1 \leq \varepsilon$$
$$\delta_2 \leq \varepsilon$$
$$\delta_3 \leq \varepsilon$$

If all the variant results agree within the tolerance (i.e., $\delta_i \leq \varepsilon$, for all i), then there exists an *agreement* event. If one or more disagrees, then there exists a *conflict* event. When less than a majority of the variants fail, then there is a *no_failure* event. When a majority of the variants fail, then there is a *failure* event.

The voting event types for comparison tolerances are defined as follows [33]:

- ALL_CORRECT event: *no_failure* occurs with an *agreement*.

- FALSE_ALARM event: *no_failure* with *conflict* (where the difference between two values is greater than the tolerance, for example, $|x - z| > \varepsilon$). This indicates that the tolerance is too small for this set of results.

- UN_DETECTED_FAILURE event: *failure* with *agreement*; in which the difference between a result and the correct result is outside the tolerance, but is not detected. This can occur if the tolerance is too large. This is the most undesirable failure event.

- DETECTED_FAILURE event: *failure* with *conflict* ($|x - y| > \varepsilon$, $|x - z| > \varepsilon$).

7.1.5.1 Operation

Adjudication functions using information in addition to the variant outputs (such as the comparison tolerance) can be grouped into those that perform their operations in two steps and those that do not. The operation of such a two-step adjudication function consists of the following steps:

1. First define a feasibility set (FS) by disregarding the variant outputs judged to be erroneous by some criterion. A usual criterion is an AT or a requirement that all elements in the FS differ by less than ε.

2. Then, choose $r*$ among the values in FS. Possible criteria for this choice include the majority, median, average, or a random selection.

The effectiveness of a two-step adjudication function depends on the choice of ε. If ε is too large, the feasibility set may contain incorrect values, one of which may be adjudged $r*$ (particularly if $r*$ is selected randomly). If ε is too small, however, the feasibility set may be empty even when there exist correct variant outputs.

Let R be the set of variant results. The formal majority voter first selects a variant output, x, and constructs the feasibility set, FS, as the subset of R containing x and all the other values in R less than ε from x. If the values in FS constitute at least a majority of all the values in R, then the value $r*$ is randomly selected from FS. Figure 7.13 illustrates the result options for using the formal majority voter. In the figure, $n = 3$ and variant result x is chosen as the base of the comparison. In Figure 7.13(a), both of the other variant results, A and B, are within ε of x, so they and x are included in the feasibility set, FS. The FS = {x, A, B}, so the adjudicated result is a randomly selected value from the FS. $r* = x$ or A or B. Figure 7.13(b) illustrates a variant result, B, greater than the allowed distance, ε, from x. Variant result A is within tolerance of x and is included in the FS with x. The FS = {x, A}. The adjudicated result is randomly selected from the FS, so $r* = x$ or A. Figure 7.13(c) is similar, but with variant result A being outside the tolerance on the low end. The FS is {x, B} and $r*$ is randomly selected from the FS. $r* = x$ or B. Figure 7.13(d) illustrates the case where no variant results are within tolerance. No result can be adjudicated as the correct result, so an exception is raised (or a flag is set to indicate that the exception should be handled in the function that called the adjudicator).

Table 7.7 provides brief examples to illustrate the formal majority voter (also see Section 7.1.5.2).

Table 7.8 provides a list of syndromes and the results of using the formal majority voter, given several sets of example inputs to the voter. The examples are provided for $n = 3$. In this table, we use the following notations:

r_i The result of the ith variant;

C_i = 1 if r_i is a correct result;

      = 0 if r_i is incorrect;

FS_i = 1 if r_i is in the FS;

      = 0 if r_i is not in the FS;

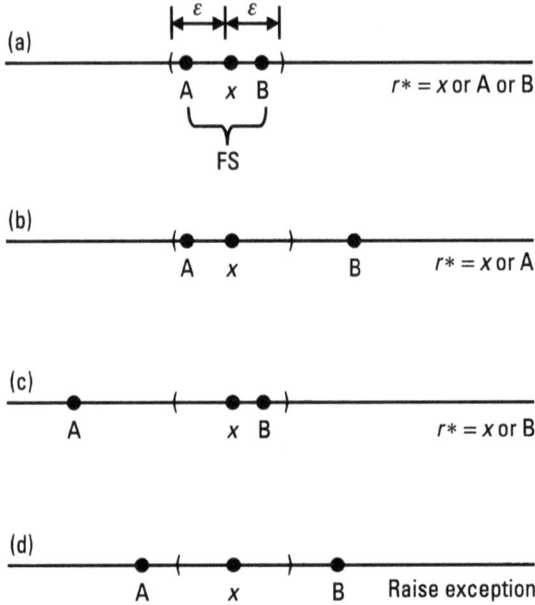

Figure 7.13 Result options for the formal majority voter.

Table 7.7
Examples of Formal Majority Voter Results

Variant Results, R	Let $x = r_2$	FS, with $\varepsilon = 0.1$	Formal Majority Voter Result, $r*$
(5.0, 5.0, 5.0)	$x = 5.0$	{5.0, 5.0, 5.0}	$r* = 5.0$ All variant results in FS. Randomly select $r*$.
(4.95, 5.0, 6.0)	$x = 5.0$	{4.95, 5.0}	$r* = 4.95$ Unequal variant results in FS. Randomly select $r*$.
(3.0, 5.0, 5.05)	$x = 5.0$	{5.0, 5.05}	$r* = 5.0$ Unequal variant results in FS. Randomly select $r*$.
(1.0, 2.0, 3.0)	$x = 2.0$	{}	$r* = \varnothing$ (exception) Empty FS.

$r*$ The adjudged correct answer;

$\varnothing$ Indicates that no result was produced by the corresponding variant. An exception is raised if an adjudged correct result can not be determined by the adjudication function. The basic formal majority voter expects a correct result from each variant.

Table 7.8

Formal Majority Voter Syndromes, $n = 3$.

C_1	C_2	C_3	FS_1	FS_2	FS_3	Voter Result, $r*$	Notes
1	1	1	1	1	1	any r_i	ALL_CORRECT.
1	1	1	1	1	0	r_1 or r_2	—
1	1	1	1	0	1	r_1 or r_3	—
1	1	1	0	1	1	r_2 or r_3	—
1	1	1	1	0	0	r_1	—
1	1	1	0	1	0	r_2	—
1	1	1	0	0	1	r_3	—
1	1	1	0	0	0	Exception	FALSE_ALARM.
1	1	0	1	1	1	any r_i	Error if r_3 (incorrect) selected.
1	1	0	1	1	0	r_1 or r_2	—
1	1	0	1	0	1	r_1 or r_3	Error if r_3 (incorrect) selected.
1	1	0	0	1	1	r_2 or r_3	Error if r_3 (incorrect) selected.
1	1	0	1	0	0	r_1	—
1	1	0	0	1	0	r_2	—
1	1	0	0	0	1	r_3	Error, r_3 incorrect. UN_DETECTED_FAILURE
1	1	0	0	0	0	Exception	FALSE_ALARM.
Similar pattern when $(C_1, C_2, C_3) = (1, 0, 1)$ or $(0, 1, 1)$, (2 correct results).							
1	0	0	1	1	1	any r_i	Error if r_2 or r_3 (incorrect) selected.
1	0	0	1	1	0	r_1 or r_2	Error if r_2 (incorrect) selected.
1	0	0	1	0	1	r_1 or r_3	Error if r_3 (incorrect) selected.
1	0	0	0	1	1	r_2 or r_3	Error, r_2 and r_3 incorrect. UN_DETECTED_FAILURE
1	0	0	1	0	0	r_1	—
1	0	0	0	1	0	r_2	Error, r_2 incorrect. UN_DETECTED_FAILURE
1	0	0	0	0	1	r_3	Error, r_3 incorrect. UN_DETECTED_FAILURE
1	0	0	0	0	0	Exception	FALSE_ALARM.

Table 7.8 (continued)

Correct Result			In FS			Voter Result, $r*$	Notes
C_1	C_2	C_3	FS_1	FS_2	FS_3		
Similar pattern when $(C_1, C_2, C_3) = (0, 1, 0)$ or $(0, 0, 1)$, (1 correct result).							
0	0	0	1	1	1	any r_i	Error, all r_i incorrect. UN_DETECTED_FAILURE
0	0	0	1	1	0	r_1 or r_2	Error, all r_i incorrect. UN_DETECTED_FAILURE
0	0	0	1	0	1	r_1 or r_3	Error, all r_i incorrect. UN_DETECTED_FAILURE
0	0	0	0	1	1	r_2 or r_3	Error, all r_i incorrect. UN_DETECTED_FAILURE
0	0	0	1	0	0	r_1	Error, all r_i incorrect. UN_DETECTED_FAILURE
0	0	0	0	1	0	r_2	Error, all r_i incorrect. UN_DETECTED_FAILURE
0	0	0	0	0	1	r_3	Error, all r_i incorrect. UN_DETECTED_FAILURE
0	0	0	0	0	0	Exception	DETECTED_FAILURE
1	1	$\varnothing$	...	...	...	Exception	See dynamic voter (Section 7.1.6) and discussion in Section 7.1.5.3.

The formal majority voter functionality is illustrated in Figure 7.14. The variable Status indicates the state of the voter, for example, as follows:

Status = NIL   The voter has not completed examining the variant results. Status is initialized to this value. If the Status returned from the voter is NIL, then an error occurred during adjudication. Ignore the returned $r*$.

Status = NO CORRECT RESULT   The voter was not able to find a correct result given the input variant results and ε. Ignore the returned $r*$.

Status = SUCCESS   The voter completed processing and found an (assumed) correct result, $r*$.

The following pseudocode illustrates the formal majority voter. Recall that $r*$ is the adjudicated or correct result. Values for Status are used as defined above.

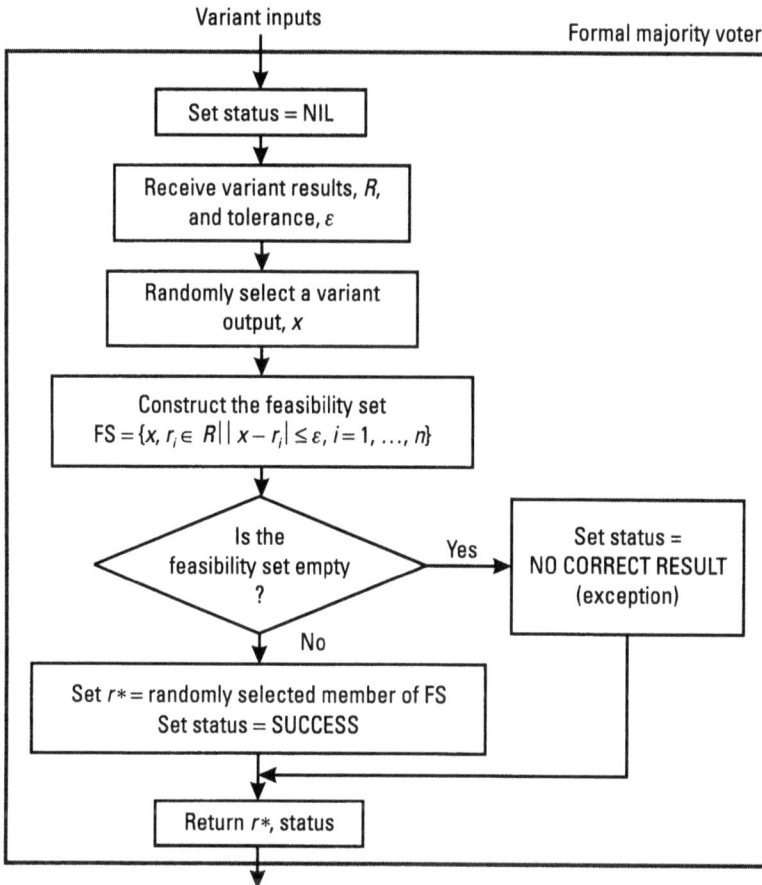

Figure 7.14 Formal majority voter operation.

```
FormalMajorityVoter (input_vector, e, r*)
//   This Decision Mechanism determines the correct or
//   adjudicated result (r*), given the input vector
//   (input_vector) of variant results and the maximum
//   allowed distance (e), via the Formal Majority
//   adjudication algorithm.

     Set Status = NIL, r* = NIL, FS = NIL
     Receive Variant Results, input_vector, e

     Was a Result Received from each Variant?
     No: Set Status = NO CORRECT RESULT (Exception), Go To Out
```

```
Yes: Continue

Randomly Select a Variant Output, x.
Construct the Feasibility Set (FS), where
    FS = {x, y in input_vector |  |x - y| ≤ z}
Is FS empty?
    No: Set r* = Randomly Selected Value in FS
        Set Status = SUCCESS
    Yes: Set Status = NO CORRECT RESULT
                     (Exception)

Out Return r*, Status
// FormalMajorityVoter
```

7.1.5.2 Example

An example of the formal majority voter operation is shown in Figure 7.15. Suppose we have a fault-tolerant component with three variants, $n = 3$. If the results of the variants are

$r_1 = 17.632;$

$r_2 = 17.674;$

$r_3 = 18.795;$

then the input vector to the voter is (17.632, 17.674, 18.795).

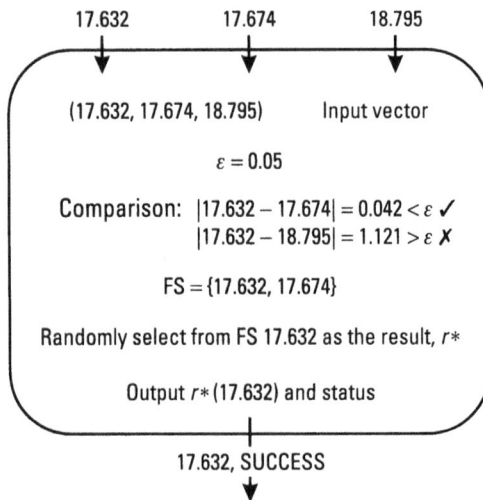

Figure 7.15 Example of formal majority voter.

Suppose the variant result selected as the "focal point," x, is r_2. The other variant results are checked to see if they are within the tolerance, $\varepsilon = 0.05$, of x.

$$|x - r_1| = |17.674 - 17.632| = 0.042 < 0.05 \quad \checkmark$$
$$|x - r_3| = |17.674 - 18.795| = 1.121 > 0.05 \quad \text{✗}$$

Since r_1 matches x (r_2) within ε, the FS = $\{r_1, r_2\}$ = $\{17.632, 17.674\}$. One of these values, say 17.632, is randomly selected from FS as the adjudicated result.

7.1.5.3 Discussion

The formal majority voter expects a result from each variant and when all variant results are not present, the voter can fail. A way to avoid this type of failure is to make the formal majority dynamic (see Section 7.1.6).

For data diverse software fault tolerance techniques, this type of DM is quite useful when the DRA is approximate (causing the copies to produce similar, but not exact, acceptable results).

The formal majority voter is sometimes called a tolerance voter because of the "tolerance" on the values of the results. The value of this tolerance is important. If it is too large, then it masks failure events. If it is too small, it will lead to too many conflict events (e.g., false alarms that can lead to increased testing costs [35] and degraded operation or critical system failure).

The formal majority voter uses a two-step adjudication function [36]. Other voters using a two-step adjudication function include: formalized plurality voter [28], modified interactive convergence algorithm (MCNV) [37], sliding majority decision algorithm (SLIDE) [37], filter strategy [38], the adjudication function used in the DEDIX system [39], and the adjudication function used in the CRB [24].

7.1.6 Dynamic Majority and Consensus Voters

The dynamic majority and consensus voters [40–42] operate in a way similar to their nondynamic counterparts (i.e., the majority and consensus voters, respectively), with the exception that these dynamic voters can handle a varying number of inputs. The dynamic voters can process from zero to n inputs. The reasons a voter may receive less than n inputs include catastrophic failure of some or all of the variants, some or all variants not providing their results in a timely manner, or some or all variant results failing an AT prior to being sent to the voter.

Suppose we have a dynamic voter with $n = 5$. If two of the variants fail to provide results to the voter, then the voter will vote upon the existing three variant results. If there are only two results, a comparison takes place. When comparing, if the results do not match, then the results fail. Otherwise, the matching value will be output as the correct result. If only one variant result makes it to the voter, and if that result has passed an AT prior to reaching the voter, then the dynamic voter assumes the single result is correct. If, however, no AT is involved, the dynamic voter designer must decide whether or not to pass the single result on as a correct result. This decision can be based on the criticality of the function implemented by the variant and the confidence in the reliability of the variant.

7.1.6.1 Operation

The dynamic majority voter selects as the "correct" output, $r*$, the variant output occurring most frequently, if such a value exists, from the available variant results. In contrast to the exact majority voter, the dynamic majority voter does not require all variants to provide a result in order to function. Recall m, the agreement number from the exact majority voter discussion (the number of versions required to match for system success), and n, the total number of variants. For the dynamic majority voter, m is equal to $\lceil (k + 1)/2 \rceil$, where $\lceil \; \rceil$ is the ceiling function and $k \leq n$. k is the number of variant results that made it to the voter. If three or more variant results make it to the dynamic voter, then the voter operates as a majority voter in evaluating those results. If two results make it to the voter, then they must match to be considered correct. For our discussions and the examples in this section, if a single variant result makes it to the voter, we will assume it is correct and output it as the result of the dynamic majority voter. The dynamic consensus voter operates as the consensus voter (described in Section 7.1.4) with the variant results available to the voter at the time of each vote.

Table 7.9 provides brief examples to illustrate the dynamic majority voter (also see Section 7.1.6.2). $r_i = \varnothing$ indicates that the ith variant's result did not make it to the voter.

Table 7.10 presents a list of syndromes and provides the results of using the dynamic majority voter, given several sets of example inputs to the voter. The examples are provided for $n = 3$. r_i is the result of the ith variant. Table entries A, B, and C are numeric values, although they could be character strings or other results of execution of the variants. The symbol $\varnothing$ indicates that no result was produced by the corresponding variant. The symbol

Table 7.9
Examples of Dynamic Majority Voter Results

Variant Results, *R*	Dynamic Majority Voter Result, *r**
(5.0, 5.0, 5.0, 4.0, 5.0)	$r* = 5.0$ All variant results to the voter (i.e., $k = n = 5$). Majority exists.
(4.95, 5.0, 6.0, 5.0, 6.0)	$r* = \varnothing$ (exception) All variant results to the voter (i.e., $k = n = 5$). Majority does not exist.
(3.0, 5.0, 5.0, 5.0, $\varnothing$)	$r* = 5.0$ $3 \le k \le n$. Majority exists.
(1.0, 2.0, 3.0, 4.0, $\varnothing$)	$r* = \varnothing$ (exception) $3 \le k \le n$. Majority does not exist.
(5.0, $\varnothing$, 5.0, $\varnothing$, 4.5)	$r* = 5.0$ $3 \le k \le n$. Majority exists.
(5.0, $\varnothing$, 4.1, $\varnothing$, 4.7)	$r* = \varnothing$ (exception) $3 \le k \le n$. Majority does not exist.
(5.0, $\varnothing$, $\varnothing$, 5.0, $\varnothing$)	$r* = 5.0$ $k = 2$. Compare results - match.
(5.0, $\varnothing$, $\varnothing$, 4.7, $\varnothing$)	$r* = \varnothing$ (exception) $k = 2$. Compare results - no match.
($\varnothing$, $\varnothing$, $\varnothing$, 4.7, $\varnothing$)	$r* = 4.7$ $k = 1$. Assume result is correct.
($\varnothing$, $\varnothing$, $\varnothing$, $\varnothing$, $\varnothing$)	$r* = \varnothing$ (exception) $k = 0$. No variant results to adjudicate.

ε_i is a very small value relative to the value of A, B, or C. An exception is raised if a correct result cannot be determined by the adjudication function.

The dynamic majority voter functionality is illustrated in Figure 7.16. The variable Status indicates the state of the voter, for example, as follows:

Status = NIL   The voter has not completed examining the variant results. Status is initialized to this value. If the Status returned from the voter is NIL, then an error occurred during adjudication. Ignore the returned *r**.

Status = NO CORRECT RESULT   The voter was not able to find a correct result given the available input variant results. Ignore the returned *r**.

Status = SUCCESS   The voter completed processing and found an (assumed) correct result, *r**.

The following pseudocode illustrates the dynamic majority voter. Recall that *r** is the adjudicated or correct result. Values for Status are used as defined above.

Table 7.10
Dynamic Majority Voter Syndromes, $n = 3$

Variant Results(r_1, r_2, r_3)	Voter Result, $r*$	Notes
(A, A, A)	A	Majority vote.
(A, A, B)	A	Majority vote.
(A, B, A)	A	Majority vote.
(B, A, A)	A	Majority vote.
(A, A, ∅)	A	Comparison.
(A, ∅, A)	A	Comparison.
(∅, A, A)	A	Comparison.
(A, B, ∅)	Exception	Comparison.
(A, ∅, B)	Exception	Comparison.
(∅, A, B)	Exception	Comparison.
(A, ∅, ∅)	A	Assumed correct.
(∅, A, ∅)	A	Assumed correct.
(∅, ∅, A)	A	Assumed correct.
(∅, ∅, ∅)	Exception	—
(A, B, C)	Exception	Multiple correct or incorrect results. See discussion in Section 7.1.6.3.
(A, A + ε_1, A − ε_2)	Exception	With a tolerance voter (Section 7.1.5), $r* = A$ if tolerance > ε_1 or ε_2. Also see discussion in Section 7.1.6.3.
Other combinations with small variances between variant results.	Exception	See tolerance voter (Section 7.1.5) and discussion in Section 7.1.6.3.

```
DynamicMajorityVoter (input_vector, r*)
// This Decision Mechanism determines the correct or
// adjudicated result (r*), given the input vector of
// variant results (input_vector), via the Dynamic
// Majority Voter adjudication function.

    Set Status = NIL, r* = NIL, k = 0
    Receive Variant Results (input_vector)
    Set k = Number of Variant Results Received

    If k > 2
        Is there a Majority Match?
            No: Set Status = NO CORRECT RESULT
            (Exception), Go To Out
```

Variant inputs

Dynamic majority voter

Set status = NIL, $r* = $ NIL, $k = 0$

Receive variant results, R
Set $k = $ number of variant results received

$k > 2$?

Yes

Majority exists ?

Yes

Set $r* = $ Majority result

Set status = SUCCESS

No

No

$k = 2$?

No

Yes

Results match?

No

Set status = NO CORRECT RESULT

Yes

Set $r* = $ matching result
Set status = SUCCESS

$k = 1$?

Yes

Set $r* = $ only result
Set status = SUCCESS

No

Set status = NO CORRECT RESULT

Return $r*$, status

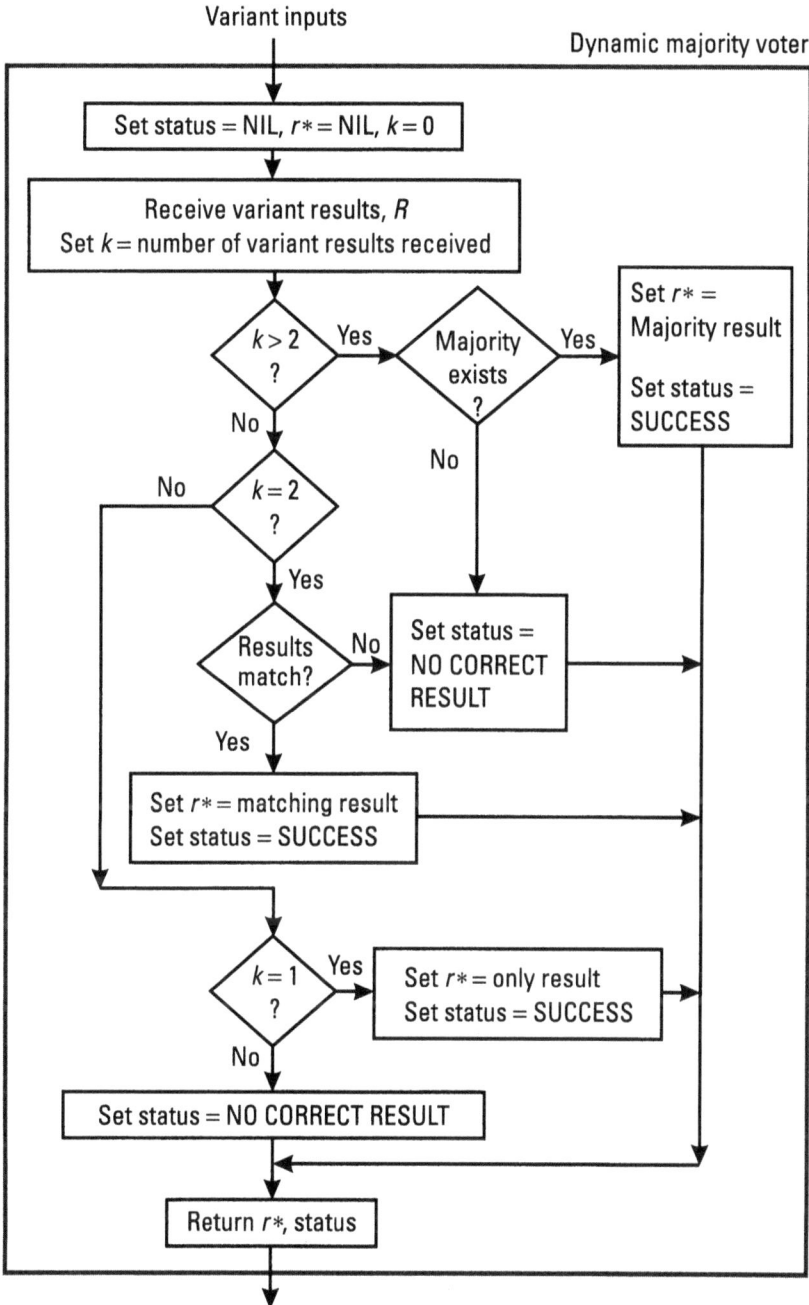

Figure 7.16 Dynamic majority voter operation.

```
                    Yes: Set r* = Majority Value
                    Set Status = SUCCESS

        If k = 2
            Do the 2 values Match?
                    Yes: Set r* = Matching Results
                    Set Status = SUCCESS
                    No: Set Status = NO CORRECT RESULT (Exception)
        Else If k = 1
            Yes: Set r* = the Only Result
                    Set Status = SUCCESS
        Else
            Set Status = NO CORRECT RESULT (Exception)
        End If

Out Return r*, Status
// DynamicMajorityVoter
```

7.1.6.2 Example

An example of the consensus voter operation is shown in Figure 7.17. Suppose we have a fault-tolerant component with five variants, $n = 5$. Let the results of the variants be

$r_1 = 17.6;$

$r_2 = \emptyset;$

$r_3 = 18.7;$

$r_4 = \emptyset;$

$r_5 = 17.6;$

then the input vector to the voter is $(17.6, \emptyset, 18.7, \emptyset, 17.6)$.

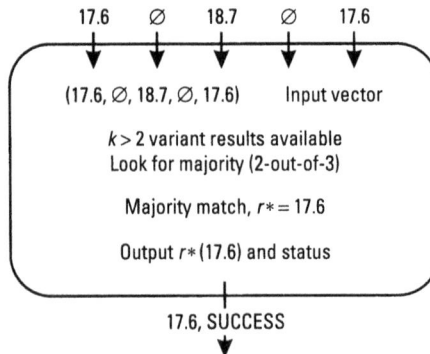

```
       17.6    Ø    18.7    Ø    17.6
        ↓      ↓      ↓      ↓      ↓

    (17.6, Ø, 18.7, Ø, 17.6)    Input vector

      k > 2 variant results available
      Look for majority (2-out-of-3)

        Majority match, r* = 17.6

        Output r* (17.6) and status
```

17.6, SUCCESS

Figure 7.17 Example of dynamic majority voter.

The basic majority voter would fail, given this input set, because it expects a result from each variant. However, the dynamic majority voter is made to handle just this situation. As we see, only three of five variant results are sent to the voter. In this case, the dynamic majority voter takes the three available results and tries to find a majority match. In this example, there is a majority result, 17.6, and it is output as the adjudicated result, $r*$.

7.1.6.3 Discussion

FPA and MCR (see Chapter 3) can yield different, but approximately equal correct results. This can defeat any DM that attempts to find exact matches among variant results. If these are the types of correct results expected for an application, it is appropriate to use comparison tolerances in the voter (see Section 7.1.5). Comparison tolerances can be used with the dynamic voter to make a more powerful and robust voter for floating-point algorithms.

7.1.7 Summary of Voters Discussed

The first part of this chapter presented the detailed operation of eight voters. Before continuing, we summarize some details of those voters in Table 7.11 (which was fashioned after a summary table found in [28]). The table states the resulting output of a fault-tolerant technique, given the type of variant results provided to the voter and the type of voter. The voter outputs are:

- *Correct:* The voter outputs a correct result;
- *Possibly correct:* The voter outputs a result that may be correct;
- *Possibly incorrect:* The voter outputs a result that may be incorrect;
- *Incorrect:* The voter outputs an incorrect result;
- *No output:* The voter does not output a result; an exception is raised.

The "Variant Results Type" column is not exhaustive, for example, it does not include the various cases of missing results that the dynamic voters handle.

To use this table, consider the primary concerns surrounding the software's application and some details about the output space and variant results. If safety is the primary concern, then select the voter that most avoids outputting an incorrect result. That is, the voter would rather raise an exception and produce no selected output than present an incorrect output as correct. Of the voters examined in this chapter, the safest (based on this criterion) are the majority voters: exact majority voter, formal majority voter,

Table 7.11
Voter Results Given Variant Output Type

Variant Results Type	Exact Majority Voter	Median Voter	Mean Voter	Weighted Average Voter	Consensus Voter	Formal Majority Voter	Dynamic Majority Voter	Dynamic Consensus Voter
All outputs identical and correct	Correct	Correct	Correct	Possibly correct	Correct	Correct	Correct	Correct
Majority identical and correct	Correct	Correct	Possibly correct	Possibly correct	Correct	Correct	Correct	Correct
Plurality identical and correct	No output	Possibly correct	Possibly correct	Possibly correct	Correct	No output	No output	Correct
Distinct outputs, All correct	No output	Correct	Possibly correct	Possibly correct	No output	No output	No output	No output
Distinct outputs, All incorrect	No output	Incorrect	Possibly incorrect	Possibly incorrect	No output	No output	No output	No output
Plurality identical and wrong	No output	Possibly incorrect	Possibly incorrect	Possibly incorrect	Incorrect	No output	No output	Incorrect
Majority identical and wrong	Incorrect	Incorrect	Possibly incorrect	Possibly incorrect	Incorrect	Incorrect	Incorrect	Incorrect
All outputs identical and wrong	Incorrect	Incorrect	Incorrect	Incorrect	Incorrect	Incorrect	Incorrect	Incorrect

and dynamic majority voter. These voters produce incorrect output "only" in cases where most or all of the variants produce identical and wrong results.

If *an* answer is better than no answer, that is, if the primary goal is to avoid cases in which the voter does not reach a decision, then select the voter that reaches a "No output" result least often. Of the voters discussed, the median, mean, and weighted average voters always reach a decision, unless they themselves fail. The performance of the weighted average voter, in particular, is difficult to generalize in this fashion without additional information about the output space [66]. Specifically, one needs information on the statistical distribution of the variant outputs. Then, one could examine the deviation of the voter's results (as a function of the weights) from a correct solution.

7.1.8 Other Voters

The preceding sections have covered several of the most used voters. As seen throughout this discussion, there are many possible variations on the basic voting schemes. Many of the variations are made to provide desired handling of the expected faults in specific applications or to overcome inadequacies of the basic voting schemes. For these same reasons, new voters have been developed. Some of the other existing voters are: generalized median adjudicator [8, 28], two-step adjudication function [9, 36], formalized plurality (consensus) voter [28], MCNV [37], SLIDE [37], filter strategy [38], DEDIX decision function [43], counter strategy [38], stepwise negotiating voting [44], confidence voter [45], maximum likelihood voter (MLV) [46, 64], fuzzy MLV and fuzzy consensus voting [47], and the self-configuring optimal programming (SCOP) adjudicator [48]. Other voters and voter performance are discussed in [60–63, 65, and 67–69].

7.2 Acceptance Tests

Acceptance tests are the most basic approach to self-checking software. They are typically used with the RcB, CRB, distributed recovery block (DRB), RtB, and acceptance voting (AV) techniques. The AT is used to verify that the system's behavior is acceptable based on an assertion on the anticipated system state. It returns the value TRUE or FALSE (see Figure 7.18). An AT needs to be simple, effective, and highly reliable to reduce the chance of introducing additional design faults, to keep run-time overhead reasonable, to ensure that anticipated faults are detected, and to ensure that nonfaulty

Variant input

General AT

```
┌─────────────────────────────────────────────────────┐
│                         ▼                             │
│         ┌───────────────────────────────────┐        │
│         │      Receive variant result       │        │
│         └───────────────────────────────────┘        │
│                         ▼                             │
│         ┌───────────────────────────────────┐        │
│         │            Apply AT               │        │
│         └───────────────────────────────────┘        │
│                         ▼                             │
│     ┌─────────────────────────────────────────┐      │
│     │   Set pass/fail indicator (TRUE/FALSE)   │      │
│     └─────────────────────────────────────────┘      │
│                         ▼                             │
│           ┌───────────────────────────┐              │
│           │        Return status       │              │
│           └───────────────────────────┘              │
└─────────────────────────────────────────────────────┘
                          ▼
```

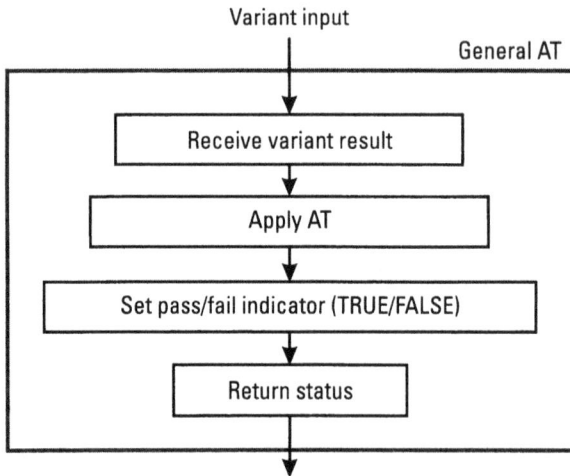

Figure 7.18 General acceptance test functionality.

behavior is not incorrectly "detected." ATs can thus be difficult to develop, depending on the specification. The form of the AT depends on the application. The coverage of an AT is an indicator of its complexity, where an increase in coverage generally requires a more complicated implementation of the test [49]. A program's execution time and fault manifestation probabilities also increase as the complexity increases.

There may be a different AT for each module or try block in the fault tolerant software. However, in practice, one is typically used.

A methodology is needed to determine the most appropriate AT test for a given situation. Criteria that could be used include run-time, cost, storage, and error detection requirements. Saglietti investigated the impact of the type of AT on the safety of an RcB system [2, 50]. Saglietti also provides a model of the trade-off between the extremes of an AT in the form of a simple check and one in the form of a comprehensive test (e.g., where the AT is another complete module performing the same functionality as the primary algorithm). The characteristics of cursory and comprehensive ATs [50] are listed below. These characteristics can help in determining the comprehensiveness of the AT.

Cursory Test Characteristics

- Error detection capability in terms of coarseness:
  - Low degree of exhaustiveness;

- Low test coverage.

- Error detection capability in terms of correctness:
  - Low design complexity;
  - Low design fault proneness.

- Cost:
  - Low development costs;
  - Short run time;
  - Low storage requirements.

Comprehensive Test Characteristics

- Error detection capability in terms of coarseness:
  - High degree of exhaustiveness;
  - High test coverage.

- Error detection capability in terms of correctness:
  - High design complexity;
  - High design fault proneness.

- Cost:
  - High development costs;
  - Long run time;
  - High storage requirements.

Program characteristics are another important driver in the determination of the most appropriate AT for a given situation. ATs can be designed so that they test for what a program should do or for what a program should not do. Testing for a violation of safety conditions (what the program should not do) may be simpler and provide a higher degree of independence between the AT and the primary routine than testing for conformance to specified performance criterion (what the program should do). Several useful principles for deriving cost-effective ATs have been identified [51–53]. These will be included in the following subsections. Most ATs currently used can be classified as one of the following types: satisfaction of requirements, accounting tests, reasonableness tests, and computer run-time checks. These AT types are covered in the subsections that follow.

7.2.1 Satisfaction of Requirements

In many situations, the problem statement or the software specifications impose conditions that must be met at the completion of program execution. When these conditions are used to construct an AT, we have a "satisfaction of requirements" type AT. Several examples of this type of AT follow.

The simplest example of a satisfaction of requirements AT is the inversion of mathematical operations. This is a useful and effective test, if the mathematical operation has an inverse, particularly if determining the inverse is simpler and faster than the original operation. Suppose the routine computes the square root. A possible AT is to square the result of the square-root operation and test to see if it equals the original operand. That is, does $(\sqrt{x})^2 = |x|$? Of course, some logical and algebraic operations do not have a unique inverse, for example: OR, AND, absolute value, and trigonometric operations.

Another simple illustration of a satisfaction of requirements AT is the sort operation AT, described by Randell [54]. When a sort operation is completed, the AT checks that the elements in the sorted set are in uniformly descending order and that the number of elements in the sorted set is equal to the number of elements in the original set. However, this test is not complete because it would not detect changes in an element during execution. To make the test exhaustive, we can add an additional test that ensures that every element in the sorted set was in the unsorted set. The problem with this additional check is that it requires too much overhead to be useful.

It is crucial that the AT and the program being tested are independent. This may be difficult to attain for satisfaction of requirements tests. An example often used to illustrate this point is the famous "eight queens" problem. The problem statement requires that eight queens be located on a chessboard such that no two queens threaten each other. An AT based on satisfaction of requirements might check that the horizontal, vertical, and two diagonals associated with each queen do not contain the location of any other queen. However, if the primary routine involves this same check as part of its solution algorithm, then this AT is not independent and, therefore, not suitable.

Testing for satisfaction of requirements is usually most effective when carried out on small segments of code [51]. (Accounting tests and reasonableness tests can handle larger sections of code.) For certain systems, such as text-editing systems, compilers, and similar programs, testing using satisfaction of requirements is the most promising current AT approach [51].

7.2.2 Accounting Tests

As stated above, accounting tests can handle larger sections of code than satisfaction of requirements tests. Accounting ATs are suitable for transaction-oriented applications with simple mathematical operations. Examples of such systems include airline reservation systems, library records, retail inventory systems, and the control of hazardous materials. Manual accounting accuracy checks in use for hundreds of years have been an effective means of detecting errors due to incorrect transcriptions or information loss. These procedures were carried over to the computerized data processing field (financial computing) and are applicable to other high-volume transaction-type applications.

The simplest form of accounting check is the checksum. When a large number of records is transmitted or reordered, a tally is made of both the total number of records and the sum over all records of a particular data field. These results can be compared between the source and the destination to implement an accounting check AT.

Inventory systems provide another opportunity for effective use of accounting checks. When the software involves control of physically measurable inventories such as nuclear material, dangerous drugs, or precious metals, the reconciliation of authorized transactions with changes in the physical inventory can be used as an AT. Determination of the physical quantity can sometimes be automated so that the process is handled without operator intervention, further reducing the risk of realizing errors.

Accounting ATs are best applied to transaction-oriented applications using simple mathematical operations. They can test large segments of code. Although limited in their range of applicability, they are very effective for these data processing applications.

In the examples above, inconsistencies detected by the AT may be due to a software failure, deliberate alteration of input or internal data, or actual theft. The lack of distinction between the results of a breakdown in software reliability and security illustrates that software reliability and fault tolerance techniques can be used in computerized security applications, and vice versa [52].

7.2.3 Reasonableness Tests

Reasonableness tests are used as ATs to determine if the state of an object in the system is reasonable. The results of many computations are bounded by some constraints. These constraints (e.g., precomputed ranges, expected sequences of program states, or other expected relationships) can be used to detect software failures. The difference between satisfaction of requirements tests and reasonableness tests is that reasonableness tests are based on physical constraints, while satisfaction of requirements tests are based on logical or mathematical relationships.

Reasonableness tests are flexible and effective, and are specifically applicable to process control and switching systems. (They can also be used effectively with many other systems.) In these systems, physical constraints can be used to determine the expected ranges for reasonable results. Kim [55] found that in real-time applications, the design of an effective AT based on physical laws or apparent boundary conditions existing in application environments is much easier than producing an effective AT in many non-real-time data processing applications. Timing tests are also essential parts of the AT in real-time systems. Timing tests typically use absolute or interval timers to invoke the detection mechanism (AT or voter). They detect operations that failed to satisfy a specified time bound. The timing tests are very powerful and simple to implement, and are thus very popular for computer-embedded systems.

The continuity properties of controlled systems also provide criteria for reasonableness tests. The rate of change of some value in a control system must be continuous and hence the rate of change can be checked for compliance to a specified range. Note that a range is used because of two primary reasons. First, determining the exact correct value for a parameter would, in the types of systems being discussed, likely require an AT as complex as the routine being checked. Second, as discussed with regards to the tolerance voters (Section 7.1.5), FPA predominantly results in values that are inexact or approximately equal to an ideal correct result. The ranges used in bounds tests will include both the correct value and incorrect values. The bounds test will indicate whether the variant result is within range of the expected correct result.

Assertions are derived from the system specification and can also be used as range bounds. An assertion is a logical expression on the value of a variable. It evaluates to TRUE if the value is consistent with the assertion, otherwise it returns FALSE. Another form of range test is a run-time system range check. Many languages include the ability to set limits for the sizes of variables or data structures when they are declared. The system then automatically generates run-time range checks based on the developer-declared variables. If, during execution, the value is outside these limits, then program execution is aborted and any required (error) signals are generated.

One example of a physical constraint involves the properties of water [56]. It is physically impossible to have water in liquid state under 1 atm pressure at a temperature higher than 100°C. The knowledge of such range bounds can be used as the basis for reasonableness tests on computed results.

Hecht [52] provides an example that illustrates the principle of the reasonableness test. In a flight control system, true airspeed is computed from the indicated airspeed (a sensed quantity). An AT based on a precomputed range arrived at from physical constraints is that the speed must be within the structural capabilities of the airframe (e.g., 140 to 1,100 km/h for a commercial subsonic aircraft). If the true airspeed is outside this range, then there is something wrong with the sensor, the computer, or the aircraft is out of control.

Continuing with Hecht's example, this test can be further refined by using a reasonable range of changes to true airspeed. If changes between the current airspeed and the previous value indicate accelerations beyond the design limit of the aircraft, an abnormal condition exists. This test is considerably more powerful than the first test because much smaller deviations can be detected. For example, if the previous true airspeed is 1,000 km/h and the subsequent calculation, which may occur in the next tenth of a second, results in an airspeed of 1,020 km/h, the AT will detect an error because the implied acceleration is almost 6g [52].

Another example (also provided in [52]) of a reasonableness test is based on progression between subsequent system states. In an electronic telephone switching system, it is not reasonable to proceed from a connected state to a ringing state or line-busy state. However, a test based on this criterion is not exhaustive, since it would not detect the premature termination of a connection [52].

As stated, the range or bounds AT is a reasonableness test type of AT. It simply determines whether a result is within preset minimum and/or maximum limits. If the result is within the bounds, it is accepted. This test is very simple, thus minimizing the potential for adding design faults to the system implementing the AT. Figure 7.19 illustrates the operation of the range bounds AT.

The following pseudocode illustrates the range bounds AT that checks both the minimum and maximum value of the result. Modifications to implement the minimum or maximum checks alone are trivial.

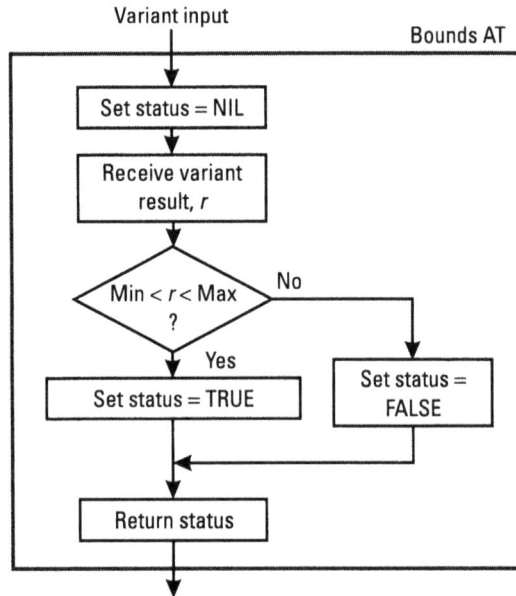

Figure 7.19 Range bounds acceptance test operation.

```
BoundsAT (input, Min, Max, Status)
//   This Decision Mechanism determines if the input
//   result (input) is acceptable given lower (Min) and
//   upper (Max) bounds, via the Bounds Acceptance Test.
     Set Status = NIL
     Receive algorithm result (input)
     // Bounds may be pre-set within AT
     Retrieve bounds (Min < and < Max)

     If input is within bounds (i.e., Min < input < Max)
     then Set Status = TRUE
     else Set Status = FALSE (Exception)
     end

     Return Status
// BoundsAT
```

7.2.4   Computer Run-Time Tests

This computer run-time test class of AT is the most cursory class. These test
only for anomalous states in the program without regard to the logical nature

of the program specification. Run-time tests detect anomalous states such as divide-by-zero, overflow, underflow, undefined operation code, end of file, or write-protection violations. Computer run-time tests are not exhaustive; rather, they can serve as additional ATs. They can be used to supplement other types of AT for critical systems, and they can be used by themselves as the AT for noncritical program segments. Run-time tests require very little development time or other resources.

Run-time checks can incorporate support software or operating system data structure and procedure-oriented tests. Examples include array subscript and value checking [57], unauthorized entries to subroutines, and other run-time monitoring techniques (described in [57–59]).

7.3 Summary

We have presented the adjudicators or "result judges" as an entity separable from the software fault tolerance techniques. In fact, in many techniques the adjudicator can be a "plug-and-play" component. In this chapter, we described a taxonomy that basically divided adjudicators into voters, ATs, and "other" or hybrid categories.

Voters, described first, are typically used in forward recovery techniques. A summary of the eight voters described here in detail was provided in Section 7.1.7. This summary compared the voters' performance under different variant result scenarios. The voter summary table and accompanying discussion provide a means of selecting among the voters based on the system goal and the output space characteristics.

ATs are the most basic approach to self-checking software and are typically used in backward recovery techniques. General AT functionality and characteristics of cursory and comprehensive ATs were described. The types of AT—satisfaction of requirements, accounting tests, reasonableness tests, and computer run-time tests—were described and examples given of each. A means of determining the best type of AT to use in a given system would be a welcome addition to the software fault tolerance field. Experience with similar systems, subject-matter expertise, and the hints provided in this chapter are so far all there is available to this end. Some of this expertise is codified in SWFTDA [70].

The first three chapters of this book provided background, and design and programming guidelines and techniques for software fault tolerance. The next three chapters described design diverse, data diverse, and other software fault tolerance techniques. The techniques are built on the foundations presented in Chapters 1–3 and typically present a result or set of results to an adjudicator. This chapter presented the voters and DMs that decide whether the world outside the software fault tolerance technique receives a result it can use, whether it should try again, or whether a failure occurs that should be handled outside the software fault tolerance technique.

References

[1]   Pradhan, D. K., *Fault-Tolerant Computer System Design*, Upper Saddle River, NJ: Prentice Hall PTR, 1996.

[2]   Saglietti, F., "The Impact of Voter Granularity in Fault-Tolerant Software on System Reliability and Availability," in M. Kersken and F. Saglietti (eds.), *Software Fault Tolerance: Achievement and Assessment Strategies*, Berlin: Springer-Verlag, 1992, pp. 199–212.

[3]   Avizienis, A., "The N-Version Approach to Fault-Tolerant Software," *IEEE Transactions on Software Engineering*, Vol. SE-11, No. 12, 1985, pp. 1491–1501.

[4]   Lyu, M. R. (ed.), *Handbook of Software Reliability Engineering*, New York: McGraw-Hill, 1996.

[5]   Eckhardt, D. E., and L. D. Lee, "A Theoretical Basis for the Analysis of Multi-Version Software Subject to Coincident Errors," *IEEE Transactions on Software Engineering*, Vol. SE-11, No. 12, 1985, pp. 1511–1517.

[6]   Trivedi, K. S., *Probability and Statistics with Reliability, Queuing, and Computer Science Applications*, Englewood Cliffs, NJ: Prentice-Hall, 1982.

[7]   Siewiorek, D. P., and R. S. Swarz, *Reliable Computer Systems—Design and Evaluation*, 2nd edition, Bedford, MA: Digital Press, 1992.

[8]   Blough, D. M., and G. F. Sullivan, "A Comparison of Voting Strategies for Fault-Tolerant Distributed Systems," *Proceedings: 9th Symposium on Reliable Distributed Systems*, Huntsville, AL, 1990, pp. 136–145.

[9]   Di Giandomenico, F., and L. Stringini, "Adjudicators for Diverse-Redundant Components," *Proceedings: 9th Symposium on Reliable Distributed Systems*, Huntsville, AL, 1990, pp. 114–123.

[10]   Avizienis, A., and L. Chen, "On the Implementation of N-Version Programming for Software Fault-Tolerance during Program Execution," *Proceedings COMPSAC '77*, New York, 1977, pp. 149–155.

[11]   Grnarov, A., J. Arlat, and A. Avizienis, "On the Performance of Software Fault Tolerance Strategies," *Proceedings of the 10th International Symposium on Fault-Tolerant Computing (FTCS-10)*, Kyoto, Japan, 1980, pp. 251–253.

[12]   Bishop, P. G., et al., "PODS—A Project on Diverse Software," *IEEE Transactions on Software Engineering*, Vol. SE-12, No. 9, 1986, pp. 929–940.

[13] Deb, A. K., "Stochastic Modeling for Execution Time and Reliability of Fault-Tolerant Programs Using Recovery Block and N-Version Schemes," Ph.D. thesis, Syracuse University, 1988.

[14] Dugan, J. B., S. Bavuso, and M. Boyd, "Fault Trees and Markov Models for Reliability Analysis of Fault Tolerant Systems," *Journal of Reliability Engineering and System Safety*, Vol. 39, 1993, pp. 291-307.

[15] Eckhardt, D. E., et al., "An Experimental Evaluation of Software Redundancy as a Strategy for Improving Reliability," *IEEE Transactions on Software Engineering*, Vol. 17, No. 12, 1991, pp. 692–702.

[16] Gersting, J., et al., "A Comparison of Voting Algorithms for N-Version Programming," *Proceedings of the 24th Annual Hawaii International Conference on System Sciences*, Big Island, Hawaii, 1991, Vol. II, pp. 253–262.

[17] Kanoun, K., et al., "Reliability Growth of Fault-Tolerant Software," *IEEE Transactions on Reliability*, Vol. 42, No. 2, 1993, pp. 205–219.

[18] Knight, J. C., and N. G. Leveson, "An Experimental Evaluation of the Assumption of Independence in Multiversion Programming," *IEEE Transactions on Software Engineering*, Vol. SE-12, No. 1, 1986, pp. 96–109.

[19] Littlewood, B., and D. R. Miller, "Conceptual Modeling of Coincident Failures in Multiversion Software," *IEEE Transactions on Software Engineering*, Vol. SE-15, No. 12, 1989, pp. 1596–1614.

[20] Lyu, M. R., and Y. He, "Improving the N-Version Programming Process through the Evolution of Design Paradigm," *IEEE Transactions on Reliability*, Vol. 42, No. 2, 1993, pp. 179–189.

[21] Lyu, M. R. (ed.), *Software Fault Tolerance*, Chichester, U.K.: John Wiley and Sons, 1995.

[22] Scott, R. K., et al., "Investigating Version Dependence in Fault-Tolerant Software," *AGARD 361*, 1984, pp. 21.1–21.10.

[23] Scott, R. K., et al., "Experimental Validation of Six Fault-Tolerant Software Reliability Models," *Proceedings of the 14th International Symposium on Fault-Tolerant Computing (FTCS-14)*, Orlando, FL, 1984, pp. 102–107.

[24] Scott, R. K., J. W. Gault, and D. F. McAllister, "Fault-Tolerant Reliability Modeling," *IEEE Transactions on Software Engineering*, Vol. SE-13, No. 5, 1987, pp. 582–592.

[25] Shimeal, T. J., and N. G. Leveson, "An Empirical Comparison of Software Fault-Tolerance and Fault Elimination," *Proceedings of the 2nd Workshop on Software Testing, Verification, and Analysis*, Banff, 1988, pp. 180–187.

[26] Voges, U. (ed.), *Software Diversity in Computerized Control Systems*, Vol. 2 of *Dependable Computing and Fault-Tolerant Systems*, A. Avizienis, H. Kopetz, and J. -C. Laprie (eds.), New York: Springer-Verlag, 1987.

[27]	Vouk, M. A., et al., "An Empirical Evaluation of Consensus Voting and Consensus Recovery Block Reliability in the Presence of Failure Correlation," *Journal of Computer and Software Engineering*, Vol. 1, No. 4, 1993, pp. 367–388.

[28]	Lorczak, P. R., A. K. Caglayan, and D. E. Eckhardt, "A Theoretical Investigation of Generalized Voters for Redundant Systems," *Proceedings of the 19th International Symposium on Fault-Tolerant Computing (FTCS-19)*, Chicago, IL, 1989, pp. 444–451.

[29]	McAllister, D. F., and M. A. Vouk, "Fault-Tolerant Software Reliability Engineering," in M. R. Lyu (ed.), *Handbook of Software Reliability Engineering*, New York: McGraw-Hill, 1996, pp. 567–614.

[30]	Broen, R. B., "New Voters for Redundant Systems," *Journal of Dynamic Systems, Measurement, and Control*, March, 1985.

[31]	Pierce, W. H., "Adaptive Decision Elements to Improve the Reliability of Redundant Systems," *IRE International Convention Record*, 1962, pp. 124–131.

[32]	Tong, Z., and R. Kahn, "Vote Assignments in Weighted Voting Mechanisms," *Proceedings of the 7th Symposium on Reliable Distributed Systems*, Columbus, OH, 1988, pp. 138–143.

[33]	McAllister, D. F., C. E. Sun, and M. A. Vouk, "Reliability of Voting in Fault-Tolerant Software Systems for Small Output Spaces," *IEEE Transactions on Reliability*, Vol. 39, No. 5, 1990, pp. 524–534.

[34]	Chen, L., and A. Avizienis, "N-Version Programming: A Fault-Tolerance Approach to Reliability of Software Operation," *Proceedings of the 8th International Symposium on Fault-Tolerant Computing (FTCS-8)*, Toulouse, France, 1978, pp. 3–9.

[35]	Vouk, M. A., "On Engineering of Fault-Tolerant Software," *10th International Symposium*, "Computer at the University," *Cavtat88*, Cavtat, Croatia, 1988.

[36]	Anderson, T., "A Structured Decision Mechanism for Diverse Software," *Proceedings: 5th Symposium on Reliable Distributed Systems*, Los Angeles, CA, 1986, pp. 125–129.

[37]	Makam, S. V., and A. Avizienis, "An Event-Synchronized System Architecture for Integrated Hardware and Software Fault-Tolerance," *Proceedings of the IEEE 4th International Conference on Distributed Computing Systems*, San Francisco, CA, 1982, pp. 526–532.

[38]	Echtle, K., "Fault Diagnosis by Combination of Absolute and Relative Tests," *EWDC-1, 1st European Workshop on Dependable Computing*, 1989.

[39]	Avizienis, A., et al., "Software by Design Diversity; DEDIX: a Tool for Experiment," *Proceedings: IFAC Workshop SAFECOMP '85*, Como, Italy, 1985, pp. 173–178.

[40]	Athavale, A., "Performance Evaluation of Hybrid Voting Schemes." M.S. thesis, North Carolina State University, 1989.

[41]	Belli, F., and P. Jedrzejowicz, "Comparative Analysis of Concurrent Fault-Tolerance Techniques for Real-Time Applications," *Proceedings of the Second International Symposium on Software Reliability Engineering*, Austin, TX, 1991.

[42] Gantenbein, R. E., S. Y. Shin, and J. R. Cowles, "Evaluation of Combined Approaches to Distributed Software-Based Fault Tolerance," *Pacific Rim International Symposium on Fault Tolerant Systems,* 1991, pp. 70–75.

[43] Avizienis, A., and J. P. J. Kelly, "Fault Tolerance by Design Diversity: Concepts and Experiments," *IEEE Computer,* Vol. 17, No. 8, 1984, pp. 67–80.

[44] Kanekawa, K., et al., "Dependable Onboard Computer Systems with a New Method —Stepwise Negotiating Voting," *Proceedings of the 19th International Symposium on Fault-Tolerant Computing (FTCS-19),* Chicago, IL, 1989, pp. 13–19.

[45] Lala, J. H., and L. S. Alger, "Hardware and Software Fault Tolerance: A Unified Architectural Approach," *Proceedings of the 18th International Symposium on Fault-Tolerant Computing (FTCS-18),* Tokyo, Japan, 1988, pp. 240–245.

[46] Leung, Y., "Maximum Likelihood Voting for Fault-Tolerant Software with Finite Output Space," *IEEE Transactions on Software Reliability,* Vol. 44, No. 3, 1995.

[47] K. Kim, M. A. Vouk, and D. F. McAllister, "Fault-Tolerant Software Voters Based on Fuzzy Equivalence Relations," *Proceedings of the IEEE Aerospace Conference,* Snowmass/Aspen, CO, 1998, Vol. 4, pp. 5–19.

[48] Bondavalli, A., F. Di Giandomenico, and J. Xu, "A Cost-Effective and Flexible Scheme for Software Fault Tolerance," *Journal of Computer Systems Science and Engineering,* Vol. 8, No. 4, pp. 234–244, 1993.

[49] Tai, A. T., J. F. Meyer, and A. Avizienis, *Software Performability: From Concepts to Applications,* Norwell, MA: Kluwer Academic Publishers, 1996.

[50] Saglietti, F., "A Theoretical Evaluation of the Acceptance Test as a Means to Achieve Software Fault-Tolerance," in J. Zalewski and W. Ehrenberger (eds.), *Hardware and Software for Real Time Process Control,* Elsevier Science Publishers B.V., North-Holland, 1989.

[51] Hecht, H., "Fault-Tolerant Software," *IEEE Transactions on Reliability,* Vol. R-28, No. 3, 1979, pp. 227–232.

[52] Hecht, H., and M. Hecht, "Fault-Tolerant Software," in D. K. Pradhan (ed.), *Fault-Tolerant Computing: Theory and Techniques,* Vol. 2, Upper Saddle River, NJ: Prentice-Hall, 1986, pp. 658–696.

[53] Randell, B. and J. Xu, "The Evolution of the Recovery Block Technique," in M. R. Lyu (ed.), *Software Fault Tolerance,* Chichester, U.K.: John Wiley and Sons, 1995, pp. 1–21.

[54] Randell, B., "System Structure for Software Fault-Tolerance," *IEEE Transactions on Software Engineering,* Vol. SE-1, 1975, pp. 220–232.

[55] Kim, K. H., "The Distributed Recovery Block Scheme," in M. R, Lyu (ed.), *Software Fault Tolerance,* Chichester, U.K.: John Wiley and Sons, 1995, pp. 189–209.

[56] Levi, S. -T., and A. K. Agrawala, *Fault Tolerant System Design,* New York: McGraw-Hill, 1994.

[57] Stucki, L. G., and G. L. Foshee, "New Assertion Concepts for Self-Metric Software Validation," *Proceedings of the 1975 International Conference on Reliable Software*, 1975, pp. 59–71.

[58] Yau, S. S., and R. C. Cheung, "Design of Self-Checking Software," *Proceedings of the 1975 International Conference on Reliable Software*, 1975, pp. 450–457.

[59] Yau, S. S., R. C. Cheung, and D. C. Cochrane, "An Approach to Error-Resistant Software Design," *Proceedings of the Second International Conference on Software Engineering*, 1976, pp. 429–436.

[60] Bass, J. M., G. Latif-Shabgahi, and S. Bennett, "Experimental Comparison of Voting Algorithms in Cases of Disagreement," *EUROMICRO 97, New Frontiers of Information Technology, Proceedings of the 23rd EUROMICRO Conference*, Berlin, Germany, 1997, pp. 516–523.

[61] Blough, D. M., and G. F. Sullivan, "Voting using Predispositions," *IEEE Transactions on Reliability*, Vol. 43, No. 4, 1994, pp. 604–616.

[62] Hecht, H., "Issues in Fault-Tolerant Software for Real-Time Control Applications," *Proceedings of COMPAC '80*, 1980, pp. 603–607.

[63] Hecht, H., and M. Hecht, "Fault Tolerance in Software." in D. K. Pradhan (ed.), *Fault-Tolerant Computer System Design*, Upper Saddle River, NJ: Prentice-Hall, 1996, pp. 428–477.

[64] Kim, K., M. A. Vouk, and D. F. McAllister, "An Empirical Evaluation of Maximum-Likelihood Voting in Failure Correlation Conditions," *Proceedings - 7th International Symposium on Software Reliability Engineering*, Albuquerque, NM, 1996, pp. 330–339.

[65] Lorczak, P. R., and A. K. Caglayan, "A Large-Scale Second Generation Experiment in Multi-Version Software: Analysis of Software Specification Faults," Charles River Analytics Inc., Report R8903, NASA Contract NAS-1-17705, Jan. 1989.

[66] Nordmann, L., and H. Pham, "Weighted Voting Systems," *IEEE Transactions on Reliability*, Vol. 48, No. 1, 1999, pp. 42–49.

[67] Parhami, B., "Voting Algorithms," *IEEE Transactions on Reliability*, Vol. 43, No. 4, 1994, pp. 617–629.

[68] Pullum, L. L., R. Dziegiel, Jr., and G. S. Wakefield, "Templates for Software Fault Tolerant Voting on Results of Floating Point Arithmetic," *Proceedings: AIAA Computing in Aerospace*, San Diego, CA, 1993.

[69] Pullum, L. L., "A New Adjudicator for Fault Tolerant Software Applications Resulting in Multiple Solutions," *Proceedings: IEEE/AIAA Digital Avionics Systems Conference*, Ft. Worth, TX, 1993.

[70] Pullum, L. L., "Software Fault Tolerance Design Assistant (SWFTDA) User's Manual," Quality Research Associates Technical Report, QRA-SWFTDA-SUM, 1997.

List of Acronyms

AECB   Canadian Atomic Energy Control

AT   acceptance test

ATB   acceptance test for backup algorithm

AV   acceptance voting

CAS   currently active set

CCP   consistent comparison problem

CED   concurrent error-detection

CER   community error recovery

CRB   consensus recovery block

CT   certification trail

CV   consensus voting

DB   database

DM   decision mechanism

DRA   data re-expression algorithm

DRB   distributed recovery block

d-tag   dependability tag

EAB   elementary asserted block

FPA   floating point arithmetic

FS   feasibility set

HECA   hardware error confinement area

HNVP   hierarchical N-version programming

IAW   identical and wrong

MCNV   modified interactive convergence algorithm

MCR   multiple correct results

MLV   maximum likelihood voter

MV   majority voting

MVS   multiversion software

NCP N-copy programming

NSCP N self-checking programming

NVP N-version programming

NVP3   3 variant N-version programming system

NVP-AT N-version programming with an acceptance test

NVP-TB *N*-version programming with a tie-breaker

NVP-TB-AT *N*-version programming with a tie-breaker and an acceptance test

NVS *N*-version software

NVX *N*-version executive

OO object-oriented

PSP pair of self-checking processors

PTC programmer transparent coordination

RcB recovery block

RcB3 recovery block with 3 alternates

RtB retry block

SAR safety analysis report

SCOP self-configuring optimal programming

SECA software error confinement area

SWFTDA Software Fault Tolerance Design Assistant

SLIDE sliding majority decision mechanism

t/(*n*-1)-VP *t*/(*n*-1)-variant programming

TB tie-breaker

TPA two-pass adjudicator(s)

V&V verification and validation

WDT watchdog timer

About the Author

Laura L. Pullum has performed research and development in the dependable software areas of software fault tolerance, safety, reliability, and security for more than 15 years. Dr. Pullum has written more than 100 papers and reports on dependable software and has a patent (as coinventor) in the area of fault tolerant agents. She holds a B.S. in mathematics, and an M.S. in operations research from the University of Alabama in Huntsville, and an M.B.A. and a D.Sc. in systems engineering and operations research from the Southeastern Institute of Technology. Dr. Pullum is a member of the IEEE Reliability and Software societies, IEEE Computer Society Technical Committee on Fault Tolerant Computing, Mensa, Women in Technology, and the U.S. Software System Safety Working Group.

Index

Multimedia Database Management Systems, Guojun Lu

Practical Guide to Software Quality Management, John W. Horch

Practical Process Simulation Using Object-Oriented Techniques and C++, José Garrido

Secure Messaging with PGP and S/MIME, Rolf Oppliger

Security Fundamentals for E-Commerce, Vesna Hassler

Security Technologies for the World Wide Web, Rolf Oppliger

Software Fault Tolerance Techniques and Implementation, Laura L. Pullum

Software Verification and Validation for Practitioners and Managers, Second Edition, Steven R. Rakitin

Strategic Software Production with Domain-Oriented Reuse, Paolo Predonzani, Giancarlo Succi, and Tullio Vernazza

Systems Modeling for Business Process Improvement, David Bustard, Peter Kawalek, and Mark Norris, editors

User-Centered Information Design for Improved Software Usability, Pradeep Henry

Workflow Modeling: Tools for Process Improvement and Application Development, Alec Sharp and Patrick McDermott

For further information on these and other Artech House titles, including previously considered out-of-print books now available through our In-Print-Forever® (IPF®) program, contact:

Artech House
685 Canton Street
Norwood, MA 02062
Phone: 781-769-9750
Fax: 781-769-6334
e-mail: artech@artechhouse.com

Artech House
46 Gillingham Street
London SW1V 1AH UK
Phone: +44 (0)20 7596-8750
Fax: +44 (0)20 7630-0166
e-mail: artech-uk@artechhouse.com

Find us on the World Wide Web at:
www.artechhouse.com

www.ingramcontent.com/pod-product-compliance
Lightning Source LLC
Chambersburg PA
CBHW050521190326
41458CB00005B/1622